KUNST
HISTORISCHES
MUSEUM
VIENNA

Guide to the Collections

Published by the Kunsthistorische Museum

The Kunsthistorische Museum as a Monument of "Ringstrasse"-Architecture	Georg Kugler Translator: Gitta Holroyd-Reece
Egyptian and Near Eastern Collection	Elfriede Haslauer Helmut Satzinger Translator: Janet Turković
Collection of Greek and Roman Antiquities	Alfred Bernhard-Walcher Kurt Gschwantler Wolfgang Oberleitner Translator: Peter Waugh
Collection of Sculpture and Decorative Arts	Alfred Auer Rotraud Bauer Bernard Descheemaeker Rudolf Distelberger Stefan Krenn Manfred Leithe-Jasper Helmut Trnek Translator: Christine Wessely
Picture Gallery	Martina Haja Gabriele Helke Wolfgang Prohaska Karl Schütz Christoph Zuschlag Translators: Katherine D. Crawford, Gitta Holroyd-Reece, Sophie Kidd, Janet Turković and Peter Waugh
Coin Cabinet	Günther Dembski Helmut Jungwirth Karl Schulz Translator: Maria Clay
Collection of Ancient Musical Instruments	Gerhard Stradner Translator: Janet Turković
Collection of Arms and Armour	Christian Beaufort-Spontin Johannes Ramharter Translator: Dorothy Alexander

KUNST HISTORISCHES MUSEUM VIENNA

Guide to the Collections

Verlag Christian Brandstätter · Wien

Kunsthistorisches Museum
Burgring 5
A-1010 Vienna
Tel. (0 222) 93 45 41–44

Opening Hours

Main Building
Entrance Maria Theresien-Platz
Tue–Fri   10–4
Sat–Sun   9–4
(Dec 26–Jan 10 and Apr 1–Oct 31
till 6 p. m.)

Neue Burg
Entrance Heldenplatz
Mon, Thu, Fri   10–4
Sat–Sun   9–4

Bookshop
Main Building, Entrance Hall

Coffee-shop
Main Building, first floor, Cupola Hall

Telephone
Main Building, Entrance Hall

Information Desk of the "Museums friends"
Main Building, Entrance Hall
Tel. (0 222) 93 06 20/489

The guide contains 747 illustrations, 446 in colour (supplied by the Kunsthistorische Museum). Photographs by Marianne Haller, Inge Kitlitschka, Erich Lessing, Albrecht Meyer, Udo Otto, Thomas Römer, Else Schwenk, Gerhard Trumler, Herbert Tscherni and Johann Willsberger.

Published by the Kunsthistorische Museum Vienna

Cover design (based on a photograph by Inge Fink, Atelier Prader, A-1130 Vienna): Hofbauer & Partner, Vienna
Layout: Christian Brandstätter
Editor: Martina Haja

1st Edition, March 1989
Set and printed in Austria by Druckerei Gutenberg, Wiener Neustadt

Christian Brandstätter Verlag & Edition
Gesellschaft m. b. H. & Co. KG
A-1080 Vienna, Wickenburggasse 26
Tel. (0 222) 48 38 14–15

CONTENTS

Groundfloor

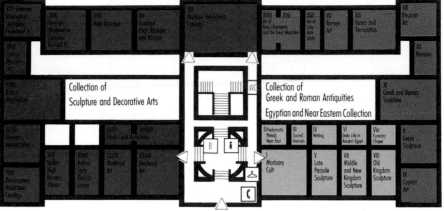

Maria Theresien-Platz

1st Floor

2nd Floor

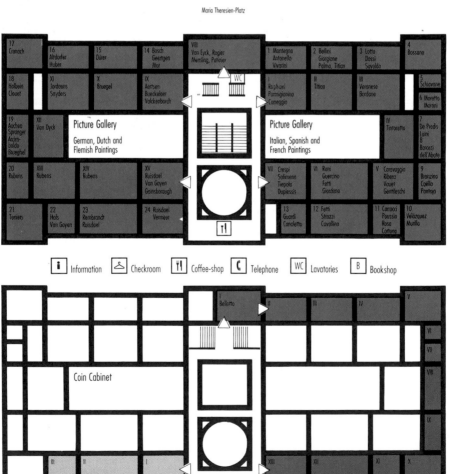

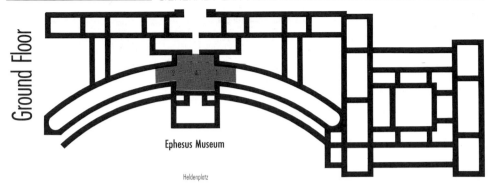

Ground Floor

Ephesus Museum

Heldenplatz

Intermediate Floor

Ephesus Museum

Upper Floor

XVIII XVII XVI XV XIV Marble Hall XIII XII XI X

Entrance Gallery

Gallery of the Hunt II

Gallery of the Hunt III

Gallery of the Hunt I

Collection of Arms and Armour
Collection of Ancient Musical Instruments

VIII VII VI IX Gallery C V Gallery B I Gallery A II III IV

Egyptian and
Near Eastern Collection

Collection of Greek
and Roman Antiquities

Coin Cabinet

Collection of
Ancient Musical Instruments

Collection of Sculpture
and Decorative Arts

Picture Gallery

Ephesus Museum

Collection of
Arms and Armour

Guide to the Collections of the Kunsthistorische Museum
No. 37

INTRODUCTION

It gives us great pleasure to be able to present the English edition of our new guide to the collections of the Kunsthistorische Museum. Since it is primarily intended as an aid to those visitors who have only a restricted amount of time in which to marvel at some of the Museum's world-famous exhibits, we have made a selection from among the vast number of items on display. We hope that this will provide the visitor with a sense of orientation and draw his attention to the most important exhibits. The brief descriptions are meant to serve as explanatory background material for the contemplation of the works of art themselves, while the purpose of the illustrations is to enable visitors to evoke the memory of what they have seen afterwards. In our opinion, the fact that increasing tourism tends to reduce the traveller's chances of viewing the art and culture of a country or city at his own leisure justifies the publication of a selective volume such as this one. However, this book also has another, more important feature: in contrast to the specialised catalogues for the various individual collections of the Kunsthistorische Museum, this volume is able to reveal the underlying unity of the collections.

Originating as far back as the Middle Ages from a variety of interests, they were built up over the centuries by the Habsburg dynasty. In 1891 they came to be housed collectively in the present magnificent building designed by Karl Hasenauer, which is a work of art in its own right and a monument to the intellectual climate of the time. In acknowledgment of this last fact, the present catalogue is prefaced by a short description of the building itself and its architectural and historical significance. Hasenauer himself did the same in the Museum's first general catalogue of 1891.

In this way, the present catalogue continues a tradition. Yet a tradition only achieves significance when it lives on within the context of the changing present. This is the goal of the forthcoming renovation work, the commencement of which will coincide – almost to the day – with the publication of this book and the completion of which will take several years. It is a work which would be only half-hearted if it did not include plans for structural improvements to the Museum and adjustment to the interests and problems of our time. This new guide is a small visible contribution in this direction.

Univ.-Prof. Dr. Hermann Fillitz
Der Erste Direktor
des Kunsthistorischen Museums

The Kunsthistorische Museum, built between 1871 and 1891 according to plans by Karl Hasenauer and Gottfried von Semper

THE KUNSTHISTORISCHE MUSEUM AS A MONUMENT OF "RINGSTRASSE"- ARCHITECTURE

Many of Europe's largest and most famous collections are still housed in the former royal or imperial palaces of their capitals – the Palais du Louvre, the Czar's Eremitage, the Medicis' Palazzo Pitti, or the Belvedere – and, despite many alterations, they still convey to this day an imposing impression of private princely collections. The building of special museums to house the rapidly growing collections in London, Amsterdam, Munich or Berlin only started in the 19th century. Such plans also existed in Vienna since the beginning of the 19th century; the majority of the Imperial collections were then kept at the Belvedere Palace, the former summer residence of Prince Eugene of Savoy; the rest was stored in various wings of the Imperial Winter Palace, the Hofburg. After 1860, in the course of planning Vienna's Ringstrasse, space was provided opposite the entrance to the Hofburg for the museums of the Imperial collections. Together with the Neue Burg (the new wing of the Hofburg) – which also houses collections today – and the Imperial Stables, the museums were intended to enclose a wide square as an "Imperial Forum". Two large museums were planned – one for the collections of fine arts, the other for those of natural history. After lengthy consideration of the designs of other architects taking part in a competition in 1866 – among them Ferstel and Hansen – the Viennese architect Karl Hasenauer (1833–1894) was commissioned with the plans. His designs were superbly revised by the great German architect Gottfried von Semper (1803–1879), thus achieving that impression of solemnity which the buildings convey to us today.

The construction of the two museums was started in the autumn of 1871; their outside structure was already completed in about 1880. The work on the rich interior of the Kunsthistorische Museum continued until 1891, and was Hasenauer's own achievement. Only in the two Imperial theatres – the Hofoper (Vienna State Opera) and the Burgtheater – can the "Ringstrasse-style" be found in equal perfection. Unlike the two theatres which were completely burned out during the

Second World War, the interior decoration of the Kunsthistorische Museum largely survived, despite serious bomb damage in all parts of the building. Hasenauer did not have to economize, he was able to use the most costly materials and to employ the most distinguished artists of his day. According to the taste of the period, the interior appointments also demanded the most opulent decorations to provide an adequately magnificent frame for the immensely valuable works of art. In addition, very thorough examinations and considerations took place in order to achieve the most favourable light conditions, not only in the skylight rooms of the Picture Gallery but also in the large halls on the ground floor at the front of the building. They are divided by a continuous row of pillars which support the central wall of the first floor as well as representing an important decorative component, as the monoliths consist of polished granite, mounted in part with gilded bronze: In the two rooms of the Egyptian Collection, three old Egyptian columns of red granite were installed. Consequently the furnishings in all the rooms of this collection eventually included Egyptian murals, door surroundings and show cases.

The ceiling frescos on the ground floor also largely reflect the epochs and masters of the works of art exhibited in these rooms. The large hall housing the Collection of Greek and Roman Antiquities is based on the architecture of imperial Rome and decorated with a relief frieze depicting the myths of the gods, by August Eisenmenger. The main hall in the other half of the building was intended as a counterpart and meant to house the Collection of Arms and Armour which is now accomodated in the Neue Burg; the ceiling was decorated with 32 coats of arms belonging to Habsburg domains at the time of Emperor Charles V, executed by Friedrich Schönbrunner after designs by Karl Krahl.

The central room on the ground floor situated behind the staircase is accentuated by a large ceiling fresco by Julius Berger. This oil painting on canvas shows the most important patrons of the

M. Munkácsy, Apotheosis of the Renaissance

Habsburg dynasty, often based on portraits of the great masters, as in the case of Maximilian I by Dürer (in the centre). The doors connecting the rooms of the Picture Gallery on the first floor were decorated by Viktor Tilgner with 49 portrait busts of great painters; they now only survive in the central Hall VIII. On the landing of the magnificently appointed staircase the visitor can see Antonio Canova's sculpture "Theseus and the Centaur", for which the so-called Theseus Temple in the Volksgarten was built in 1820; but the group was later chosen as an effective showpiece in its present place.

The large ceiling fresco entitled "Apotheosis of the Renaissance" is by the Hungarian painter Michael (Mihály) von Munkácsy (1844–1900). On its left side we can see old Leonardo descending the stairs in conversation with young Raphael. Above them, on a scaffold, facing a canvas, stands Veronese; Michelangelo is on the

J. Berger, The Habsburgs as patrons of art

The staircase with Theseus and the Centaur by Antonio Canova

The Kunsthistorische Museum, built between 1871 and 1891 according to plans by Karl Hasenauer and Gottfried von Semper

right, behind the balustrade. In the centre above the stairs we see Titian with a number of pupils in front of two female life models. In a private box in the centre Pope Giulio II, studying a sheet of paper. Floating above them are the figures of Glory and Fame.

The twelve fanlights in the staircase were decorated by Hans Makart with presentations of the great artists Dürer, Holbein, Leonardo, Raphael, Michelangelo, Titian, Rubens, Rembrandt, van Dyck and Velázquez, as well as with the allegory "Law and Truth" facing the stairs, and the personification of religious and secular painting opposite. The spandrel pictures between the capitals of the huge columns made of "Grand-antique" (marble from Aubert at the foot of the Pyrenees) and mounted with gilded bronze, were painted by the brothers Ernst und Gustav Klimt and Franz Matsch and depict the development of art. The early work of Gustav Klimt – later to become world-famous – is of interest today, particularly his "Egypt", "Greek Classicism", "Old Itallan Art", "Florentine Cinquecento" and his "Roman and Venetian Quatrocento".

Finally, the enormous cupola hall was turned into

a Hall of Fame for the collectors of the Habsburg dynasty. The Emperors Maximilian I, Charles V and Rudolph II, the Archdukes Ferdinand (II), Albrecht (VII) and Leopold Wilhelm, the Emperors Charles VI and Francis Joseph I are depicted in the cupola by Johann Benk as portrait medallions whereas Rudolph Weyr united in large reliefs the most distinguished artists working for these Habsburg princes.

The Fin de siècle had a special preference and feeling for the use of precious materials, multicoloured granites and marble varieties which were collected from the whole of Austria – from Bohemia to Istria –, from France, Italy, Belgium and Sweden; but also for the use of best quality stucco lustro, whose distinctive colourfulness is greatly admired to this day.

Great emphasis was put on the sculptural decoration of the façades, following designs by von Semper. They were meant to symbolize the different branches of art as well as representing great artists and philosophers of every era. The lantern in the cupola is crowned with a statue of Pallas Athena as the patroness of art and science, by Johann Benk. An inscription above

The Neue Burg, built between 1881 and 1906 according to plans by Gottfried von Semper, Karl Hasenauer and others. Today this new wing of the Hofburg houses the Ephesus Museum, the Collection of Arms and Armour and the Collection of Ancient Musical Instruments.

the entrance reads: "To the monuments of art and antiquity Emperor Francis Joseph I. 1881" — and refers to the predominantly scientific intention of the court museums at the time of their foundation.

In 1881, virtually contemporaneous with the building of the museums, work began on the large semi-circular wing of the Hofburg, designed by Semper. Hasenauer was in charge of the building operations, and later E. Ritter von Förster, Friedrich Ohmann and Ludwig Baumann. The completion of this building dragged on till the First World War, and it is still not quite finished today. Plans for another wing on the opposite side, which was to have enclosed the "Imperial Forum" to the north-west, were never realized. The building, known as Neue Burg, has accommodated collections since 1908: first, the World Travel Collection of Archduke Franz Ferdinand; after his assassination in 1914 it became part of the Imperial collections under the name of Este Collection. Gradually, more and more collections were transferred from the Kunsthistorische Museum to the Neue Burg. Since 1935 the main floor has housed the Collection of Arms and Armour, and, after a first exhibition, still as a part of the Este Collection, the Collection of Ancient Musical Instruments was established in 1947. In 1978 the Ephesus Museum was set up in the magnificent staircase.

G. K.

Initials of the Authors

Alfred Auer	A. A.
Rotraud Bauer	R. B.
Christian Beaufort-Spontin	C. B.
Alfred Bernhard-Walcher	A. B.-W.
Bernard Descheemaeker	B. D.
Günther Dembski	G. D.
Rudolf Distelberger	R. D.
Kurt Gschwantler	K. G.
Martina Haja	M. H.
Elfriede Haslauer	E. H.
Gabriele Helke	G. H.
Helmut Jungwirth	H. J.
Stefan Krenn	S. K.
Georg Kugler	G. K.
Manfred Leithe-Jasper	M. L.-J.
Wolfgang Oberleitner	W. O.
Wolfgang Prohaska	W. P.
Johannes Ramharter	J. R.
Helmut Satzinger	H. S.
Karl Schütz	K. S.
Karl Schulz	K. Sch.
Gerhard Stradner	G. S.
Helmut Trnek	H. T.
Christoph Zuschlag	C. Z.

List of Abbreviations

b.	born
BL	Body Length
c.	circa
d.	died
D	Depth
Diam.	Diameter
H	Height
Inv. No.	Inventory Number
L	Length
ment.	mentioned
TH	Total Height
TL	Total Length
TW	Total Width
W	Width
WT	Weight

THE EGYPTIAN AND NEAR EASTERN COLLECTION

In the 18th century, the Egyptian antiquities owned by the Habsburg dynasty were still very few. They did not form a collection of their own, but were rather part of the Cabinet of Coins and Antiquities. At the beginning of the 19th century this field gained more public estimation than ever before, due to Napoleon's spectacular expedition to Egypt in 1798/1799. This increase in interest resulted in a certain emancipation of the Egyptian collection, as it was continuously enlarged by substantial donations. The greatest increment was effected by a large-scale purchase in 1821 in Egypt which brought the number of items to several thousands. This increase necessitated a change of premises. Until then, the collection had been housed in rooms behind the Court Library, together with the Classical antiquities. From 1824 onward it was eventually displayed to the public in a palace in the Johannesgasse. This propitious period of independent location did not last long. In 1837, the collection had to move to the Lower Belvedere Palace, rejoining there the Classical antiquities. Plans were not, however, abandoned for granting the Egyptian collection independent rooms. In the reign of Emperor Francis Joseph I, the erection of a new art museum was designed that was to unite all of the dynasty's art collections. In this Kunsthistorische Museum, the Egyptian rooms are set apart stylistically from the rest of the museum, emphasizing the independent character of the collection.

A very substantial increment was effected around 1880 (that is, well ahead of the inauguration of the new museum, which was to occur in 1891) by acquiring the Egyptian Miramar collection. This was a particularly rich assemblage of Egyptian art and antiquities, gathered by Archduke Ferdinand Max (the later Emperor Maximilian of Mexico, d. 1867) from the fifties onward at Miramar Castle near Trieste.

Twentieth-century acquisitions have come largely from Austrian archæological endeavours. Especially worthy of mention is the work Hermann Junker did in the area of the Great Pyramids of Giza in 1912/29. Most of the Egyptian monuments of the Old Kingdom can be credited to his efforts. Although this was the most rewarding enterprise in terms of works of art, excavations in several other places have yielded a wealth of objects of historical and cultural interest.

The most important part of the Near-Eastern Collection are the monuments of ancient South Arabia. Most of these we owe to the activities of the Austrian explorer, Eduard Glaser (d. 1908).

H. S.

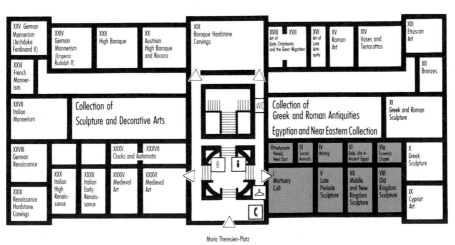

Maria Theresien-Platz

TOMB CHAPEL OF KA-NI-NISUT
Pyramid district of Giza
5th Dynasty, c. 2400 B. C.
Limestone; W 360 cm, D 143 cm (interior measurements)
Inv. No. 8006

Typical of tomb forms in the Old Kingdom is the *mastaba*. With its masonry walls and block shape, it is a monumental stone memorial. The burial chamber is located deeply underground. Egyptian mortuary ritual stipulated that the dead be regularly cared for, a task relegated to special funeral priests (*ka*-priests, or "soul servants"). Worship consisted of praying, partaking of food and drink, incense-burning and sprinkling of water. Even early *mastaba* blocks contained a separate room specifically for these rites. This room represented the reception room in the deceased's home and was designed as a place for offering and commemoration by the bereaved. Although a few earlier examples are attested, the development of these tomb chapels begins practically at the close of the 4th Dynasty, after the period of construction of the two largest pyramids. The impressive relief pictures in the chapels are still rather severe in style and content in this early period, eventually becoming more relaxed towards the end of the Old Kingdom. The tumb chapel of Ka-ni-nisut dates from the beginning of this development. The pictures are full of simple beauty and harmony. The most noteworthy sections are: on the west wall, the tomb-owner with his family and servants; on the north partition, Ka-ni-nisut (large-sized), visiting his administrative offices; and above the entrance, both his ships, awaiting his use, even after death.

H. S.

FALSE DOOR OF IHA
Pyramid district of Giza
6ᵗʰ Dynasty, c. 23ʳᵈ century B. C.
Limestone; H 205 cm, W 72 cm, D 17 cm
Inv. No. 7445

The false door is the imaginary connection between the cultic chamber with its offering table and the realm of the dead tombowner, the sealed statuary chamber *(serdâb)*. In the centre is the suggestion of a passageway in the form of a narrow vertical groove; at its uppermost end, we see rolled-up matting. A structure of transverse and vertical beams frames the false passage; the upper section of the structure, a panel, is a canonical depiction of the deceased in front of the offering table. The false door is carved in one piece. The spendid hieroglyphics are cut and painted in exquisite relief.   H. S.

INNER COFFIN FOR MERI-IB
Pyramid district of Giza
Late 6ᵗʰ Dynasty, c. 2200 B. C.
Wood; L 214 cm, W 59.5 cm, H 53.5 cm
Inv. No. 7803

In the Old Kingdom, coffins were either house-shaped or were simple crates with a flat lid. The inner coffin was enclosed in a similar outer coffin. Drawings of a head and legs indicate the head and foot ends of the coffin. On the left side of the head end is a pair of *wedjat* eyes; the inside of the coffin is covered with elaborate offering lists.
                                                             E. H.

RESERVE HEAD
Pyramid district of Giza
4th Dynasty, c. 26th century B. C.
Limestone; H 27 cm, W 17.5 cm, D 23.1 cm
Inv. No. 7787

The *Portrait* or *Reserve Head* is one of the major works of the Viennese Collection. Found in an early tomb in the burial grounds of Giza, it was not in the above-ground statuary chamber, but below the earth – at the entrance to the underground burial chamber. Of some thirty heads that have been found to date, this one is considered to be the most beautiful. The portrayal while stylized is still full of life, with idealized, very regular features. Scholars still disagree about the purpose of this type of object. Traditional explanations proffer their use as surrogate heads for the soul (mummifying having then been only in its earliest stages).   H. S.

LADY KHENT AND HER YOUNGEST CHILD
Pyramid district of Giza
5th Dynasty, c. 2300 B. C.
Limestone; H 54 cm, W 25 cm, D 38 cm
Inv. No. 7507

SNEFRU-NOFER
Pyramid district of Giza
5th Dynasty, c. 2400 B. C.
Limestone; H 79 cm, W 23 cm, D 30 cm
Inv. No. 7506

The funerary statues of the *mastaba* tombs in the Old Kingdom were kept in sealed rooms called *serdâbs*. The statues were felt to be an *alter ego* of the deceased, apt to receive the mortuary rites, which were then completed in the adjacent tomb chapel. Khent (full name, Khentit-ka) was the wife of a high official. In his *mastaba,* she had her own *serdâb.* The sculpture is a magnificent example of Old Kingdom canonical sculpture in the round.

H. S.

Statue of the inspector of singers and royal supervisor of entertainment, from his own tomb. It is one of the rare portrayals of a nude standing youth. It may well be expressing one aspect of Egyptian funerary beliefs, such as "vitality" or "rejuvenation". The statue represents the pinnacle of idealized Egyptian art, especially of sculpture in the round, in its immobility, symmetry, cubic form, straight-forward-looking gaze, and idealization.

H. S.

21

KAI-PU-PTAH AND IPEP
Pyramid district of Giza
5th Dynasty, c. 2300 B. C.
Limestone; H 50 cm, W 27 cm, D 22 cm
Inv. No. 7444

Funerary statue of a man and woman. The woman's gestures are in keeping with the canonical
expression for loving devotion – she has her right
hand laid on the man's back and her left resting on
his left arm. The man is wearing the round curled
wig and a short, smooth kilt. The woman has a
shoulder-length striated wig and the usual long,
close-fitting dress.   H. S.

BA'EF-BA
Pyramid district of Giza
5th Dynasty, c. 2300 B. C.
Calcite   ("alabaster");   H 50 cm,   W 16 cm,
D 22 cm
Inv. No. 7785

Funerary statue of a high official, portrayed in the
partially pleated "gala" kilt. He gazes distinctly
upwards. Especially characteristic of Old Kingdom
portrayal is the athletic stance seen in his massive, broad shoulders, muscular limbs and erect
bearing.   H. S.

SQUATTING FIGURE
Pyramid district of Giza
6ᵗʰ Dynasty, c. 2250 B. C.
Granite; H 38.5 cm, W 27 cm, D 18 cm
Inv. No. 7442

This funerary statue represents a man sitting oriental-style, cross-legged on a mat. In a shoulder-length striated wig and a short kilt, he sits bolt upright with his gaze directed straight ahead. Hard, grainy granite was much in use in the Old Kingdom for architectural detail and sculpture. Even with their primitive methods, sculptors and stone-masons of that time showed great prowess in working the stone.   H. S.

ITJEF WITH WIFE AND CHILDREN
Pyramid district of Giza
6ᵗʰ Dynasty, c. 2200 B. C.
Limestone; H 93 cm, W 62 cm, D 60 cm
Inv. No. 8410

Family group from a *serdâb*. The parents are seated on a simple bench with no arm or back rests. On either side of them, left and right, are two children, a boy and a girl, done in such miniature proportions that their heads remain below the level of the seat. The husband wears a wig with short curles and a simple kilt. The wife is clothed in the usual long, close-fitting dress and wears a shoulder-lenght striated wig. The children are nude.   H. S.

TOMB RELIEF OF NI-UI-NETJER
Pyramid district of Giza
6ᵗʰ Dynasty, c. 2200 B. C.
Limestone; H 78 cm, W 190 cm
Inv. No. 8028

These tomb chapel reliefs of Ni-ui-netjer show a more advanced stage of development than those of Ka-ni-nisut. On the left, the tomb-owner and his relatives are depicted at a funerary repast. The upper right-hand side shows the slaughter of two bulls; on the lower right is a dance provided for the entertainment of the banquet guests. Performing it are seven young women. Some of them are shaking sistra while under their feet a dwarf prances. The three women on the left are clapping in time to their singing.   H. S.

RELIEF SLAB OF KHETI

Beginning of 12ᵗʰ Dynasty, c. 1980 B. C.
Limestone; H 44 cm, W 77.2 cm, D 11.2 cm
Inv. No. 202

The period following the Old Kingdom was a time of political and economic decline. The difficult process of consolidation could only be resumed after the kings of the late 11ᵗʰ Dynasty reunited the empire. This development is mirrored in the art of the time. In the First Intermediate Period, the classical style was discontinued only to be gradually reinstated in the early Middle Kingdom. The Relief of Kheti, while showing stylistic traces of the foregoing intermediate period, nevertheless follows the new proportion scheme (for which the grid lines are still visible). The relief's special appeal comes from the seemingly naive form along with the precision of detail and the well-preserved colour composition. Depicted are a man and wife receiving funerary equipment and rich offerings from their son.   H. S.

STELA FOR SENBEF

Abydos
Middle Kingdom, c. 1800 B. C.
Limestone; H 45.5 cm, W 35 cm, D 7 cm
Inv. No. 109

In Abydos, the cultic place of pilgrimage to Osiris, it was the custom to erect cenotaphs. Many stelae from these Middle Kingdom monuments remain. Here we see one unique form in that the symbol of life (ankh) is carved in open-work in the middle of the window-like opening in the slab. Three mummy figures in demi-ronde are set in niches around the ankh.   H. S.

HEAD OF A SPHINX OF SESOSTRIS III
12ᵗʰ Dynasty, c. 1850 B. C.
Green schist; H 21.9 cm, W 33.2 cm, D 32.1 cm
Inv. No. 5813

The 12ᵗʰ Dynasty was the most important period of the Middle Kingdom. Its founder, Amenemhat I, vizier to the last Mentu-hotep (11ᵗʰ Dynasty), usurped the throne. His greatest challenge was to reintegrate the two parts of the country, Upper und Lower Egypt, which had split and subsequently grown apart during the First Intermediate Period. Specially, he had to rechannel disparate spiritual movements. Amenemhat I's successors too, were concerned with strengthening the power of the throne and establishing political absolutism. In the royal sculpture done under the reigns of Sesostris III and his son, Amenemhet III, these aspirations are stylistically evident in the hard realistic features and serious expressions. The impressive royal head is, because of its style, attributed to Sesostris III and is one of the most magnificent portraits of this ruler. The side view of the headdress and details of the break show that the head was not atop a human form, but part of a leonine sphinx body.

H. S.

SENI-ONKH
Coptos (Upper Egypt)?
12th Dynasty, c. 1900 B. C.
Granodiorite; H 53 cm, W 15.5 cm, D 33 cm
Inv. No. 61

This is a typical statue of a private person in the Middle Kingdom, as found in temples more often than in tombs. The steward Seni-onkh is seated on a chair with a low back rest. His long-haired wig, shoulder length, has its lower edge slanting to points in the front. He is dressed in the typical ankle-length kilt (knotted under the breast) of high-ranking officials. The sober facial features seem very portraitlike.   H. S

SHRINE OF HORI
Abydos
13th Dynasty, 18th century B. C.
Limestone; H 49 cm, W 39 cm, D 25.5 cm
Inv. No. 186

The construction of the upper side of the squared stone block suggests a barrel vault with raised end walls, an ancient sacral architectural form. A male figure has been sculpted as seated in a niche in the façade. All four sides of the memorial are inscribed. From these texts, we know that the shrine was erected in Abydos as a cenotaph, so that Hori and his many relatives could partake of the cult and mysteries of Osiris.   H. S.

KING SEKHEM-KA-RE AMENEMHAT V
Elephantine
13th Dynasty, c. 1750 B. C.
Metasandstone; H 35 cm, W 17.5 cm, D 20 cm
Inv. No. 37

The bust of a royal statue in gray-green stone was only recently identified as belonging to the six fragments of the body. The latter, found in 1932 in the temple area of Elephantine, are inscribed with the names of one of the first kings of the 13th Dynasty (1785– c. 1650). The royal sculpture still retains the form and style of the 12th Dynasty in its construction; however, the smooth, independent style of the successive period is already evident.
H. S.

SEBEK-EM-SAUF
Armant (Upper Egypt)
13th Dynasty, c. 1700 B. C.
Granodiorite; H 150 cm, W 43 cm, D 61.5 cm
Inv. Nos. 5051, 5801

One of the most exquisite non-royal statues from
the time of the decline preceding the Hyksos
reign. The subject, portrayed as particularly
corpulent, was an important personality. His father
before him, a high-ranking official, appears in
numerous monuments as well as his sister (the
wife of a king). Sebek-em-sauf is presented as
bald. His dress consists of an ankle-length kilt
knotted under the breast.   H. S.

HIPPOPOTAMUS ▽
11th/12th Dynasty, c. 2000 B. C.
Faience, blue glaze, painted;   L 20.5 cm,
W 7.65 cm, H 11 cm
Inv. No. 4211

Diminutive hippopotamus figures were included
in tomb contents of the Middle Kingdom. Hippopotamus hunting was a royal privilege bestowed as a favour on private citizens. Painted on the
hippo's ample body are signs of its habitat (papyrus, lotus, a bird) as if it were wallowing through
lush swamp vegetation.   E. H.

KING THUTMOSIS III
Thebes?
18th Dynasty, c. 1460 B. C.
Granodiorite; H 46.5 cm, W 30.6 cm, D 20.3 cm
Inv. No. 70

Royal portrait with headdress, uraeus snake and wide ritual beard, upper part of the body nude. Remnant of a standing or kneeling figure. As a standing statue, its height must have reached 1.20 meters without the pedestal. In the fine features, the sharp profile and the hooked nose, we recognize King Thutmosis III, the mighty conqueror under whose reign the Egyptian realm reached its greatest size: from Syria on the North to below the Fourth Nile Cataract in the South.

H. S.

TJENENA
Thebes?
18th Dynasty, end of 15th century B. C.
Limestone, painted; H 56 cm, W 15.8 cm, D 35.7 cm
Inv. No. 63

Seated statue of a high official, possibly from a tomb known to be in Western Thebes. The carefully painted sculpture shows a man with a long striated wig, short beard and long cloak covering one shoulder. The back of his chair has the form of a rounded stela. The inscriptions on the back have been partially chiseled away, while those on the base are completely obliterated. Destruction of inscriptions and reliefs is also found in the Theban Tomb from where this statue is believed to have come. This indicates that the chief stewart fell from grace during his lifetime.

H. S.

28

BUNDLED PAPYRUS STALK COLUMNS
18ᵗʰ Dynasty, c. 1410 B. C.
Pink granite; H 596 cm and 630 cm, resp.
Diam. 112 cm and 110 cm, resp.

Egyptian architectural design in stone structures was wont to include imitations of its own ancient prototypes in other kinds of material. Supports of bound papyrus stalks used in lightweight hut-building find their counterpart in the columns of the mid-18ᵗʰ Dynasty. The columns, with a few items of the cartouche of Thutmosis IV, were usurped two hundred years later by Merenptah (1224–1214) and Sethos II (1210–1204); most of the remaining cartouches name these two kings. The most recent use of the columns has been in the construction of the Kunsthistorische Museum.   H. S.

KING AMENOPHIS III (SHABTI STATUETTE)
Thebes
New Kingdom, c. 1360 B. C.
Red granite; H 38 cm, W 15.9 cm, D 12.5 cm
Inv. No. 8188

As Thutmosis III's most eminent successor, Amenophis III ruled the empire for almost forty years (1403–1365). In his politically absolute, outwardly peaceful reign, he made many important contributions. Among these were extensive

STELA OF AMENOPHIS II
Elephantine?
18th Dynasty, c. 1435 B. C.
Metasandstone; H 166 cm, W 128 cm, D 38 cm
Inv. No. 5909

The imposing monument (the missing lower section is in Cairo) was erected by Amenophis II upon his return from his first Syrian campaign. He had a stela with the same text erected in Amada (Nubia). The king is shown being led from the right, by the cataract goddess, Anukis, to Amun, the supreme Egyptian god; on the left he pays tribute to Khnum, the god of Elephantine. The lengthy text extols foremost the military exploits of the Pharaoh and then his bequests and structural restorations of temples. There follow historical accounts (on the Cairo Fragment).   H. S.

construction activity and the erection of a great deal of colossal royal sculpture. Certain aspects of these royal portraits tend to a unique realism, like this *shabti* statuette: the rather full facial features and ample body depart from the traditional concept of the ideal and the athletic.   H. S.

COMMEMORATIVE SCARAB ▷
18th Dynasty, 1393 B. C.
Gneiss; L 8.5 cm, W 5.8 cm, H 3.6 cm
Inv. No. 6730

On special occasions, Amenophis III issued large scarabs on which appropriate descriptions of the event were inscribed, for example, a wedding with a foreign princess, or successful hunting expeditions. This scarab relates the Pharaoh's having slain (by himself) 102 wild lions in the first decade of his reign.   E. H.

REVERENT BABOON WITH PHARAOH FIGURE
Memphis?
New Kingdom, c. 1400 B. C.
Pink granite; H 130 cm, W 42 cm, D 61.5 cm
Inv. No. 5782

The loud rejoicing of the Hamadryas baboon at sunrise and sunset in its rocky habitat served as a model for the Egyptian celebration of the ascent and descent of the sun at the critical stages of its cycle. Baboons with upraised hands – the Egyptian gesture of reverence – became symbols for the "eastern souls", the gods who cheer the sun at its appearance above the horizon. The king joins these gods in his role as sun priest.   H. S.

GODDESS SEKHMET ▽
Mut-Temple, Karnak (Thebes)
18th Dynasty, beginning of 14th century B. C.
Granodiorite; H 197 cm, W 45.9 cm, D 107.7 cm
Inv. No. 77

The goddess, whose name means "the powerful one", is portrayed with a lioness' head. She is known for her predominantly wild and dangerous temperament, an attribute only brought to the fore in protecting the king. In the Mut Temple of Karnak, King Amenophis III had a tremendous monument erected to Sekhmet, consisting of 600 colossal statues. This would indicate that there had been a kind of dogmatic merging of the two goddesses, Mut and Sekhmet, both of whom were members of the Memphite and Theban triads respectively. The Viennese Collection contains five of these sitting statues, four of which are exhibited.   H. S.

◁ **HORUS AND KING HOREMHEB**
18th Dynasty, end of 14th century B. C.
Limestone; H 152 cm, W 73.1 cm, D 77 cm
Inv. No. 8301

Horemheb was not of royal descent. He began his military career under Amenophis IV, Echnaton, the son of Amenophis III. He witnessed the rise and fall of the great ideological reform of Amarna and survived both youthful successors to Echnaton (Smenkhkara and Tutankhamon), as well as aged Ay. During these years of declining royal power, he was made supreme head of the military, regent and finally king. Facing him was the tremendous task of bringing about domestic order and rebuilding Egypt's damaged military reputation in the Near East. Horus wears the double crown of Upper and Lower Egypt. His wig provides the transition between the falcon head and the human body. Horemheb wears the double crown surmounting the Pharaonic headcloth. Both are clothed in short, pleated ritual kilts. Horemheb has his tomb in the Theban Valley of the Kings. Before he was made king, however, he had built himself a splendid sepulcher in the necropolis of Memphis. One of its relief slabs is in the Viennese Collection.   H. S.

TOMB RELIEF OF MERI-RE
Memphis
18th Dynasty, beginning of 14th century B. C.
Limestone; H 128 cm, W 85 cm
Inv. No. 5814

The shining era of Amenophis III Is mIrrored In the art of that time, especially in the region of the northern capital, Memphis. Reliefs from that time have a special richness not only in form but also in their depiction of personal adornment, such as apparel, wigs and jewellery. The two reliefs (Inv. Nos. 5814 and 5815) from the tomb of the tutor of the king's son are especially beautiful. After its discovery in mid-nineteenth century, the tomb filled up again sand and its traces became lost. Only recently has it been rediscovered.   H. S

PEDESTAL FOR A PORTABLE CULTIC BARK
Auaris (Tell el-Dab'a, Lower Egypt)
19th Dynasty, beginning of 13th century B. C.
Silicified sandstone; H 97 cm, W 106 cm, D 110 cm
Inv. No. 5106

The heart of an Egyptian temple is its shrine, concealed deep within its most sacred recesses. There, the cult image or divine statuette, is found.

During festivals, this was taken on procession in a model-sized portable bark. This testifies to the supreme importance of the ship as a means of transportation in ancient Egypt. In the temple, the bark was kept near the Holy of Holies and usually rested on a massive stone base. This particular base, from Auaris, was erected by Sethos I for the bark of the god Seth in his temple, known to us from literary sources.

H. S.

HUI'S STELA
Memphis
New Kingdom, c. 1300 B. C.
Limestone; H 106.5 cm, W 72 cm, D 11 cm
Inv. No. 126

Sepulchral stela for the Royal Treasurer, Hui. In the upper scene, Hui makes an offering to Osiris, the king of the dead, who is joined by Isis, Horus and Wepwawet. Directly below Hui with his wife and brother is making an offering to the deceased parents and grandparents. In the lowermost register Hui, together with his wife, receives funerary offerings from his many siblings.   H. S.

MERI-PTAH, SI-ESE AND KAFI ▷
Western Thebes
19th Dynasty, 13th century B. C.
Calcareous sandstone;   H 70 cm,   W 55 cm,
D 45 cm
Inv. No. 48

Three people are seated on a bench. They are wearing wigs and long cloaklike garments. The men have large amulets on their chests. The right hands grasp the edge of the cloak in front of the stomach; the left hands lie flat on the chest. It has been proven that the group comes from the rear niche of a particular Theban rock tomb. The inscription and reliefs in that tomb are all dedicated to the same persons. Meri-ptah and Si-ese are brothers and the woman is their mother, Kafi.
                                                                H. S.

KHAI-HAPI
Heliopolis
19th Dynasty, 13th century B. C.?
Gneiss; H 49.5 cm, W 19.8 cm, D 31.4 cm
Inv. No. 64

This small crouching statue was excavated in Vienna around 1800 along with Roman artifacts. It may have been part of a shrine to Serapis or Isis. But its origin was elsewhere. Judging from the style and inscriptions, it must have stood in a temple in Heliopolis one and a half millennia before Roman times. Khai-hapi holds the emblem of the goddess Hathor in front of him: a stylized sistrum bearing Hathor's face with cow's ears.
                                                                H. S.

TILES DEPICTING FOREIGNERS

Tell el-Yahudiya (Lower Egypt)
20th Dynasty, beginning of 12th century B. C.
Glazed clay; largest fragment: H 13.4 cm,
W 12.5 cm
Inv. Nos. 3896, 3897

Egyptian Pharaonic philosophy included inter alia the subjugation of alien enemies. The enemy, depicted as conquered and paying homage, appeared in the canonical decoration of royal monuments. In the palace of Ramses III (at Tell el-Yahudiya) these decorations took the form of exquisite glazed clay reliefs set into the walls of the Throne Room. The standard groups, Hittites, Mesopotamians, Libyans and Black Africans, are shown kneeling in splendid dress.　　　　H. S

◁ **SI-ESE, CHIEF OF GRANARY AFFAIRS**
Asyut (Upper Egypt)
19th Dynasty, c. 1220 B. C.
Granodiorite; H 105 cm, W 35 cm, D 36 cm
Inv. No. 34

A man in formal dress of the Ramesside period: a wavy wig, a shirt with pleated sleeves and a long, fully-pleated kilt. The standing figure is holding a tall staff on the left, topped with the jackal's head of the god Wepwawet. The cult of the sacred staffs is documented as coincident with the New Kingdom and must have had a close affiliation with the kingship.　　　　H. S.

HIGH PRIEST OF PTAH ▽
Memphis
22nd Dynasty, 10th–8th centuries B. C.?
Limestone; H 105 cm, W 37.5 cm, D 58 cm
Inv. No. 5773

The First Priest of Ptah, the High Priest of the god of the age-old city of Memphis, played an essential role in that region's religious, political and cultural life. His attire is characterized by the side lock and the animal skin hung over the shoulder. The sculpture shows the priest kneeling, holding a little shrine before him containing the falcon-headed Sokar, deity of the Memphite necropolis. The statue is severely weathered, the greatest loss being the inscriptions with the name of the portrayed.   H. S.

THE GOD IM-KHENT-WER
Memphis?
New Kingdom or Third Intermediate Period?
Metasandstone; H 115 cm, W 50 cm, D 36 cm
Inv. No. 5770

Standing figure with wig, broad collar, and typical features of a god's attire, such as the braided beard and the short, pleated kilt, also belonging to the gods. The upper part of the body is nude. Inscribed in large hieroglyphics on the back pillar of the statue is the name of the god (about whom very little is known). Also inscribed is just the beginning of the first of the two cartouche names of the royal donor unfortunately precluding any identification. The sculpture is also difficult to identify stylistically, even more so since it was changed: The high forehead section was redone and even the inscription may be secondary. H. S.

NAMARUT (NIMLOT)
Heliopolis?
22nd Dynasty, second half of 10th century B. C.
Basalt; H 77.5 cm, W 35 cm, D 35.5 cm
Inv. No. 5791

Block statue of the son of Osorkon I and brother of Shoshenq I of the 22nd Dynasty, a Libyan princely family. Namarut's garment is ankle-length. According to the style of the times, three sides of the cubic sculpture contain both inscriptions and pictures of the gods in relief: on the front is Amun (with the double feather crown); on the right, the sun-god, Re-Harakhte; and on the left, Ptah. H. S.

GEMNEF-HOR-BAK
Sais (Lower Egypt)?
26th Dynasty, c. 600 B. C.?
Granodiorite; H 51 cm, W 18 cm, D 25.7 cm
Inv. No. 62

This statuette is documented as having been with the Viennese Collection the longest. It was acquired in 1560 in Constantinople, where it had probably been brought during the Imperial Roman period. Gemnef-hor-bak is wearing the bag wig so popular in the Late Period; neither apparel nor jewellery are visible. Kneeling, he holds a small shrine containing the figure of the goddess Neith. The lateral texts on the shrine extol the goddess; the inscription on the back pillar gives the ethical ideals of the portrayed. H. S.

INTERCOLUMNAR SLAB FROM A NEW YEAR'S PAVILION
26th Dynasty, 7th century B. C.
Green schist; H 120 cm, W 150 cm, D 38 cm
Inv. No. 213

The beginning of the Egyptian cult year was defined as the time of the annual rise of the Nile. The King, as guarantor of fertility and cosmic order, was to perform rites invoking divine intervention in bringing about adequate flooding. These observances were in all probability held in a pavilion atop a temple. Psammetichus II is named in the cartouches, but they have been altered. Judging from similar pieces, Psammetichus I could have been the builder. Especially striking in the reliefs are the very realistic royal portraits. H. S.

37

STELA OF HA-HAT
Thebes
26th Dynasty, c. 640 B. C.
Wood with stucco layer, painted; H 57.5 cm,
W 34.3 cm, D 5 cm
Inv. No. 5073

In the Late Period, stelae in the interior of the tombs were very often made of wood. The funerary concepts of this time encompass not only Osirian philosophy, but also the new idea that the deceased could become one with the sun god, previously only a royal prerogative. The stela of the Month-priest, Ha-hat, is dedicated solely to the honour of the sun god. The picture shows homage being paid to the falcon-headed Harakhte, the morning sun, on the right and, on the left, to Atum, the evening sun. The text, also divided in half, consists of hymns to both gods.

H. S.

ISIS ENTHRONED, NURSING THE HORUS CHILD
Late Period, 7th/6th centuries B. C.
Bronze; H 28 cm, W 7 cm, D 11.9 cm
Inv. No. 6622

The divine mother, Isis, is sitting on a lion throne. Her tripartite wig is covered with a vulture head-dress, surmounted by the uraeus crown, with cow's horns and solar disc. She is offering her breast to Horus, seated on her lap. He, in turn, is shown with a side lock and nude, to indicate that he is a child.   E. H.

LION, DEVOURING BULL   ▽
30th Dynasty, mid-4th century B. C.?
Green schist; L 61.5 cm, H 28 cm, W 13 cm
Inv. No. 8020

The unique subject of this piece shows a lion holding on tightly to a bull and devouring it, head-first. The prey is somewhat smaller in its proportions than the lion. The event shown is not natural, but symbolic in character. One explanation might be the symbolism of the astronomical conflict between solar and lunar cycles. The sculpture may have served as the cult image of a lion god, and as such would habe been kept in the sanctuary of his temple.   H. S.

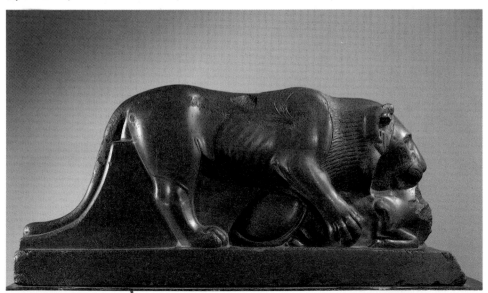

UPPER SECTION OF A MALE STATUE
Probably end of 4th century B. C.
Gabbro; H 25 cm, W 18.5 cm, D 13.2 cm
Inv. No. 20

The features of the portrayed are well-defined and his smile is typical of Late Period sculpture. He is wearing the bag wig. His garments consist of an undershirt with a V-necked shirt over it. His kilt is knotted under his chest. For the most part, the long inscription (in four columns along the back pillar) is missing, affording us with no means of identification.   H. S.

SPHINX OF WAH-IB-RE ▷
End of 4th century B. C.
Limestone; L 105.5 cm, W 29 cm, H 60.5 cm
Inv. No. 76

The sphinx (almost always male in Egypt) along with the pyramid and the obelisk is one of the best-known symbols of Pharaonic culture. Normally it has a leonine body and a royal head. A perfect transition between the head and the body is provided by the striped headcloth. Since ancient times the lion has symbolized the sun. In the sphinx form, therefore, the sun and royalty are one. The usual function of a sphinx was to protect holy places and in this particular case, the inscription tells us that the sphinx was guarding the tomb of General Wah-ib-re.   H. S.

◁ **GODDESS**
Probably 3rd century B. C.
Syenite; H 66 cm, W 24.7 cm. D 15.9 cm
Inv. No. 5809

The head and lower legs of the statue are missing. The sculpture belongs to a well-documented form of the early Ptolemaic period, representing a goddess (or a queen posing as a goddess). The wig and the pearl collar are worked in plain forms and lines.

The long dress (which would have been obvious through the lower hem, here missing) is so close-fitting as to give the impression of a nude body. One leg is slightly in front of the other; the arms hang down alongside the body with the hands flat on the thighs. The style of that period emphasized the plasticity of the female body. Another of its features are the elongated limbs.　　　　　H. S.

BOY IN PHARAONIC ATTIRE
1st century A. D.?
Granite; H 96 cm, W 86 cm, D 45 cm
Inv. No. 5780

Sculpture of Caesar's successors often portrayed them as Lords of Egypt in the royal array of a Pharaoh. In this particular case, the curls showing under the front of the regal headdress are a concession to the tastes of the time. We find the age easily recognisable in the youthful facial features as well as the side lock. Probably an imperial prince, he is portrayed as "Horus, the child" (Harpocrates).　　　　　H. S.

HEAD OF AN AGED MAN (PTOLEMY X?)
c. 100 B. C.?
Green schist; H 32.5 cm, W 15.5 cm, D 15.5 cm
Inv. No. 42

The head – now only face and neck – was part of a larger-than-life-sized statue. What was once a smooth head gear is still discernible; the chest was probably bare. The aging face done in such realism is fascinating. Based on comparable portraits, it has been argued that the head is that of King Ptolemy X Alexander (110–109 and 107–88 B. C.). It is without a doubt one of the most splendid examples of the successful synthesis of Egyptian and Hellenistic sculpture.

　　　　　H. S.

WRITING BOARD ▽
19th Dynasty, c. 13th century B. C.
Wood, stucco; H 18.5 cm, W 14.8 cm
Inv. No. 3924

The surface of the thin wooden board has been smoothed with a layer of stucco. The board was on both sides used for practicing hieratic script and drawing baboons. Many more script, drawing and sculpture studies survive on stone (*ostraca* and sculptor's trial pieces).   E. H.

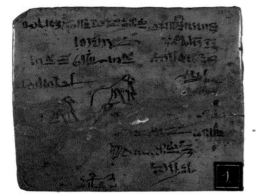

HEAD REST
Giza
6th Dynasty, 2290–2150 B. C.
Calcite; H 21 cm, W 20 cm, D 7.5 cm
Inv. No. 7798

Head rest with fluted column as base.

HEAD REST
New Kingdom, c. 1300–1200 B. C.
Wood; H 19 cm, W 31.2 cm, D 8 cm
Inv. No. 5068

Head rest with carvings of the luck-bringing dwarf-god, Bes. Head rests were most often used in a side position, and were frequently uphol-stered. Noteworthy is that the upper surface of the sickel-shaped part was rounded and slanted out-wards. Head rest amulets placed on mummies' necks were supposed to protect their heads. E. H.

FRAME OF A SHORT BED
1st Dynasty, c. 2800 B. C.
Wood; L 119 cm, W 56 cm, H 18 cm
Inv. No. 6128

The frame has two long poles ending in carrying handles, two connecting, mortised crosspieces and four feet shaped like cow's legs. In the frame are regularly-spaced slits where interwoven leath-er strips were to be attached. The legs were bound to the frame with narrow leather thongs as well, for extra durability. Traces of the leather are still visible. The shortened form is clear from its usage as bier for the crouching corpse of Early Period tombs, before coffins came into use.

E. H.

MODEL OF A NILE BOAT
Middle Kingdom, c. 1900 B. C.
Wood, stucco, painted; L 54.3 cm, W 10.2 cm,
H 20.1 cm
Inv. No. 3923

During the Middle Kingdom, the entire household
was often placed, in miniature form, in the tomb,
including the house, the farm and outbuildings
complete with cattle and servants. The pleasure
boat was also included. Here, the married couple
is sitting in the cabin, attended by a servant. E. H.

FISH-SHAPED COSMETIC PALETTE
c. 3000 B. C.
Slate; L 18.5 cm, W 8.7 cm, H 1.5 cm
Inv. No. 9067

Slate palettes were used for grinding mineral
pigments. This one takes the form of a common
Nile fish. Palettes with relief work are rare. Here
the area for rubbing and mixing the colour is set
off by a ring; encircling it are various aquatic life
forms, like fish, a crocodile, a stork and a goose
with goslings. The eye recess was originally set
with bone. Beneath the mouth, a hole has been
drilled for a string.   E. H.

KOHL CONTAINER
6th Dynasty, 2268–2228 B. C.
Calcite; H 14.4 cm, W 6 cm, D 6.5 cm
Inv. No. 3886

The receptacle is shaped like a monkey with her
baby. The (now missing) collar and bracelets
show it to have been a house pet. Its upper right
arm bears the name-ring of the throne name,
Meri-re, of King Pepi I, indicating that this was a
present from him to some private personage.
Kohl is the black eye make-up worn by both men
and women.   E. H.

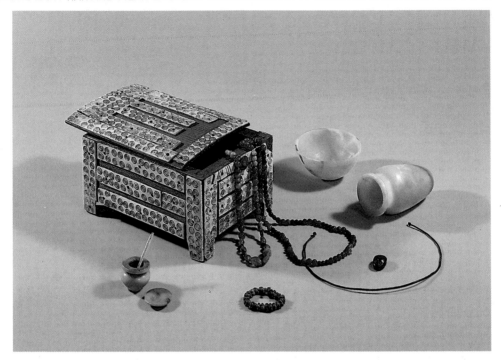

SMALL COSMETIC CHEST WITH JEWELLERY
El-Kubaniya-North
12th Dynasty, 1990–1785 B. C.
Wood with ivory, calcite, precious stones, copper;
L 17 cm, W 12.5 cm, H 10 cm
Inv. Nos. 7108–7116

Funerary equipment for a girl. The small wooden chest is decorated with ivory bands in the Nubian fashion. Inside was a little kohl pot out of light blue stone, complete with lid and applicator. The body had been adorned with the copper fillet, the strings of amethyst, carnelian and turquoise beads and a scarab out of serpentine. The two small calcite vessels symbolize nourishment.
E. H.

BROAD COLLAR AND BRACELET ▷
Giza
End of 5th Dynasty, c. 2290 B. C.
Faience, gold foil; H c. 20 cm, W c. 26 cm
Inv. Nos. 9072, 9073

Broad collars were standard adornment of both men and women. This particular collar is a durable imitation of a broad necklace made of flowers and foliage. Here, glazed faience in different colour was covered with gold foil, making it more valuable for the corpse to wear.
E. H.

FEMALE HEAD

19th Dynasty, beginning of 13th century B. C.
Limestone; H 22.5 cm, W 25.6 cm
Inv. No. 73

Canonical representation of a lady's face in bas-relief, with an artistically curled wig, earrings and a diadem with a lotus flower. The eyes and brows bear evidence of make-up. It could have been a model study for a sculpture studio.　　　　H. S.

WOMAN GRINDING GRAIN ▽

Pyramid district of Giza
6th Dynasty, c. 2200 B. C.
Limestone; L 29.5 cm, W 7.8 cm, H 18 cm
Inv. No. 7500

An expressive, living portrayal of a woman grinding grain into flour using a grindstone on an oval slab. Sometimes the *serdâbs* of the Old Kingdom *mastaba* tombs contained such servant statues along with the statues of the tomb-owner and his family. According to the magical ideas of the time these servants were "real" and could provide the dead with food and drink in the afterlife.　　　H. S.

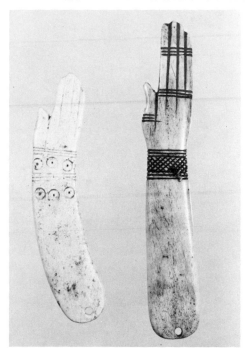

TWO CLAPPERS
Middle Kingdom, 2000–1750 B. C.
Ivory; L 12.4 cm and 15.5 cm, resp. W 2.4 cm
and 2.5 cm, resp.
Inv. Nos. 7236, 8263

Two hand-shaped clappers were used together
as rhythm instruments instead of handclapping.
They were usually decorated with eye symbols,
bracelets and rings.   E. H.

SISTRUM ▽
Ptolemaic/Roman, 1st century B. C.?
Bronze; H 23 cm, W 4.7 cm, D 2.85 cm
Inv. No. 324

The arched sistrum is a percussion instrument
similar to a rattle. This one may be attributed to the
Bastet cult because of the small cat figure on the
top.   E. H.

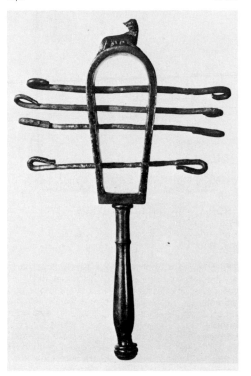

OFFERING TABLET ▷
12th Dynasty, c. 1900 B. C.
Limestone; L 32 cm, W 28.5 cm, H 7.5 cm
Inv. No. 98

Such offering tablets were used for daily food
offerings in the tomb, in this case, for an entire
family (according to the inscription). Shown in
relief are bread, meat, drink and two water basins
for any and all the needs of eternity.   E. H.

"HORUS ON THE CROCODILES"
Ptolemaic Period, 3rd–1st centuries B. C.?
Serpentine; H 13.6 cm, W 8.9 cm, D 2.9 cm
Inv. No. 4137

The obverse side of the *Horus Stelae* consists of a statuette of the child Horus standing on crocodiles and holding fast to various dangerous animals (snakes, scorpions and lions). All the other surfaces contain magic spells, even the bottom. The slabs were usually carved out of serpentine ("snake-stone"!) and were intended as a defence against the dangers of harmful animals. Water poured over the stone would have become imbued with magical powers.　　H. S.

FALCON
Prehistoric, end of 4th millennium B. C.
Breccia; L 13 cm, W 4 cm, H 3.7 cm
Inv. No. 1186

The eyes and legs were made of another material and are missing.　　E. H.

RAM'S HEAD ▽
19th/20th Dynasty, c. 1150 B. C.
Serpentine; H 16.1 cm, W 8.3 cm, D 9.3 cm
Inv. No. 1029

The ram was the sacred animal of Amun. This ram's head rests on a high base. The inscription tells us it was a votive offering to the god Amun of Karnak from Pentaweret. King Amenophis I (18th Dynasty) is depicted on the front. In later periods he was to be honoured as an oracular god.　　E. H.

BAT ▽
Prehistoric, end of 4th millennium B. C.
Serpentine; H 5.2 cm, W 13.2 cm, D 3 cm
Inv. No. 1180

Two holes are drilled next to the feet so that the bat could be hung in its natural upside-down sleeping position. This bat is represented flapping its wings.　　E. H.

ICHNEUMON
Late Period, 6th–4th centuries B. C.
Green schist; L 28 cm, W 6.3 cm, H 10.5 cm
Inv. No. 1062

The mongoose, a small beast of prey, was greatly loved and respected as a killer of mice and

snakes. It is associated with the god of creation, Atum of Heliopolis, and destroys the demon serpent, Apophis. In accordance with customary Egyptian style, the animal emerges from the geometrical block of stone underneath it. The front of the stone is formed into an obelisk. Atum of Heliopolis is mentioned in the inscription. E. H.

STANDING FALCON
Late Period, 6th–4th centuries B. C.
Bronze; H 21 cm, W 8.7 cm, D 21.5 cm
Inv. No. 304

As the sacred animal of the god Horus, falcons were mummified and buried, for example, in a hollow falcon figure. Engraved in the bronze are the feathers, the ornamental collar and an amulet. Occasionally this fine decorative work was inlaid with silver and gold. A suitable plate sealed up the rectangular opening in the underside of the tail.
E. H.

HYKSOS WEAPONS FROM TELL EL-DAB'A
1675–1575 B. C.

SCIMITAR
Bronze; L 22.3 cm, W 3.5 cm
Inv. No. A 1278

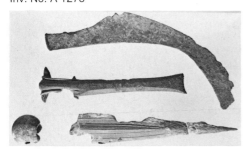

BATTLE-AXE
Bronze; L 16 cm, W 2.4 cm
Inv. No. A 1285

DAGGER
Bronze; L 19 cm, W 3.7 cm
Inv. No. A 1282

These three kinds of weapons, as well as the horse and chariot, were unknown in Egypt before the foreign rule of the Hyksos. With the new weapons came new fighting techniques. E. H.

SMALL PAINTED CLAY VESSEL
El-Kubaniya-South
Prehistoric, 4000–3000 B. C.
Fired clay, painted; H 10.5 cm, Diam. 4.6 cm
Inv. No. 7469

On either side of the vessel are lugs for attaching a rope, enabling it to be hung or carried. Below these, the sides are decorated with row boats (with cabins), flamingos and mountain peaks. The predynastic period in Egypt was known for its beautifully painted ceramic work, but usually the decorative motives were geometric in nature or imitations of speckled or veined stone. Pictures of objects or figures are rare. E. H.

LARGE JAR WITH POTTER'S MARK
Tura
Predynastic, end of 4th millennium B. C.
Fired clay; H 50 cm, Diam. 26 cm
Inv. No. 6756

The large cylindrical storage vessel of red clay was formed by hand on a slowly revolving potter's wheel. The exterior is coated with red slip and carefully smoothed. Just under the rim is an incised string decoration. Nearly halfway down are two marks, one in the shape of a bull. E. H.

BIG JUG, TELL EL-YAHUDIYA WARE
Tell el-Dab'a
End of the Middle Kingdom, c. 1700 B. C.
Fired clay, encrusted in white, with modern restoration; H 30.3 cm, Diam. 28.5 cm
Inv. No. A 1691

Tell el-Yahudiya jugs of this size are rare. As part of the funerary equipment they were always of small size. In the densely stratified layers of the settlement they were not preserved. The design is also unusual: a narrow row of fish bounded by geometric areas. Tell el-Dab'a is a settlement found in the eastern Nile Delta. The levels from the Hyksos era (ca. 1675–1550 B. C.), a time of foreign (Asian) rule, are especially interesting to historians. The Egyptians called this group "Hyksos" which means "Rulers of Foreign Lands".
E. H.

49

◁ **MUMMY BOARD AND INNER COFFIN FOR NES-PAUTI-TAUI**
From Deir el-Bahari Cachette
21st Dynasty, c. 1000 B. C.
Wood covered with linen cartonnage, painted, varnished;
Mummy board: L 173 cm, W 36 cm; coffin: L 183 cm, W 50 cm, H 35.5 cm
Inv. Nos. 6261, 6262

Another, outer coffin of mummy-form shape belongs to this mummy board and inner coffin. The entire set of coffins was made in Thebes for the Amun priest, Nes-pauti-taui. The mummy board and both coffin lids bear the same decorative scheme. We see enormous ornamental collars of foliage and flowers. The hands are separately applied and hold the *djed*-pillar and the Blood of Isis. The faces and wigs were also superimposed. The decoration of the body is divided into squares showing various deities in a symmetrical arrangement: The rising sun as scarab is flanked by the throned Osiris, winged guardian goddesses, serpents and throned gods in shrines. The geometrical divisions in the lower half follow the vertical and horizontal wrappings of the mummy bindings and are used here as lines of script. The short lines declare the deceased to have been "vindicated by the Great God, the Ruler of the Underworld". The longer lines consist of the spells of Osiris and offering formulas naming the deceased by title. Typical for this period are the mummy-form shape, the large collars, hands with amulets, rich and ornate painting, body and sun disc in stucco relief and *horror vacui,* meaning the avoidance of an empty background. Every square centimeter is covered with symbols and hieroglyphics. Amun temple priests were interred in the so-called *cachette,* a system of underground passages in western Thebes. In 1891, the priestly tombs were opened up and many coffins and funerary objects were given to European collections by the Egyptian government.   E. H.

MUMMY-SHAPED INNER COFFIN OF PEDE-ESE
25th Dynasty, 7th century B. C.
Wood covered with linen cartonnage, painted;
L 183 cm, W 44 cm, H 35 cm
Inv. No. 8902

The accompanying outer coffin and mummy still exist. Rich ornamentation: adoration of the Abydos fetish, Osiris and Re-Harachte, the mummy on a bier and Osiris in a tree. The outer coffin is decorated with the four sons of Horus, Thoth leading the dead to Osiris, Isis and Nephthys.
          E. H.

MUMMY-SHAPED SARCOPHAGUS OF PA-NEHEM-ESE

Saqqara
Ptolemaic, 2nd century B. C.
Basalt; L 205 cm, W 66.5 cm, H 47.5 cm
Inv. No. 4

The hard stone has been painstakingly polished and engraved. The finely textured figures provide a strong contrast to the polished surface. The floral collar is small and insignificant. Dominant are the representations of gods of the hereafter, worship of the sun, the *Ba*-bird and the mummy on a bier. On the rear of the head, Isis and Nephthys embrace the Abydos fetish. Lengthy inscriptions contain passages for the hereafter and an idealized biography.   E. H.

SARCOPHAGUS OF NES-SHU-TEFNUT ▽

Early Ptolemaic, c. 300 B. C.
Metaamphibolite; L 290 cm, W 115 cm, H 108 cm
Inv. No. 1

This exceptionally large sarcophagus contained the wooden mummy-shaped coffin (or two nesting coffins) and the mummy. The interior and exterior are richly decorated with pictures and passages from the so-called Book of the Caverns first appearing in the royal tombs of the 19th Dynasty. Described is the voyage of the sun god, Re, through the underworld, going past caves guarded by demons and punishing the enemies. Inside, Isis and Nephthys, Neith and Selket, Nekhbet and Uto, as well as Anubis guard the mummy. On the top of the lid the *Ba*-bird of Nes-shu-tefnut soars. On the underside of the lid are the starry heavens with the goddess of the sky, Nut.   E. H.

HEAD SECTION FROM THE STUCCO COFFIN OF A WOMAN

Roman, first quarter of 2nd century A. D.
Stucco, painted; L 60.5 cm, W 25 cm, H 30 cm
Inv. No. 8513

In Roman times, mummy coffins were modelled in fine plaster over stiffened linen or papyrus forms. The heads were mass-produced in moulds and then given their individual features through painting. They show the native dress of that time. This woman is wearing a curled wig with a stylized floral wreath and is heavily bejewelled.   E. H.

FOUR CANOPIC JARS FOR PRINCESS TJES-BAST-PER

Thebes
22nd Dynasty, c. 870 B. C.
Limestone, yellow sandstone; H 35.6 cm, Diam. 20.4 cm
Inv. No. 3561
Calcite; H 42.4 cm, Diam. 17 cm
Inv. No. 3562
Calcite; H 37.2 cm, Diam. 19.4 cm
Inv. No. 3563
Calcite; H 41.2 cm, Diam. 15.5 cm
Inv. No. 3564

Canopic jars are clay or stone vessels (seldom out of any other material) used for storage of the viscera which were removed from the body during the mummification process. They were kept alongside the coffin. In the Old Kingdom, the lids were flat. In the First Intermediate Period, they are shaped like a human head, either male or female, corresponding to the gender of the deceased. From the 19th Dynasty on, they usually resembled the four sons of Horus who were to guard the viscera. The four were the human-headed Imsety, the ape-headed Hapy, the jackal-headed Duamutef and the falcon-headed Qebehsenuef. Tjes-bast-per was the daughter of King Osorkon II and his (concubinary) wife Ast-em-achbit; this, courtesy of the four-lined inscription. Tjes-bast-per had been married to the High Priest Takeloth.
                                                                E. H.

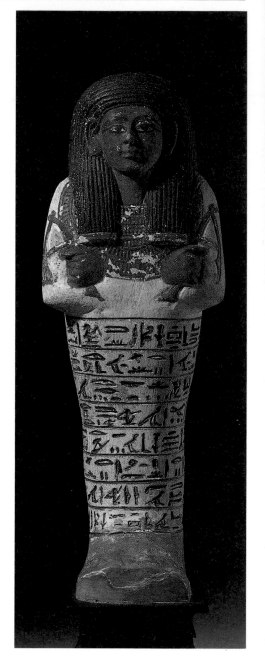

SHABTI IN THE DRESS OF DAILY LIFE FOR RAI
Early 19th Dynasty, c. 1290 B. C.
Blue paste; H 17.3 cm, W 5.9 cm, D 3.35 cm
Inv. No. 17

SHABTI IN MUMMY FORM FOR SEN-NEDJEM
Found in 1885 in Deir el-Medina
19th Dynasty, c. 1300 B. C.
Limestone, painted; H 28.3 cm, W 9.95 cm,
D 8.8 cm
Inv. No. 6614

Shabti, or „answerer", is a mummy-like figure of a worker. Its function in the tomb was to act as a proxy in whatever work there might be in the domains of the hereafter. This explains the great number of them: 365, one for each day of the year and, in addition, a minimum of thirty-six over-seers. Their intended usage and the work they were to do are inscribed on the figures them-selves. They hold two hoes and carry baskets.

E. H.

SHABTI FOR KING PINODJEM I
From Deir el-Bahari Cachette
21st Dynasty, 1054 – 1032 B. C.
Faience, blue glaze; H 14.2 cm, W 4.04 cm,
D 2.58 cm
Inv. No. 3905

The uraeus snake about the forehead distinguishes this *shabti* from the worker figures of private persons. He was High Priest of Amun in Thebes and also carried a full royal titulary. The cartouche encircles the throne name, Pinodjem mer-amun.   E. H.

SHABTI FOR TJAI-HAR-PTA ▽
30th Dynasty, c. 360–342 B. C.
Faience, light green glaze; H 24.8 cm, W 6.6 cm,
D 3.9 cm
Inv. No. 8373

This mummy-shaped figure with its sharply chiseled features is an especially superior example of its time. The finely grained faience has a thin, beautifully gleaming glaze enabling all the detail work to be appreciated. The text consists of the *shabti*-spell and the title of its owner – Sage, Prophet.   E. H.

SHABTI FOR NES-TA-NEBT-ASHRU △
From Deir el-Bahari Cachette
21st Dynasty, c. 965 B. C.
Faience, blue glaze; H 14.5 cm, W 5.8 cm,
D 3.5 cm
Inv. No. 6062

She was the daughter of King Pinodjem II and carried the title: "Chief of the Harem and foremost of the Noblewomen of Amun". The *shabti*-spell in this particular example runs around the figure in columns.   E. H.

SHABTI FOR KING PSAMMETICHUS △
26th Dynasty, c. 600 B. C.
Faience, pale blue green glaze; H 19.2 cm,
W 5.7 cm, D 3.8 cm
Inv. No. 8354

This worker figure has the pharaoh's facial features and is distinguished by his royal headdress with the uraeus on the forehead.   E. H.

SHABTI BOX OR CANOPIC CHEST
21st Dynasty, 11th/10th century B. C.
Wood and stucco, painted; H 34 cm, W 30 cm,
D 17 cm
Inv. No. 960

The chest consists of a triad of shrines or store
rooms with barrel vaults. On the four sides may be
seen the deceased in adoration of Osiris, the tree
goddess giving water to the *Ba* and the four sons
of Horus.   E. H.

BOOK OF THE DEAD OF KHONSU-MES
21st Dynasty, c. 1000 B. C.
Papyrus, painted; L 410 cm, H c. 15.5 cm
Inv. No. 3859

The so-called Book of the Dead is found with the
mummy. Selected chapters contained vital
information for life in the hereafter. The papyrus of
Khonsu-mes is unusual because it only consists
of illustrations. Short captions providing names
are found solely in the case of the deceased
(described as Chief Archivist of the Treasury of
the Amun Temple) and a few deities. Noteworthy
are the elegant drawings and the polychromatic
treatment. The contents include entering the
underworld, coming before the judgement of the
dead and the completion of the mummy by
Anubis. One important chapter describes the gift
of bread and water by the goddess of the sky, Nut,
in the tree.   E. H.

LION PASSANT
Babylon
Beginning of 6th century B. C.
Glazed brick; W 230 cm, H 107 cm
Inv. No. Sem 951

Nebuchadnezzar II (605–562 B. C.), monarch of the late Babylonian Empire had the Ishtar Gate built as one of the gates to the city of Babylon. Its highly colourful and richly decorated façade was done in glazed brick reliefs. Whereas the main motifs of the Gate are the Dragon of Marduk and the Bull of Adad, the Lions of Ishtar adorn the walls of the processional avenue running towards the Portal. The structure has been, to a great extent, rebuilt in (East) Berlin's Pergamon Museum.

H. S.

MALE HEAD
South Arabia
Beginning of 1st millennium A. D.
Alabaster; H 25 cm, W 14 cm, D 11.5 cm
Inv. No. Sem 114

South Arabia (Yemen) has always been famous for its incense. The cultivation and wide-spread trade of this desirable product turned Yemen into a very important region in the first millennium B. C. Earliest literary information is found in the Old Testament, in the story of Solomon (10th century) and the Queen of Sheba. Here in a marginal region of the Near East a highly autonomous culture developed. This kind of heads, in sculpture on the tombstones, portrayed the bearer partly in abstract idealization and then again – as here – in a very naturalistic way.   H. S.

SOUTH ARABIAN INSCRIPTION
South Arabia
Probably 4th century A. D.
Limestone; H 65 cm, W 32 cm
Inv. No. Sem 673

South Arabia adopted – in the first half of the 1st millenium B. C. – the semitic alphabet that had originated about 1000 B. C. in Syria's coastal regions. In South Arabia it assumed a beautifully geometric form, especially well-suited to stone inscription. Architectural inscriptions, inserted in façades were often done using a negative engraving method, that is, the spaces were cut out so that the letters projected. The same was done with the vertical slashes used to separate words.

On the left and right, here, are monograms. They are formed as a combination of three letters.

H. S.

PROTECTIVE SLAB
South Arabia
Beginning of 1st millennium A. D.
Limestone; H 27 cm, W 23 cm
Inv. No. Sem 24

Early cultures often believed that bulls' heads could ward off evil. Slabs, such as this one, were mounted on building exteriors. The two-line inscription reads: "Protective magic of 'LZ'D and his brother HLQH from (the tribe) HB'T". South Arabian writing did not represent vowels.   H. S.

OIL LAMP
Shabwa (South Arabia)
1st century A. D.?
Bronze; H 34 cm, W 11 cm, D 25.5 cm
Inv. No. Sem 694

By the beginning of the first Christian millennium, Hellenistic influence had reached South Arabia. It is clearly evident in the ornate decorative style of the oil lamp. (There are several parallel examples.) South Arabian symbolism is unmistakable in the leaping ram and the flat knot of the handle. In addition, both sides of the base carry short inscriptions in late, richly ornate South Arabian letters. On one side is the word „lamp" and on the other, possibly, the owner's name.   H. S.

THE COLLECTION OF GREEK AND ROMAN ANTIQUITIES

The Collection of Greek and Roman Antiquities in Vienna's Kunsthistorische Museum is among the most important of its kind in the world. The exhibits cover a period of history extending from Cypriot Bronze Age pottery from the 3rd millennium B. C. to Slavic finds from around the turn of the first millennium A. D. Above all, the collection is internationally renowned as the home of the unique cameos and archaeological treasures dating from the Great Migration and the Early Middle Ages.

The Collection originates from the former estate of the Habsburgs. The Viennese Court had begun to collect ancient works of art as far back as the 16th century and some of the most outstanding exhibits were acquired at a very early date indeed; for example, the priceless Gemma Augustea under Rudolph II (1576–1612), the Amazonian sarcophagus in the 17th century, or the Senatus Consultum de Bacchanalibus under Karl VI (1711–1740). Yet the actual basis of the present collection was provided by Franz II (1792–1835) with the organisation of the Cabinet of Coins and Antiquities in the Hofburg.

In the 18th century the revival of interest in ancient Greece and Rome, aroused by the finds in the cities around Vesuvius and by German Classicism, produced an enthusiasm for collect-

ing which in its turn brought some remarkable results. A variety of archaeological finds from all parts of the Monarchy made their way into the Imperial collection at Vienna, some of accidental nature but others originating from excavations or acquired on travels. Although some of the discoveries of important treasures from the Eastern regions of the Monarchy can be attributed to pure chance, the subsequent organisation of the numerous antiquities in the various Imperial art collections, libraries and palaces was undertaken in a highly systematic fashion. In 1779 Maria Theresa had the antique gems transferred from the Treasury to the Coin Cabinet which since 1798 also received sculptures and inscriptions from the Court Library and the two Palaces of Belvedere and Schönbrunn, with the aim of founding a "complete gallery of antiquities". Of significance were also the purchases from private collections, which came to form the basis of the collection of ancient vases and bronzes. In 1802, the painter M. Wutky acquired numerous antiquities in Rome and Naples, amounting to a value of more than 9,000 gulden. In 1804 sculptures, vases and bronzes were purchased from the collection of M.V. von Rainer in exchange for an life annuity of 2,500 gulden a year; in 1808 30,000 gulden were paid for a variety of objects from the estate

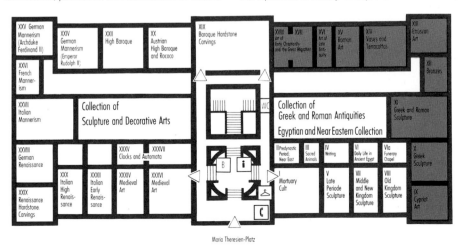

Maria Theresien-Platz

of the late J. de France, and in 1815 the fantastic sum of 125,000 gulden was paid for Count Lamberg's collection, containing sculptures and more than 600 vases. In the following periods such vast amounts of money were never again available, which is why the Collection was never systematically extended. Nevertheless, apart from small acquisitions, donations and bequests, there have been several major additions since then. The sculptural and architectural sections were considerably enriched by the Austrian archaeological excavations in Eastern Greece (Samothrace, Gölbaşı-Trysa and Ephesus); the complete inventory of the antiquities of the Ambras collection were obtained in 1880, as were those of the Este-Catajo collection in 1923; and with the incorporation of the antiquities of the then Austrian Museum of Art and Industry in 1940, numerous valuable pieces enlarged the collection of Greek vases.

Due to all these new acquisitions the Collection of Classical Antiquities (its official title ever since it was separated from the Coin Cabinet in 1900) has suffered from a continual lack of space. As early as 1891, when the ancient works of art were being transferred to the new museum on the Ringstraße, the relief frieze of the Heroon of Trysa had to be put into storage. The finds from Ephesus too, which began to arrive in 1896, were either provisionally installed in other buildings or put into storage, and it was only in 1978 that the treasures from Ephesus and Samothrace found a suitable home in the collection's new Ephesus Museum in the Neue Hofburg. Thus it was that the Collection became the second largest department of the Kunsthistorische Museum, though the severe lack of space still prevents it from being appreciated in its entirety even today.

A. B.-W.

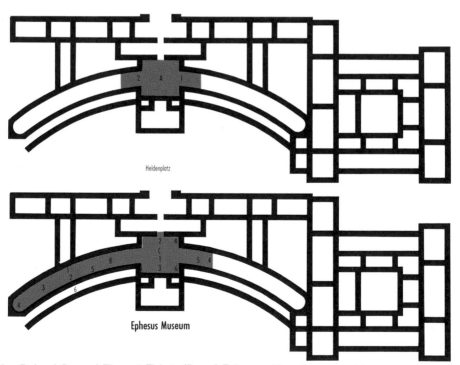

Heldenplatz

Ephesus Museum

A – Raised Ground Floor: 1 Ticket office · 2 Ephesus: Altar of the Artemision

B – Intermediate Floor: 1 Theatre · 2 City model · 3 Parthian monument · 4 Oktogon · 5 Rotunda · 6 Documentation

C – Upper Floor: 1 Ideal sculpture · 2 Ideal sculpture and reliefs · 3 Portraits and minor finds · 4 Samothrace: Hieron, Propylon · 5 Arsinoeion · 6 Ptolemaion

LIDDED BOX
Cypriot – Bronze Age
2000–1800 B. C.
Clay; H 9.3 cm, L 18.5 cm
Inv. No. IV 1857

From earliest times, due to its position at the crossroads of the major civilisations of the ancient world, the island of Cyprus was subject to a variety of influences in its cultural development. Nevertheless, its works of art preserved an unmistakeable Cypriot originality. During the Bronze Age, when the exploitation of the island's extensive copper resources led to a flourishing of its trade, a characteristic red or black polished pottery began to be produced. Often decorated with incised or applied patterns, it was exported to Syria, Egypt and Crete. To this form belongs the handmade lidded box *(pyxis)*, the decoration of which is restricted to simple linear patterns and circles.   A. B.-W.

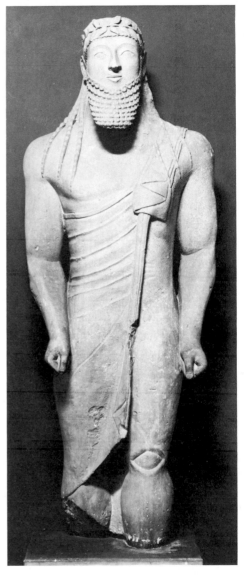

VOTIVE STATUE ▷
Cypro – Archaic
c. 500 B. C.
Limestone; H 201 cm
Inv. No. I 341

In its mode of construction and motific stance this larger-than-life statue of a priest, discovered in a sanctuary near Pyla in Cyprus in 1868, displays the typical characteristics of large-scale Greek archaic sculpture. The head, which is adorned with a wreath of leaves, is dominated by the flat, almond-shaped eyes and the highly stylised ringlets of the beard. With its broad structure, designed for a purely frontal view, the statue embodies the style which flourished on Cyprus in the 6th century B. C. and which combined elements of Greek, Egyptian and Oriental art. A great number of similar votive statues, originally painted and often standing back to back, have been found in the sanctuaries of the island.   A. B.-W.

◁ **INVENTORY OF THE TEMPLE OF JUPITER DOLICHENUS FROM MAUER AN DER URL**
Roman
1st half of 3rd century A. D.
Silver, bronze, iron
Jupiter: Bronze; H 32 cm; Inv. No. M 1
Victoria: Bronze; H 25.1 cm; Inv. No. M 3
Triangular panel: Bronze; H 54.2 cm; Inv. No. M5

Containing more than 100 objects, this Roman Age find was the most extensive archaeological discovery ever made in Austria. The whole complex was discovered in 1937, not far from the Roman fort of Mauer an der Url (near Amstetten in Lower Austria). On the site were found the contents of a temple to the god Jupiter Dolichenus, whose cult had originated in the Syrian city of Doliche and been brought to the west largely by soldiers, for whom the god was a protector. The treasure, which had been buried in the first half of the 3rd century A. D. in the face of attacks by Germanic tribes, gives us a picture of the inventory of a provincial temple on the outer reaches of the Roman Empire (Noricum). The objects can be divided into two groups: those with a religious or cultic function (statuettes, standards, miniature silver votive plates) and those with a profane function (vessels, lamps, bells and various instruments and tools). A statuette of Jupiter Dolichenus shows him standing on the back of a bull and wearing a Phrygian cap, cuirass and buskins, holding a bundle of thunderbolts and a double-headed axe (of which only the handle remains). The goddess Victoria would have held the symbols of victory, a crown and a palm leaf, in her right and left hands respectively. Her roundish rustic face and the elongated proportions, as well as the unnaturally fluted hem of her skirts with their graphically defined pleats, all help to make this statuette one of the most important examples of the local conception of art. The triangular panel decorated with repoussé (an eagle, the sun god Sol, the moon goddess Luna, Jupiter Dolichenus, Juno Regina, Victoria etc.) was once mounted on a wooden shaft and would have been carried in processions as a standard. Dedicatory inscriptions are to be found on the bases of the two statuettes as also on the triangular panel.   K. G.

TOMB RELIEF OF A WOMAN
Palmyran
2nd half of 2nd century A. D.
Limestone; H 38 cm
Inv. No. I 1503

In the 2nd and 3rd centuries A. D. a unique kind of art developed in the desert city of Palmyra in Northern Syria. Fusing elements of the Hellenistic-Roman and Persian-Parthian styles, it found its highest expression in the lavish decoration of tombstones. An example is this relief fragment displaying a half-length portrait of a young woman of high-ranking family. It once served as the sealing slab of a tower-tomb. Spool and spindle characterise the deceased as a virtuous housewife.   A. B.-W.

YOUTH FROM MAGDALENSBERG ▷
16th century cast after the Roman original
Bronze; H 183.5 cm
Inv. No. VI 1

In 1983 the Collection of Greek and Roman Antiquities began a research project which had the primary aim of clarifying the methods used in the casting and moulding of the Magdalensberg statue. The results caused some surprise, for it was discovered that the statue is not the ancient original but rather a cast from the 16th century.

The original was found in 1502 by a farmer ploughing his field. It then arrived in Salzburg through the initiative of Matthäus Lang von Wellenburg, at first Bishop of Gurk, after 1519 Archbishop of Salzburg. News of the sensational discovery spread quickly and it is possible that Albrecht Dürer saw the statue on his way to Italy in 1505. The first representation of it was a woodcut which appeared in a book of inscriptions in 1534, and the Salzburg artist Hans Bocksberger the Elder made it the subject of a fresco he painted in the residence of the Duke of Bavaria in Landshut in 1542. In 1551 the Salzburg Cathedral chapter acceded to a request of King Ferdinand I and presented the statue to him (the record of the transaction is still extant), and in order to possess at least a copy of the original a cast of it was made. However, the knowledge of this procedure was then forgotten, so that the cast came to be considered the original, and as such it found its way into the Collection of Greek and Roman Antiquities in Vienna in 1806. The original has long since disappeared, although its trail seems to lead towards Spain.

The most important evidence in support of the argument that the statue is an example of a Renaissance cast and not an ancient original, derived from examination of its casting and moulding. The method of casting involved the use of auxiliary negatives taken from the original – a method unknown to the ancient world, yet one for which there is evidence that it was employed in the 16th century and which also accounts for the thick walls of the bronze and the fact that it was cast in one piece. Scientific analyses (using radiography, analysis of alloy and core etc.), have all provided further corroboration. The prominent traces of surface work (hammer strokes, file and scraper marks) did in part derive from a later reworking, as had earlier been presumed, yet in a much greater extent from cold-work undertaken during roughcasting. A complete burnishing of the surface had been dispensed with and the statue given a coating of some kind of black laquer, traces of which still remain today. We do not know the exact date of casting (sometime after 1551), nor the workshop where it was carried out, only that the statue in the Collection of Greek and Roman Antiquities is one of the earliest examples of a Renaissance cast of a large-scale ancient bronze.

The original must have been a work of early Roman ideal sculpture from the 1st century B. C. based on classical Greek statues (Polykleitos). On the right thigh is an inscription, presumed to have also appeared on the original, according to which the statue on Magdalensberg was donated by two freedmen, Aulus Poblicius Antiocus and Tiberius Barbius Tiberi(a)nus.

K. G.

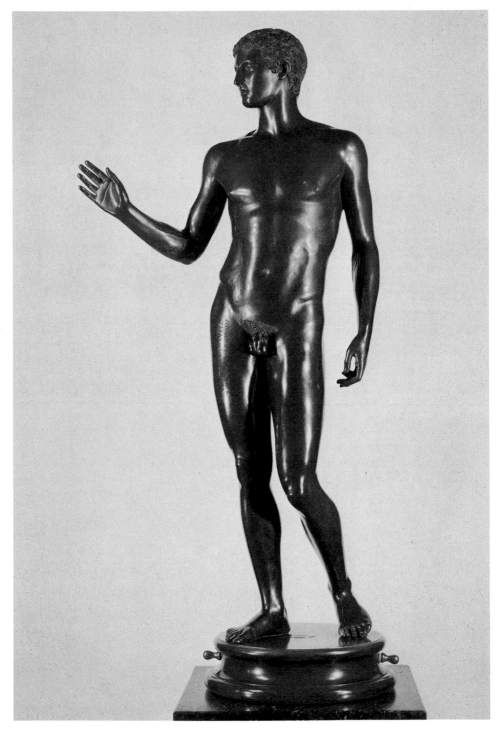

FRAGMENT OF THE PARTHENON FRIEZE
Greek
c. 440 B. C.
Marble; H 26 cm
Inv. No. I 1092

The climax of the Great Panatheneion, the chief festival of Athens held in honour of Athene, was a procession which ended with the presentation of the newly woven peplos (a woman's garment) to the tutelary goddess of the city. This is the subject of the frieze around the cella of the Parthenon, the temple on the Athenian Acropolis. It depicts the garment being handed over in the presence of the goddess, with the festival procession approaching from both sides: girls with sacrificial instruments, young men with sacrificial animals, old men, chariots, youths on horseback. This fragment shows two bearded elder citizens of Athens in conversation. W. O.

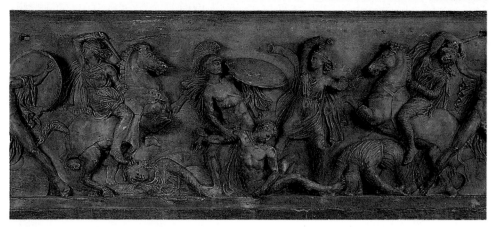

AMAZONIAN SARCOPHAGUS
Greek
2nd half of 4th century B. C.
Marble; L 264 cm
Inv. No. I 169

The relief art of the Greek sarcophagi first reached its peak not in the mother country, but rather among the Greeks further east. Thus it was that the Amazonian sarcophagus was first discovered in a burial chamber in Cyprus in the 16th century, later arriving in Vienna via the Fuggers, a family of Augsburg merchants. The symmetrical composition masterfully depicts the struggle between the Greek heroes and the mythical female warriors in a series of dramatic individual scenes. In the middle group, a Greek is seen defending himself with his shield against an Amazon's axeblow while trying to rescue his fallen comrade.

K. G.

PORTRAIT OF ARISTOTLE
Roman
Copy after Greek original of 4th century B. C.
Marble; H 30.5 cm
Inv. No. I 246

The Greek philosopher Aristotle (384–322 B. C.), a native of Macedonia, was a pupil of Plato, the teacher of Alexander the Great and the founder of a school of philosophy in Athens. Towards the end of the 4th century, the importance attached to portraiture increased in proportion to the growth of interest in the individual form. Characteristic of the depiction of Aristotle, represented in this bust with a short beard and sparse hair on his brow, are the broad skull, the furrows of age and the small, penetrating eyes.

W. O.

HEAD OF ARTEMIS
Greek
2nd century B.C.
Marble; H 29 cm
Inv. No. I 26

ARTEMIS
Hellenistic
3rd century B.C.
Marble; H 78 cm
Inv. No. I 603

This statuette of Artemis, found in ancient Kition (present-day Larnaka) in Cyprus in 1881, clearly demonstrates – as a delightful contrast – the change of style in the depiction of clothed female figures. The goddess, having made her appearance at her archaic votive statue, seems to be awaiting the pious visitor, leaning upon the idol that represents her. The pictorial character of this typically Hellenistic work, in which the influence of Praxiteles is still to be felt, was originally strengthened by the use of colour, which at the time of its discovery was much more evident than the present pale traces imply.   A. B.-W.

HEAD OF EROS ▷
Greek
3rd century B.C.
Marble; H 23.5 cm
Inv. No. I 1563

This head of the love god, who is wearing a band in his hair, originally belonged to a statue and is almost certainly a Hellenistic adaption of the arrow-stringing Eros of Lysippus, one of the most important sculptors of the 4th century B.C.   W. O.

The continuing effect of the legacy of the great sculptor Praxiteles is here revealed in this head of the goddess of the chase, which was designed to be set into a statue. Through the wavy hair runs a ribbon in which a hole has been bored – evidently for securing a piece of jewellery. The gentle grace and loveliness of her face, the remote gaze in her eyes and the fullness of her lips are all expressions of an almost rococo sensuousness.   W. O.

TOMB RELIEF ▽
Greek (Thasian)
3rd century B.C.
Marble; H 140.5 cm
Inv. No. I 1553

Although a law passed in the year 317 B.C. brought excessive burial luxuries in Attica to an abrupt end, gravestone decoration still lived on in other regions of Greece. This tomb relief from the North Aegean island of Thasos is a particularly good example. It presents an oblique view of the deceased sitting in a chair skillfully turned towards the spectator, with her robe drawn over the back of the head and her eyes staring fixedly into the distance. To her left stands a small servant girl, her eyes upturned towards her mistress, in her hands a cylindrical box *(pyxis)* for the safekeeping of jewellery or articles for her toilette.   K. G.

GRAVE STELE OF PARMENISKOS
Greek
c. 200 B.C.
Limestone; H 108 cm
Inv. No. I 1024

The upper section of this grave stele is a fusion of various elements of the Ionic style: a pediment with a Gorgon head to ward off evil; underneath it the cornice *(geison)*, a dentil border and a frieze depicting a battle against the Amazons. Immediately below are oak dwarfs and sirens standing upon rosettes, and composite creatures half-fish, half-woman who perform the threnody. In the lowest part are two griffons, one on each side of a *crater* (mixing bowl), Dionysian symbols of the afterlife.   K. G.

PORTRAIT OF A RULER ▽
Ptolemaic
3rd quarter of 2nd century B.C.
Marble; H 28 cm
Inv. No. I 1764

Another example of a head designed to be set into a statue, this bust displays a technical characteristic found in many Ptolemaic portrait sculptures; namely, that the missing fore and rear parts of the head would originally not have been worked from the marble block but, rather, completed with another piece of coloured plaster. That the person represented is a ruler is indicated by the diadem he wears. The portrait is possibly of the young Memphitis, one of the sons of King Ptolemy VIII of Egypt.   W. O.

HEAD OF A PRIESTESS (?)
Egyptian-Hellenistic
2nd century B.C. ?
Basalt; H 31 cm
Inv. No. I 406

A portrait of an old woman with full face and double-chin, small spiral ringlets across her forehead and corkscrew curls over her ears and neck. The expressive face, the eyes of which were once set with some other material (ivory?), is subdivided by two deep furrows running from the corners of the mouth to those of the nose, and the band in her hair suggests a portrait of a priestess or a sovereign. The use of such black stone finds its precedent in the tradition of ancient Egyptian art.   W. O.

GRIMANI RELIEF
Roman
Mid-1ˢᵗ century A.D.
Marble; H 94 cm
Inv. No. I 605

In a grotto at the foot of a gnarled plane-tree a lioness looks round alertly as she suckles her two young. Beside the tree is a small rustic temple to the god Dionysus, consisting of a stone-built altar with fruits on it, a sacred relief adorned with garlands, and two of the god's attributes: the torch and the thyrsus rod surmounted by a pine-cone. The counterpart to this idyllic relief, that of a suckling ewe, is also to be found in the Collection of Greek and Roman Antiquities. Both pieces came to Vienna from Palazzo Grimani in Venice, having once belonged to a Roman well-head in the ancient settlement of Praeneste, south-east of Rome, as is attested by a third relief found there which displays a suckling wild-boar.

K. G.

MITHRAIC RELIEF
Roman
2nd half of 2nd century A.D.
Marble; H 61 cm
Inv. No. I 624

Of all the oriental mystery religions, the cult of Mithras, the god of light (originally of Persian origin), was the most widely practised under the rule of the Roman Emperors. The central ritualistic scene depicted in the temples was that of Mithras killing the bull, an act which symbolised the regeneration of the world. Having overpowered the bull in a cave, Mithras then forces it to the ground with his knee and thrusts a dagger into its flank. To the left and right of Mithras stand his companions Cautes and Cautopates, their torches raised and lowered respectively, both of them clad, like the god himself, in Phrygian garments. A scorpion, a serpent and a dog drink the seed and blood of the dying animal. In the upper corners are to be seen the sun god Sol (right) in his four-horsed chariot and the moon goddess Luna (left) with her crescent sickle. K. G.

EAGLE-HEADED GRIFFON
Roman
Early Roman Empire
Bronze; H 40 cm
Inv. No. VI 324

The motif of this composite mythological creature, which originates from the orient and combines the winged body of a lion with an eagle's head, first occurs in Creto-Mycenaean art. The superbly finished statuette we have here was discovered on Magdalensberg, in Carinthia, and belongs to a group which once surrounded an Apollo, who would have rested his lyre on the profiled bridge between the animal's outspread wings. Sitting with its right foreleg raised, the griffon gazes up attentively at the god, waiting for him to resume his music.   K. G.

TOMBSTONE OF T. CALIDIUS SEVERUS

Roman
Mid-1st century A.D.
Limestone; H 205 cm
Inv. No. III 365

From the inscription we learn that Titus Calidius Severus died at the age of 58, after 34 years of service. At the end of his life he was centurion of the 15th legion, stationed in Carnuntum (Lower Austria). In the area of the pedestal are depictions of various pieces of military equipment (cuirass, centurion's staff, helmet and greaves) as well as a stable boy with the horse of the deceased.   K. G.

LION-HUNT SARCOPHAGUS

Roman
2nd half of 3rd century A. D.
Marble; L 222 cm
Inv. No. I 1133

The relief on the lion-hunt sarcophagus achieves a similar effect to that of the art of the Baroque. The scene is full of an ardent pathos, expressed in the throng of figures, the animated facial features, the wealth of gesture and the flowing garments. The master of the hunt, for whom the sarcophagus was intended, is seen at the centre of the composition, riding with his lance raised towards a charging lion. To the man's left stands the goddess Virtus, the embodiment of his courage. The unfinished heads of both the huntsman and the goddess betray the fact that a whole stock of such sarcophagi were frequently produced in advance.
K. G.

THESEUS AND THE MINOTAUR

Roman
4th century A. D.
Marble and limestone mosaic
Total size 410 × 420 cm
Central picture 58 × 57 cm
Inv. No. II 20

The Theseus mosaic – a floor mosaic discovered in the Roman "Villa auf den Loigerfeldern", near Salzburg in 1815 – is one of the most beautiful in Austria, reproducing scenes from the myth of Theseus within a framework of ornamental decoration. The large central picture shows the Attic hero killing the monstrous bull-headed Minotaur at the heart of the Cretan labyrinth, the symmetrical convolutions of which also serve to embellish the greater part of the mosaic. Theseus is able to reach the outside world safely again with the aid of the red thread which the King's daughter Ariadne had given him beforehand as a precaution – the scene represented in the picture to the left. In the upper picture the hero and Ariadne are seen boarding a ship rigged with ominously black sails about to return to Athens. At the behest of the gods Theseus was forced to leave his beloved on the island of Naxos, and the right-hand picture shows Ariadne in sorrow.   A. B.-W.

NAKED MALE FIGURE (KUROS)
Greek (Corinthian)
c. 560 B. C.
Bronze; H 12.7 cm
Inv. No. VI 2333

This statuette displays traits which are very characteristic of early Greek sculpture; for example: the standing posture, with the left leg somewhat to the fore; the graphic reproduction of the stomach muscles; the unusual hairstyle; and the face with its large, wide-open eyes and so-called archaic smile. Statues depicting a naked, standing youth *(kuros)* used to be generally regarded as a representation of the god Apollo, but in fact the same *kuros* model was used to depict humans as well as gods.   K. G.

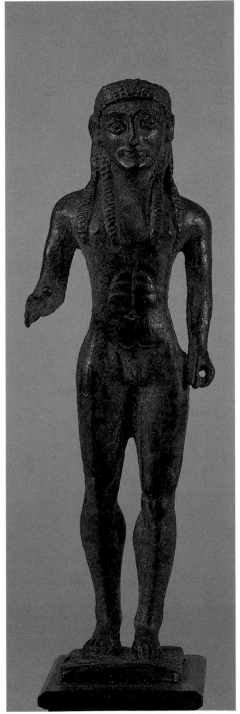

MINIATURE HORSE ▽
Greek-geometric (Laconian)
2nd half of 8th century B. C.
Bronze; H 7.5 cm
Inv. No. VI 3064

The various anatomical parts of this miniature horse have been constructed from abstract geometric forms. The legs are exceptionally long, with the roundness of the joints strongly emphasized; the barrel and head are cylindrical in shape, the bladebone juts out at an angle and even the bronze base displays a triangular pattern. Such statuettes were offered as votive gifts in the temples of ancient Greece. During the course of the 8th century B.C. they began to exhibit regional characteristics as individual styles developed.   K. G.

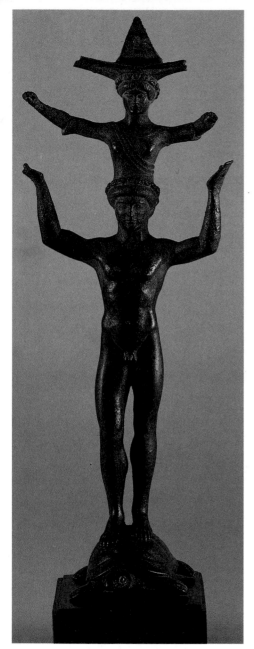

MIRROR STAND

Greek (Southern Italy)
c. 460 B. C.
Bronze; H 28.5 cm
Inv. No. VI 107

Upon the back of a turtle stands a naked youth with his arms raised, the upturned palms of his hands having once supported the necks of two horses. From his head grows the top half of a female figure, a mistress of animals who used to hold the reins of the horses in her hands. On her head is still to be seen the support piece for the mirror which today is missing.   K. G.

DISCUS

Greek (Southern Italy)
c. 500 B. C.
Bronze; Diam. 28.3 cm
Inv. No. VI 2889

The representation of a dolphin, incised on this discus as a symbol of its trajectory, was apparently chased in polychrome materials, as can be seen from the lines which clearly demarcate the snout, belly and fins from the rest of the body. Such a costly finishing process indicates that this discus was probably never used as a piece of sports equipment but would rather have served as a votive offering. In Homer, discus throwing is still counted as a discipline in its own right, although later it is only found in combination with running, the long-jump, spear throwing and wrestling as one of the events in the Pentathlon.   K. G.

FOREPART OF A CENTAUR
Greco-Hellenistic
c. 170 B. C.
Silver, partly gilded; H 22 cm
Inv. No. VII A 49

What we find represented here is not simply one of the wild, mythological creatures, half-man and half-horse, whose battle with the Lapiths had such great symbolic significance for the Greeks; but rather a Centaur of the type of Chiron, the tutor of Achilles, making music. The left hand must once have held a stringed instrument, since a plectron is to be seen in the right. It would originally have formed part of a drinking horn. The fierce pathos and finely modelled body of this Centaur make it closely related in style to the frieze of Pergamon. Technically too, it may be considered one of the masterpieces of ancient toreutics – the whole body, with the exception of the arms and legs, which were cast-moulded, having been chased from a single thin sheet of silver.   K. G.

HEAD OF JUPITER ▽
Roman
1ˢᵗ century A. D.
Bronze; H 29 cm
Inv. No. VI 9

This head came from the collection at Ambras Castle belonging to the Archduke Ferdinand of Tyrol. Originally part of a statue, the head today lacks both the eyes, which were of a coloured material, as well as the thin sheet of copper which plated the lips. The hair and the beard surround the face in a carefully worked wreath of curls. This head is a magnificent example of the classicism of the early Roman Empire, which absorbed stylistic features and tendencies from the previous epochs of Greek art to create its own distinctive mode of expression. K. G.

APOLLO
Greco-Roman
1ˢᵗ century B.C.
Bronze; H 28.5 cm
Inv. No. VI 2848

The Greek god Apollo is a god of vegetation and oracles, an averter of evil, the god of the Muses and of Light. The naked god seen here would have held a bow in his lowered right hand and a laurel branch, symbol of the purifying force of

atonement, in his left. The characteristics of old and new styles can be seen to merge in this statuette, the long spiralling locks of hair forming a contrast to the powerful and exact modelling of the body. Apart from its decorative appeal, this inclusion of older styles was certainly also intended as a testimony to the venerable tradition of the cult. The statuette, which is known as the *Apollo of Siebenbürgen* (Transsylvania) after the place where it was discovered, possibly formed part of a Roman household shrine. K. G.

MIRROR ▽
Etruscan
4th century B. C.
Bronze, bone; L 29.6 cm
Inv. No. VI 3008

The reverse side of the mirror displays the left profile of a female head wearing a headdress and earrings, engraved in outline, and surrounded by a simple tendril decoration. The actual mirror-side is slightly convex; since mirror glass was unknown until Roman Imperial times, polished metallic surfaces were used instead. The bone handle is embellished with geometric patterns.

K. G.

ETRUSCAN JEWELLERY
Etruscan
7th–5th century B. C.
Fibula: Gold; L 7.3 cm; Inv. No. VII 959
Clasp: Gold; L 6 cm; Inv. No. VII 971

This fibula of serpentine form (dating from the 7th century B.C.) and clasp of gold acorns (presumed to be from a 5th century chain), present characteristic examples of Etruscan goldsmith work. Both pieces of jewellery were decorated using the granulation and filigree techniques at which the Etruscans excelled. Fine chips of gold (granules) were laid upon the background of a thin sheet of gold and set with thin filigree wire.   A. B.-W.

BRAZIER
Etruscan
c. 500 B. C.
Bronze; H 31.9 cm
Inv. No. VI 1686a

This brazier has the form of a small cart. However, the three-spoked wheels are only for decoration, being immoveable and fixed to the box by perpendicular strips of bronze. On the short sides are handles, and on the corners seated lions, finished as flat silhouettes.   K. G.

ATHENA ROCCA D'ASPROMONTE
Italic
2ⁿᵈ half of 5ᵗʰ century B. C.
Clay; H 151 cm
Inv. No. V 115

This statue was found in the ruins of a sanctuary in
Rocca d'Aspromonte (Italy) in 1777. The Roman
goddess Minerva (Etruscan Menerva) was originally the protectress of craftsmen. As patroness
of Rome she became part of the city's triple
godhead with Jupiter and Juno, and later became
equated with the Greek Athena, the goddess of
peace, wisdom, skilfulness and war fought in
defence of one's country. This statue clearly
shows Italic-Etruscan stylistic elements, above all
in the proportions; for example, the small head
and the short trunk. The goddess is depicted
wearing a helmet, the peplos (Greek women's
garment) and on her breast the protective *Aegis*
with its Medusa's head (now missing) to ward off
evil. The broken-off arms would once have borne
shield and lance.   W. O.

BUCCHERO AMPHORA ▷
Etruscan
Mid-6ᵗʰ century B. C.
Clay; H 36 cm
Inv. No. IV 3927

Among the Bucchero ware vessels so typical of
Etruscan pottery of the 7ᵗʰ–5ᵗʰ centuries B. C. was
the amphora. A grey-black colour, its flat handles
were decorated with impressed friezes, usually
depicting animals (in this case the panther). The

MENERVA
Etruscan
1ˢᵗ half of 5ᵗʰ century B. C.
Bronze; H 24.1 cm
Inv. No. VI 7

The Etruscan goddess is here represented as a
variation of the Greek Athena Promachos, in her
role as protectress in war. In this lunging posture,
the raised right hand would have held a lance and
the left hand a shield. Menerva wears an Attic
helmet with upturned cheek flaps and a long
plume which reaches far down her back, an
unbelted chiton and the breastplate armour typical
for her, the scaled *Aegis*.

                                                     K. G.

variety of design and decoration of these vases, which served the Etruscans as burial objects and which were fashioned after models made of metal, reflects the richly imaginative character of a race which in many aspects remains enigmatic even today. The decoration was either incised or imprinted with a small cogwheel, later impressed using a roll-seal. In the 6th century the designs of the vessels became rounder, the walls thicker and the decoration took the form of reliefs obtained from negatives. A. B.-W.

CINERARY URN
Etruscan
2nd century B. C.
Alabaster; H (with lid) 99 cm
Inv. No. I 1045 a, b

The Etruscan conception of death and the afterlife is reflected in the reliefs to be found on their burial urns. Made of either stone or clay, they were placed in the tombs as early as the Hellenistic period and depict terrifying daemons of Death (here a dragon) tearing the deceased away from the arms of his companions. On the narrow sides of this box-shaped cinerary urn, made in Volterra in the 2nd century B. C., appear the threatening gods of the underworld. Upon the lid reclines the deceased, holding in his left hand a bowl raised to recieve the meal of the dead. A. B.-W.

HARIGAST HELMET ▷
Late Hallstatt
1st half of 5th century B. C.
Bronze; H 20.6 cm
Inv. No. VI 1660

This helmet comes from a cache found in 1811 near Negau (present-day Ženjak, Yugoslavia). The place of discovery gave its name to the type of helmet found there (Negau helmet), which has the appearance of a hat. Developed by the Etruscans in the 6th century B. C., its use was subsequently widespread in the Alpine regions. The *Harigast helmet* seen here is named after its dedicatory inscription, incised on the brim of the helmet in the North Etruscan alphabet and mentioning a man with the Germanic name of Harigast. The inscription dates from the 1st century B. C. and is probably the earliest surviving reference to the Germanic language. K. G.

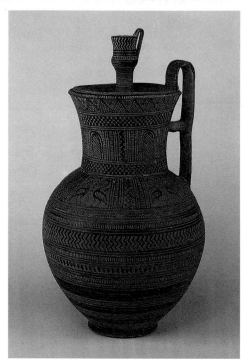

GEOMETRIC PITCHER
Attic
2nd half of 8th century B. C.
Clay; H 51 cm
Inv. No. IV 2

The 9th and 8th centuries B. C. are sometimes designated as the "geometric" period, after the decoration of the vases. This style was first developed in the pottery workshops of Athens, where it predominated, vessels often of considerable size being produced there for the furnishing of tombs. Geometric patterns such as meanders, triangles and circles are the characteristic motifs, but even the rare figurative representations (burial celebrations, animals), which first appear in the 8th century, show the same geometric traits. This richly decorated jug, which has a lid with a knob in the form of a miniature cup, also came into existence in the late geometric period, for which its cursory, impressionistic style of painting is typical.   A. B.-W.

BUSIRIS HYDRIA ▷
Eastern Greek
c. 525 B. C.
Clay; H 45.5 cm
Inv. No. IV 3576

This three-handled water jug belongs to the group of Caeretan hydriae (named after Caere, the principal place of their discovery) manufactured in a workshop run by Ionian Greeks who had emigrated to Etruria. The lower frieze shows figures in a hunting scene. Depicted in the upper frieze with colourful exuberance and cheerful naivety is the Greek national hero Heracles, seen in the act of slaying the Egyptian King Busiris. The latter, who was in the habit of seizing and putting to death every stranger who travelled through his land, has fled to an altar with his retinue.   W. O.

RHODIAN JUG
Eastern Greek
c. 600 B. C.
Clay; H 38 cm
Inv. No. IV 1622

The vase painting of the 7th century B. C. is characterised by a strong oriental influence, with new motifs from the animal and plant kingdom superceding the geometric decoration. This Rhodian jug, named after the main place in which examples of this genre were discovered, gives us a good idea of the development of this style in these eastern regions. The white surface of the vessel is decorated with a circular animal frieze (sphinx and griffon, dog and hare) and ornamental bands with interlacing patterns and lotus blossoms. The piece achieves particular charm through the hybrid style of painting combining closed silhouettes and outline drawing; as also through the exaggeration of length in the figurative motifs and the wealth of ornamental decoration.   A. B.-W.

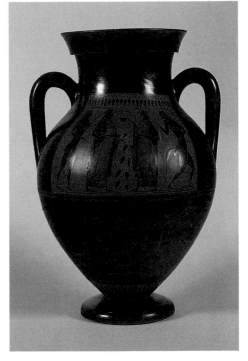

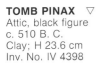

TOMB PINAX ▽
Attic, black figure
c. 510 B. C.
Clay; H 23.6 cm
Inv. No. IV 4398

The Attic vases of the archaic period are, until the
year 530 B. C., painted solely in the black figure
style. Both figures and decoration were applied to
the red background in the form of a black glaze,
the inner lines being incised. The black figure
technique was also used to paint this funerary
plaque (pinax) depicting the body of a young man
lying in state on a richly decorated bier, around
which stand men and women with arms raised in
lamentation for the deceased. Similar pinakes
also served as oblations and were nailed to the
walls of burial chambers.   A. B.-W.

AMPHORA
Attic, black figure; so-called "Affected Painter"
c. 540 B. C.
Clay; H 45 cm
Inv. No. IV 4399

Gods and heroes are among the favourite themes
of the Attic vase painters of the 6th century B. C.
The scene depicted on this black figure amphora,
a storage jar for wine or oil, is the arrival in Athens
of the wine-god Dionysos. The god, seen at the
(Continued on page 84)

centre of a group of figures, is of dignified appearance, bearded and wearing a crown of ivy; in his right hand he holds his ritual drlnking vessel, the kantharos, and in his left a vine. The Athenian Ikarios, whom he taught the art of wine-growing, raises a bowl of wine in salutation. This manneristic style of painting, in which vivid representation of the figures is sacrificed for the sake of the decorative impression made by the whole, earned the Attic potter the title of the "Affected Painter".   A. B.-W.

DOURIS CUP ▷
Attic, red figure; painted by Douris
c. 500 B. C.
Clay; Diam. 33 cm, inner picture 21.1 cm
Inv. No. IV 3694

Around 530 B. C. the red figure style of painting was invented, which was a reversal of the process used in the black figure style. The black glaze now covered the whole of the vessel except the figures and ornamentation, which were left in the original red colour of the clay. The drawing thus took on a freer form, since the details (hair,

beards, folds of garments ect.) were no longer incised with a sharp tool but applied with a fine brush. Using this new method Douris, one of the most important Attic vase painters of the early 5th century, painted the great drinking cup with scenes from the life of the warrior. Here, the inner picture depicts a farewell scene, with an armed and bearded warrior receiving the farewell drink which a woman is pouring from a jug into the bowl he is holding in his right hand.   A. B.-W.

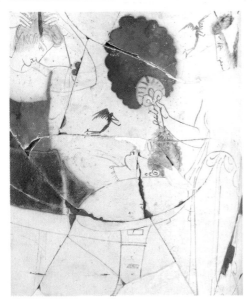

LECYTHOS
Attic, white grounded
c. 425 B. C.
Clay; H 45.8 cm (without restored foot)
Inv. No. IV 3748

The white *lecythoi* were solely used as burial objects or as containers for the ritual sacrifices made in the cult of the dead. The special finishing method involved was employed almost exclusively for this genre of Attic vases. A white slip made from a clay preparation with a low iron content served as the background, from which the outline drawing and the figures and decoration (applied in matt colouring) stand out distinctly. The deceased is seen lying on her death bed covered by a grey blanket. Three short-haired women wearing dark clothes stand around her in lamentation, the one to the right holding a fan in her hand. Between them fly three *eidola* (phantoms or souls). The sombre colours and the short hair are symbols of mourning.   K. G.

ENTOMBED WARRIOR
Apulian; red figure
c. 330 B. C.
Clay; H 64.5 cm
Inv. No. IV 94

In the 2nd half of the 5th century B. C. workshops specialising in the manufacture of red figure vases were started by the Western Greeks in Southern Italy. In the course of the 4th century, in Apulia, Campania and Lucania they even developed regional characteristics such as matt colouring, plump forms or the impoverishment of the themes depicted. Typical for Apulia are the large *craters* (mixing vessels) overlaid with figures and decoration, their use as sepulcral vessels being evident from their depictions of the tomb cult. Here, the centre of the representation is dominated by the image of a tomb containing the deceased, a warrior, in sitting position, young girls and boys appearing on either side with funerary donations made to the cult of the dead.   A. B.-W.

◁ **BRYGOS-SCYPHOS**
Attic; red figure; Brygos Painter
c. 490 B. C.
Clay; H 25 cm
Inv. No. IV 3710

Reproduced on this large drinking bowl, which was made in the workshop of the potter Brygos, is a scene from Homer's Iliad. Achilles, the much-praised Greek hero of the Trojan Wars, lies on a bier, in front of which stands a small table laid for a meal. Priam, the elderly King of Troy approaches

from the left with his retinue to ask for the corpse of his fallen son Hector, who is seen lying under the bed. To the right stands Achilles' cup-bearer, ladle and wine-sieve in his hands. The spatiality of the room in which the scene takes place is indicated by the weapons that are seen hanging on the wall. The other side of the bowl shows an assembly of the Greek heroes. Although made at the beginning of the Classical period, these pictures contain numerous traits of the late Archaic style, for example the fullness of the figures and the love of detail.   W. O.

MYCENAEAN IDOLS
Late Mycenaean
14th–13th centuries B. C.
Clay; H 10.7 cm, 11.4 cm, resp.
Inv. Nos. V 3253, 3254

These miniature clay idols of a female deity, large numbers of which were found in the graves and shrines derive from the late period of the Mycenaean culture, which reached its peak during the 14th and 13th centuries B. C. Typical for such figures is the unpretentiousness of their form and decoration, the full-length girded garment pleated above the waist, the hint of a crown and the definite positions in which the arms are held. After their similarity to the Greek letters Φ and Ψ, these two types were given the names Phi and Psi idols respectively. A. B.-W.

PLASTIC VASES ▷
Corinthian
1st half of 6th century B. C.
Clay; H 10.7 cm, 9.4 cm
Inv. Nos. V 1267, 1273

The custom of making vessels in the form of human beings, animals or mythological creatures is very ancient, sculpted vases being familiar to the Egyptians, as also to the inhabitants of Cyprus and Mycenae. Yet only in the 7th century B. C. did the pottery workshops of Greece begin to produce vessels of this type on a large scale. In doing so, the potters' imagination knew no bounds to the variety of possible forms. These two delightful vessels originated in Corinth, one of them having the form of a kneeling youth, the other that of a bearded man on his haunches. They were used for the storage of precious consecrated oils.
A. B.-W.

THRONED GODDESS
Attic
Beginning of 5th century B. C.
Clay; H 18.5 cm
Inv. No. V 401

Wearing a diadem as her headdress, the goddess sits with dignified bearing on a throne with a high backrest and a footstool. This piece of terracotta is made from a single mould and clear traces of the once vivid colouring are still to be seen. The model for this compact statuette, with its strict frontality, was perhaps the archaic cult statue of Athena in her ancient temple on the Acropolis in Athens. K. G.

GOLD JEWELLERY
Greco-Hellenistic
4th–3rd centuries B. C.
Gold, scarab; L (chain) 25 cm
Inv. Nos. VII B 217, 247, 269/70, 315/16, 323, 325, 353

The opulence with which a rich woman's tomb from the early Hellenistic period would have been furnished is revealed by these nine pieces of jewellery, found at the beginning of the 19th century in Southern Italy. The treasure, which reached Vienna apparently incomplete in 1819, consists of the following: a pair of earrings with lion-head design; a necklace of both smooth and grained pearls; a pair of fibulae; an ornamental disc in the form of a shield with a Medusa's head; a chain-clasp shaped like the Heraclean knot; a heavy gold ring with a picture of Aphrodite and Eros engraved on the face; and an Etruscan scarab on a gold bow. A. B.-W.

STANDING WOMAN WITH FAN ▷
Hellenistic (Boeotian)
c. 300 B. C.
Clay, painted; H 23.4 cm
Inv. No. V 2824

In the 2nd half of the 4th century B. C. the potteries of Boeotia, inspired by the late Classical art of Athens, began to produce large numbers of terracotta figurines in a refined and elegant style. They were mainly of aristocratic women dressed in rich and flowing garments, their appearance being characterised by the vivid colours used in their decoration. The most important centre of their manufacture was the Boeotian town of Tanagra, which gave its name to this genre of Hellenistic terracottas. From this time on, statuettes not only served as votive or burial objects but also found a place as domestic ornaments.

A. B.-W.

CAMEO: PTOLEMAIC ROYAL COUPLE
Greek
278 B. C.?
Nine-layered onyx; H 11.5 cm
Setting: gold rim; 16th century (?)
Inv. No. IX A 81

The great cameos of antiquity provide examples of miniaturism of the highest artistic quality, fascinating both for their subject matter – they form a political, cultural and religious testimony to the age – as also for their technical virtuosity and the preciousness of the materials used. They served the ends of political prestige, of the glorification of the ruler and his family, and were the pride of the imperial treasuries. In contrast to intaglios, the incision of which produces a depression in the material (they were often used as seals), cameos are miniature reliefs, i. e. layers are cut in relief from the stone, with the figures usually belonging to the light layer and the background being formed by the dark layer. In this cameo portraits of a king and queen of Egypt have been carved from the stone's nine layers, alternately dark-brown

and bluish-white. In the foreground is Ptolemy II Philadelphos who wears an Attic helmet which has the thunderbolt, an attribute of Zeus, emblazoned on the sideflaps. The serpent on the dome of the helmet is the Graecized descendant of the Uraeus asp found on the war helmets of the Pharaohs. On the neck-piece of the helmet is seen the head of the Egyptian god Ammon. In the background is Arsinoe II, the sister and wife of Philadelphos, wearing a crown like a headdress, over which is a veil. The cameo was made sometime between the marriage of the couple in the year 278 and Arsinoe's death in 270/69. It was quite possibly commissioned as an official marriage gift. From the description of the theologian and natural scientist Albertus Magnus, the cameo was to be found in the Reliquary of the Three Kings in Cologne around the middle of the 13th century A. D., the heads of the two rulers and of Ammon being interpreted as an image of the three Magi from the East. In 1574 the precious stone was stolen, then turned up in Rome before disappearing once more. The first mention of its presence in Vienna appears in 1668/69.   W. O.

GEMMA AUGUSTEA

Roman
After 10 A. D.
Two-layered onyx; H 19 cm
Setting: gold frame, reverse side in ornamented open-work; German, 17th century
Inv. No. IX A 79

In the upper row, Augustus is posed and dressed as Jupiter and holds a scepter and augur staff. On his right is Roma, the patroness of the city. Between their heads is a capricorn, the personal constellation of Augustus. To the left of the throne are allegorical figures: Oecumene (the inhabited Earth), Oceanus (the rivers of the world), and Italia with cornucopia and two boys. Next to Roma stands Augustus' great nephew, Germanicus, as well as his step-son and successor to the throne,

Tiberius, who is shown descending from a war chariot driven by Victoria. The lower scene shows the erection of a victory monument. Surrounding it are Roman soldiers and the defeated barbarians. The whole scene depicts the victory of the Romans over the Dalmatians. On January 6, 10 A. D., Tiberius, the supreme military commander of the Roman troops, entered Rome. As victor he stands before his Emperor. The cameo was first documented in 1246 as part of an inventory of the Cloister Saint Sernin in Toulouse. At the beginning of the 17th century, it came into Habsburg possession through a purchase of Rudolph II's. The Viennese collection of gems is one of the three most important in the world today; as far as the so-called *Prunkkameen* are concerned, it is without doubt the greatest.

W. O.

EAGLE CAMEO
Roman
27 B. C.
Two-layered onyx; Diam. 22 cm
Setting: silver, gilded; Milan, 3rd quarter of 16th century
Inv. No. IX A 26

The eagle, symbol of the power of the Imperium Romanum, stands with outspread wings on a palm branch. In the raised left talon he grips a wreath of oak leaves, which is a depiction of the *corona civica* (civic crown), an order of great distinction and one which was presented to the Emperor Augustus on 16th January 27 B. C. in gratitude for having saved Rome from the chaos of civil war. The state cameos were in the possession of the imperial treasury in Rome until they were stolen, along with other art treasures, and taken to Byzantium, probably in 5th century A. D. There they remained until 1204, when they returned to the Occident following the sacking of the city by the Crusaders. The eagle cameo was installed in Aachen Cathedral directly after this, presumably in the ambry of Henry II. The first evidence of it in Vienna is dated 1750. W. O.

LION CAMEO ▽
Roman
Claudian
Three-layered onyx; TH 20 cm
Setting by Johann Boÿ, 1651
Inv. No. IX A 29

A lion is seen lying in the entrance to a cave, on the top of which a crow is perched. Since both of these animals play a role in the mysteries of the cult of Mithras, the Persian god of Light, it is possible that some connection exists between this cameo and the religion. Around 1500, when the stone, along with a relic of St. Stephen, formed part of an ostensorium in St. Stephen's Cathedral, the lion was taken to be the symbol of the evangelist. In 1651 the City of Vienna dedicated it to Emperor Ferdinand III and the magnificent setting dates from the same year. At the top is the double-headed eagle with the imperial sword, sceptre and orb, the eagle's necks supporting the crown of Rudolph II, the traditional crown of the Habsburg dynasty. W. O.

GEMMA CLAUDIA

Roman
49 A. D. ?
Five-layered onyx; H 12 cm
Setting: gold rim
Inv. No. IX A 63

Out of two cornucopia sprout four portraits in symmetry: left, the Emperor Claudius and his spouse Agrippina the Younger; opposite them, Germanicus and his wife Agrippina the Elder, the ruler's parents-in-law. The year 49 A. D. saw the beginning of Claudius' fourth marriage and great hope was being placed in Agrippina the Younger, here represented as Cybele, the goddess of Fertility, to provide the drastic change for the better which was so desperately needed after the murder of Messalina. It is possible that the stone is thus an official marriage gift to the imperial couple, for at this point nobody could suspect that the installation of this domineering and scheming woman as Augusta and the adoption of her son Nero as future emperor would have such disastrous consequences for both Claudius and the state. The unknown master carved the representation from the five alternately dark and light layers of the stone with great virtuosity. He achieves an increased transparency of the material by cutting layers which in places are of unparalled thinness (minimum 2 mm). W. O.

HEROPHILOS CAMEO
Roman
14–37 A. D.
Glass; H 5.9 cm; setting: gold rim
Inv. No. IX A 30

This portrait of a man crowned with a laurel wreath probably represents the Emperor Tiberius. The work is signed "Herophilos Dioskourid(ou)" (Herophilos, son of Dioskurides). In his choice of the colour of the glass used the artist has imitated a piece of turquoise. W. O.

DECIUS CAMEO
Roman
249–251 A. D. ?
Two-layered plasma; H 7.7 cm
Setting: gold, enamel; c. 1600
Inv. No. IX A 16

This portrait is presumably that of Decius, under whose rule a bloody persecution of Christians took place. The inscription on the front side of the setting mentions Rudolph II, that on the rear side Constantine the Great. At the time when the stone was set, the portrait was interpreted in a Christian sense, as referring to Constantine, the friend of the Christians. The role of Rudolph was compared to that of Dominus in late antiquity, who was a champion and defender of Christianity. W. O.

◁ **CLAUDIUS CAMEO**
Roman
41–54 A. D.
Chalcedon; H 14.5 cm
Setting: silver, gilded; c. 1600
Inv. No. IX A 23

A portrait of the Emperor Claudius in frontal view, crowned with a laurel wreath, bearing a sceptre and clothed in tunic and toga. His intelligent face shows signs of strain and gives the impression of a man deficient in energy; the face of a ruler whose character is marked by a certain instability, eccentricity and lack of authority. W. O.

PORTRAIT OF AUGUSTUS
Roman
Late Augustan
Marble; H 36 cm
Inv. No. I 60

This head is a product of Roman "court art". Its elegance, smoothness and lack of surface detail, as well as its idealisation of the subject, are all typical characteristics of Augustan classicism. Nonetheless, what we are here confronted with is an individual likeness from Roman times, exhibiting all the essential features for which Augustus (27 B. C. – 14 A. D.) was famous.   W. O.

PORTRAIT OF TRAJAN
Roman
After 108 A. D.
Marble; H 68 cm
Inv. No. I 104

The Emperor Trajan (98–117 A. D.) was an exceptional field-commander and it was during his reign that the Roman Empire underwent its greatest expansion. He was moreover a just and intelligent administrator, and the Senate even bestowed upon him the epithet *optimus princeps*. The likeness seen here also conveys this sense of sober judgement and simple dignity.   W. O.

PORTRAIT OF COMMODUS
Roman
180–192 A. D. (Bust: modern)
Marble; H 86 cm
Inv. No. I 15

Commodus, the degenerate son of Marcus Aurelius, was an absolutist ruler known for his megalomania, violence and favouritism; a debauchee on the imperial throne who decreed that he be divinely worshipped as the incarnation of Heracles. All of which resulted in the consequent opposition of the Senate and his eventual murder. This portrait takes into account the character of the man, showing a bloated face with sallow cheeks and sensuous lips; the image of a morbidly decadent voluptuary, whose proclivity to acts of cruelty is clearly noticeable in the leering, protruding eyes. There is little trace here of the Classicism of the portrait of Augustus (above left); dominant is rather the realism so in keeping with the Roman character.   W. O.

PATERA FROM AQUILEIA
Roman
1st half of 1st century A. D.
Silver, gilded; Diam. 30 cm
Inv. No. VII A 47

MOSAIC FROM CENTOCELLE
Roman
1st century A. D.
Marble fragments; H 40 cm, W 40 cm
Inv. No. II 9

At the centre of the plate Triptolemos is to be seen performing a sacrifice, the requisites for which are being handed him by children. His gaze is directed up to the right where the goddess Ceres is seated. Beneath her is the serpent cart upon which, according to Greek legend, the hero brought grain to mankind at the behest of the goddess. The scene is framed by allegorical figures: to the right of the cart as well as above left are seen the four seasons (Hores); top centre, Caelus looks down from the sky; and at the bottom lies Tellus, the personification of the Earth.
K. G.

The love scene depicted in this small mosaic, found in Centocelle near Rome in 1865, was based on an earlier Hellenistic model. The focus of the picture is a couple settled on a couch. A young woman in a reclining position, and resting on cushions, is looking up at a man, who is sitting on the couch and leaning towards her. A statue of the god Dionysos and a tree, to which an awning is fastened, suggest that the scene takes place outdoors. A similar representation of the same theme is to be found preserved on one of the folding panels in the Villa Farnesina in Rome.
A. B.-W.

FLASK FROM PINGUENTE
Gallo-Roman
2nd half of 2nd century A. D.
Bronze with enamel inserts; H 17.5 cm
Inv. No. VI 1197

The whole surface of this vessel, reminiscent in its form of a field-flask, has been decorated in blue, red and orange using the so-called "groove enamelling" technique. The ornamentation, which is derived from pre-Roman La Tène art, consists partly of spherical motifs, partly of linear patterns of chequered and triangular design. The flask from Pinguente (present-day Pazin, Yugoslavia) perhaps belonged to the inventory of a horseman's grave, to judge from other objects found alongside it (riding snaffles etc.). Other centres of Roman enamel work were Gaul and the Rhineland area.
K. G.

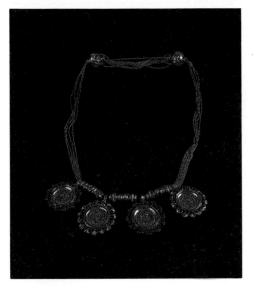

NECKLACE
Roman
3rd century A. D.
Gold; L 42.5 cm, WT 172.7 g
Inv. No. VII 813

The fashion of working coins into pieces of jewellery first became widespread in Roman imperial times. The beginning of the 3rd century A. D. saw the appearance of gold coins mounted in broad settings and worn as pendants on necklaces. From archaeological evidence and the representations to be found on mummy portraits, this type of jewellery was above all extremely popular in Egypt. The necklace here, apparently discovered in Aswan, is among the few surviving examples of this genre. Four gold coins, bearing the heads of Faustina the Elder, Marcus Aurelius, Antoninus Pius and Gordian III, each provided with an ornate setting, have been used as pendant decoration for a chain which can be adjusted in length.   A. B.-W.

SENATUS CONSULTUM DE BACCHANALIBUS
Roman
186 B. C.
Bronze; L 27.3 cm, W 28.5 cm
Inv. No. III 168

This inscription from the year 186 B. C. is the oldest surviving Senatorial Decree and an important document in the history of the Latin language. It stipulates the regulations to be observed during the rites of the mystery cult of the Bacchanalia, ecstatic festivals held in honour of the god Dionysos/Bacchus, in the wake of which severe excesses occurred at the beginning of the 2nd century B. C. The text of the original was copied and its contents promulgated even among the rural communities. The copy seen here was destined for Ager Teuranus, today the region around Tiriolo in Calabria. The late baroque frame, inlaid with mother-of-pearl and gold, dates from the year 1727.   K. G.

LARARIUM FROM MONTORIO
Roman
2nd–3rd centuries A. D.
Bronze
Jupiter: H 17.8 cm; Inv. No. VI 409
Mercury: H 25.5 cm; Inv. No. VI 423
Cupid: H 19 cm; Inv. No. VI 121
Porter: H 30 cm; Inv. No. VI 337

These eleven objects comprising the inventory of a Roman household shrine (Lararium) were found in 1830 at Montorio, near Verona. Apart from the more esteemed deities (here Jupiter, Mercury and Cupid), Lararia also contained the guardian spirits of the home and the family (Penates, Lares and Genii). Jupiter is seen here holding a sceptre in his right hand, while in his left he grips the thunderbolt. Beside him is a tree-stump (struck by lightning?) and on the front of the plinth are two miniature Lares. Mercury is seated on a rock and holds the herald's staff in his right hand, his left resting on a purse, his attribute as the god of trade. The rocky terrain below him is inhabited by several animals: tortoise, lizard, goat and a ram ridden by a small Cupid. The god of love is also represented here in his own right, by a roughly-worked statuette, obviously added to the Lararium

at a later date. As a contrast to the rest of the group are two porters (only one of which is pictured here). Bearded farmers or slaves, they are wearing high-heeled sandals and short work-aprons. With their left hands the men shoulder carrying-poles, which would have been attached to some kind of vessels.   K. G.

SILVER DRINKING-CUP ▷
Roman
3rd century A. D.
Silver; H 7.2 cm
Inv. No. VII A 12

The outer surface of this beaker, found as early as the 16th century in Arras (France), is decorated with dionysian reliefs. On the upper, slightly concave area is depicted a sequence of masks, animals (panther, goat, stag, deer) and dionysian attributes (Thyrsos rod, tympana, cornucopia, pine-cones and syrinx). In the lower, convex zone are mythological creatures which combine the front parts of griffon, bull and horse with convo-luted fish-tails.   K. G.

ROMAN POTTERY
Roman
1ˢᵗ–3ʳᵈ centuries A. D.
Bowl: H 12.8 cm; Inv. No. IV 1399
Beaker: H 25.5 cm; Inv. No. IV 439
Jug: H 20 cm; Inv. No. IV 2940

The chief characteristics of numerous genres of Roman pottery were their monochrome colouring and their relief decoration, the latter being achieved using either a die or a mould. Made from hard-baked clay and with a burnished red slip usually displaying ornamental or figurative decoration, terra sigillata vessels had been produced as fine tableware in Italy since the 1ˢᵗ century B. C., as they later were on a large scale in Gaul and in the Rhineland area. The bowl is decorated with representations of gladiators and comes from a pottery in southern Gaul. Rare types of vessel with a lead glaze slip, like the jug from 1ˢᵗ century A. D., imitate the glaze, colour and relief decoration of metalware models. Among the examples of painted pottery are often found mottoed drinking-cups, typical products of the potteries of Trier since the 3ʳᵈ century A. D. The drinking motto is painted in white lettering ("Let us drink as befits us").   A. B.-W.

ROMAN GLASSWORK   ▽
Roman
1ˢᵗ–4ᵗʰ centuries A. D.
Small jug: H 13 cm; Inv. No. XI 981
Double-handled jug: H 24 cm; Inv. No. XI 1530
Dish: H 6.5 cm; Inv. No. XI A 185

The use of glass had already been known in Egypt for three millennia when the Syrian invention of the glass-blowing pipe in the 1ˢᵗ century B. C. brought about a complete revolution in glass production. Using the blow pipe, it suddenly became possible to mass-produce glassware, at the same time achieving the required effects of colour or colourlessness through the addition of minerals. First in Alexandria and Syria, then in Italy and on the Rhine, glassworks were founded in which the various applications of the new methods were developed to perfection. An example of the precious pieces of glasswork which have come down to us from early Roman imperial times is this ribbed dish produced from a mould, the decorative design of which resembles banded agate. Examples of free-blown glass are the

double-handled jug of blue glass with white feather decoration (1ˢᵗ century A. D.) and a small jug with brown threading from Syria (4ᵗʰ century A. D.).   A. B.-W.

BUST OF JUPITER
Roman
After a Greek model of 2ⁿᵈ half of 4ᵗʰ century B. C.
Bronze; H 17.5 cm
Inv. No. VI 288

Jupiter (Gr. *Zeus*) is wearing an oak leaf crown on his head. Draped over the back of his head is a cloth, whose left edge hangs down the side of his body while the right rests on his shoulder. The veiling of the head is part of sacral symbolism. The hair is swept back from the furrowed brow as in the portraits of Alexander the Great and frames the large surface of the face with fluid, softly modelled curls. On the right-hand side leans a winged thunderbolt, Jupiter's weapon.   K. G.

VENUS AND CUPID
Roman
Middle imperial times
Bronze; H (without base) 24 cm
Inv. No. VI 333

The tiny Cupid, having flown to his mother, is trying to get a grip on her naked body with his little hands. Venus presses him against her with her left hand, holding a round fruit as enticement in her right. This idyllic scene of the goddess of love lost in play with her little son is a Hellenistic invention which has also been given literary expression. The fullness of the body of Venus, her curling African-style hair and the form of the diadem with its top shaped like a palmetto, all suggest oriental (Egyptian) provenance.

K. G.

PORTRAIT BUST OF EUTROPIOS ▽
Early Byzantine
2nd half of 5th century A. D.
Marble; H 32 cm
Inv. No. I 880

During the Austrian excavations in Ephesus a console which presumably belonged to this bust was found not far away from it, bearing an inscription which mentioned a citizen by the name of Eutropios. In the bust we not only see that the Greek conception of an ideal beauty of the human face was already a thing of the past, but also that little was now left of Roman realism. Individual characteristics here take second place to the new Christian spirituality. A heightened facial expression is manifest in the ascetic gauntness of the head and above all in the large eyes, whose gaze reaches out beyond the spectator.   W. O.

MUMMY PORTRAIT
Egyptian-Roman
Beginning of 4th century A. D.
Wax painting on wood; H 36.9 cm
Inv. No. X 301

After Augustus' conquest of Egypt, the Egyptians adopted the custom of binding a painted likeness of the deceased onto the front of the mummy, a custom which was closely connected to the ancient Egyptian tendency to preserve the facial features of the deceased for the other world. The lady wears a red garment, two golden necklaces and earrings decorated with pearls. The face presents a strictly frontal view, with the large eyes gazing directly at the observer.   W. O.

DIPTYCH
Early Byzantine, Constantinople
c. 500 A. D.
Ivory: H 26.5 cm
Inv. No. X 39

The centre section of a five-panelled imperial diptych, this carving conveys an impressive picture of early Byzantine court ceremony the Empress being depicted in the act of receiving homage from the court in the throne room. Seated beneath a cupola supported by pillars, she is adorned in richly ornate vestments, including a diadem, luxurious drop earrings and a jewelled collar. In her left hand is the globe surmounted by the cross. The Empress is most probably Ariadne (died 515 A. D.), at first married to the Emperor Zenon and after his death to Anastasius. The style of this period is typified by matrimonial ceremony, rigidity, frontality, diminishing tonal values in the carving and the neglect of individual facial features in favour of a heightened expression. W. O.

CAGE-CUP ▷
Roman – late antiquity
4th century A. D.
Glass; H 9.5 cm
Inv. No. XI A 186

This fragment of a cage-cup, found in 1785 in Daruvar (Croatia), belongs to the masterpieces of the glass-cutting work of late antiquity. The glass cup, which has the form of a goblet, is surrounded by a basket-like filigree lattice which has been cut from the body of the glass itself. The inscription may be completed to read *FAVENTIBUS* ("for the favoured"). The immensely complicated technique involved in the production of such cups, which were also called *diatret* glasses and of which only a few examples still survive today, made them objects of high value even in antiquity. Under the Emperor Constantine the glass-cutters were treated as the equals of artists and exempted from paying tax. A. B.-W.

SILVER FLASK
Late antiquity (early Byzantine?)
4th–5th centuries A. D.
Silver; H 33.7 cm
Inv. No. VII A 45 a

The neck, body and foot of this vessel from ancient Siscia (Sisak, Yugoslavia) do not comprise an organic unity at all; instead they appear to be three different parts which have been joined together to make a whole. The square foot curves upward to support the wide protrusive drum of the body, from which rises the long conical neck with its beaked spout. The relief decoration consists of a female head in profile on the front and back, with animal representations (lion, bull, dog, goat, tiger and stag) and tendrilled embellishment on the narrow side, and acanthus leaves on the bottle's neck. K. G.

GEMMA LANCKOROŃSKI
Early Byzantine, Constantinople
Beginning of 7th century A. D.
Three-layered onyx; H 9.8 cm
Inv. No. IX 2607

MONOGRAMMATIC CROSS
Early Christian
5th century A. D.
Bronze; H 54.7 cm
Inv. No. VI 612

Effective despite its simplicity, this monogrammatic cross, found in Monastero, near Aquileia, is a significant example of the ritual symbolism of early Chistianity and served as a cult object in its own right. It is a cross of the so-called Latin form which has been transformed into a christogramm by the addition of the Greek P (= R) at the top. The first and last letters of the Greek alphabet, Alpha and Omega, which hang from the arms of the cross-beam, symbolize the Christ of the Revelation of John (1,8; 21,6; 22,13): "I am Alpha and Omega, the beginning and the end." A. B.-W.

In contrast to the cameos, on which the reliefs are worked away from the stone in layers, the representations on the gems are incised to produce a depression in the material. Above the cross we see the bearded Christ, with St. Peter carrying a cross and St. Paul with a book. Underneath are the flowers of the Garden of Eden, above the inscription EMMA-NOUEL ("God with us!"). The largest and most significant gem of the late period, this was probably the resplendent insignia of a high dignitary of the Church, perhaps even of the Patriarch himself, who would have worn it, at that time complete with a magnificent setting, at his breast. W. O.

TEXTILE PANEL WITH DIONYSOS ▷
Coptic – late antiquity
4th century A. D.
Knitted wool on cloth; H 27.5 cm, W 30 cm
Inv. No. XIII 1b

Weaving and knitting are among the oldest skilled crafts known to humanity. Although in most regions of the ancient world the old fabrics have disintegrated, in Egypt – thanks to the desert climate so favourable to their preservation – a large number of textiles descending from late antiquity and early Christian times, and known as Coptic textiles, have survived. Our example shows a half-length portrait of the god Dionysos against a violet background set within a tendrilled border containing blossoms and birds. The por-

trait was found during excavations in Akhmim; together with its counterpart, which depicts Ariadne, it would once have served as the decoration for a shroud. A. B.-W.

101

RELIQUARY VESSEL
Early Christian
c. 400 A. D.
Silver; H 12.3 cm
Inv. No. VII 760

This silver box *(pyxis)* belongs to a reliquary find discovered in an altar grave in the former Basilica of San Tommaso in Pola (present-day Pula, Yugoslavia). The greater part of the reliquaries have today disappeared, this box and a small gold one being all that remains (both finds arrived in Vienna in 1888). The sections of the six-sided lower box, as also the vaulted dome-shaped lid, are decorated with full and half-length figures in repoussé and representing Christ surrounded by five Apostles. Made in the workshop of a north Italian silversmith around the year 400 A. D., the box first came to be used for reliquaries at a later date (presumably in the 6th century).   A. B.-W.

FIBULA ▽
Germanic
2nd half of 4th century A. D.
Gold with semi-precious inlays; L 19.5 cm
Inv. No. VII B 307

In its imposing splendour, this ornate fibula with its three pendant chains reminds one of the large disk fibula featured in the portraits of the Roman Emperors of the 4th century A. D. The settings of the face-ground almandine (Indian garnet) have been placed close together on the gold body of the fibula so as to create a network of cells. From this emerges a splendid geometrical decoration, in the centre of which is a huge resplendent onyx (light-brown upon a layer of black). This is an example of the so-called polychromatic style, the effect of which is achieved through the contrast between the coloured stones and the gleaming gold. The Germanic tribes had become acquainted with it on the shores of the Black Sea, whence it had been brought by Scythians and Sarmatians from the Orient.   K. G.

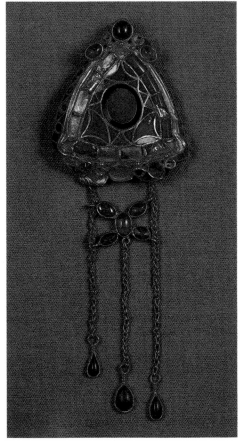

PAIR OF FIBULAE
Germanic
Beginning of 5th century A. D.
Gold sheet on silver with semi-precious inlays
L 15.9 cm and 16.0 cm
Inv. Nos. U 1,2

These two ornate fibulae were among the burial objects of the Princess of Untersiebenbrunn (Marchfeld, Lower Austria). Her tomb has provided the most precious examples of Germanic art from the time of the Great Migration ever to be found on Austrian soil. The surface of the cast silver body of each fibula is plated with a thin sheet of gold and the whole studded with coloured semi-precious stones, chiefly almandines, and with glass pastes and green enamel. All the inlays are individually mounted, some of the stones being convex (en cabochon), others faceground. Further decorative features are the filigree work and the granulated embellishment.

K. G.

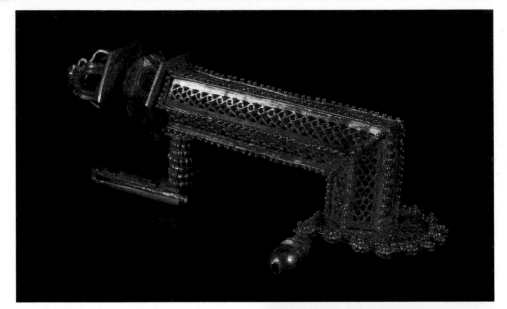

FIBULA

Roman
End of 3rd century A. D.
Gold; L 9.8 cm, WT 71.8 g
Inv. No. VII B 349

Exhibiting the most exquisite ornamental work (opus interrasile), this fibula is a masterpiece of Roman goldsmith work. On the upper side of the bow is an inscription reading *VTERE FELIX* ("Use with luck!"). The piece belongs to a German treasure hoard, found in 1790 in Osztropataka (present-day Ostrovany, Slovakia), containing tableware and ornamental objects, mostly of gold and silver, from various historical periods and cultures, including both the Germanic and the Roman.   A. B.-W.

CHAIN WITH 52 PENDANTS ▷

Germanic
c. 400 A. D.
Gold, smoky topaz; L 177.5 cm, WT 712.8 g
Inv. No. VII B 1

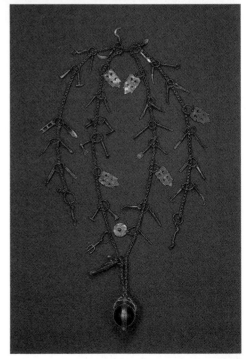

The showpiece of the Germanic gold treasure found in Szilágysomlyó (present-day Şimleul Sievaniei, Rumania) was this chain of honour, unique for its symbolic content. The central breast ornament is a bead of smoky topaz (cairngorm), mounted with two standing panthers, one on either side of a tiny mixing-bowl. Above this is a pendant which has been worked into the form of a man in a boat. To the cairngorm is attributed the power to avert evil, a fact which indicates the magical and religious nature of the chain. The other pendants are mostly arranged in pairs (miniature tools, weapons and vine-leaves) and symbolize the dominion of the prince over all the occupations practised by his tribe, whether in agriculture, trade or soldiery.   A. B.-W.

GOLD TREASURE FROM NAGYSZENTMIKLÓS
Protobulgarian?
2nd half of 9th century A. D.
Gold; WT (total) 9926 g
Medalled pitcher: H 22 cm, WT 608 g
Inv. No. VII B 33

The unique gold treasure found in 1799 in Nagy-szentmiklós (now Sînicolaul Mare, Rumania) consists of twenty-three pure gold vessels weighing a total of ten kilograms. The treasure represents many different cultural, stylistic and religious influences. Central Asian, Persian-Sassanidic idiosyncracies are found next to Greco-Roman and Byzantine; heathen features stand next to the crucifix. Some of the vessels bear Greek, Turkish and rune-like inscriptions that have yet to be fully deciphered. The differences between the pieces make it difficult to define the ethnic and artistic origins of the treasure. Most probably it originated in the 9th century as a product of ancient Bulgarian art. The conversion of the Bulgarians to Christianity in 864 could explain the Christian motifs among the heathen elements. The treasure, in its last use as ecclesiastical treasury, was probably buried during the Hungarian invasion in 896.

Fourteen of the vessels (pitchers, bowls, goblets and drinking horn) are shown below.

Braiding on the medalled pitcher frames four circular medallions of figures: an eagle, carrying off a woman; a rider astride a character of fable who is shooting with bow and arrow at a panther; a griffin tearing at a doe; and the most important scene of a victorious prince dragging a prisoner by the hair while a decapitated head dangles from the saddle (see above picture).   A. B.-W.

SILVER BUCKET: MARS AND VENUS
Byzantine
1st half of 7th century A. D.
Silver; H 25.8 cm, WT 2044 g
Inv. No. VII A 95

The silver treasure from Kuczurmare, found in 1814 in the former Austrian province of Bucovina, represents a find of particular importance and consists of nine silver vessels: a bucket, a small cauldron and seven bowls. The bucket, which originates from Constantinople and can be dated to the time of the Emperor Heraclius (610–641 A. D.) from the Byzantine stamps to be found on the bottom, is a noteworthy example of the continuation of the pictorial tradition of heathen antiquity, presenting six gods arranged in pairs divided by laurel wreaths: Mars and Venus, Hercules and Minerva, Apollo and Diana.

A. B.-W.

HEROON OF TRYSA

Greco-Lycian
Beginning of 4th century B. C.
Limestone; wall corner: 22 × 26 m
Inv. Nos. I 445–592

The peninsular of Lycia is a wild and rugged region of karst mountains broken only by a few wide river valleys with luxurious vegetation. There it was that in 1841 a school teacher from Posen by the name of J. A. Schönborn discovered, not far from the village of Gölbaşı, the Heroon of Trysa. After Schönborn's death the monument was forgotten and it was not until 1881 that Otto Benndorf, Professor of Classical Archaeology at the University of Vienna, succeeded in rediscovering the site. When the first scientific analyses had been made, photographs taken and permission granted by the Turkish authorities, the present frieze, the monumental gateway to the cemetery and a 5 metre high sarcophagus in the form of a Lycian house were all transported to Vienna.

The Lycians, who were of Indo-Germanic descent and originally a matrilinear society, had settled on the peninsular in the south-west of Turkey in the 2nd millennium B. C. They managed to preserve their independence for eight centuries, until their land became a Persian satrapy in the 6th century B. C. It was during this period that their aristocratic social structure, headed by princes who were continuously attempting to enlarge their territories, produced a cultural golden age. A characteristic type of architecture and numerous tombs, inscriptions and reliefs all bear testimony to this epoch. Later they came under the dominion of Athens, were conquered by Alexander the Great and then incorporated into the Roman Empire, but they finally played a not unimportant role in early Christian times.

The Heroon of Trysa, which constitutes Lycia's largest monument and the one richest in the variety of its representations, was built in a period when the Lycian rulers were inviting Greek artists to work in their country. For this reason the reliefs combine certain intrinsic elements of pure Hellenism with native Lycian and oriental characteristics. Noticeable is the incorporation of perspective into the designs.

In antiquity, a heroon was originally the walled tomb of a hero from the distant past; later the same hero worship and thus cultic veneration also grew up around benefactors, commanders and kings as well. The Heroon of Trysa was a square sacred area, enclosed by a wall decorated on all of the inner sides and both of the outer entrance sides with two rows of relief one above the other. The total length of the frieze amounts to 211 metres; almost 600 figures having been chiselled out of the stone. In one of the sarcophagi in the inner area a Lycian ruler was entombed, though his name is unknown because no inscription has survived and there are no written records about him. His life is related in the reliefs, real in their representation of historical events and heroic deeds, symbolic in their pictures drawn from legend: an enemy army landing on the coast; a city being stormed; hunting scenes; the feast of the dead; the battle of the seven against Thebes; the rape of the daughters of Leucippus; figures of Perseus and Theseus; battles of Centaurs and Amazons.

After the frieze had arrived in Vienna its pieces had to be put into storage for reasons of space. Out of their original order they are difficult to understand in their thematic context and thus prove rather inaccessible for the public. Whether the plan to erect the monument in its original state can be realized in the near or far future remains questionable.   W. O.

MODEL OF THE HEROON
Paul Kohl, 1889
Plaster, painted; proportions 1 : 30
Inv. No. XIV 265

SIEGE OF THE CITY (WEST FRIEZE)
H 124 cm

Enemy troops are storming the walls and gates of the city. Behind the battlements soldiers are hurrying to the defences. On the left a warrior is seen killing a ram (a sacrifice to the gods?), while beside him a commander is praying for victory, his right arm raised. In the centre are the king and queen on their throne. When, as here, the Greeks' siege of Troy is represented (in this case the enthroned king is Priam) it is certainly a substitution for an important event from Lycian history. W. O.

RULER IN FOUR-HORSED CHARIOT
(INNER SOUTH FRIEZE)
H 66 cm

The owner of the tomb is seen equipped with helmet, armour and shield standing on a four-horsed chariot, his driver beside him. Beneath this scene is a depiction of the Greek hero Bellerophon killing the Chimera. He is one of the mythical forefathers of the Lycian prince. W. O.

ODYSSEUS MURDERING A SUITOR
(INNER SOUTH FRIEZE)
H 59 cm

After twenty years spent fighting at Troy and trying
to return home, Odysseus finally reaches Ithaca.
In the palace, his wife Penelope is being pressed
by suitors. As the executor of divine judgement,
Odysseus shoots the transgressors one after
another with his bow and arrow. The foremost of
them, Eurymachos, raises his arm as he begs for
mercy. Next to Odysseus stands his son Tele-
machos with drawn sword.   W. O.

DUEL (WEST FRIEZE) ▷
H 61.5 cm

Two opponents attack each other with sword and
lance, their bodies protected by shields. This
relief frieze stands at the end of another depicting
a battle on the sea-coast.   W. O.

EPHESUS MUSEUM

The Parthian monument in the Ephesus Museum

The ruins of Ephesus (Turkey), an important city of the ancient Greek world and later a metropolis of the Roman Empire, have been under excavation by Austrian archaeologists ever since 1895. Up until 1906 numerous high-quality finds entered the Collection of Greek and Roman Antiquities, where they unfortunately had to be put into storage due to lack of space. It was only in 1978, that the Ephesus Museum could be opened in the neo-baroque halls of the Neue Burg, as an annexe to the Collection of Greek and Roman Antiquities. W. O.

AMAZON FROM THE ALTAR OF THE ARTEMISION
Greek
2nd half of 4th century B. C.
Marble; H 65.5 cm
Inv. No. I 811

When the Greeks founded the city of Ephesus in about 1000 B. C., they found the cult of an ancient Asiatic Mother and Nature goddess already in existence there. They were able to identify it with their own cult of the goddess Artemis and in the 6th century B. C. the Ephesians constructed in her honour the first great temple, considered to be one of the seven wonders of the world. This later burnt down and in the process of its reconstruction in the 2nd half of the 4th century B. C., an ornamental wall *(thrinkos)* was built around the sacrificial altar in front of the temple of Artemis Ephesia. The *thrinkos* was decorated with a figurative frieze on which appeared this upper half of a wounded Amazon, her right hand laid wearily on her head. The relief figure is a late Classical reproduction of a statue made in the 5th century B. C. by the sculptor Cresilas for an artistic competition.   W. O.

PARTHIAN MONUMENT
Roman
After 169 A. D.
Marble; L (preserved frieze) c. 40 m

The Parthian monument, the most important relief frieze from Roman times ever found in Asia Minor, was erected on the occasion of the victorious conclusion of the Parthian wars (161–165 A. D.) to commemorate the Emperor Lucius Verus, commander of the Roman forces, who had set up his headquarters in Ephesus. The Emperor is glorified in a series of five scenes: his adoption by Antoninus Pius in 138; Lucius Verus in battle; as

Emperor with the personifications of the most important cities of the Empire; enthroned among the gods; his apotheosis. All the relief slabs and their remains were found in second or third use, making the accuracy of the reconstruction questionable. The original memorial presumably took the form of a monumental altar enclosing the sacrificial one, the outer walls being decorated by the circa 70 metre long figurative frieze, of which 40 metres still survive as exhibits in the Ephesus Museum. It is possible that the remains of a monumental altar recently excavated in the Library square of Ephesus once formed the foundations of the Parthian monument.

◁ BATTLE SCENE
W 146 cm
Inv. No. I 866

Central event of this frieze is the battle between Romans and barbarians, with the opponents attacking each other on foot, on horseback and in chariots in a furious surge of fighting, the dead and wounded lying scattered upon the battlefield. The intensity and turbulence of a quasi-baroque style influenced by the altar of Zeus in Pergamon is well adapted to the subject. The illustration shows a Roman warrior in front of a rearing horse; wearing a short chiton, helmet and boots and carrying a shield, his sword is raised ready to strike a barbarian who has fallen to his knees.

APOTHEOSIS OF LUCIUS VERUS
W 306 cm (2 relief slabs)
Inv. No. I 867

◁ ADOPTION: THE EMPERORS
W 150 cm
Inv. No. I 864

During his reign the Emperor Hadrian (figure right) adopted Antoninus Pius (centre left), and he in turn adopted the 17 year-old Marcus Aurelius (left) and the 8 year-old Lucius Verus. A head stares from behind Hadrian's left shoulder, presumably representing the guardian spirit of Aelius Verus, the late father of Lucius. The sacrifice of a bull is being offered to the gods in connection with this state occasion, with the Emperor's family and court dignitaries also taking part.

Led by the winged goddess of Victory, the Emperor is seen mounting the four-horsed chariot of the Sun god Sol, visible in the background wearing a crown of light. The Emperor is about to ride up to Olympus (he was deified after his death in 169 A. D., i. e. made a state god by order of the Senate). Virtus, the personification of military virtue, stands in front of the horses, holding their reins. Just as the presence of Victoria and Virtus refers the Emperor's triumph in the Parthian Wars, so Tellus, the Earth Mother and goddess of Fertility (seen here sitting beneath the horses, her cornucopia overflowing with fruits), symbolizes the prosperity of the Empire under the rule of Lucius Verus and Marcus Aurelius.   W. O.

MODEL OF THE OKTOGON
Made 1977/78
Plexiglass, sprayed white; proportions 1 : 25
Inv. No. XIV 268

OKTOGON

Roman
2nd half of 1st century A. D.
Marble; H 565 cm
Inv. Nos. I 1633 A–M

The oktogon in the street of the Curetes is an eight-sided tomb, the cella or solid centre of which is surrounded by an equal number of columns. The burial chamber is located in the socle, where the skeleton of a woman aged about

20 was discovered in a coffin. One side of the oktogon has been reconstructed. Two Corinthian pillars support a triple-fascia Ionic architrave and a frieze decorated with tendrils and palmettos, and on palmettos and the foreparts of lions rests the corona of the cornice. The fascia board displays lion heads in the form of mock water fountains. A coffered ceiling reaches from the architrave to the cella, where it is supported by the wall architrave, this being carried by a frieze of garlands and bulls' heads. At the base of the cella wall is a bench (modern cast).   W. O.

CHILD WITH A GOOSE

Roman
Copy after a Hellenistic bronze original from the 3rd century B. C.
Marble; H 62 cm
Inv. No. I 816

Found in the quayside Gymnasium of Ephesus in 1896, this piece of sculpture depicts a boy of about two years sitting on the ground and presumably being talked to by an adult, since he is stretching his arm up towards somebody. At the same time he is half squashing his playmate, a small Egyptian goose. In contrast to Archaic and Classical Greek art, in which children were portrayed as small adults, Hellenistic art knew how to represent the typical features of an infant's body, as can be seen from the large head and the fat little arms and legs of this Roman copy.   A. B.-W.

HERACLES AND THE CENTAUR ▽
Greco-Hellenistic
2nd half of 2nd century B. C.
Bronze; H (Heracles) 38 cm
Inv. No. VI 3169

Engaged in a struggle with a Centaur, Heracles is about to strike a blow with his club. The mythological creature, half-man, half-horse, has reared up on his hind legs and is trying to get out of the hero's way. The effect of the group depends more than anything else on the contrast between the almost relief-like conception of the powerful but collected Heracles and the fierce agitation and three-dimensional composition of the Centaur. The background to the pair is provided by a tree which ends at a round socket decorated with leaves. This was almost certainly the foot of a lamp, so that the group would have served as a costly table candelabrum.　　K. G.

ATHLETE
Roman
Copy after a Greek original from the last quarter of the 4th century B. C.
Bronze; H 192 cm
Inv. No. VI 3168

After competitions in the Palestra, or sports arena, it was customary for athletes to clean the sand from their oiled bodies with a *strigil,* or scraping iron. This is the activity depicted in the famous "Apoxyomenos" by the Greek artist Lysippos, to

be found in the Vatican. The Ephesian athlete seen here has already finished this task and with his hair still wet with sweat, is now in the process of cleaning the *strigil* itself, which he once held in his right hand. Using the index finger and thumb of his left hand for the purpose, this in itself trivial matter commands the youth's complete attention. The statue cannot be attributed to any Greek artist with certainty, yet Roman reproductions in marble and depictions on pottery reliefs and engraved stones testify to a high degree of familiarity with the original.　　K. G.

115

FRIEZE OF A CAVALRY BATTLE
Greco-Hellenistic
After 166 B. C.
Marble; H 99 cm
Inv. No. I 814

This frieze depicts a battle between the Ionian
Greeks and the Galatians, which ended in a
victory for the Greeks. This, the best-preserved
scene, shows an ironclad Greek cavalryman to
the front and right of a *signum* (standard), with his
horse springing over the body of a fallen Galatian.
To the left is a Galatian infantryman seeking to
protect himself with his shield against the charging Greek, and another tumbling head-first from
his mount. As early as the 3rd century B. C. the
Celtic Galatians had penetrated into Asia Minor,
and in the ensuing period there were recurrent
heavy clashes with the forces of Pergamon and
Rome. The cavalry battle relief is probably related
to the last war between Pergamon and Galatia
which took place in the years 168–166 B. C., from
which the King of Pergamon, Eumenes II, finally
emerged as the triumphant victor. Ephesus, like
Miletus, Sardis and Pergamon, would certainly
have made a contribution to the tribute paid to
their deliverer from the constant Galatian threat,
and this frieze presumably once formed part of a
monument to Eumenes.   W. O.

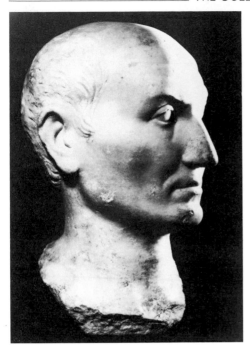

◁ **PORTRAIT HEAD**
Roman
3rd quarter of 1st century B. C.
Marble; H 43 cm
Inv. No. I 817

This head of a Roman man at the age of about fifty exhibits a high forehead and a bald crown with a broad, protruding skull, lean cheeks, an angular chin and a thin, tight mouth, a penetrating stare and a markedly sharp nose, and a bone structure that is visible through the fine layer of skin and muscle. Energy, intelligence and willpower are the most striking features of this personage, portrayed by an Ephesian sculptor during the twilight years of the Roman Empire.   W. O.

CORINTHIAN CAPITAL
Roman
Imperial times
Marble; H 68 cm
Inv. No. I 840

The capital of the Corinthian order (to be understood as a variant of the Ionic) displays the floriform element of Greek and Roman architecture in its clearest and most naturalistic form. The capital's flared fruit basket, or *calathus,* is wreathed by two rows of acanthus leaves, between which sprout forth the tendrils of the volute, supporting the corners of the abacus. At the respective centres of the curved sides of the abaci are single palmettos.   W. O.

◁ **HEAD OF ARTEMIS**
Roman
Copy after a Greek original from 460 B. C.
Marble; H 31 cm
Inv. No. I 829

This impressive head of the goddess Artemis derives from a work of early Classical art dating to about 460 B. C. Severe, harmonious and emphasizing only the most essential features of the human face, it was originally set into a robed statue. Its model, the bronze cult statue of the goddess with bow and torch, stood in the Temple of Artemis in Athens and was frequently copied in Roman times.   A. B.-W.

Apart from the archaeological finds from Ephesus itself, the Ephesus Museum also houses architectural specimens and sculptures from the sanctuary of a mystery cult excavated by Austrian archaeologists in 1873 and 1875 on the Greek island of **SAMOTHRACE.**

PEDIMENT SCULPTURE FROM THE HIERON
Greco-Hellenistic
150–125 B. C.
Marble; H 58 cm
Inv. No. I 342

This reclining female figure comes from the right-hand corner of the temple's pediment and has her head turned towards its centre. Her legs are crossed beneath a garment covering only the lower half of her body. The symbolism of the pediment is presumably related to the legend of the founding of the Samothracian mysteries. K. G.

NIKE FROM THE HIERON
Roman
1st half of 1st century A. D.
Marble; H 145 cm
Inv. No. I 680

This statue of Nike, the goddess of victory, of which now only the torso remains, depicts her wearing a heavily pleated garment covered by a cloak which is folded back across her left shoulder. The raised left arm once held a jug, the lowered right a sacrificial bowl. For stylistic reasons it is believed that this Nike, which would have served as lateral roof decoration on the top of the Hieron, is not the Hellenistic original but rather a Roman replacement. K. G.

CENTAUR FROM THE HIERON
Greco-Hellenistic
150–125 B. C.
Marble; 102 × 85 cm
Inv. No. I 347

This relief, which has been reconstructed from numerous fragments, was part of the decoration of the coffered ceiling in the *pronaos* (vestibule). The Hieron did not have the usual function of a temple in the sense of housing the cultic image, but rather that of a religious centre in which initiation into the higher levels of the mysteries took place. While the construction of the cella was begun in 325 B. C., the vestibule and the whole range of sculptural decoration, including this impressive artistic relief of the Centaur, only came into being in late Hellenistic times.   K. G.

IONIC CAPITAL FROM THE PTOLEMAION
Greco-Hellenistic
285–280 B. C.
Marble; H 38 cm
Inv. No. I 420

This fragmented capital, displaying a three-scrolled volute and a wealth of floriform decoration on the cushion, originates from the so-called Ptolemaion, a gateway built in Samothrace for the Egyptian king Ptolemy II Philadelphos. The gateway provided access to the temple from the city and its form corresponded to that of a temple with extended columned halls at both ends. The columns on the city side were of the Ionic order, those on the sanctuary side of the Corinthian order.   K. G.

LOTUS AND PALMETTO FRIEZE FROM THE ARSINOEION
Greco-Hellenistic
289–281 B. C.
Marble; L 117 cm
Inv. No. 698

Beneath leaf-shaped decoration (Lesbian Kyma-tion) we see a frieze of lotus blossoms and alternately open and closed palmettos. This cornice block comes from the inside of the so-called Arsinoeion, a circular building named after its foundress Arsinoe, the wife of King Lysimachos of Macedonia. With an inner diameter of almost 17 metres, it was the largest covered rotunda in Greece.   K. G.

THE COLLECTION
OF SCULPTURE
AND DECORATIVE ARTS

The Collection of Sculpture and Decorative Arts has its roots in the Habsburg treasuries and the Kunstkammern *(Chambers of Art and marvels) of the late Middle Ages, the Renaissance and the Baroque. Individual collectors contributed decisively to the number of objects on view today. Here first of all should be mentioned the* Kunstkammer *of Archduke Ferdinand II (d. 1595) in Ambras Castle near Innsbruck, the* Kunstkammer *of Emperor Rudolph II (d. 1612) in Prague, the* Kunstkammer *of Archduke Leopold Wilhelm (d. 1662) in Vienna and the Imperial Treasury in Vienna. This last included above all Rudolph's collection, as well as parts of Leopold Wilhelm's collection. Our knowledge of the history of these collections is mainly due to the preservation of inventories which provide us with informative clues considering these personages and their collections. The objects of the Ambras* Kunstkammer *were taken to safety at Napoleon's invasion and were brought to Vienna, where they were at first independently installed in the Lower Belvedere Palace. Not until 1875, when the Emperor Francis Joseph initiated the great reorganization of all the Imperial collections, were all their various parts joined*

together in the Kunsthistorische Museum, opened in 1891. Only Imperial and Royal insignia as well as mementoes of members of the Imperial family remained in the Treasury.

The new collection was at first entitled Sammlung kunstindustrieller Gegenstände *(i. e. Collection of Art and Artefacts). In 1919 the name was changed to* Sammlung für Plastik und Kunstgewerbe *(Collection of Sculpture and Decorative Arts). This latter name is usually misunderstood as well as being misleading. The collection contains very few large sculptures and almost no utilitarian objects made by master artisans. Most of these items, instead, were not intended for practical use, but were specially created for princely* Kunstkammern *for no special purpose of their own. The most salient works of art of this collection, its numerous examples of goldsmith's and stone cutter's work, of bronze figurines and figurative as well as turned ivories, owe their high artistic value to the demands of the princely treasuries for which they were commissioned. The* Kunstkammer *was to a certain degree a mirror of the cosmos, and represented the sum of contemporary knowledge about the world. This is the reason*

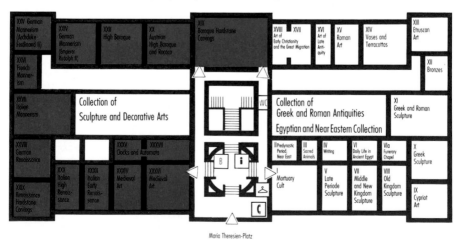

Maria Theresien-Platz

120

why a Kunstkammer does not only contain works of art, so-called artefacta, but also products of nature and „exotics". Furthermore, we find the so-called scientifica, instruments designed to assist the scientists of the day in their quest for discovering the universe. Then there are etchings and woodcuts related with all these, and, finally, bizarre "miracles" of nature and equally miraculous specimens of arts and crafts – the mirabilia – and of science.

Kunstkammer collectibles are, therefore, showpieces of non-utilitarian character of the highest artistic and technical rank, rarities of nature or apparatus from the natural sciences which frequently belong to the pioneer contrivances or gadgets of technical development. The Kunstkammer thus became a miniature universe ruled by the prince and his claim to universal dominion. As in this case the prince was the Emperor himself or at least a member of the arch-house, the claim to the Kunstkammer was as universal as was the claim for the absolute best concerning the objects that went into the collection.

The Collection of Sculpture and Decorative Arts therefore is still unrivalled and counts among the best documented art collections of the world.

The high rank of these collections was famous even in the 16th and 17th centuries. Many a European prince of the blood felt especially honoured to increase its splendour by suitable presents. It used to be common knowledge that e. g. Emperor Rudolph II was extremely susceptible to "diplomatic gifts" of this kind. With the 18th century, the artistic ambitions of the Habsburgs increasingly shifted to architecture, music and the dramatic arts and later on were dedicated to the re-organisation of the collections and the building of the Kunsthistorische Museum; but during all this time the collection was continually enlarged by singular remarkable objects.

After the breakdown of the monarchy in 1918 the collections of the Austrian line of the Este dynasty as well as the tapestry collection (which hitherto had been under the administration of the garde-meuble) were added to it. The tapestry collection is among the most renowned of its kind and is only surpassed by the collection in the possession of the Spanish Crown. Only shortly before the end of Austria as a sovereign state in 1938, the collection of Gustav von Benda by legacy completed the collection in a most advantageous way as it brought some of the most select main œuvres of Florentine early Renaissance. Fortunately, the Collection of Sculpture and Decorative Arts survived World War II with only minor losses. There was only one grievous loss, as the specimens of tapestry taken to Berlin and to Marshall Göring's private domicile Karin-Hall for interior decoration have disappeared since 1945.

Since 1963, the collection has been on display again in the Kunsthistorische Museum. M. L.-J.

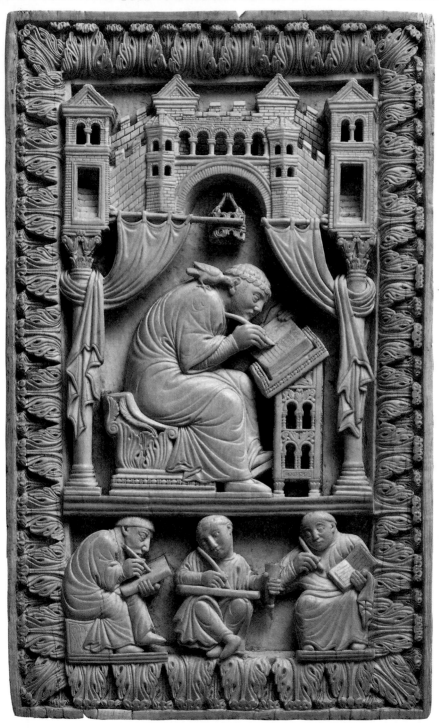

◁ ST. GREGORY WITH THE SCRIBES
Carolingian
Late 9th century
Ivory; H 20.5 cm, W 12.5 cm
Inv. No. 8399

Pope Gregory the Great is considered to be the author of the Roman book of forms for the Holy Mass. The use of it became obligatory under Charlemagne in the Carolingian Empire. The sacramentary contains the celebrant's part of the mass together with prayers for baptisms, blessings, ordinations etc. The core is the canon of the mass, the poem of which starts with the "Vere dignum". The ivory plaque illustrates the very moment, when Gregory the Great is about to write down this text which divine inspiration brought to his mind. The legend tells that one of his scribes secretly watched the author reassuming his dictation only after the dove of the Holy Spirit had stopped whispering in his ear. The anecdote of the watching scribe is left out in this ivory; Gregory is shown according to the well known prototype of an author's portrait, culminating in the moment when divine inspiration makes him personally write down the text the dove of the Holy Spirit whispers into his ear. The scribe crouching in the right lower corner seems to be listening to the saint but, as may be discovered with a magnifying glass, he is writing down a different text. These scribes are evidently occupied with copying the Roman book of forms. The typical Carolingian element in this ivory carving is the reduced size of the palace exterior, indicating a view from a distance. Its dominant motif, the central arch, reappears in the palace's façade, a conglomeration of staircases, mural walkways, towers and galleries, but also in the draperies and their extensions, although there is no real arch bridging the two supporting interior columns. While they are an indication of place, and as such part of the central scene, the constructional elements at the same time serve as a tectonic frame for the picture of the saint. In this Franco-Saxon prototype we encounter a precursor of the typical architectural frame constructions which evolved during an aesthetic dialogue carried on for two hundred years in England as well as on the continent, and which ended up in the brilliant artistic concept of the canopy-crowned framing arch as a congenial manifestation of early Romanesque art. The ivory's compositional concept is Carolingian, harking back to earlier artistic sources: An early Byzantine model stimulated not only the Carolingian version of an architecturally structured canopy, it was also the source of the realistic conception in rendering all the details as well. Contrary to any such Byzantine sources, the main composition and its additional register show-

DEATH OF THE VIRGIN MARY (KOIMESIS)
Constantinople
2nd half of 10th century
Steatite, partially gilt; H 13 cm, W 11.2 cm
Inv. No. 8797

The term "icon" refers to a sacred picture which is particularly venerated. Throughout the Orthodox Church iconolatry was part of the liturgical divine office in which the icon holds a sublime position. The painted icon holds equal spiritual significance as the written word. Small portable icons were preferably made of ivory. When ivory became scarce, steatite was used, as its soft, soapy surface resembles ivory, apart from its olive hue. This steatite icon is one of the earliest specimens known. Gilding adds to their value. A canopy vaults the death scene in which the Virgin is conceived of as "fallen asleep". Jesus Christ appears to receive his mother's soul which is wrapped in swaddling clothes like a newborn infant.   H. T.

ing the scribes at their work is framed by an acanthus frieze which holds together both zones with their very cramped figural narratives into one visual representation.   H. T.

ASCENSION OF CHRIST ▽
Metz, c. 980
Ivory; H 20.6 cm, W 14.4 cm
Inv. No. 7284

The Ottonian bone-carver was evidently inspired by two different models: Byzantine for the lower part of the panel and western for the upper part. Jesus Christ is seen from behind, a perspective signifying his turning away from the world. He elevates himself up into the spheres, reaching for the hand of God the Father, a Roman motif implying his sharing in the divine power. He is no longer part of this world, only the movement of the angels establishes a connection with the perplexed, agitated disciples below. Christ ascends through a funnel of clouds, a sculptural transformation of the text from the Scriptures into visual representation. Antique elements of western and eastern Roman origin have been integrated into a mediaeval concept, vanquishing the gravity of matter. In a similar way, the apostles do not touch the ground any longer, but seem to float. The composition is well-balanced along the vertical and horizontal axes of the picture, while giving priority to the correlation of projective form in the images' planes. Following Byzantine models, an acanthus frieze makes a perfect frame for the scene.   H. T.

SS. PETER AND ANDREW
Constantinople
Middle of 10th century (before 959)
Ivory; H 24.6 cm, W 13.5 cm
Inv. No. 8136

This panel was made in the workshop of an artisan working for the imperial court in the reign of Constantine VII Porphyrogenetos (912–959) and of Romanos II (945–963). The Greek inscription, an invocation of the apostles for intercession on his behalf, refers to Constantine VII. Romanos II gave the name to the entire "Romanos-group" of stylistically coherent ivories, distinguished by a style which combines refinement, artistic subtlety, and formal precision. At the peak of the so-called Macedonian renaissance, Byzantine art reached a second apogee. An aesthetic balance is achieved between the revival of a classic sense of proportion and an artistic effort serving exclusively religious purposes and aiming at the dematerialisation of the physical.   H. T.

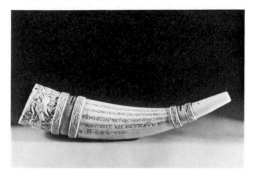

OLIFANT
South Italian (Saracen)
11th century
Ivory, partially coloured; L 51.8 cm
Inv. No. 4073

In mediaeval hunting, so-called Saracens' horns were widely used for transmitting signals. Usually, they were decorated with an ornamental frieze round the bell as well as around the mouthpiece, together with a broad figured border representing hunting scenes or animal combats. Probably in consequence of a re-dedication during the High Middle Ages, this *olifant* was engraved with an inscription on its middle section. It informs us that in 1199 Count Albrecht III of Habsburg, grandfather of King Rudolph I, presented the horn, filled with relics, to the Swiss Abbey Muri. Highly prized secular possessions were frequently made into reliquaries. In 1702, the *olifant* was returned to the Habsburgs in the form of a present from the then Abbot of Muri to the Emperor.　　　　H. T.

"PÜSTERICH" (FIRE-BLOWER, AELOPILE)
North Italian (?)
1st half of 12th century
Bronze cast; H 23.5 cm
Inv. No. 5702

It remains open to speculation whether this bizarre Romanesque *aeolopile* was an ordinary part of household equipment and was simply used for fanning the fire or served for the demonstration of experiments with steam power. It was filled with water and put among the embers where it puffed steam from small holes in nose and mouth (the hole in the belly is a damage). Already the antique specimens used to crouch or kneel, while shading their eyes with one hand. As a rule, the mediaeval fire-blowers are naked, usually with a special emphasis on the representation of their genitals. These characteristic traits may well indicate origins even beyond their antique models, deriving ultimately from prehistoric fertility idols.　　H. T.

CASKET ▷
Alpine
Early 12th century
Wood, gilt copper, bone, with tinged engravings;
H 21.8 cm, W 16.6 cm, L 15.5 cm
Inv. No. 10.006

The rectangular body of the casket is topped by a lid formed like the frustum of a pyramid. The entire surface is abundantly decorated; walls and tilts of the roof follow the same concept of ornamentation. The flat border is ornamentally engraved. It frames a centre piece in open work decoration with a delicately interlaced relief, the à jour facets underlaid in gold. Fabulous beasts inhabit the ornamental foliage of the tilts, becoming entwined and interlaced. This ornamental form of decoration which got to be known as "Langobardic style" in reference to its origin especially in the alpine region was in use over a long period.　H. T.

◁ GRIFFIN EWER (AQUAMANILE)

Circle of Roger of Helmarshausen
Lower Saxony, 1st quarter of 12th century
Gilt bronze, partially silver-encrusted, with
niello; H 17.3 cm, W 8.5 cm, L 14.5 cm
Inv. No. 83

The exotic fascination of this flagon evokes several differing associations. It is a utensil in the form of a daemonic animal, an upright sitting bird of prey with an eagle's beak, in fact a griffin. The griffin symbolizes Jesus Christ purifying the soul of man. All these allusions continuously shift, change and run into one another. Created after oriental models, aquamaniles were frequently of a profane character. Today, they remind us of the high standard of civilization of even household equipment in the days of chivalry. But such artefacts also served for the liturgical ceremony of ritual hand-washing. Thus, the inventory of the Mainz Cathedral treasure of 1253 lists "several vessels of different form called *manilia,* as they are used for pouring water over the hands of the priests. Some are formed like lions, others like dragons, griffins etc." As U. Mende found out, the Viennese specimen belongs to the artistic circle of Roger of Helmarshausen, a monk who worked in Lower Saxony around 1100. He is regarded as one of the outstanding artisans of the Middle Ages. The perfect bronze casting pleases by the swelling roundness of its smooth form and its elegantly flowing lines. Shallow decorative elements of inlaid niello and silver corresponding with comprehensive hot-gilding, determine the accord of colouring which is established by the black of the inserted eye beads, anthracite grey, silver sheen, and the glimmer of gold. Whereas the artistic roots have hitherto been ascribed to the tradition of the Mosan arts and crafts, these technical characteristics rather point to the Anglo-Saxon tradition. At the same time as Roger von Helmarshausen was working in Lower Saxony, the Gloucester candelabra (1107/1113) was produced in England, where the use of such inset pupils of silver and niello decoration was common. Some artefacts of Lower Saxon origin combine in a similar way the techniques of goldsmiths' works and the characteristics of bronze casting, usually strictly kept apart in the mediaeval workshop traditions.

H. T.

COMMUNION CHALICE FROM THE ARCH-ABBEY ST. PETER IN SALZBURG

Salzburg
c. 1160/80
Silver gilt, node beryl, incrusted stones; H 23 cm
Inv. No. 9983

The inscription on the covered upper rim of the stem indicates that the twelve half figures rising out of the pinnacles represent the twelve tribes of Israel led by Aaron. Through the flowering of Aaron's rod God appointed Aaron's Levites to the priesthood. The High Priests of the Old Testament were seen in close connection with Christ. The inscription on the upper rim of the chalice refers to the twelve representatives of the Old Testament according to Moses, who in their prayers entreat that the Holy Blood should revive that which has been slain by sin. Finally, the highpriestly act inaugurating the New Testament is represented in the scene of the Last Supper on the paten. The chalice should be seen as an object of living faith, while the pictorial representations point to the spiritual reality of Christian doctrine.

H. T.

COMMUNION CHALICE, THE SO-CALLED "WILTEN CHALICE"
Lower Saxony
c. 1160/70
Silver partially gilt, with niello; H 16.7 cm
Inv. No. 8924

The celebration of the Christian mass necessitates altar equipment designed for specific purposes. The chalice and paten have the noblest rôle, since they are in contact with the Holiest of Holies. According to Catholic doctrine, bread and wine are transformed into the Body and Blood of Christ in the hands of the priest when he pronounces the words of the Last Supper. The two Romanesque communion chalices on display are two-handled chalices used only for dispensing the Eucharist in the form of wine which the faithful drank by means of a *fistula*, a drinking tube. The sequence of scenes depicting the story of the Salvation and the inscriptions on the chalice and the paten from Wilten explain the meaning of the Eucharist sacrifice by means of representations

from the history of the Old and New Testament. On the paten they culminate with the Crucifixion of Christ and his victory over death. On the base of the chalice there are scenes from the Old Testament, among them the fall of man as the cause of Christ's redeeming sacrifice, as well as the sacrifices of Noah, Abraham and Melchisedech. On the outer side of the cup there are scenes from the New Testament, from the Annunciation to the carrying of the cross. The events around the Last Supper are given ample space. Above the four Cardinal Virtues on the stem there are reliefs on the node representing the four rivers of Paradise. Thus, the chalice represents the fountain of life from which wells the blood of Christ. Probably, this altar equipment was presented to the Abbey of Wilten in Tyrol by Count Berthold III of Andechs (1148–1188), if indeed he is the *BERTOLDVS* mentioned in the donor's inscription. This masterpiece of Romanesque goldsmith's work is mainly executed in niello technique, which aims at graphic effects. It originates from the artistic circle under the patronage of Henry the Lion.   H. T.

ST. JOHN THE BAPTIST ▽
Constantinople
11th/12th century
Heliotrope, set in gold; Diam. 4.6 cm
Inv. No. IX a 20

After Christ and Mary, John the Baptist is the third personage to be invoked in prayer by orthodox Christians. St. John, the forerunner of Jesus Christ, is here seen in relief in the form of a *clipeus*. In antiquity, this representation was used in particular for imperial portraits. When Christian artisans began to make use of the circular form, they intentionally alluded to the special meaning of the *clipeus*. This cameo was used as jewellery and served the need for luxury of aristocratic circles. Nevertheless, the saint represented on the medallion was assured of the veneration of the wearer. Thus, in the Byzantine Empire the ambivalent desire for ostentation and veneration came into conflict with the meaning and intention of a devotional object.   H. T.

POSEIDON AS RULER OF THE ISTHMIAN GAMES
Southern Italy (staufian)
1st half of 13th century
Cameo: onyx; setting (early 19th century): gold; H 7 cm, W 8.8 cm
Inv. No. IX a 62

As in the case of many works imitating an antique style, the significance of this representation is unclear. Separate antique motifs were obviously strung together. As central figure Poseidon, the god of the sea, is standing on a rock, with a team of tethered horses on each side. Under Emperor Frederick II glyptic art reached its apogee in the kingdom of Southern Italy-Sicily. Admiration for antiquity is one characteristic of this art form, particularly where figurative cameo carving was concerned. Hardstone carving was also promoted by the patronage of princely connoisseurs. Emperor Frederick II was notorious for his passionate interest in precious stones.   H. T.

CRUCIFIXION OF CHRIST ▷
Italian
2nd half of 13th century
Cameo: onyx; setting (French, 2nd half of 16th century): gold enamelled
H 9.2 cm, W 6.7 cm
Inv. No. IX a 4

To the left of the suffering Christ on the cross are the three Marys with St John the Evangelist, Christ's favourite disciple, lamenting. They unite harmoniously in grief and compassion. The same feeling is evident in the floating angels, with the same gesture of sorrow of the hand pressed against the cheek. On the right stand Christ's enemies. The model for this representation was a Byzantine crucifixion scene, in which, since the days of the Comnene dynasty, the emotional

appeal had been predominant. It was via Venice that those Byzantine influences came to Western Europe after the fall of Constantinople.   H. T.

129

TWO-HANDLED VESSEL OF ROCK CRYSTAL
Southern Italy? Venice?
13th century?
Rock crystal; setting (18th century): silver gilt;
H 41.3 cm, Diam. 31 cm
Inv. No. 2316

JUG OF ROCK CRYSTAL
Paris?
14th century?
Rock crystal; H 26.1 cm, Diam. 17.5 cm
Inv. No. 2272

A group of masterpieces carved in hardstone are the claim to fame of the mediaeval section of the Collection of Sculpture an Decorative Arts. Opinions diverge widely as to the origin and date of the faceted monolithic rock-crystal vessels with their handles carved out of the same block. Analyses of form and cutting technique have not so far led to precise results. Only Constantinople possessed a more or less continuous tradition from antique times in this technically difficult, time-consuming and truly noble art. The revival of antique stone-carving in the West is probably connected with the fall of Constantinople in 1204, which resulted not only in a great number of objects but also many artists and entire stone-carving work-shops moving to Western Europe. The earliest guild rules (1259 Paris, 1284 Venice) already distinguished between two crafts: the *arte minuta,* or subtle gem-cutting, and the *arte grossa* which comprised the cutting of vessels out of hardstones. Venice secured an option on the best pieces of oriental raw material. Yet it seems certain that a passionate amateur collector of precious stones like Emperor Frederick II, with his well known contacts in the Islamic world, had no difficulty in acquiring the very best for himself and for the Imperial workshops in his Norman-Hohenstaufian kingdom of Lower Italy-Sicily. It must be stressed, however, that only in the case of cameos glyptographing is documented as a branch of Frederick's court art.

The large double-handled ewer weighing 12.8 kilograms is unique. The size of the uncut block of quartz must have been impressive. Its flawless purity – apart from a few flaws – probably only became apparent during the progress of work. The massive character of the block was preserved in the ample, tectonically conceived outline characterized by the balance between the purely crystalline handles and the swelling roundness of the vessel itself.

According to the criteria used for evaluating hardstone vessels – purity of the crystal, beauty of outline, and cutting precision – the onehandled ewer of purest crystal with its elegantly curved outline is among the most remarkable achieve-

ments of the *arte grossa* as such. Its handle in the shape of an E is considered the most graceful as well as the most complicated formal solution of the late Middle Ages. In no other vessel of that time was the same perfect regularity of cut achieved. Specialists agree to ascribe it to the French court workshops of the 14th century. Such vessels decorated princely tables and sideboards. French queens used to present them as gifts to princes of the blood.

H. T.

CHRIST ENTHRONED
Venice
End of 13th century
Marble, traces of gilding and polychromy;
H 90 cm, W. 209 cm
Inv. No. 7394

Tomb decoration was closely connected with the Christian belief in a life hereafter. Persons of importance secured for themselves tombs inside a church in order to be as near as possible to the

relics of the saints. The saints intercede for the salvation of the soul from eternal damnation. This tombstone sculpture in relief from a workshop that copied Byzantine models is intended to evoke the monumental art connected with this belief. The centre-piece of the three marble slabs of a mural sarcophagus depicts Christ enthroned, whose image the resurrected hope to perceive. Floating angels support the throne, a motif derived from the Byzantine conception of the Ascension.

H. T.

AMETHYST BOWL △
Venice
Late 14th or early 15th century
Amethyst; mounting: silver gilt; H 16.3 cm,
W 23.8 cm
Inv. No. 86

The vessel belongs to the common category of incense boats. Its lid has been lost. The mounting with a pomegranate motif and with its traces of enamel enables us to ascribe it to Venice and to fix an approximate date. The mount proves the close collaboration between goldsmiths and hardstone cutters who joined forces to form the Venetian confraternity of the *cristalleri* in the middle of the 13th century. Since this time, Venice became the most important centre for stone cutting. Its production was mostly exported. According to its Greek name (*amethyein* = to preserve from drunkenness) the amethyst is meant to protect and to disperse evil thoughts.

H. T.

AGATE BOWL ▷
Prague (?)
2nd half of 14th century
Agate; mounting: silver gilt; H 18.6 cm,
Diam. 27.2 cm
Inv. No. 6699

Although Venice knew an apogee of hardstone carving during the late Middle Ages, we know also of stone cutters in Prague who worked in the New Town and were usually called "polishers". The pious Emperor Karl IV felt a strong inclination towards the symbiotic union of the cult of relics and the belief in the magic power of precious stones. He ordered walls inlaid with precious stones and costly vessels to be made for him. The simple form of the setting, with its smooth base and the quatrefoil openwork round the foot follows the artistic tradition of the Prague court artisans. An even more certain indication of the Bohemian origin of the bowl is the fact that only in the Bohemian kingdom this kind of agate with traces of amethyst was quarried. The site of the ancient quarry has recently been rediscovered. H. T.

ENTHRONED MADONNA, VENERATED BY A KNEELING BISHOP
Siena
c. 1320
Copper gilt; H 5.5 cm, W 9 cm, L 3.8 cm
Inv. No. 53

This group of three figures – the Virgin with child enthroned, on her own pedestal, and a kneeling bishop in front of her – are joined by a hexagonal base. The bishop in full regalia raises his folded hands in a formal gesture of prayer. The group originally decorated the curve of a crosier's head. The most closely related object known is the completely preserved *pastorale* of Città di Castello – a goldsmith's work from Siena dated about 1324. Both evidently follow the same model but were not cast from an identical mold. They come from different workshops, the Viennese group being considered the older of the two. Possibly, the spatial concept of the eternal adoration goes back to a design of Nicola Pisano, one of the most gifted sculptors of the 13th century.   H. T.

LITTLE FOLDING ALTAR
French (?)
2nd quarter of 14th century
Silver gilt, enamel; H 9 cm, W 15.5 cm
Inv. No. 8878

Because of their tiny format, folding altars were used as travelling altars. Their precious materials and finish made them valuable objects for princely treasuries. This item was part of the Salzburg Cathedral Treasure. It consists of four plaques connected by hinges with open work tops. Both sides, the enamel pictures as well as the cast relief figures on an enamel background depict scenes from the passion and resurrection of Christ. The light reflected by the engraved back of each panel lends sparkle and shimmer to the translucid enamel. Such a precious object is apt to provoke spontaneous appreciation for its artistic achievement rather than religious fervour suited to the sombre character of the passion scenes.
                H. T.

IVORY CASKET ▽
French
Mid-14th century
Ivory; mounting and handle: silver gilt; H 21 cm, W 10.2 cm, L 7 cm
Inv. No. 115

Chivalric self-assurance and aristocratic habits are reflected in the graceful reliefs of the lid and the sides of this jewellery casket. These scenes from the *Châtelaine de Vergi*, a popular troubadour poem, served as a visual reminder of the well-known ballad. Most probably such delicate profane carvings were once presented to high-born ladies whose sense of beauty they would please. These objects were not made to order but produced in great number by French workshops. Travelling merchants sold them to the European nobility.   H. T.

GAMES BOARD

Venice
c. 1380
Inlaid wood, jasper, chalcedony, bone, painted
clay reliefs, miniatures under rock crystal;
H 38 cm, W 38 cm
Inv. No. 168

This games board consists of two folding panels
joined by hinges. One side is a chess board, while
the other is a backgammon board. Chess was the
courtly game par excellence. The figures in polychrome earthen ware represent motifs from courtly chivalry, which were taken at random from the
reserve stock of a large workshop. The inlay *alla
certosina* consists of wood coloured with boiling
oil and different chemicals. This was a popular
Northern Italian technique, which was mostly
practiced in the Venetian workshops of the Embriachi family.   H. T.

OCTOGONAL JEWEL CASKET

Workshop of Baldassare degli Embriachi
Venice
Late 14th/early 15th century
Wood with *certosina-intarsia,* bone; H 43 cm
Inv. No. 8020

The lateral plaques depict a series of mythological
representations such as the history of Paris, the
rape of Helen, and the birth of Adonis. The
more educated among the mostly aristocratic owners of
such objects were familiar with antique mythology, at least from translations or contemporary
versions. The lid in the shape of a roof depicts
scenes of naked lovers, which was very daring for
the times. Two of the figures are seen holding
shields to cover their nakedness. The buyer's
coat of arms would normally have been blazoned
onto the blank shield. A special technique characterizes the abundant production of the Venetian
family workshop of the Embriachi; pieces of
cheap bone replace often the rare and expensive
Ivory.   H. T.

BUST OF A PROPHET ▽
Circle of Pier Paolo and Jacopo dalle Masegne
Venice
c. 1400
Marble; H 41 cm
Inv. No. 7432

This bust is one of six half length figures which
may have decorated the sarcophagus of the tomb
of Margherita Gonzaga in Mantua. Originally, the
busts of the prophets were placed in the wall
niches of the sarcophagus. The figures of the
prophets evidently engaged in lively dispute
prove that the Venetian masters who produced
them about 1400 had joined the main-stream of
European art trends in their graceful delicacy and
expressive movement.   H. T.

DRINKING HORN ("GRIFFIN'S CLAW")
Lower German,
2nd half of 15th century
Buffalo horn; mounting: silver gilt; foot: bronze
gilt; H 26 cm, L 24.5 cm
Inv. No. 80

Materials whose origin was more or less unknown
(and nobody really cared to search further) left
more scope to fantasy. Popular imagination liked
to interpret the strange, fossilized buffalo horns as
claws of the legendary griffin. The support of the
vessel in the shape of a griffin gives further
evidence why it was customary in the late Middle
Ages to refer to such drinking horns as "griffins'
claws". They were supposed to make poison in
drinks visible and harmless. The form and ornamentation of the six-lobe tracery of the mouth
piece allow us to date it in the late 15th century.
                                              H. T.

lenses in the Burgundian court goblet of Duke Philip the Good (today in the Vienna treasury). The owner's motto as well as the date of 1449 on the base of the cup show it to have been the property of Emperor Frederick III. Emperor Ferdinand I inherited it from Maximilian I. In 1564 Ferdinand left it to his son Archduke Karl II of Inner Austria who resided in Graz. The latter presented it in the same year to his chamberlain Caspar Baron Herberstein and linked it to the proviso that the cup should only be inherited through the male line. The donation and the proviso are inscribed on the setting of the lid which was added in 1564. The knob bears the Herberstein coat of arms.

The pieces of rock crystal which form part of the so-called "double goblet" are possibly much older than the goldsmith's work dating from the middle of the 15th century. Due to the hallmark of Nuremberg, the origin of the setting can be safely traced.   S. K.

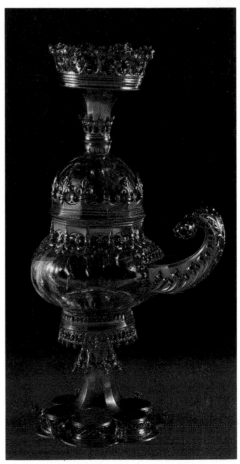

ROCK CRYSTAL GOBLET WITH LID
Burgundy or Venice?
1st half of 15th century
Rock crystal; mounting (Nuremberg? 1449 and Graz? 1564): silver gilt; H 25.7 cm
Inv. No. 6896

ROCK CRYSTAL "DOUBLE GOBLET" ▷
Burgundy or Venice?
1st half of 15th century?
Rock crystal; mounting (Nuremberg, mid-15th century): silver gilt, partially enamelled; H 24.5 cm
Inv. No. 82

The origin of both rock crystal goblets cannot be certified. Venice and Burgundy are both possible centres of origin. The goblet with lid is modelled on two-handled ewers of the late Middle Ages (cf. p. 130 r.). The lenses cut at irregular intervals into the body of the vessel remind one of similar

TABLE DECORATION (EPERGNE WITH "ADDERS' TONGUES")
German
Mid-15th century
Silver gilt, fossilized sharks' teeth, citrine;
H 27 cm
Inv. No. 89

In the Middle Ages people imagined that fossilized sharks' teeth were adders' tongues (or dragons' tongues) and ascribed to them the power of neutralizing poison in food and drink.

Princes commissioned specially designed table ornaments decorated with the much sought-after "adders' tongues". They were suspended on such epergnes like fruits on a tree. Above a conventional base with a knob covered with foliage there sprouts a bouquet of these "adders' tongues". The centre is formed by a citrine. Two of the three remaining epergnes with "adders' tongues" have survived in Viennese treasuries, others, however, were listed in inventories not only of Frederick III in Vienna, but also in those of the Duke of Burgundy.   H. T.

KRUMAU MADONNA
Prague?
c. 1390–1400
Calcareous sandstone; originally painted (robe: outside white, inside blue) with gilding on hair and border of robe.
H 112 cm
Dep. Prot. 1

This Madonna was found in Krumau in southern Bohemia, but in style and artistic technique it is a product of the court art of Prague. These statues of the Virgin Mary represent the most delicate expression of international Gothic in its south-eastern variant, the so-called *Weicher Stil* ("soft" style), as well as one of the highest achievements of court art. They possess an emotional appeal and are known as "Beautiful Madonnas"; delicate masterpieces, embodying an ideal, which affect us with their grace and loveliness. The Virgin Mary presents her Son as the Redeemer, yet is depicted in a spirit of maternal playfulness: in its complete state the Child would have been playing with an apple. The statue, designed to be viewed from the front, is given plasticity by the play of light and dark caused by the rhythmical profusion of drapery which conceals her body. Lateral cascades frame the deep hollows between the folds of material. The drapery is characterized by a singularly soft fluidity of line, which has less to do with the flowing lines of the robe's borders than with the undulating surfaces and the delicately modelled structure, from which the "soft" style derives its name.   H. T.

BUST RELIQUARY (ST. CASSIAN?)
South Tyrol?
Late 14th century
Copper gilt; H 45 cm, W 38 cm
Inv. No. 8867

Reliquaries were frequently shaped according to that part of the saint's body the specific relic had been taken from. Thus, reliquaries in the shape of a bust were used for skull relics. This bust may represent an idealized portrait of St. Cassian, one of the patron saints of the Brixen diocese. The vividly expressive bust originated from South Tyrol, but seems to have been modelled after the sculpted stone portraits of St. Vitus' Cathedral in Prague. These busts, executed by the stone-masons' lodge of Peter Parler in Prague, are counted among the masterpieces of a new realistic form of portraiture which was just beginning in the late 14th century. H. T.

"WIENER MUSTERBUCH"
Bohemia, 1st quarter of the 15th century
Fourteen tablets of maplewood, held together by strips of parchment; on each tablet four small pieces of green tinted paper have been pasted; silverpoint, pen, white and red brush; protected by a leather case; each tablet H 9.5 cm, W 9 cm
Inv. Nos. 5003, 5004

Mediaeval model books were used in workshops and by itinerant artists in order to have a stock of forms and motifs. These prototypes were de-signed to transmit iconographic and formal elements from place to place and from generation to generation. In this sumptuous edition of a model book a painter working in the international Gothic style of 1400 captured various types of human and animal heads. Except for two portraits added at a later date, all drawings were executed by the same hand. The assemblage in the manner of a folding book and the precious leather casing seem to indicate that it was intended as a present for an important patron from whom the artist hoped to obtain commissions. H. T.

GAME OF CARDS ("AMBRASER HOFJAGDSPIEL") ▽
Circle of Konrad Witz
Upper Rhine
c. 1440/50
Set of 54 cards (formerly 56); layers of paper glued together, pen drawings, water colours; each card c. H 15.6 cm, W 9.5 cm
Inv. Nos. 5018–5071

This set of cards depicts courtly falconry. The "suits" are chosen accordingly. The falcon is represented as a hunting bird of prey, the silver heron as prey. The dog retrieves the wounded heron, and the bait entices the falcon to return to his master. The vivid rendering of dramatic scenes on some cards and even more a remarkable series of landscapes characterize this game of cards. The immediacy of the nature scenes and a feeling for light and composition combine with stylistic idiosyncrasies of the new trend towards realistic depiction. Stylistically, many details point to Konrad Witz from Basle. H. T.

GAME OF CARDS ("HOFÄMTERSPIEL")
Vienna?
c. 1455
Complete set of 48 playing cards; layers of paper glued together, wood cuts and pen drawings, water colours and gold and silver leaf; each card c. H 14 cm, W 10 cm
Inv. Nos. 5077–5124

The four suits of this set depicting court functions are represented by means of four heraldic colours (Bohemia, German Empire, France, Hungary), while the suits themselves reflect the court hierarchy. The individual values of the cards conform to the precedence of the court functions. The aristocratic court functions were enlarged with court servants and purveyors. Each card carries the title of the function depicted and the respective Roman number. The cards are unique as a series of profane wood cuts. The virtuosity of their carving makes the contours resemble finely drawn lines. The careful finishing and colouring with gold and silver leaf intensify the effect of the engraving. All these points indicate that this set of cards can only have been intended for princely entertainment. Some details suggest that it was commissioned by Ladislaus "Postumus" (d. 1457), Duke of Austria, King of Hungary and Bohemia. H. T.

BOSS OF A CRIB SADDLE ▽
Southern Low Countries
3rd quarter of 15th century
Braziery; H 23.5 cm, W 21.8 cm
Inv. No. 139

The picture of a young lady decorates this metal plaque. Her hair is divided into two plaits and tied above her temples, topped by a winged head-dress, whose veil is held across her forehead by a piece of jewellery, descending over her shoulders. Hairdo and cap follow the refined taste of the fashion around 1470 of Burgundy and the Low Countries. The crib saddle itself is another typical example of the courtly culture of aristocratic society. The southern Low Countries and Brussels in particular, were at that time a centre for figurative bronze and brass casting. This object is closely related to the figures on the tomb of Isabella of Bourbon in the Rijksmuseum in Amsterdam.   M. L.-J.

VEINED "DOUBLE CUP"
Nuremberg ?
Mid-15th century
Veined elm-wood; mounting: silvergilt; H 18 cm
Inv. No. 73

Veined wood, obtained from deformations of the trunks of different deciduous tress, is very hard and compact. Because of its beautiful veining, it was frequently used for making drinking vessels in the Middle Ages. It was further thought to possess the ability to neutralize poison or at least to heighten the taste of drink. Such a flattened bowl, made on a wood turning lathe, was a *Kopf* (from Latin *cuppa*) in German. A second cup was sometimes placed on top, thus forming a "double cup" (*Doppelkopf*). This upper cup could be removed and served as a separate drinking vessel.   S. K.

TROUBADOUR CASKET
Upper or Middle Rhenish
c. 1460/1470
Boxwood; H 12 cm, W 16 cm, L 12 cm
Inv. No. 118

The side panels show an informal series of scenes from the life of the Wild Man. The Wild People are the personification of the vital forces of nature. Their playful activities – making love, enjoying leisure, hunting, bringing up children – are counterbalanced by dangers they must face. They have to fend off the attacks of wild beasts. In contrast to these scenes in which the Wild Men are framed by stylised, overlapping foliage, the lid depicts the return from the hunt in a wooded landscape resembling a tapestry. The erotic *leitmotif* is initially represented by their prey, the captured Wild Woman riding on a unicorn. In its stress on loyalty and family closeness the behaviour of the Wild People rather corresponds to the bourgeois conception of married life.   H. T.

PRAYER NUT (ROSARY BEAD)
Low Countries
Early 16th century
Boxwood; Diam. 6.2 cm
Inv. No. 4206

When open, the pendant reveals on its lower part Christ in front of Pontius Pilate with the Scourging as background scene. On the side wings, in shallow relief, we find the Carrying of the Cross on the left and the Lamentation and Burial on the right. In the middle a "crowded Crucifixion" can be seen. In contrast to the wings, the two many-figured central scenes are deeply carved. Such prayer nuts – masterpieces of virtuoso miniature carving – were intended as pendants for rosaries. They served for private devotion and meditation. Dexterity, patience and artistic skill were needed in order to create an entire world in miniature. H. T.

143

ADAM ▽
Tilman Riemenschneider
(Osterode/Harz c. 1460 – 1531 Würzburg)
Würzburg
c. 1510
Pearwood; H 24 cm, W 8.5 cm
Inv. No. 43

This statuette formed part of a group depicting the Fall from Grace and arranged on a single base representing the Garden of Paradise. Adam's attitude evidently compliments that of Eve, his figurative counterpart. The scene must have conveyed the idea of temptation as well as of the final expulsion from Eden. The biblical theme is used as a pretext for representing the naked human body. Adam is represented at the moment when he is stepping from one leg onto the other, thereby transferring his weight. If this movement brings to mind the dawning of the Renaissance, the delicate figure caught in its unstable balance nevertheless remains late Gothic in form with its elongated, affected posture.   H. T.

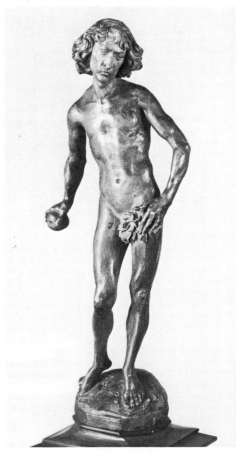

VIRGIN WITH CHILD
Tilman Riemenschneider
(Osterode/Harz 1460 – Würzburg 1531)
Würzburg
c. 1495
Limewood, ancient colouring; H 145 cm
Inv. No. 8899

Religiosity, and his high opinion of his own quality as an artist are already apparent in Riemenschneider's early work. This statue from about 1495, belongs to this early period. It is apt to evoke deep devotional meditation, yet it does not produce a confusion between the figure's reality and the religious message it intends to convey. Although the faces of the Virgin and Child follow the tenets of realistic bourgeois appearance of the time, Riemenschneider aimed at a universal canon by idealizing their features. Intending it for a strictly frontal presentation, Riemenschneider utilized all the possibilities of the natural contours of the wood.   H. T.

FALCONER ▽
Ascribed to Hans Syfer
(d. 1509 Heilbronn)
Heilbronn ?
c. 1495
Pearwood, partially tinted, polychromed base;
H 31.3 cm
Inv. No. 3968

The falconer is represented at the moment when he launches the bird of prey (no longer extant). The young man's long stride conveys a sense of energy. Daring motifs and abrupt movements are nevertheless deeply rooted in the late Gothic spatial concept. In its remarkable consciousness of form and the perfection of its execution, this work of art in his own right was clearly a collector's item intended for aesthetic pleasure, and therefore a creation indicating the transition to the Renaissance. Undisputed is the specific Upper Rhenish character of this sculpture, which it shares with a burial group by the same artist, dated 1496.   H. T.

ENTHRONED MADONNA WITH CHILD ON A CRESCENT
Ascribed to Niklaus Weckmann
(mentioned as a burgher 1481–1526)
Ulm
c. 1510
Limewood, original polychromy;   H 113 cm,
W 90 cm, D 20 cm
Inv. No. 30

This figure, supposedly from a convent church in Ulm, must have been part of a carved altar shrine. (In its basic concept of a flat upright box, the shrine constitutes the centre piece of a winged altar. These altars were probably the most impressive achievement of late Gothic art, wood carving playing a decisive part in this.) The top half of the madonna's body is represented in full; below, the body disappears in a high relief of widely spread drapery. Statuesque calm is replaced by a dynamic rippling of folds. The carved throne – which is more of a projecting form rather than an actual seat – and the crescent moon frame the Virgin and Child.   H. T.

DÜRER GOBLET (right) ▷
Nuremberg
c. 1500
Silver gilt; H 47.5 cm
Inv. No. 109

MAXIMILIAN GOBLET (left) ▷
Nuremberg
c. 1510
Silver, partially gilt; H 56 cm
Inv. No. 110

Goblets with lid formed a *leitmotif* of German goldsmiths' work executed during the late Gothic and the Renaissance period. Sketch books, paintings and engravings by Albrecht Dürer prove that he concerned himself with the design of this traditional mediaeval vessel. Goldsmiths probably executed cups according to his ideas. Among the cups and goblets still extant, two prime examples, the so-called *Dürer goblet* and the *Maximilian goblet*, specifically suggest this. The *Dürer goblet* was probably acquired by Archduke Ferdinand II of Tyrol from the legacy of the Counts of Montfort-Werdenberg, as the *Wild Man* clad in animal skins on the knob of the lid holds this family's coat of arms. The sophisticated yet seemingly "natural" construction of the bosses is a development of late Gothic concepts probably due to Dürer. The characteristic motif of three intertwined bosses appears in a cup design in Dürer's Dresden scrap book.

In the *Maximilian goblet*, executed ten years later, this concept has been further transformed in line with Renaissance design. Realistically shaped pears have replaced the bosses, and out of the lid sprouts a twig carrying pomegranates, the symbol of princely virtues. The inside shows Maximilian I's coat of arms.   S. K.

ALLEGORY OF VANITY (TRANSIENCY)
Gregor Erhart
(Ulm c. 1468 – 1540 Augsburg)
Hans Holbein the Elder? (colouring)
(Augsburg c. 1465 – 1524 Augsburg)
Augsburg
c. 1500
Limewood with original polychromy; H 46 cm
Inv. No. 1

This regularly composed group of three figures contrasts youth and beauty on one side to old age on the other, the former represented by a young man and young girl, the latter in the shape of an old woman with drastic signs of decrepitude. The chastity of the beautiful young couple is in sharp opposition to the shameless exhibition of ugliness on the part of the old woman, which borders on travesty. The moralizing tendency – all is vain – is linked to certain puritan principles. The natural approach towards the naked body characteristic of antiquity has not yet been regained. The shimmering quality of the enamel-like colouring and the richness of surface texture are typical of Holbein the Elder.   H. T.

TWO GOBLETS WITH LID
Ludwig Krug
(Nuremberg c. 1489/90 – 1532 Nuremberg)
Nuremberg
c. 1510 and 1525, resp.
Silver gilt; H 32 cm
Inv. No. 979
Silver, partially gilt; H 44 cm
Inv. No. 898

Krug was not only one of the foremost goldsmiths of the 16th century but was also a successful painter, engraver and sculptor. His art is closely related to that of Dürer. On the goblet with the figure of the *Landsknecht* on top (the coat of arms was only added in 1582) the taut, round bosses of the cup are contrasted to nineteen narrow ones around stem and lid. The tiny figures of three crouching hooded miners support the second richly structured goblet, whose lid is crowned by the figure of a woman at a well. These works are closely connected with sketches from Dürer's Dresden scrap book. The combination of old and newly developed forms is characteristic of these vessels. S. K.

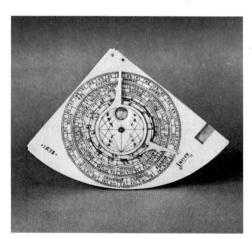

QUADRANT OF EMPEROR FREDERICK III
Vienna
1438
Ivory, with engraved curves, shadow square and signs of the zodiac; H 91 cm, W 87 cm
Inv. No. 166

The sun quadrant is a greatly simplified version of an astrolabe. Of the original full circle only a quarter circle remains. Apart from determining the height of the sun and of buildings, the sun quadrant after its further development by Johann of Gmunden (before 1385–1442) could then also be used to tell the time. A copy of his design of 1434 proves that Johann of Gmunden developed this sun quadrant. He was one of the leading members of the Vienna School of mathematics and astronomy and had personal connections with the Emperor's court. Frederick III was fascinated by astronomy and carried out astronomical observations from a tower in the *Hofburg* in Vienna. The quadrant, dated 1438 and marked with the Emperor's personal motto *AEIOU*, must have been very useful to him. H. T.

ARMILLARY SPHERE
Pierre de Fobis
(working in Lyons 1507 – c. 1575)
Lyons, late 16th century
Gilt brass, glass; mechanism: iron; H 53 cm
Inv. No. 9843

Since antique times, astronomers had used mechanical models, and the armillary sphere above all was especially suited to purposes of demonstration. It may be considered a forerunner of our present-day planetariums. It was able to convey to the audience the idea of the celestial sphere and of the regular movements of the universe by means of the most important circles of reference. When such a geocentric model was slowly set in motion by means of a mechanism, it correctly simulated the daily changes in the sky, but only when they were adjusted to correspond to one revolution of the sphere. One oft the main tasks of *scientifica*, a special department of the princely treasuries, was to vividly portray the movements of the planets. H. T.

CELESTIAL GLOBE ▽
Georg Roll
(Liegnitz 1546 – 1592 Augsburg)
Johann Reinhold
(Liegnitz, c. 1550 – 1590 Augsburg)
Augsburg
1583/84
Bronze, gilt brass, partly painted silver, wood; mechanism: iron; H 54 cm
Inv. No. 854

This clockwork driven globe served as a model to demonstrate the cosmos. These mechanical models of the sky simulated the movements of the sun, the moon and the stars. In addition, they made it possible to project the movements of the celestial bodies into the past and the future. Also they were suitable calculators which could be used to tell the time by analogy from the position of the stars, and vice versa. In 1584, Georg Roll, an entrepreneur from Augsburg, delivered two globes to Emperor Rudolph II and to his brother, Archduke Ernst. When the Emperor's globe which was the more expensive of the two soon became defective, Rudolf was so angry that he had Roll imprisoned for some time, as he "had presented him with foul fish". H. T.

TABLE CLOCK
Jeremias Metzker
(working in Augsburg 1555 – 1599)
Augsburg
1564
Gilt bronze; mechanism: iron; H 29.7 cm
Inv. No. 852

When in the 16th century men of science once more began to precisely survey the earth, the mechanical clock for telling the time became the most important instrument of all. No other implement for measuring time could surpass its possibilities. The mechanical clock could tell the time, but could also demonstrate the cosmic movements with the help of an astrolabe. The table clock made by Jeremias Metzker possesses particularly varied indicators, among them a 24-hour clock dial, shutters for the Nuremberg hours, a calender for the days of the year and a dial for the position of the sun in the zodiac. It also has an alarm. The clock is among the most remarkable exemples in a series of south German Renaissance table clocks. It is crowned by a wide housing for the bell. H. T.

ROLLING BALL CLOCK ▽
Christoph Margraf
(active Prague 1587 – 1620/24)
Prague
1596
Gilt copper, glass, unrefined silver, opaque colouring; mechanism: iron; H 40.3 cm, W 28 cm, L 23 cm
Inv. No. 845

The mechanism of this clock was developed by the Imperial clockmaker Margraf in Prague. For this invention he received a charter of privilege from Emperor Rudolph II. This signed clock of 1596 is the oldest of its kind still extant. A ball races down a tilted pane of glass guided by zigzagging wires. The time needed for one run is always the same. When one ball has reached the end of its course, the second ball is sent on its way after having been raised by a return mechanism. The hand of the clock is moved forward mechanically. In the lid of the clock case the run of the ball is reflected by a mirror in front of one of two scenic images one of Diana and Actaeon in unrefined silver, and the other, a painted Perseus and Andromeda. For the beholder, the reflected ball seems to ascend without being impeded by the force of gravity. H. T.

PLANETARY CLOCK ▽
Jost Bürgi
(Lichtensteig, Canton of St. Gallen 1552 – 1632 Kassel)
Prague
c. 1604
Bronze, gilt brass, painting on parchment, glass, rock crystal; mechanism: brass, iron; H 39,3 cm
Inv. No. 846

Jost Bürgi worked as a chamber-clockmaker at the Imperial court in Prague. Emperor Rudolph II expected him to invent new mechanisms and to find unique, strange and special objects for him. The princely residence in Cassel and the Imperial court in Prague were two centres in the Holy Roman Empire where the construction of scientific apparatus were especially encouraged. Bürgi worked for both courts. The lower clock dial represents the geocentric system, while the upper one shows the symbols the planets revolving around the sun in accordance with the Copernican system.
This clock presents a heliocentric planetarium for the first time in the history of clock making. The case of the clock was made by court craftsmen. Emperor Rudolph II was especially interested in technical masterpieces which could be regarded as works of art as well.   H. T.

ROCK CRYSTAL CLOCK
Jost Bürgi
(Lichtensteig, Canton of St. Gallen 1552 – 1632 Kassel)
Prag
c. 1623
Gilt brass, silver, rock crystal; mechanism: brass; H 18.6 cm
Inv. No. 1116

According to the conception of the world as a *machina mundi,* the universe seemed to resemble a clock. Conversely, the clock was considered as a functional model of the world. "Its universal analogue is to be found in astrology, the belief that there is an all encompassing relation of cause and effect between the movements of the planets and the course of things on earth (i.e. between the events in the sky and the things happening on earth within that same time)." In this incredibly complicated and precise rock crystal table clock the skilful technical and artistic elements form a perfect unity. It is the invention of Jost Bürgi, mathematician and mechanical genius of his days.
H. T.

**DEVICE FOR MEASURING DISTANCES
(WEGMESSER)** ▽
South German
c. 1580
Gilt brass, enamel; Diam. 15.1 cm
Inv. No. 9844

To measure the length of a coach ride, this abundantly decorated cylindrical box was fixed on the harness of horses. From it, a string led to one hock of the horse and transmitted the number of steps to a mechanism which was in turn connected to a measuring dire and numbers ring. Additionally, there was a contrivance for noting down any deviation from the originally chosen direction. This mechanical device for measuring distances owes its existence to the cartographers of the Renaissance. They were intent on precise geographical survey. Thus, in 1583 Christoph Schissler from Augsburg presented the Emperor Rudolf II with an *instrumentum geodeticum* which, according to his statement, had "described and noted" the entire distance he had travelled.   H. T.

TABLE CLOCK
Workshop of the Gross Family (case)
David Altenstetter (email en basse taille):
(d. 1617 Augsburg)
Augsburg
c. 1585
Silver partially gilt, enamel; mechanism: iron, brass; H 21.8 cm
Inv. No. 1121

Princely collectors liked to commission objects from eminent craftsmen of the guilds in free imperial cities. The skill of these artisans by far surpassed the abilities of the average craftmen. These usually contented themselves with the production of a series of almost identical types of objects. Imperial cities such as Nuremberg or Augsburg gave Germany a leading position in the construction of mechanical instruments. The case of this table clock is covered with incised ornaments filled with enamel. The corner posts, which carry the concave bell-house are ornamented with the same technique. The grotesques consisting of tendrils, animals and garlands gleam like gems, thus emphasizing the preciousness of time. A new appreciation of the value of time is apparent in this masterpiece.   H. T.

AUTOMATON WITH TRUMPETERS ▽
Hans Schlottheim
(Naumburg/Saale c. 1545 – 1625 Augsburg)
Augsburg
1582
Ebony, silver inlaid with cold enamel, gilt brass;
mechanism: iron; H 33.4 cm
Inv. No. 855

The ebony base holds the works of a tiny organ
with ten pipes. When the organ is started, the
eleven figurines are set in motion as well. The
trumpeters raise and lower their instruments and
the drummer begins to drum. The front of the
base shows two enamelled shields, one with the
coat of arms of Duke Wilhelm V of Bavaria, the
other with his initials W. H. I.B. and the date 1582.
The automaton is listed in the inventory of the
Ambras Collection of 1596. This indicates that it
had been presented by the Bavarian Duke to his
uncle, Archduke Ferdinand II, sovereign of Tyrol,
probably on the occasion of the latter's second
marriage to Anna Catarina Gonzaga in 1582.
H. T.

**AUTOMATON WITH MUSICAL MECHANISM,
IN THE FORM OF A SHIP (SHIP CLOCK)**
Hans Schlottheim
(Naumburg/Saale c. 1545 – 1625 Augsburg)
Augsburg
1585
Silver gilt, figurines and sails painted; mecha-
nism: iron; H 67 cm, W 66 cm
Inv. No. 874

Automatons like this musical clock in the form of a
ship were used as festive table decorations intended to amuse and entertain the diners. The
effect was increased when they were designed to
mechanically imitate real-life action and could
produce a melody as well. Gradually, the traditional epergnes lost their original function and developed into mechanically moving toys and
gadgets, and finally into automatons proper. A
mechanism and a musical clockwork allowed this
ship automaton to roll across the table, while the
tiny musicians on it could be heard and seen to
play their instruments. The date 1585 in the
inscription and the Imperial double eagle on flags
and banners suggest that the ship was intended
for Rudolph II. Hans Schlottheim, who built several of these mechanical ships, was staying in
Prague in 1587.   H. T.

CLOCK: DIANA ON A CENTAUR
Melchior Mair (goldsmith's work)
(c. 1565–1613 Augsburg)
Augsburg
c. 1605
Silver partially gilt, deeply incised enamel, precious stones, wood; H 39.5 cm
Inv. No. 1166

After the gearing in the base has been started, the clock moves forward, propelled by wheels. The centaur rolls his eyes and sends off an arrow. Diana and one of the hounds turn their heads, while the second hound opens its mouth. The clockwork also strikes the hour. The mechanical clock is listed in the inventory of Emperor Rudolph II's collections of 1607–1611. So-called *Trinkspiele* were much esteemed table decorations of the period. Among the most common motifs used in figurative decoration was "Diana riding a stag"; hence the goddess' name has been applied to this huntress on the centaur. This figurative clock does not offer any drinking vessel, nevertheless it could be used for playful drinking games. The guest in whose direction the centaur's arrow pointed, had to offer a toast before emptying his cup.   H. T.

THE TRIUMPH OF BACCHUS ("TRINKSPIEL") ▷
Sylvester II Eberlin (?)
(d. 1639 Augsburg; master c. 1604)
Hans Schlottheim (organ works)
(Naumburg/Saale, c. 1545 – 1625 Augsburg)
Augsburg
c. 1605
Silver gilt, traces of painting; two mechanical works: iron, brass; H 44 cm, L 53 cm
Inv. No. 959

Trinkspiele (drinking automatons) are among the most charming inventions of the Augsburg goldsmiths around 1600. Commissioned as a princely table decoration, this playful piece of machinery in the shape of a triumphal wagon with a removable top crowned by a Bacchic group soon found its way into the collection of Emperor Rudolph II in Prague. By means of a gearing mechanism hidden inside, the vehicle could move across the table all by itself. Two satyrs busy themselves at the volutes of the pole. On the abundantly decorated box-shaped top, the youthful god Bacchus sits on a resting billy-goat, accompanied by his playmates. The interior of the wagon holds an organ mechanism, which, according to the research of J. H. Leopold, closely resembles that of the mechanical ship also on display here. The wagon may, therefore, also be ascribed to Hans Schlottheim. Movement of the figures is likewise impelled by this mechanism. Bacchus raises his arm, a parrot flaps its wings, a musician starts using his instrument. The reason why the entire top can be taken off may probably be the goat; in keeping with the idea of drinking-pieces in general, it can be used as a drinking vessel. Its head could be removed so that the entire company was able to drink the wine filled into his body. Even more than the two frolicking youthful satyr boys in front, the musician with the bagpipes sitting in the back of the wagon and dangling his legs determines the mood of unimpeded serenity conveyed by this centre-piece.   H. T.

MECHANICAL DOLL (CITTERN PLAYER)
Spain?
Mid-16ᵗʰ or 2ⁿᵈ half of 16ᵗʰ century
Upper part, hands and feet: painted wood;
mechanism: iron; dress: linen and silk brocade;
H 44 cm
Inv. No. 10,000

The mechanical doll plays the cittern, turns its head and seems to mince along with tiny steps while in fact running on wheels. Movement conveys the impression of life. The imitation of life is among the ancient dreams of mankind, already reflected in the myths of antiquity. At that period, technology and the arts were still considered to be identical. With the help of mechanisms, artists and artisans tried to imitate God's creation as if by magic. Androids like this mechanical doll are automatons that are not able to act by themselves. Once started, they can only function on a pre-programmed basis, yet the amazed on-looker is prepared to take the inanimate doll as having magically come to life for as long as the movement lasts.   H. T.

VIRGIN AND CHILD
Donatello
(Florence 1386 – 1466 Florence)
Florence
c. 1444
Bronze, fire gilt; Diam. 27 cm
Frame: marble; H 88 cm, W 51 cm
Inv. No. 7462

This bronze *tondo* depicts the Virgin Mary sitting on the ground in the manner of a *madonna della umiltà*. She venerates the infant Jesus who rests in her lap toying with her veil. Two putti stand beside and behind the madonna with raised arms clinging to a garland fixed at the narrow rim of the *tondo*. This motif lends depth to the extremely shallow moulded delicate relief. It was created by Donatello, probably shortly before his departure for Padua 1444. The *tondo* is set into a splendidly decorated frame resembling a window, which was executed by an unknown artist approximately two decades later. M. L.-J.

ODYSSEUS AND IRUS ▽
Antonio Averlino, called Filarete
(Florence c. 1400 – 1469 Rome)
Florence
c. 1450
Bronze; H 27.5 cm, W 16.4 cm
Inv. No. 6127

After wandering the Mediterranean for twenty years, Ulysses (Odysseus) returned from the Trojan War to his native Ithaca. He entered his own palace in the disguise of a beggar to find his faithful wife Penelope besieged by numerous suitors competing for her hand. When the young beggar Irus did not want to share his alms with him, Ulysses challenged him to a boxing match which he won, thereby disclosing his identity. This scene from the *Odyssey* was set by Filarete in a vaulted pillared hall modelled after Roman antiquity. Thus, as also by the Greek and Latin inscriptions the artist shows off his knowledge of antiquity. However, his style resembles that of Donatello's reliefs. M. L.-J.

ALEXANDER THE GREAT
Ascribed to Andrea Verrocchio (moulding)
(Florence 1435 – 1488 Venice)
Andrea della Robbia (glazing)
(Florence 1435 – 1525 Florence)
Florence
c. 1480
Terracotta, polychrome glazing: Diam. 61 cm
Inv. No. 7491

The *tondo*, framed by a colourful garland, presents the relief bust of a young warrior facing to the right, white on blue ground. His fanciful armour is decorated by a gorgon's head at the breast, while a dragon adorns the helmet. Probably, this relief is one of a series of variants of the bronze „Alexander relief" by Verrocchio. Around 1480, Verrocchio's relief, together with a companion piece by the same artist depicting Darius, was supposedly sent to King Matthias Corvinus of Hungary by Lorenzo de' Medici. Both reliefs have been lost. The most delicate moulding of the *tondo* shown here also suggests that it is the work of Verrocchio himself. The glazing and burning can undoubtedly be ascribed to Andrea della Robbia.   M. L.-J.

LAUGHING BOY ▽
Desiderio da Settignano
(Settignano 1429/30 – 1464 Florence)
Florence
c. 1464
Marble; H 33 cm, W 21.5 cm
Inv. No. 9104

The representation of children belongs among the most charming motifs revived by Renaissance art under the influence of Hellenism. Although himself neither innovator nor pioneer as regards this subject matter – parts most certainly played by Donatello and Luca della Robbia – Desiderio da Settignano could be compared to no one else in his time whenever he tried to catch the expression of spontaneity characteristic of children. Like a number of similar statuettes of equally unaffected charm, this one is probably the portrait of a child conceived as the infant Jesus. Such statuettes were commissioned to be set up in private chapels. The *Laughing Boy* is considered to be the last work of Desiderio da Settignano, who died young in 1464.   M.-L. J.

VIRGIN AND CHILD
Antonio Rosselino
(Settignano 1427 – 1479 Florence)
Florence
c. 1465
Marble; H 69.5 cm, W 52 cm
Inv. No. 5455

This relief marks an apogee in the work of Rosselino. He succeeds in a masterly manner, in depicting a close and heartfelt connection between mother and child, paying heed to the scene's aspect of Salvation through an incomparably graceful attitude and a certain reticent dignity in his personages. This expressivity is matched by a kind of monumentality of mother and child who nearly fill the entire surface of the relief. The subtly treated surface appears as if painted with a chisel. The relief greatly influenced many Florentine artists of the early Renaissance, first of all Verrocchio.   M. L.-J.

PUTTO WITH FIG AND GRAPES
Florentine
2nd half of 15th century
Polychrome terracotta; H 65 cm
Inv. No. 9111

This figure of a little boy probably was once part of the crowning of an architectural structure, a motif introduced into the arts by Donatello. Because of the lovely spontaneity of expression as well as the sensual grasp of the characteristic details of the infantile body, however, we must address the figure as work of an artist from a later period who could already benefit from the accomplishments of Rosselino and Desiderio da Settignano and was close to Andrea Verrocchio. He may have been Andrea di Simone Ferrucci. A similar putto is in the possession of the Victoria and Albert Museum in London.   M. L.-J.

BELLEROPHON TAMING PEGASUS
Bertoldo di Giovanni (model)
(Florence c. 1440 – 1491 Poggio a Caiano)
Adriano Florentino (casting)
(Florence c. 1450/60 – 1499 Florence)
c. 1480
Bronze; H 32.5 cm
Inv. No. 5596

Aided by Pallas Athena, Bellerophon succeeded in taming Pegasus, the winged horse serving Zeus. It had sprung from the body of the Medusa after her decapitation by Perseus. Riding Pegasus, Bellerophon performed many heroic deeds. However, when he set out to take Olympus by storm, Pegasus shook him off, and Bellerophon went mad. Thus, he became a symbol of boundless ambition and of pride going before the fall. At the bottom of the base there are the signatures of the artists, of the sculptor as well as of the bronze founder – *EXPRESSIT ME BERTHOLDVS CONFLAVIT HADRIANUS* –, a rare feature at this time. Bertoldo modelled this group after a detail from the relief of a Roman sarcophagus and after the *Horse-tamers* still in place on Monte Cavallo at the Quirinal in Rome since antiquity. In this sculpture Bertoldo created one of the first autonomous bronze statuettes of the Renaissance. In his capacity as a pupil of Donatello and the teacher of Michelangelo he plays a key

role in linking early and High Renaissance. His special connections with the Medici contributed to his important position in the world of art. M. L.-J.

POLYHYMNIA
Ascribed to Pier Maria Serbaldi della Pescia
(Pescia c. 1445 – after 1525 Rome ?)
Florence
c. 1500
Porphyry; H 41 cm
Inv. No. 3529

ISABELLA OF ARAGON ?
Francesco Laurana
(Vrana 1430 – 1502 France)
Naples
c. 1488 ?
Painted marble; H 44 cm
Inv. No. 3405

In antiquity, porphyry, because of its red colour, was strictly reserved for purposes of imperial representation. In the Renaissance this hard rock material was only rarely found in sculpture. In using it, the artist probably intended a deliberate reference to antiquity. Serbaldi was a seal and stone carver especially highly esteemed in Rome and Florence. In the collection of the Medici in the Palazzo Pitti in Florence is another porphyry statuette by him, a figure of Venus also signed with Greek letters. Serbaldi's excellent skill is documented by the mastery with which he achieved grace and poetic expression in a bust of this extremely hard stone and also an explanation for the high regard paid to him. .   M. L.-J.

Francesco Laurana from Dalmatia was one of the important itinerant artists of the early Italian Renaissance. He probably executed this bust of a lady during his third stay in Naples. It presumably represents Isabella of Aragon, daughter of King Alfonso II of Naples, who in 1489 married Gian Galeazzo Sforza, Duke of Milan. The bust is abstract in conception and executed in smooth spherical forms. The lifelike quality was then achieved by the application of coloured wax. Even the red flowers in the network of the gold wimple are made of wax, while a precious jewel was to have decorated the graceful lady's forehead. This is the only portrait by Laurana where the polychrome colouring has been preserved.   M. L.-J.

◁ **ALFONSO I OF ARAGON, KING OF**
NAPLES
Neapolitan?
Mid-15ᵗʰ century?
Marble; H 96 cm
Inv. No. 5441

The king's head emerges from a hollow cuirass. He wears the necklace of the Order of the Golden Fleece, an order which was presented to him by Philip the Good of Burgundy in 1446 and ac-

cepted on condition that he would only wear it on Sundays. The date and origin of the bust are controversial. Although modelled on the medallions of Pisanello and Christoforo di Geremia, as well as on the triumphal figure of the Castelvecchio gateway in Naples, the form of the bust, the ornamentation and the conception of the necklace point to a later date (i. e. to a posthumous portrait from a time in which there was renewed interest in the king's membership of the Order of the Golden Fleece).   M. L.-J.

ENTOMBMENT OF CHRIST
Upper Italian
c. 1470/80
Bronze, partially fire gilt; H 24.4 cm, W 44.9 cm
Inv. No. 6059

The expression of grief which characterizes the mourners on this relief would be hard to surpass. The artist, unknown up to the present time, had this representation of the *Entombment* based on works by Donatello as well as Mantegna. Even the technique of the relief which is extremely shallow, at times even undercut, shows his indebtedness to Donatello's later work. On the other hand, the remarkably graphic treatment of the surface suggests that the artist was a goldsmith from the circle around Mantegna. He probably worked for the Gonzaga in Mantua, whence the relief originates. This assumption is further strengthened by the courtly refinement of the partial gilding. Donatello's prototype of the scene gave birth to a long line of similar works of art reaching from Riccio to Titian. The composition of this *Entombment* makes it an important link in the chain of this tradition.   M. L.-J.

BASIN
Padua
c. 1520/30
Bronze; H 26 cm, Diam. 42.2 cm
Inv. No. 550

This basin cast in thick bronze probably served for cooling drinks. It was modelled after antique Roman forms in its classically harmonious proportions, as well as in its ornamental details. The frieze of recurring tritons and groups of Nereids is based on reliefs on Roman sarcophagi and was a decorative motif much used in the late 15th century by sculptors in Lombardy and the Veneto. The shells and snakes of the handles were not formed by hand, but were cast directly from nature. This technique, called "life casting" was frequently used in the foundries of the 16th century in Padua,

a place well known for its naturalistic approach to art.   M. L.-J.

YOUNG COUPLE (BACCHUS AND ARIADNE)
Tullio Lombardo
(first ment. 1475 – 1532 Venice)
Venice
c. 1500/10
Marble; H 56 cm, W 71.5 cm, D 22 cm
Inv. No. 7471

A characteristic feature of this relief (and of a similar piece in the Cà d'Oro in Venice) is that the busts of the young couple seem to be placed on a slim base in front of a neutral background. These busts were modelled on a type of double portrait taken from antique tomb sculpture, as well as from paintings north of the Alps, taken up by the Venetian painters in the early 16th century. This particular piece is probably a double portrait of a young Venetian patrician pair represented as Bacchus and Ariadne. In 1499 there appeared in Venice an allegorical love story by Francesco Colonna – *Hypnerotomachia Polyphili* – which contained wood cuts remarkably similar to works by Tullio Lombardo. The story was conceived as a transcendental projection of a pair of human lovers into the spiritual unity of the mythological couple of Bacchus and Ariadne, thereby giving their human love an aspect of immortality. This idea is also expressed by the young couple's eyes converging in eternity. Around 1500 Tullio Lombardo was the leading sculptor of Venice. With these reliefs he introduced poetry into sculpture, a comparable achievement to that accomplished by Giorgione in painting.　　M. L.-J.

BACCHUS AND ARIADNE
Jacopo Alari-Bonicolsi, called Antico
(Mantua, c. 1460 – 1528 Gazzuolo)
Mantua, c. 1520/25
Bronze, partially oil gilt; H 59 cm and 50 cm, resp.
Inv. Nos. 5987 and 5991

While Bacchus is characterized by his crown of wine leaves and grapes, Ariadne can be recognized by the sheafs of hops wound into her hair, hops being a symbol of sleep, out of which Bacchus woke her after Theseus had abandoned her on the island of Naxos. Antico only rarely gave his figures such a poetic expression as we find in these two busts. The subtle rendering of their nostalgic emotions can be admired as much as the meticulous care in execution. Antico, who served several generations of the Gonzaga, created these two busts in his later period, probably about 1520/25, for the *grotta* of Isabella d'Este in the ducal palace of Mantua.   M. L.-J.

VENUS FELIX
Jacopo Alari-Bonacolsi, called Antico
(Mantua c. 1460 – 1528 Gazzuolo)
Mantua, c. 1500
Bronze, partially fire gilt;
Base: limewood, inlaid with Roman coins;
H (without base) 29.8 cm
Inv. No. 5726

This statuette is a free variation on an antique marble sculpture which was found at the end of the 15th century in Rome and ordered before 1509 by Pope Julius II to be set up in the Vatican.

Antico had frequently worked in Rome as a restorer of antique sculptures as well as a buyer and copyist of antique pieces for the Gonzaga. When modelling his small-scale statuettes after monumental marble sculptures, he rarely contented himself with merely copying them. Instead, he introduced concepts of his own into the only partially preserved originals. All the bronzes that Antico executed on commission for Bishop Ludovico Gonzaga of Mantua around 1500 are characterized by the extraordinary quality of their modelling, casting, chiselling, gilding and patination.   M. L.-J.

HERCULES AND ANTAEUS
Jacopo Alari-Bonicolsi, called Antico
(Mantua, c. 1460 – 1528 Gazzuolo)
Mantua, c. 1519
Bronze; H 43.5 cm (with base)
Inv. No. 5767

The inscription under the base *D/ISABEL/LA/ME MAR* proves this item to have been the property of Isabella d'Este, Marchioness of Mantua. In 1519 Antico agreed at her request to make replicas of some of the models still in his possession which he had previously cast. Among these was the small-scale reproduction of the monumental Hercules and Antaeus-group (nowadays in Florence) which Antico had seen as a torso in Rome. The bronze represents his suggestion for its completion. A letter of Antico's to Isabella also proves him to have been a pioneer in the refinement of casting techniques, finally enabling the production of replicas. M. L.-J.

VENUS OF CARDINAL GRANVELLA ▷
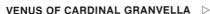
North Italian
1500
Bronze, silver; H 18.5 cm
Inv. No. 7343

This statue of Venus was the property of Cardinal Antoine Perrenot de Granvella. Emperor Rudolph II bought it from Count Cantecroy, Granvella's nephew and heir. At this time it was considered a famous work of antiquity whose particularity were the silver feet contrasting with the verdigris bronze patina. Granvella had the statuette mounted on that silver pedestal which carries the hallmark of Besançon. Rudolph II kept this Venus in a gilt case. Today, we know the statue to be a deliberate Renaissance forgery of an antique object. The forgery was so well made, however, that its authenticity was believed in until 1919.
M. L.-J.

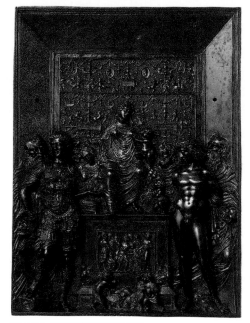

THE SCOURGING OF CHRIST
Moderno (Galeazzo Mondella?)
(working 1490 – 1540)
Rome
c. 1510
Silver, fire gilding; H 13.8 cm, W 10.2 cm
Inv. No. 1105

The figure of Christ tied to the scourging column derives directly from the antique figure of Laocoön which was excavated in Rome in 1506. On the other hand, the two guards with the scourges go back to the figures of the *Tyrant's Murderers,* which were placed in the courtyard of the Palazzo Madama in Rome at the beginning of the 16th century. But the artist did not only fall back on antique models for reasons of form, but also of content. Pliny the Elder had already referred to the Laocoön group as an *exemplum doloris.* Even the Counter-Reformation, in general rather hostile to antiquity, recommended artists to use the Laocoön group as a model in their representations of Christ.   M. L.-J.

SACRA CONVERSAZIONE
Moderno (Galeazzo Mondella?)
(working 1490 – 1540)
Rome
1510
Silver, fire gilding; H 13.9 cm, W 10.2 cm
Inv. No. 1107

Also this plaquette bears a strikingly antique character. The Virgin with the infant Jesus may be interpreted as Isis and Harpocrates or Venus and Cupid, St. Sebastian and St. George as Hercules and Bacchus. They all may be traced back to antique sculptures that could already be seen in Rome at the beginning of the 16th century. Like in its companion piece (the plaquette depicting the *Scourging of Christ)* the adoption of antique patterns was not only intended to enlarge the accepted canon of forms. It also served to imply an affinity between the ancient myths and Christianity, as taught by the humanist hermetics. The artist's significant pseudonym "Moderno" suggests similar connotations. He received his artistic training in Northern Italy and later on worked in Rome.   M. L.-J.

WOOD CUTTER TAKING A REST
Andrea Briosco, called Riccio
(Trento ?, c. 1470 – 1532, Padua)
Padua
c. 1500
Painted terracotta; H 37 cm
Inv. No. 7345

The workman, identified as a carpenter or wood cutter by his tools, has seated himself on the stump of a tree to take a rest, his cheek leaning against his right hand. The rendering of this haggard figure marked by hard work and constant want, of his ragged dress and of the tired and resigned look on his face is characterized by extreme naturalism. The question arises what the meaning of this, probably early, work of Riccio really was. Whether it represented just another genre figure, or whether it once belonged in the context of a larger group and was fraught with a deeper significance as in the case of a carpenter who mourns that it was he who had been assigned to set up the cross of Christ.   M. L.-J.

DRINKING SATYR
Andrea Briosco, called Riccio
(Trento ?, c. 1470 – 1532 Padua)
Padua
c. 1520
Bronze; H 21.7 cm
Inv. No. 5539

Riccio frequented the learned circles around the University of Padua. This is the reason why his work is so strongly influenced by ideas of Neoplatonism and Aristotelian metaphysics and the natural philosophy of his time. This splendid figurine, monumental despite its minute size, symbolizes the elemental forces of nature in every line. The hammering of the surface lending it vibrant warmth and a lifelike quality, are characteristic features of Riccio's best works. Both the Louvre and the museum in Padua preserve replicas, but they cannot match the quality of this figurine probably executed after the Easter candelabra completed by Riccio between 1507 and 1516 in the Santo of Padua.   M. L.-J.

BOY WITH A GOOSE
Andrea Briosco, called Riccio
(Trento ?, c. 1470 – 1532 Padua)
Padua
c. 1515
Bronze; H 19.6 cm
Inv. Nr. 5518

This bronze figurine is based on one of the numerous hellenistic replicas of the *Boy with a Goose* by Boethos of Calchedon. However, it is more expressive and dynamic than the antique model, and more realistic in detail. The dramatic composition based on the idea of two triangles is achieved by means of a balance between movement and counter movement of the two figures, the turning point being of crucial importance. This miniature group, one of the most mature works of Riccio's, was possibly conceived as top of a fountain, or at least could have been adapted for such use.   M. L.-J.

STRIDING YOUTH
North Italian
Beginning of 16th century
Bronze, verdigris patina; H 71.5 cm
Inv. No. 6023

This figure of a youth was placed in a niche of the *Camerino dei Cesari* in the ducal palace of Mantua the decoration of which was completed in 1537 with the arrival of Titian's portraits of Roman emperors. The statue was certainly not imported from the workshop of Peter Vischer in Nuremberg, as previously thought, but is rather the work of an as yet unidentified, probably Northern Italian artist. It was modelled on an antique Roman figure of Apollo. Characteristic for the Tuscan taste in the 15th and 16th centuries was the addition of a real cloth soaked in plaster of Paris to the wax model before casting. The artist, therefore, may have come from the circle around Andrea Sansovino. A variant without drapery is preserved in Munich.   M. L.-J.

JUG
Milan ?
Mid-16th century
Rock crystal; H 32.9 cm
Inv. No. 2224

BEZOAR STONE
Spanish
3rd quarter of 16th century
Gold, emeralds, rubies; H 25.5 cm
Inv. No. 981

Uniting the masterly cutting of crystal vessels and their skilful decoration was regarded as a revival of an antique art form. Nevertheless, the antique model served rather as an incitement to the expression of new forms. Milan was the undisputed centre for the carving of such vessels. Crystal vessels of the High Renaissance were relatively thickly cut but the purity of the material and the sparseness of the decoration were characteristic. This jug is optically partitioned by festooned garlands hanging from a decorative border below the jug-handle, and by dotted and palmetto friezes. The form of the massive, high handle points to the middle of the 16th century.

H. T.

The bezoar – from Persian *bâd-sahr* (antidote to poison) – builds up in the stomach or entrails of certain ruminants. Until the 18th century it was considered an effective cure for various illnesses (e. g. melancholy and epilepsy). It was also looked upon, as its name indicates, as a mysterious remedy against poisoning. Because of these curative qualities, the bezoar was highly prized and often preciously mounted and presented as a princely gift. This bezoar is placed on a gold ring set with emeralds and resting on three ornamental lions. Four ribbons set with emeralds and dragon-like volutes support the bezoar. It is topped by a crown set with emeralds.

R. B.

◁ **SMALL HOUSE ALTAR WITH JESUS
CHRIST AND THE WOMAN FROM SAMARIA**
Gian Ambrogio Caroni (frame)
(d. 1611 Florence)
Jacques Byliveldt (goldsmith's work)
(Delft 1550 – 1603 Florence)
Bernardino Gaffuri (walls of aedicula)
(d. 1606 Florence)
Christofani Gaffuri (centre of aedicula)
d. 1626 Florence)
Florence
finished 1600
Commessi in pietre dure; frame: rock crystal;
H 37.8 cm, W 32.5 cm
Inv. No. 1542

This small house altar executed for Grand Duke
Ferdinand de' Medici is among the most remarkable art objects owing its existence to princely
patronage. It took an entire decade to produce
this masterpiece. The altar came into being
through a complex collaboration between the
various artisans in the ducal workshops, which
had been founded in 1572 and reorganized by
Ferdinand I in 1588. Out of them grew the *Opificio
delle pietre dure,* still extant today. The splendid
window-like frame of rock crystal impresses by its
strictly architectural construction and harmonious
proportions, as well as by the charming idea of a
crowning vase in the split pediment. It is based on
a design by the architect Buontalenti. Gian Ambrogio Caroni, who usually carved vessels, created the richly carved aedicula within one year. In
accordance with the very demanding intentions of
the Grand Duke the goldsmith Jacques Byliveldt
richly decorated the narrow sides of the frame
with golden female hermas, flower garlands, festoons, masks and cartouches in gold enamel. This
elaborate aedicula was mentioned, still without
picture, in a Medici inventory of 1598. Two years
later, Cristofano Gaffuri completed the cen-
trepiece, a sculptured group of figures placed in
front of a vivid landscape. The scene represented
is of Christ and the woman of Samaria at the well.
The well is cut out of a single emerald. The jamb
of the architecturally conceived niche was executed a few months later by Cristofano's brother,
Bernardino. He used narrow gold bridges to
separate the small plaques of the panelling.
Cristofano Gaffuri himself was considered the
most remarkable of the stone carvers, especially
where the Florentine mosaic was concerned (as
to technique, cf. page 200). In *Commesso in
pietre dure* it was possible to realize the old dream
of an indestructible work of art. The Florentine
master artisans developed an infallible instinct for
using the natural colouring as well as the original
veining of the stone for their representations. By
their sophisticated treatment of the slightest irre-
gularities in the configuration of the material they
could even produce minute details. The lower

**DOUBLE GOBLET WITH SCENES FROM
OVID'S "METAMORPHOSES"**
Milan
c. 1570
Rock crystal; mounting: gold with enamel;
H 25.9 cm
Inv. No. 2360

**GOBLET WITH LID WITH REPRESENTATION
OF THE PROSERPINE MYTH**
Annibale Fontana
(Milan 1540 – 1587 Milan)
Milan
c. 1570
Rock crystal; mounting: gold with enamel;
H 23.8 cm
Inv. No. 1415

Differences in style are to be found in the formal
composition of the representations carved onto
the goblets *(intagli).* In the case of the double
goblet, the stone cutter *(intagliatore)* has transferred the technique of gem cutting directly to vessel
cutting. The artistic possibilities found in crystal in
the contrast between the transparent and opaque
cutting are not taken advantage of. Annibale
Fontana, on the contrary, makes use of the
transparent material by cutting the clearly
silhouetted figures as freely as possible into the
polished surface of the Proserpine-goblet. His
masterly skill as a cutter and his perfect understanding of human anatomy allow him to fully
unfold the mythological scenes in an illusionistic
depth.   H. T.

cartouche, with the coat of arms of Emperor Karl
VI added later, was commissioned by Franz
Stephan of Lorraine who, as reigning Grand Duke
of Tuscany from 1737 to 1740, presented this little
altar to his father-in-law.   H. T.

DRAGON CUP WITH HANDLE ▷
Milan
c. 1580
Lapis lazuli; setting: gold, enamel, emeralds, rubies, pearls; H 17 cm, L 18.9 cm
Inv. No. 1851

This ceremonial cup harmoniously combines the techniques of the gem cutter and the goldsmith to achieve a phantastic composition.
A dragon with glowing ruby eyes opens his gullet wide; his long neck curves upward. The beast seems ready to attack. Its wings stretch forward spanning the back of the vessel. This dragon motif is characteristic of the Milan workshop of Miseroni. An abstract ornamentation of volutes and the mask under the handle turn the daemonic beast into a grotesque decoration. The object was the property of Emperor Rudolph II.   H. T.

PRASEM CUP WITH LID
Milan
c. 1580
Prasem, onyx cameos, rubies, pearls; setting: gold, enamel; H 19.3 cm
Inv. No. 2014

Prasem is a semi-precious stone of the quartz group which was already much prized in antiquity. This remarkable masterpiece of Italian hardstone carving from about 1580 derives its effect from its perfect proportions and the discreet elegance of its cutting, but most of all from the colour harmony between the warm olive green of the stone, the gold shimmer of the setting, the enamel colouring and the precious stones and pearls. The characteristic details of the setting as well as the cameos on the knob of the lid point to the artistic tradition of Milan. The cup is listed in the inventory of the treasury of Rudolph II, 1607/11.   H. T.

LAPIS LAZULI RECEPTACLE ▷
Gian Stefano Caroni (carving)
(d. 1611 Florence)
Jacques Byliveldt (mounting)
(Delft 1550–1603 Florence)
Florence
1575/76 and 1576/81
Mounting and handle: gold enamel; H 36 cm
Inv. No. 1655

It is difficult to distinguish between stone vessels carved in Milan on the one hand and Florence on the other, but in this case the execution and later history of the vessel can be traced. Gian Stefano Caroni was commissioned in 1575 to carve this receptacle, and lapis lazuli was a material much used in Florence. Bernardo Buontalenti's generous design achieves maximum effect with this material. The imaginative execution of the mobile handle complements the purity of form in the shape of the vase. The goldsmith Jacques Byliveldt owes his fame to his precious settings and mountings. Such ceremonial items reflect Grand Duke Francesco's personal taste, and represent the apogee of Florentine mannerist art. Grand Duke Ferdinand II presented the receptacle to Emperor Ferdinand II in Prague in 1628 on the occasion of an official state visit.   H. T.

TWO HERONS
Workshop of the Saracchi
Milan
End of 16th century
Rock crystal; mount: gold, enamel, precious
stones, cameos, pearls
Large heron: H 40.9 cm
Inv. No. 2401
Small heron: H 23.1 cm
Inv. No. 2238

Searching for an opportunity to show their formal
skill as *cristallari,* the Saracchi workshop developed vessels in the shape of animals. It was
Giovanni Ambrogio Saraccho who accomplished
the carving and polishing of these table decorations in bird form which in old inventories were
called *Reiger* (heron). His brother Simone did the
fine *intagli* work. All the animal characteristics are
concentrated on the upper part of the objects, the
abstract form of the receptacle is found in the
lower part, with its carved scenes and ornamentation. Natural egret feathers were set diagonally
back from the head, emphasizing the birdlike
shape of the vessels.   H. T.

FIGURINES FROM THE COMMEDIA DELL'ARTE

Venetian (Murano)
c. 1600
Coloured glass; H 21.4 cm
Inv. No. 2705

The *commedia dell'arte* was an impromptu performance the theatrical action of which was mostly played by masked characters. Individual performers adhered all their lives to one chosen role and acted it with the lively expressive gestures of their southern temperament. This Venetian figurine flanked by two others is giving a fiery burlesque rendering of a character known as the *Capitano*. These statuettes are timeless in their style and do not correspond to the sculptural concept of the day. Not unlike caricatures, they are executed in an exaggeratedly theatrical form.

H. T.

LUCRETIA
Jacopo da Trezzo (cameo)
(Milan c. 1514 – 1589 Madrid)
Madrid, c. 1570
Jan Vermeyen (setting)
(Brussels before 1559 – 1606 Prague)
Prague, c. 1602
Cameo: agate; H 3.5 cm, W 2.4 cm
Setting: gold enamel; H 5.8 cm, W 5.2 cm
Inv. No. XII 97

Lucretia, a Roman woman much admired for her
virtue and beauty, in despair plunges a knife into
her breast being unable to bear the dishonour
inflicted on her by Tarquin. This piece of jewellery
is an example of the large collection of cameos
produced by Milanese stone cutters during the 2nd
half of the 16th century. Jacopo da Trezzo who left
Milan in 1555 in order to work at the court of Philip
II of Spain, showed a masterly skill in using the
natural colours of the agate. On a bluish background a reddish layer forms the flesh of the
body. A thin white layer covers the body with a
draped gown. Jan Vermeyen, the creator of the
Rudolph Crown (Secular Treasury, Vienna) executed the precious setting about 1602.   R. D.

ROCK CRYSTAL VASE WITH COVER
Miseroni workshop ?
Milan, late 16th century
Rock crystal; setting: gold, enamel; H 28.9 cm
Inv. No. 2353

When hardstone carving of the Renaissance was
still in its infancy the attempt was made to cut the
vessels from the precious stone or crystal in one
piece, in imitation of antiquity. This, however,
resulted in such a lack of smoothness that they
soon afterwards began to be to put together from
several pieces, with the additional advantage that
vessels could now be produced in a greater
variety of forms. The breeding grounds for this
whole genre were the princely *Kunstkammern*.
The vases, goblets and bowls were extremely
valuable and it would take a craftsman about a
year to complete an average piece. Since Gasparo Miseroni died in 1573 and his brother
Girolamo went to Spain in 1584, it is probable that
this vase was made by one of Gasparo's sons,
whose names are unknown to us. The frieze on
the bowl, depicting the triumph of Bacchus, is
after an engraving by Etienne Delaune.   R. D.

175

CUPIDS PLAYING
Hans Daucher
(Ulm 1486 – 1538 Stuttgart)
Augsburg
c. 1530
Pearwood; H 42 cm, W 16.2 cm, L 76 cm
Inv. No. 8920

of spatial composition which nevertheless preserves the imaginary contours of a single log. H. T.

About 1530, Hans Daucher completely renounced certain linear qualities of his early period and achieved an artistic freedom which is also reflected in this carved group of three playful cupids. A male putto in the characteristic posture of early childhood tries to separate his two female playmates who resist his efforts. The fragments of an inscription on the pedestal explain that attraction and repulsion in the play of children symbolize the passion of grown up persons. The theme is without doubt influenced by erotic motifs. The group possesses a certain sensuous appeal which was also decisive for the formal treatment of this precious item designed for a *Kunstkammer*. Its masterly carving and the amazing wealth of its differentiated treatment of the surfaces points to Italian influence. The putto, a much loved subject of Florentine Renaissance sculpture, is seen with the eyes of a "northerner" from the other side of the Alps. Hans Daucher with touching realism renders certain details of the infant bodies otherwise reduced to more general structures. His familiarity with Italian art is shown in the harmony of the proportions and the relaxed gaiety. Noteworthy is also the mastery

HAT MEDALLION ▽
Spanish or French
1520
Gold, enamel; Diam. 5.72 cm
Inv. No. 1610

The medallion shows a portrait of the youthful Charles V wearing the chain of the Order of the Golden Fleece. The circumscription of the medallion *CHARLES R(OI) DE CASTILLE LEÉON GRE-* *NADE ARRAGON CECILLES 1520,* shows Charles to be King of Spain at a time when he already had a claim to the title of Emperor. This suggests that the medallion was intended – perhaps as a present – for the Spanish part of the realm. It may originate from there or from a French-speaking part of the country. The object itself indicates how such a trinket was used – Charles has a similar piece pinned on the broad brim of his hat.   R. B.

◁ ANNUNCIATION
Hans Daucher
(Ulm c. 1486 – 1538 Stuttgart)
Augsburg, c. 1515
Limestone from Solnhofen/Germany; H 18 cm, W 15 cm
Inv. No. 4422

Hans Daucher received the title of master of his craft in 1514, when he was 28. This relief signed *HD* and depicting the Annunciation was probably executed at the same time. The figurative part is a free variant of Dürer's Annunciation from the series of wood cuts devoted to the Life of the Virgin. Dürer integrated his figures into the spatial continuum in a masterly way. This problem did not even arise in the case of the relief cutter. Hans Daucher executed his bas-relief in a very careful manner, smoothing and even polishing its surface. Yet angel and Virgin somehow seem to be detached from the space surrounding them. Instead, they convey the impression of *staffage* figures added to a stage set. The step towards the restrained new Italian style of the period has not yet been taken. The ornamental tendencies of the artist still prevail, as does a pleasant spreading of forms on the plain.   H. T.

ADAM AND EVE
Conrat Meit
(Worms c. 1475/80 – 1550/51 Antwerp)
Mecheln
c. 1520
Boxwood; H 25.5 cm and 24 cm, resp.
Inv. Nos. 9888 and 9889

Dürer once made the laudatory remark that he had never seen another wood carver the equal of Conrat Meit. Meit worked for Archduchess Margaret, Regent of the Netherlands, in Mecheln since the year 1512. On the one hand, Dürer's canon of proportions distinctly influenced Meit's figures. On the other, Conrat Meit was a keen observer of the function and structure of the human body and thus formed his ideally conceived sculptures in a most vivid and realistic way. An indication of the extent to which Conrat Meit carried his studies in anatomical realism can be assessed from the way in which he portrays the different stances without so much as disturbing the flux of the movement.   H. T.

CIRCULAR BOX WITH THE PORTRAIT OF ELECTOR FREDERICK THE WISE OF SAXONY
Hans Daucher ▷
(Ulm 1486 – 1538 Stuttgart)
Augsburg, 1525
Nutwood; portrait: pearwood; Diam. 22 cm
Inv. No. 3878

The head of the elector, which nearly fills the entire surface of the lid, is slightly turned to the left. It is a laterally inverted replica of Dürer's engraving of the elector of 1524. The circumscription of the portrait gives the date of 1525, which was the year of Frederick's death. Earlier research tried to identify the artist as an individual artistic personality given the provisional name "Meister der Dosenköpfe" (= master of decorated box-tops). Characteristic details of his style – like the square conception of the slightly turned faces with their high cheekbones and their peculiarly shaped eyes and eyebrows – have recently proved him to be identical with Hans Daucher, whose personal style of the mature years they closely resemble. The elaborate execution of the portrait fulfills the demands of a cabinet piece for the *Kunstkammer*.

H. T.

CARITAS
Peter Flötner
(Thurgau ?, 1485 – 1546 Nuremberg)
Nuremberg
1540/46
Slate from Solnhofen; H 7.9 cm, W 6.7 cm
Inv. No. 4401

The *Caritas*-relief is the only known model for a plaque by Peter Flötner complete with title and the initials of the sculptor. Any monograph dealing with the plaques of this most versatile of the German Renaissance artists must take this work into consideration. Flötner's prototypes were cast in lead, bronze or silver and were used as models by generations of goldsmiths and artisans of all sorts. The *Caritas*-relief is one of a series of seven seated allegories of the Virtues. Only three models executed in slate from Solnhofen have been preserved; apart from the *Caritas* the Kunsthistorische Museum also owns a *Justitia*. Flötner probably produced this series during the last years of his life. M. L.-J.

ADAM AND EVE ▷
Augsburg?
c. 1600
Pearwood; H 32 cm and 31.2 cm, resp.
Inv. Nos. 3965 and 3967

The figures of Adam and Eve are depicted in similar, but complementary positions, each of them holding an apple. While Eve presents hers with an alluring smile, Adam has already taken his, casting a final reluctant glance at the seductress. Dürer's previous versions of the Adam and Eve motif were an obvious inspiration for the execution of this group. Up to now, these two outstanding figures were considered to be the main work of the sculptor Christoph Weidlitz in Augsburg, around 1540. The slender proportions, the fragile limbs and the graphic elegance of the heads, however, point to a later period, when the ideal of the naked human body was already influenced by Mannerism. The group probably belongs to the era of the Dürer revival around 1600. S. K.

BUST OF A YOUNG MAN
Upper Rhenish?
c. 1540/45
Terracotta, painted; H 48 cm
Inv. No. 8919

Details of men's fashion in Upper Germany around 1540/45 included closely cropped hair and a high-necked shirt with frilled collar rimmed by black embroidery. The young man depicted in this bust is wearing a broad-shouldered doublet over his shirt, a coat and a cape. The bust ends immediately below the shoulders; the radical abstraction of form imparts a great intensity of physiognomic expressivity. This may be the reason for the earlier theory that the bust portrays Dr. Faustus, an indication of its origin from the Upper Rhine area. This assumption, however, has not been authenticated.   M. L.-J.

EMPEROR CHARLES V
Ascribed to Thomas Herings
(? c. 1510–1549 Munich)
Munich
c. 1540/45
Alabaster, traces of gilding, garnets; H 14.2 cm, B 12.9 cm
Inv. No. XII a 82

This shallow relief made of white alabaster originally was certainly mounted on a stone slab of different colour. The Emperor's half-length figure, leaning against a balustrade, is dressed in costly raiments, his arms resting on a brocade pillow. The head is turned to present the Emperor's profile which, with hook nose, protruding lower lip and goatee, borders on the caricature. The ribbon which holds the drawn collar of the shirt in place shows traces of gilding; on the broad cuffs of the sleeves seven small garnets polished *en cabochon* and added for decoration have been preserved. Where the garnets have been lost, the yellowish wax underlay has been preserved. R. B.

TRICKTRACK BOARD
Hans Kels the Elder
(Kaufbeuren c. 1480 – 1559/60 Kaufbeuren)
Kaufbeuren
c. 1537
Oak, walnut, rose-wood, mahogany, briar-wood.
Hinges: bronze; H 56 cm, W 56 cm
Inv. No. 3419

Two wooden panels with hinges unfold to form the tricktrack board. The exterior with its intricate heraldic and genealogical motifs is dedicated to the glorification of Emperor Charles V and his brother King Ferdinand I (Emperor Ferdinand I after 1588). The side depicted above shows an equestrian portrait of Ferdinand I, probably the owner of the board, in the centre, surrounded by four medallions. Executed in most delicate miniature carving, they show the youthful portraits of King Ferdinand the Catholic (above, left), Ferdinand's maternal grandfather, and King Ladislaus

of Poland (below, left), his father-in-law. The portraits of Duke Charles the Bold (above), his great-grandfather, and of King Louis of Hungary (below), his brother-in-law, are shown on the right side. The tiny corner medallions represent the rulers of the four great monarchies of the antique world: Ninus of Assyria, Cyrus of Persia, Alexander the Great, and the Roman Romulus. The initials *AF* refer to Ferdinand and his wife Anna. On the insides of the board the six points for the tricktrack game – a variety of backgammon called *Langer Puff* in German – are executed in precious inlay work. The border rim is formed by minutely carved foliage populated by birds and animals and studded with medallions showing mythological scenes of a moralizing character as told by Giovanni Boccaccio and referring to the representations on the thirty-two playing pieces of the set. The game was possibly designed by Jörg Breu the Elder (1475–1537) or by his son Jörg Breu the Younger (1510–1557), both from Augsburg. R. B.

SALT CELLAR, SO-CALLED "SALIERA"
Benvenuto Cellini
(Florence 1500 – 1572 Florence)
Paris
1540/1543
Gold, partially enamelled; base: ebony; H 26 cm,
L 33.5 cm
Inv. No. 881

The salt cellar is the only authenticated example of the goldsmith's art by Benvenuto Cellini still existing. It was executed during Cellini's stay in Paris 1540–1543 commissioned by King François I of France. In 1570 it was presented to Archduke Ferdinand II of Tyrol by King Charles IX on the occasion of his serving as a proxy for Charles at his wedding to Archduchess Elizabeth. This exceedingly precious table decoration, by Cellini's own account formed by his own hand out of pure gold foil, is at the same time an allegorical representation of the planet Earth. In his autobiography, Cellini states that in order to show how the sea united with earth he made "two figures, palm-sized and sitting opposite each other with crossed legs" resembling the sea embracing the earth. The sea-god Neptune, trident in hand and supported by sea-horses, dispenses salt from a richly ornamented boat large enough for a copious supply of the mineral. The goddess of the Earth is a female, "as beautiful and graceful a figure as I could make it". Next to it stands a lavishly decorated small temple designed to hold pepper. On its side "were the most beautiful animals the earth brings forth". The concave base shows allegories of the Four Winds, Morning, Noon, Evening and Midnight as well as emblems symbolizing human activities.

M. L.-J.

CABINET
Giovanni Battista Serabaglio
(ment. in Milan 1560)
Marco Antonio Fava
(ment. in Milan 1560)
Giuseppe de Vico
(1569–1576 Court Sculptor of Emperor Maximilian II)
Milan, 1567
Embossed iron, fire gilt, with niello in gold and silver, blued, etched, engraved; bronze, wood, partially painted; H 90.5 cm, L 68.5 cm, W 47.5 cm
Inv. No. 879

For reasons of style and form, this preciously decorated iron case in the shape of a *tempietto* is considered to be a work by the armourer Giovanni Battista Serabaglio from Milan and the goldsmith Marco Antonio Fava. The front of the iron cabinet

YOUTHFUL HERCULES
Florentine
c. 1550
Bronze; H 30.8 cm
Inv. No. 5658

Setting out from the three points of the trifoil base, the movement of the figure resembles the turn of a screw, offering a perfect aspect from any angle reaching its zenith in the head of the youth. The bended head at the same time becomes the turning point of the spiral, so that from here the lines of composition flow back again. The figure reminds one of Benedetto Varchi, who, in 1546, invited some Florentine artists to debate whether painting or sculpture were to be regarded as the nobler art. Benvenuto Cellini responded that sculpture was the easy winner as a statue had to present at least eight views of equally good standard to the observer, whereas a painting contented itself with a single one.   M. L.-J.

JUPITER
Ascribed to Jacopo Tatti, called Sansovino
(Florence 1486 – 1570 Venice)
Venice
Mid-16th century
Bronze; H 43 cm
Inv. No. 5655

This softly modelled ageing body is quite unusual in sculptures representing Jupiter, supreme god of Olympus. On the other hand, the distinctly well-balanced stance – a *contrapposto* of body and limbs – is definitely inspired by antiquity, the head of the sculpture even calling Greek models to mind. The traditional ascription to Jacopo Sansovino that was mainly based on the specific attitude of the body of Jupiter has recently been called in question, and perhaps rightly so. However, no alternatives have been put forward until now, apart from the observation that the modelling of the body and of the fine strands of hair resemble works by Guglielmo della Porta.
M. L.-J.

case is hinged at the bottom and can be opened to reveal a wooden box with 53 drawers for holding jewellery and similar precious items. The additional bronze figurettes signed *JOSEF DE VICO FECIT 1567* are part of the complex programme of allegorical representations. Referring to monarchy and rulership, they personify the Virtues, the Muses, and certain gods from antique mythology, suggesting an owner of distinguished rank, probably Emperor Maximilian II.   A. A.

QUEEN MARIA OF HUNGARY
Leone Leoni
(Arezzo c. 1509 – 1590 Milan)
Milan
1555
Bronze; H 67.5 cm
Inv. No. 5496

EMPEROR CHARLES V
Leone Leoni
(Arezzo c. 1509 – 1590 Milan)
Milan
1555
Bronze; H 113 cm
Inv. No. 5504

The base of this remarkably designed bust is formed by an eagle and two supporting nude figures, probably Hercules and Minerva. The bust itself is conceived in deliberate imitation of the busts of Roman emperors with the sole exception that Charles V is wearing a costume of his own period (i. e. the armour in which he fought the Battle of Mühlberg in 1547). Today, this armour is in the possession of the *Armeria* in Madrid. Leone Leoni had executed the bust for Cardinal Granvella, Chancellor of Charles V. After his decease it was bought by Emperor Rudolph II in 1600. Adriaen de Vries used it as a model for his official portrait bust of Rudolph II in 1603 (cf. p. 200).
M. L.-J.

Maria, younger sister of Emperor Charles V and widow of the Hungarian King Louis II (killed at the Battle of Mohács in 1526) was Regent of the Low Countries from 1530 to 1556. There she, as well as Charles V and other members of the Imperial family, were portrayed by Leone Leoni who had come to Brussels in 1549 and 1551 through the mediation of Cardinal Granvella. The modelling and casting of the busts were done in Milan.
One copy of each of these busts was sent to the Cardinal. Whereas the realism in the rendering of physiognomy and costume has been carried to an extreme, the bust derives its formal balance from the rigorous outlines of the widow's costume and the majestic attitude of the Queen. M. L.-J.

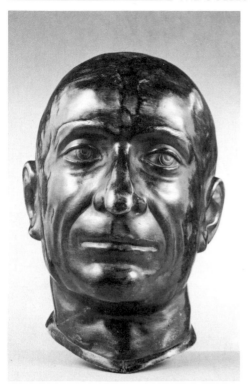

ST. CARLO BORROMEO
Milan
c. 1610 ?
Bronze; H 25 cm
Inv. No. 6015

Carlo Borromeo (1538–1584) was Archbishop of Milan, Cardinal, executor of the resolutions of the Council of Trent and one of the most powerful personalities in the Roman Catholic church of his time. He was an ascetic and deeply concerned with improving the slackening morale within the church, as well as the theological training of the priests. During the Great Plague of 1576 his pastoral and social commitment was exemplary, which probably explains his unusually expedited canonisation in 1610. Numerous likenesses of the saint were produced at that time, most of all in Milan. This most expressive bronze head probably was mounted on a bust of red marble and may be traced back to a model by Giovan Andrea Biffi.   M. L.-J.

KING PHILIP II OF SPAIN
Pompeo Leoni (head)
(? c. 1533 – 1608 Madrid)
Balthasar Moll (bust)
(Innsbruck 1717 – 1785 Vienna)
Vienna
1753
Head: painted silver; bust: polychrome terracotta;
H 62 cm
Inv. No. 3412

This silver cast of the head of Philip II, painted in a naturalistic manner, was probably originally inserted into a real armour belonging to the King. This intensified the authentic effect of the likeness which came close to the impression otherwise only achieved by wax effigies. In 1753 at the latest, this advantageous combination of head and armour was broken up, when Balthasar Moll was commissioned to fit the head with a bust of clay suitable for setting up in the Viennese treasury. Pompeo Leoni had already entered the services of Cardinal Granvella in 1551. Through the intervention of the Cardinal, Pompeo Leoni went to Spain to take over the position formerly held by his father Leone Leoni. The portrait head was probably executed in 1556, when Philip II was raised to the throne.   M. L.-J.

LUNA
Venetian ?
Mid-16th century
Bronze; H 51 cm
Inv. No. 5511

Instead of the crescent which usually adorns the forehead of Diana, we find in this figurine a full moon covering her face. This is to emphasize Diana's rule over the starry sky of night, as opposed to her usual depiction as goddess of the hunt and patroness of wildlife, characterized by her emblems spear and horn. The statue was perhaps intended for a fountain-head as may be guessed from the tube the goddess holds over her head. Attempts to ascribe the sculpture to Danese Cattaneo, a sculptor from Tuscany resident in Venice, are called in question nowadays, as are similar attempts to ascribe it to Johann Gregor van der Schardt, an artist from the Netherlands working in Nuremberg.   M. L.-J.

STATUE OF A PHILOSOPHER
Alessandro Vittoria
(Trento 1525 – 1608 Venice)
Venice, c. 1580/85
Bronze; H 33.2 cm
Inv. No. 5664

Because of its thick, fur-lined mantle, this statuette is frequently interpreted as an allegory of Winter. An inventory of the 18th century, however, lists it as "Anacharsis", probably also inspired by

the striking costume. Anacharsis was a Scythian prince and philosopher who visited Athens at Solon's time. Later he was accounted one of the Seven Sages. As a matter of fact, the statuette resembles the pictures of philosophers by Paolo Veronese and Jacopo Tintoretto in the *Libreria Marciana* in Venice. Vittoria evidently modelled his expressive figure of an old man on them. This interpretation is reinforced by the fact that there is no evidence of further allegories by Vittoria devoted to the Seasons.   M. L.-J.

LADY FROM THE HOUSE OF ZORZI
Alessandro Vittoria
(Trento 1525 – 1608 Venice)
Venice
c. 1570/80
Terracotta; H 83 cm
Inv. No. 9905

The bust originates from the Palazzo Zorzi next to the Ponte dei Greci in Venice. Francesco Sansovino in his *Venetia Città nobilissima et singolare,* published in 1551, had already praised the stuccowork, marble sculptures and portraits by Alessandro Vittoria to be found in that palace. Vittoria was probably Jacopo Sansovino's most remarkable pupil and one of the leading artists of the second half of the 16th century in Venice. With his numerous likenesses, he created masterpieces which not only count among the highest accomplishments in the history of sculpture but also stand their ground compared to the highlights of contemporary Venetian painting, the portraits of Titian, Tintoretto, and Veronese.   M. L.-J.

OLD MAN
Venetian
c. 1540/50
Bronze; H 82 cm
Inv. No. 5442

This expressive sculpture was executed with the help of a death mask, as is clearly indicated by the haggard stubbled cheeks and the tightly compressed lips. The costume is similar to those found in portraits of scholars in Padua and Venice. The physiognomy of the old man resembles that of the physician Girolamo Fracastoro (d. 1553) from Verona, whose monument, commissioned by the city of Verona, was executed in 1555 by Danese Cattaneo. This accounts for the fact that the bust was described as a portrait of Fracastoro by the hand of Cattaneo. However, its radical realism and the unrestricted style of the modelling is hardly to be reconciled with the authenticated work of Cattaneo.   M. L.-J.

TWO-FIGURED RAPTUS GROUP
Jean Boulogne, called Giambologna
(Douai 1529 – 1608 Florence)
Antonio Susini
(working c. 1580 – 1626 Florence)
Florence, c. 1580
Bronze; H 98.2 cm
Inv. No. 6029

In this composition Giambologna did not depict a historical event. Instead, his interest was centred on the formal mastery of a group in extreme movement, of a man in full stride lifting the figure of a woman. This combination of two figures marks the beginning of a development that culminated in the famous three-figured marble group of the *Rape of the Sabine Women* which was displayed in Florence in 1583. The first version of the group with two figures was sent by Giambologna to Ottavio Farnese in 1579 (today in Naples). The Viennese version offers a tautened, more dynamic composition. The perfect finishing of the sculpture can probably be ascribed to Antonio Susini. M. L.-J.

MERCURY ▽
Jean Boulogne, called Giambologna
(Douai 1529 – 1608 Florence)
Florence, c. 1585
Bronze; H 62.7 cm
Inv. No. 5898

Mercury is shown in flight, a pose forcing Giambologna to exceed the laws of statics characteristic of sculpture. Instead, he proceeded into a field of representation hitherto reserved for painting and relief molding. With his upraised right arm Mercury, messenger of the gods and executor of Jupiter's commands, points to the place whence all wisdom emerges. From the time of his stay in Bologna in 1563 Giambologna occupied himself with this motif. In 1665 Cosimo de' Medici sent a life-sized bronze statue of Mercury to Emperor Maximilian II. The most mature compositional solution of the Mercury motif was achieved, however, in the signed Viennese version of the statuette which once was part of Emperor Rudolph II's. *Kunstkammer.*   M. L.-J.

ASTRONOMY
Jean Boulogne, called Giambologna
(Douai 1529 – 1608 Florence)
Florence, c. 1573
Bronze, fire gilt; H 38.8 cm
Inv. No. 5893

The beautiful young woman depicted in this statuette is an allegory of astronomy as can be deduced from her attributes: prisma, armillary sphere, straight edge, ruler, plumb and drawing compass. Because of these attributes the sculpture in old inventories was listed as *Venus Urania*. It marks the culmination of Giambologna's efforts to form the perfect nude. The beauty of its spiral composition demands appreciation from an infinite number of viewing positions. The statue was executed in 1573, and it was at about the same time that the artist created his *Apollo* sculpture for Francesco de' Medici's *studiolo*. The figure of *Astronomy* is its compositional counterpart.

M. L.-J.

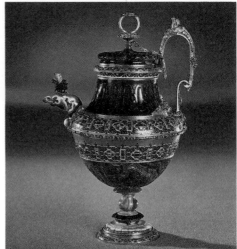

ONYX EWER
Richard Toutain the Younger
(master craftsman 1559, d. 1579 Paris)
Paris
c. 1560/70
Setting: Gold enamelled, diamonds, emeralds, rubies; H 27.1 cm
Inv. No. 1096

The onyx ewer was one of the presents received by Archduke Ferdinand II from Charles IX of France in 1570. Only a few months earlier the vessel, still unfinished, had been described in detail in an inventory listing the properties of the goldsmith Richard Toutain in Paris. The ring crowning the lid had already been mentioned as had been the several settings for the precious stones amid the broad "moorish" décor. Even the flat pearl below the nozzle had been described. The main part of the vessel can be taken apart to form a goblet and a flat jug with a lid. Today it is regarded as the main specimen of goldsmith's works from the era of the last Valois kings of France. Articles of gold from that period are very rare today. H. T.

"MICHAEL GOBLET"
Paris or Antwerp
c. 1530/40
Gold, partially enamelled, diamonds, emeralds, rubies, pearls; H 51.7 cm
Inv. No. 1120

This goblet with lid charms us with the abundant wealth of precious materials as well as by the elegance of its complex form. The base with its slender stem is crowned by a narrow cup with a frieze-like decoration of reliefs showing bacchan-

tian scenes. Delicate, freely suspended garlands are fixed between masks and bucranions with pearls dangling from them. The goblet was one of four eminent works of art presented to Archduke Ferdinand of Tyrol by King Charles IX of France on the occasion of Charles' wedding to Archduchess Elisabeth in 1570, where Ferdinand had acted as proxy for the groom. The lid is topped by a tiny figure of the Archangel Michael richly studded with diamonds. The statuette is perhaps a reference to the French *Ordre de Saint Michel*. R. B.

LOCKET
Paris
1571/72
Gold, partially enamelled; H 6.1 cm, W 4.7 cm
Inv. No. 1601

The front of the medallion shows the figures of two women in brilliantly coloured enamel. They hold a laurel wreath over a royal crown set up on pillars. The motto on the ribbon wound around the pillars reads *PIETATE ET IVSTITIA*, an indication that the fame and glory of a monarch depend on his piety and virtue. On the reverse side of the locket two intertwined Cs beneath a picture of an identical crown refer to one of the two portraits on parchment in the interior of the locket depicting King Charles IX of France. The lady in widow's weeds is his mother, Catherine de' Medici. The miniatures were painted by François Clouet (d. 1572), while the goldsmith's work may have been executed by François Dujardin. R. B.

BASIN
Pierre Reymond
(? c. 1513 – 1584 ?)
Limoges
1556–1558)
Copper, enamelled on both sides; Diam. 45.2 cm
Inv. No. 3201

The bottom of this splendid basin is decorated with a representation of the triumphal procession of Diana. The motif goes back to a design by Jacques Androuet Du Cerceau and was adopted several times by different workshops in Limoges. The detail presented here shows the goddess of the hunt and of chastity sitting in her chariot drawn by stags. On the rear platform of the wagon Venus and Cupid are carried along, bound. A tablet names the year 1556, probably the date of the design. The raised boss of the basin is decorated with the portrait of a lady in the costume of the period, while the outer rim shows a frieze of grotesques. The ornamentation is executed *en grisaille* on a black ground which is enlivened by tender golden foliage. The bottom is dominated by a decoration of scroll-work. On the rim are the initials *P. R.* and the date 1558. R. B.

"MERCURY GOBLET"
French?
c. 1560
Gold, partially enamelled, emeralds, rubies;
H 34.4 cm
Inv. No. 1095

This goblet in embossed gold rests on three open pomegranates, the kernels of which are made of small rubies. The handle on the flat lid is formed by a statue of Mercury which holds aloft an enamelled ring with a large emerald. The bosses around the goblet as well as the lid are rimmed with costly enamelled bands. These consist of a filigree décor of scroll-work and lilies set with rubies and emeralds. The form of the vessel and the feet in the shape of pomegranates stem from the German late Gothic goldsmith's tradition. The contrast between large smooth surfaces and filigree details corresponds to French taste. Possibly, the artisan may have been a German goldsmith working for the French court.   R. B.

CABINET
Augsburg
1580/90
Ebony, silver; H 75 cm, W 45 cm, L 62 cm
Inv. No. 883

This type of precious small cabinet can be considered as a forerunner of the desk and is probably of Spanish origin. When opened, it contains a great number of drawers and compartments. In the top there is a small drawer containing writing utensils. The silver decoration provides an elegant contrast to the ebony. There is no definite theme to the decoration, the motifs come from various sources. Allegories, Virtues and the Free Arts as well as mythological themes, are represented in the reliefs. The seated figures symbolize the Continents, while at the corners, on pedestals, Hercules is shown performing feats of heroism. Masks, festoons, bosses and scroll-work were used as ornamentation. R. B.

WRITING SET
Wenzel Jamnitzer
(Vienna 1508 – 1585 Nuremberg)
Nuremberg
c. 1570
Silver; H 6 cm, W 10.2 cm, L 22.7 cm
Inv. No. 1155–1164

Caskets containing writing utensils had already

been mentioned in mediaeval inventories. In the Renaissance writing sets were abundantely decorated being particularly esteemed objects. This writing set by Wenzel Jamnitzer, a goldsmith working for the Imperial court as well as for Archduke Ferdinand II and the King of France, is a fine example. It is typical of the naturalistic *style rustique* which prevailed all over Europe during the 2nd half of the 16th century. Nature was represented in every detail without artistic license, sometimes even in form of casts from natural objects. On the lid of the casket there are ten compartments with life-casts of a locust, a moth, shells, beetles, a frog and lizards placed tidily as if in the boxes of a natural scientist. They are of a purely ornamental character, like the garland of flowers, leaves and blades of grass enlivened with insects and small animals that decorates the sides of the casket. Some of the compartments of the lid can be opened or pulled out like drawers to give access to several partitions inside, an inkwell and a sandbox. The partitions of the double bottom hold several quills, tiny knives, pincers and a pair of scissors with gilt handles. R. B.

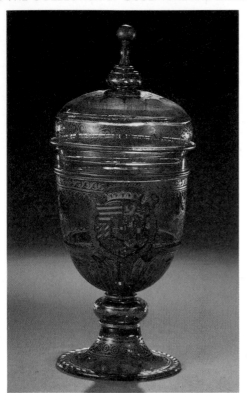

GOBLET WITH LID
Antonio Montano
(working in Hall in Tyrol 1572–1590)
Hall
after 1582
Yellowish glass, painted; H 34.1 cm
Inv. No. 3363

This thick-walled, not quite flawless glass belongs to a group of vessels that contrast with the more elegant thin glasses made by glass blowers from Murano working at the Innsbruck Court glassworks. The thick glasses are not diamond-engraved but are decorated with painted gold foliage and blossoms. This cup with lid bears the coat of arms of Archduke Ferdinand II and his second wife Anna Catharina of Mantua. The city of Venice had passed stringent laws in order to protect its monopoly of glass production. Archduke Ferdinand therefore had either officially to borrow glass blowers or have them secretly trained in Venice, as in the case of Antonio Montano.   R. B.

ARCHDUKE FERDINAND II
Francesco Segala
(working in Padua and Venice from 1557 to c. 1597)
Innsbruck
c. 1580
Coloured wax, precious stones, pearls; H 22.3 cm, W 19.9 cm
Inv. No. 3085

This portrait in wax of Archduke Ferdinand II shows a delicacy worthy of a goldsmith's work in its richly detailed execution of the silver armour with gilded decoration, the lace frills at the neck and sleeves, the necklace set with precious stones and the emblem of the Order of the Golden Fleece, and the archducal hat. The centre of the brocade drapery shows a representation of Jonah and the whale which can also be found on medallions of Ferdinand with the motto *vincit potentia fati* (the power of destiny overcomes). On the underside of the pillow on which the archducal hat rests, appears the signature *FRANC.S.P.S.F.* (Franciscus Segala Padovanus Sculptor Fecit). The frame is of the same date and a piece of Venetian work.   R. B.

DRINKING HORN
Cornelius Gross
(master craftsman before 1534, d. 1575)
Augsburg
c. 1560/70
Pressed tortoise-shell, silver gilt, partially
enamelled; H 30 cm, L 34 cm
Inv. No. 889

The vessel is in the shape of a dragon standing on
a turtle floating on the waves of the sea. This is a
post-Gothic version of the mediaeval drinking
horn, possibly reaching back to memories of the
mediaeval conception of the "griffin's claw" (cf.
p. 135). In the dragon's gullet is placed an "adder's tongue" (cf. p. 137). According to an old
belief, this was supposed to protect the person
drinking from the horn against poison. A triton is
sitting on the back of the dragon, holding the coat
of arms of the Counts of Montfort-Werdenberg.

R. B.

OSTRICH-EGG GOBLET ▷
Clement Kicklinger
(master craftsman 1561, d. 1617 Augsburg)
Augsburg, c. 1570/75
Shell of an ostrich-egg, corals, silver gilt
and silver painted; H 56.8 cm
Inv. No. 897

This goblet, with its combination of exotic natural
objects and precious goldsmith's work is a typical
item of a *Kunst- und Wunderkammer*. Above an
open-work base with thick coral stems, by means

of a long chain a Moor leads an ostrich carrying its
own egg on its back. The ostrich holds a horse
shoe in its beak which was considered to bring
luck as early as the 16th century. The motif of an
ostrich eating iron originates in mythology and
signifies "greater strength through opposition" as
the bird has such strength that it can digest stone
and iron and feed itself therewith. The corals, on
the other hand, were considered as being able to
heal "cramps in the bowels and flux in the blood"
as well as protecting against the evil eye and black
magic.

R. B.

MOUNTED HUSSAR
South German
End of 16ᵗʰ century
Silver gilt, traces of colouring; H 53.3 cm
Inv. No. 6853

The crowned *C* on the horse's back and the coat of arms on the hussar's shield indicate that he is Marquis Carl von Burgau (1560–1618), the second son of Archduke Ferdinand II from his morganatic marriage to Philippine Welser. Carl is wearing the traditional garb of a Hungarian hussar in which he is also depicted in the engravings by Johannes Agricola commemorating the festivities on the occasion of the marriage of the Archduke Ferdinand to his second wife Anna Catharina of Mantua in 1582. It is probable that the statuette was executed in 1582, either as a wedding gift of Carl's or as a variation of the engravings. The heads of rider and horse are removable, so that the object could also be used as a drinking vessel.
R. B.

HAND-STONE
Caspar Ulich
(documented after 1555, d. 1576
St. Joachimsthal)
St. Joachimsthal
c. 1565
Silver gilt, silver ore; H 31.7 cm
Inv. No. 4148

Hand-stones were a peculiarity of Bohemian goldsmiths' work. Pieces of silver ore found by miners after initial treatment and artistic decoration became cherished items in a *Kunstkammer*, and were used as representative princely gifts. This Resurection of Christ was modelled on Dürer's woodcut of the Passion, made in 1510. A contemporary describes the piece "as the most beautiful hand-stone I have ever seen". While the work was being made it happened that "the body of Christ emerged in white silver while the guardians and the tomb appeared black as lead". The back shows a representation of a meeting between Emperor Charles V and King François I of France after the Battle of Pavia in 1525, which did not in fact take place in this way.
R. B.

196

"JOLLY BOTTLE" WITH TANTALUS
Christoph Gantner
(d. 1605 Innsbruck)
Innsbruck
c. 1580/90
Clay with coloured glazing; H 26.6 cm
Inv. No. 3155

The figure of a drinker straddling a keg symbolizes the punishment of a glutton suffering the
pains of Tantalus with all sorts of delicious foods
surrounding his head beyond his reach. The head
of the figure is a removable stopper. The 16th
century's delight in drinking is as rich and varied
as the drinking vessels of that time. The following
lament has come down to us: "No drinking vessel
can be made large enough or beautiful enough or
strange enough for us Teutons. We drink out of
monkeys, priests, monks, nuns, lions and
bears . . . and I don't want to mention the incorri-
gible wine tipplers who toast each other with hats,
shoes, boots and chamber pots."   R. B.

THE BEAR AS HUNTER
Gregor Bair
(Meran? – 1604 Augsburg; master craftsman in
1573)
Augsburg
c. 1580/90
Silver, musk, gold, enamel, precious stones,
pearls; H 21.3 cm
Inv. No. 1094

The bear sitting upright with a golden shotgun
consists of a silver core coated with musk or
amber which must originally have exuded a pleasant smell. The removable head hides a vessel
which probably contained an aromatic essence. If
one moves the little dog standing next to the bear
a monkey appears riding on a dragon and holding
a book. When one moves the bear a small game
board appears. It is uncertain whether this strange
object was a princely toy or a scent dispenser. In
any case it seems to be an allegory of the topsy-
turvy world.   R. B.

JUG MADE FROM A TRITON SHELL
Abraham I. Pfleger
(master craftsman before 1558, d. 1605)
Augsburg
1585/90
Triton shell, silver gilt; H 32.6 cm
Inv. No. 4129

A bearded sea-dweller carries a triton shell on his back mounted with narrow ribbons and a beautifully curved handle. The legs, ending in fins, curl round a central pillar serving as a seat. This shell, adapted as a jug together with a basin (Inv. No. 4128), belongs to a wash-stand set. The basin consists of four Tridacna shells held together by four sea virgins. This set from Ambras Castle and probably commissioned by Archduke Ferdinand II is mentioned in the inventory of 1596 as *mörschneggengeschirr* and *gieszbeckhet* (i. e. sea snail jug and basin). R. B.

JUG WITH LID
Königsberg?
1st quarter of 17th century
Amber, silver gilt, partially enamelled;
H 23 cm
Inv. No. 3548

Amber is found mainly on the coasts of the Baltic and North Sea. The precious fossil resin exists in different shades and varying degrees of transparency. These peculiarities were cleverly combined in the production and decoration of vessels and caskets. The body of this jug is made up of six rounded transparent plaques which are decorated in turn with carvings of ancient heroes and arrangements of weapons. Slender opaque yellow strips with inlaid transparent oval medallions separate the plaques from each other. Delicately enamelled flowers and leaves decorate the silver gilt handle and rim. The lower end of the handle finishes in a coat of arms – a golden sceptre on a blue background (sceptre of the Elector of Brandenburg as Lord Chamberlain of the Holy Roman Empire). R. B.

TOILET CASKET
Venice
Mid-16th century
Mother-of-pearl, bone, lacquer, silver;
H 22.5 cm, W 13.5 cm, L 13.5 cm
Inv. No. 4103

The precious casket of shimmering mother-of-pearl and applications of architectural design of bone shows a painted Renaissance décor strongly influenced by oriental art. The transparent lacquer coating lends the colours an enamelled appearance. The casket can be transported by means of a red silk cord which is threaded through rings with lion masks at the sides and under the lid. The cord is intertwined with gold strands and ends with a tassel. The casket contains ivory double combs, a mirror, a brush, gilded scissors, and other small instruments for beauty care. A small bottle of white filigree glass denotes the Venetian origin of this casket; it has been mentioned in the inventory of Ambras Castle since 1596.

R. B.

CASKET
Ceylon
2nd half of 16th century
Ivory, silver; H 14.9 cm, W 16 cm, L 25 cm
Inv. No. 4743

This casket with lid is made up of carved ivory plaques and mounted in silver, with silver feet, lock and handle. The latter are a European addition from the 2nd half of 16th century. The reliefs depict scenes from the life of Krishna. The casket is mentioned in the Ambras inventory of 1596, which proves once again how popular such exotic objects were in the *Kunst- und Wunderkammern* of the time. Apart from the European setting, this mention of the casket in the Ambras inventory is important in determining the otherwise difficult dating of the ivory work. An even more precious casket of gold with precious stones preserved in

the treasury of the Munich residence is already mentioned in a Munich inventory of 1598. R. B.

EMPEROR RUDOLPH II
Adriaen de Vries
(The Hague c. 1545 – 1626 Prague)
Prague
1603
Bronze; H 112 cm
Inv. No. 5506

Adriaen de Vries became court sculptor to Rudolph II in 1601, and made this bust at the Emperor's request as a companion piece to that of Charles V by Leone Leoni (see p. 184), which Rudolph had obtained in 1600. It is not only the freer artistic character of the modelling that fascinates here but also the formal improvements on the prototype, for by slightly twisting the body and raising the gaze, de Vries endows his portrait with a certain drama and majestic pathos, at the same time conveying a sense of greater distance to the beholder. With this bust he achieved a degree of perfection in court portraiture which by far excelled anything that had been done in this field by sculptors before him and which was only to be surpassed by Bernini's baroque busts of rulers.

M. L.-J.

VIEW OF THE HRADSCHIN IN PRAGUE ▽
Court workshop of the Castrucci
Prague
Early 17th century
Commesso in pietre dure; H 11.5 cm, W 23.5 cm
Inv. No. 3060

The two Florentine artisans Cosimo and Giovanni Castrucci were summoned to Prague by Rudolph II. They seem to have carried on the Castrucci workshop for some time even after the death of the Emperor. Their work is almost indistinguishable. The special glyptic variant, which may be described as inlay-technique, aims at achieving effects that imitate painting. These effects depend largely on the artist's skilful use of the various natural shades and veining of the stones. *Commesso in pietre dure* literally means a work composed of hard stones, a technique also known by the name of "Florentine mosaic", because the Florentine ducal workshop brought this esoteric art to perfection. The production of such inlaid stone work made of semi-precious stones was a very time-consuming and expensive art form. Besides the stone cutters' skill a large and varied stock of coloured stones was needed. In order to reproduce the details of a design, stones of suitable colour and veining had to be assembled. Thinly sawed plaques resembling pieces of fret-saw work with the contours of the intended colour are closely fitted together to form the picture.

H. T.

ADORATION OF THE MAGI
Munich court workshop
End of 16th century
Gold, enamel, ebony, precious stones, pearls;
H 17.5 cm, W 11.9 cm
Inv. No. 3218

This miniature altar made of gold enamel on an ebony plaque depicts the *Adoration of the Magi*, and is modelled on Albrecht Dürer's woodcut from 1511. Ten large sapphires and crosses of rubies are set in the frame, and between them four little figures of the Evangelists as well as putti in *email sur ronde bosse*. On the reverse, under a piece of rock crystal, there is a miniature representing the Birth of Christ modelled on Dürer's engraving of 1504. A note by Hermann Gabriel von Völcker, treasurer to Leopold I, affixed to the back indicates that this object was a gift to the Emperor by his wife Eleonora Magdalena on the occasion of his saint's day, and was placed in a so-called *geschmuck kasten,* a jewellery casket, in 1701. R. B.

PENDANT DEPICTING MOSES SMITING THE ROCK
Augsburg
c. 1600
Gold, partially enamelled, diamonds, rubies, pearls; H 7.2 cm, W 5.7 cm
Inv. No. 1616

PENDANT WITH PEARL IN THE SHAPE OF A BUNCH OF GRAPES
South German
Early 17th century
Gold, partially enamelled, rubies, giant Baroque pearl; H 5.3 cm
Inv. No. 2127

From time immemorial man has wished to adorn himself. There is proof of this in all epochs. Yet the Renaissance surpasses all other periods in the number, richness and skilled technique of the objects produced. Artistic imagination goes hand in hand with an abundance of costly materials such as precious stones, gold and enamel. In the court portraits of the 16th and 17th centuries, the sitters are shown wearing a profusion of necklaces, brooches, pendants, tiaras and rings. The heavy material of the ladies' robes is covered with pearl embroidery, buckles and studs. R. B.

MERCURY
Johann Gregor van der Schardt
(Nijmwegen c. 1530–c. 1581 Nuremberg ?)
Nuremberg
Last third of 16th century
Bronze; H 53 cm
Inv. No. 5900

Mercury is represented striding forward as becomes the messenger of the gods. Posture and gesture suggest an opposite figure. This was probably a statuette of Minerva preserved today in a private American collection. Van der Schardt, a contemporary of Giambologna, worked in Rome, Florence, Bologna and Venice, in the 1560s. He was, compared to Giambologna, more influenced by the older generation of Italian artists like Benvenuto Cellini, Baccio Bandinelli and Sansovino. This was the reason why the statuette was ascribed to different artists until a signed larger version in Stockholm became known. A replica is preserved in Stuttgart. M. L.-J.

ALLEGORY OF SPRING
Ascribed to Johann Gregor van der Schardt
(Nijmwegen c. 1530–c. 1581 Nuremberg)
Nuremberg
1569/78
Bronze, fire gilt; H 71.2 cm
Inv. No. 1118

The allegory of spring is one of four supporting figures representing the seasons which were part of a three meters high silver fountain commissioned by Emperor Maximilian II in 1569 from the goldsmith Wenzel Jamnitzer. It was, however, only delivered to his successor, Emperor Rudolph II in 1578. There exists a detailed contemporary description of the fountain which was melted down in 1748. Only the four caryatids of gilded bronze remain. They cannot be the work of Jamnitzer, but must have been designed by a sculptor. There are stylistic reasons for believing that this may have been Johann Gregor van der Schardt who worked in Nuremberg from 1570 onwards as court sculptor to Maximilian II.
M. L.-J.

MARS, VENUS AND CUPID
Hubert Gerhard
(Amsterdam ? c. 1550–1622/23 Munich)
Innsbruck
c. 1605
Bronze; H 41.4 cm
Inv. No. 5848

Like his Dutch fellow sculptors Giambologna, Adriaen de Vries and Johann Gregor van der Schardt, Hubert Gerhard also spent some years of apprenticeship in Italy. We do not know the names of his teachers, but it is certain that he was in Florence in 1581. The same year he entered the service of the Fuggers in Augsburg. For their Castle at Kirchheim he produced a monumental fountain between 1585 and 1590, which was crowned by a group of figures of Mars, Venus and Cupid and is preserved today in the Bavarian National Museum in Munich. About 1605, while in the service of Archduke Maximilian III in Innsbruck, he once again took up this motif and transformed it with more elegant and flowing proportions into a *Kunstkammer* piece.   M. L.-J.

VENUS AND CUPID
Nikolaus Pfaff
(Nuremberg 1556 ?–1612 Prague)
Prague
1601/07
Ivory, ebony; H (with base) 19.5 cm, H (without base) 12.9 cm
Inv. No. 4658

Around 1600, ivory carvings gradually came back into fashion. In the rich *Kunstkammer* of Emperor Rudolph II only four such pieces are mentioned. All four carvings were executed by Nikolaus Pfaff, among them this Venus. With graceful indifference she rests her right leg on Cupid's quiver filled with arrows. In her peaceful reflective mood she seems to overlook Cupid's wilful pleading for his weapons. The figurine evokes the spirit of antiquity. The raised leg forms a counterpart to the bent arm holding a scarf draped over her breast. The inclined head leads the observer's eye over the dangling left arm down to the supporting leg. From here Cupid's raised head directs it upward again to the slender features of Venus. From January 1st, 1601 Nikolaus Pfaff was employed as court cabinet maker and sculptor in Prague.   R. D.

EWER
Nikolaus Schmidt
(Greifswald ?–1609 Nuremberg; master crafts-man in 1582)
Nuremberg
c. 1600
Silver gilt, mother-of-pearl, garnets; H 54 cm
Inv. No. 1124

The characteristic type of oval shaped jugs and ewers of mannerist goldsmiths' workshops with their narrow necks and high drawn curved hand-les is here abundantly enriched by figurative elements in high relief. In the course of time, the smaller decorative elements gave way to figura-tive representations. A Nereid sits on the bulge of the ewer under the spout, her widely spread arms stressing the curve of her torso. Below, a mask hides the transition between her body and her divided fish tail which is reduced to a flat re-presentation on the body of the ewer. The use of mother-of-pearl inlay on this completely pre-served wash-stand set may have its origin in the predilection for copying oriental techniques pre-vailing in Nuremberg around 1600.   H. T.

ORNAMENTAL BASIN DEPICTING THE TRIUMPHAL PROCESSION OF CUPID
Christoph Jamnitzer
(Nuremberg 1563–1618 Nuremberg)
Nuremberg
c. 1605
Silver gilt, enamel; H 64.7 cm, W 53 cm
Inv. No. 1104

Cupid's triumphal procession completely fills the bowl of this quartrefoil basin. In his horse-drawn triumphal chariot, Cupid carries Jupiter as the most distinguished of his twelve prisoners. Caesar leads the "nine perfect heroes" on foot, with the crouching Hercules bringing up the rear of the bound companions. Cupid's retinue reaches into the distance as far as the eye can see. Putti seated at the spandrels of the rim personify the four continents, as can be seen from their emblems. Relief medallions on the rim – one each of gold, silver, bronze and iron – represent the four world empires (Babylon-Assyria, Persia, the Empire of Alexander the Great and the Roman Empire) in the shape of visionary symbolic animals. Delicately chiselled engravings of four mythological scenes from Ovid's *Metamorphoses* (Apollo and Daphnis; Pluto and Proserpine; Hippomenes and Atalanta; uncertain scene) appear on the smooth rim of the basin. The main theme, the triumph of Cupid, refers to the first of the six *trionfi* of Petrarch, while the last five are represented in relief on the ewer. Jamnitzer was not only inspired by the text but also by illustrations of the *trionfi* but without exactly copying a single one. Whether the enlargement of the theme should be ascribed to an ideographer from the Prague circle around Emperor Rudolph II who commissioned the set, or whether the artist himself was responsible for it, is a moot point.
Christoph Jamnitzer, who had a great family tradition behind him and was influenced by his stay in Italy was the greatest artist in Nuremberg during the 17th century being as he was a goldsmith, a designer of the sculptures for the city hall, and the engraver and author of the *Neuw Grotteßken Buch* (Book of New Grotesques). His work is characterized by its abandonment of all purely additive linear construction in order to achieve a vivid profusion of decorative elements in preference to functional use. The *trionfi* basin and ewer are mere show pieces and not meant for use. As such, they were taken to Frankfurt for the coronation ceremonies. We can easily trace the creation from design to execution because four signed sketches for the decoration of the rim and the triumphal procession have been preserved. The engraving and chasing are of a dramatic and sparkling vitality, in the reliefs the artist achieves a heightened sense of atmosphere and depth. H. T.

ORNAMENTAL EWER
Christoph Jamnitzer
(Nuremberg 1563–1618 Nuremberg)
Nuremberg
c. 1605
Silver gilt, enamel; H 43.5 cm
Inv. No. 1128

The matching ewer continues the *trionfi* series with the triumph of innocence over love (represented by unicorns), death over innocence (the buffaloes), fame over death (the elephants), time over fame (the stags), and eternity over time. This last triumph of godliness differs from Petrarch's text because pagan instead of Christian motifs are depicted. The gathering of the gods on Olympus represents a mythological, emblematically encoded programme in compressed form. Psyche's entrance into Olympus is a metaphor of the immortality of the soul, while the Graces are a metaphor for the grace of God. In the emblem of the *fata Homerica* (i.e. the "gates of Jupiter"), fate takes shape in vessels filled with good and evil. The ewer is topped by Venus (or Leda) and a swan. H. T.

ORNAMENTAL BASIN WITH REPRESENTATIONS OF THE MYTH OF EUROPA
Christoph Lencker
(Ludwigsorget 1556–1613 Augsburg)
Augsburg, late 16th century
Silver gilt, enamel; H 58.5 cm, W 69 cm
Inv. No. 1110

Originally, the rape of Europa by Jupiter in the form of a bull was represented twice on the complete wash stand set: once in the shape of the ewer – no longer extant – formed like a girl straddling a bull, and again in the relief scenes on the bowl of the basin. A plain recess for the ewer in the centre of the basin stresses the functional character of the object. On the other hand balance is achieved between the circular composition and the picture-like coherence of the scenes depicted. The emphasized inactivity of Europa's watching playmates neutralizes the fact that the story of Europa is represented in three consecutive periods. On the right Mercury rounds up the cattle herd in order to deceive the girls. On the left, the rape is successfully carried out, and above there is the lover's happy reunion.   H. T.

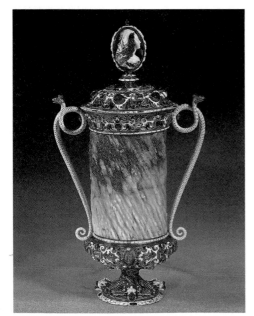

TANKARD MADE FROM THE TUSK OF A NARWHAL
Jan Vermeyen
(Brussels before 1559–1606 Prague)
Prague, c. 1600/05
Narwhal tusk (unicorn), gold enamelled, diamonds, rubies; double cameo: agate; H 22.2 cm
Inv. No. 1113

The "unicorn" forming the vessel was considered the most precious part of the item. From about 1200, the tusk of the narwhal was taken for the single horn of the mythological unicorn. Great curative powers were attributed to it. According to Anselmus Boetius de Boodt, personal physician to Emperor Rudolph II, the "unicorn" was so highly priced because it was unsurpassed in the recognition, prevention and cure of any poison. It was therefore more costly by far than gold. This explains the precious setting of the vessel. The rich gold enamel work set with precious stones was the work of Rudolph II's court jeweller Jan Vermeyen, who was summoned to Prague in the autumn of 1597. The beautiful double cameo on the lid probably originates from the Miseroni workshop in Milan.   R. D.

JASPER JUG
Ottavio Miseroni (jug)
(Milan 1567 – 1624 Prague)
Paulus van Vianen (mount)
(Utrecht c. 1570 – 1630 Prague)
Prague
Late 16th century (mount 1608)
Jasper, gold; H 35.5 cm
Inv. No. 1866

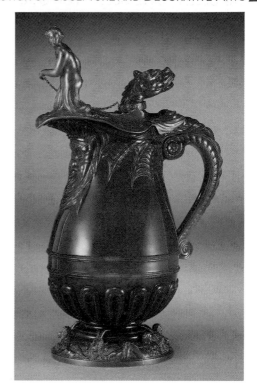

This unique piece gives the impression of having been conceived as a single unity, although it was in fact produced in two stages. Made sometime before 1600 by Ottavio Miseroni who had been working in Prague since 1588, the jug did not stand in need of any mounts in its original form, being a monolithic piece of virtuosity in its own right. Designed by Paulus van Vianen and dated 1608, the mounts were added when the dragon's head on the handle, which is made from a type of jasper with a different structure, was being restored, a piece of gold drapery being used to conceal the restoration. On the lid a Nereid rising from the water holds the dragon on a chain and this is complemented at the base of the jug by a broad gold hoop with representations of the four elements, symbolized by Jupiter (fire), Juno (air), Pluto (earth) and Amphitrite (water). These are divided by four goats' heads, whose horns form the attachments.   R. D.

GOBLET WITH COVER MADE FROM RHINOCEROS HORN
Prague
1611
Rhinoceros horn, tusks of an African warthog
Silver gilt; H 49.7 cm
Inv. No. 3709

The pictorial, expressive character of this goblet was determined by the underlying idea of warding off the demonic powers in nature by objectifying them. The formidable tusks of the warthog give the appearance of being the horns on the head of the wild beast dominating the lid. Between its bared teeth it once bore an "adder's tongue" (fossilized shark's tooth). The small creatures on the lid and the base (life casts of spiders, beetles etc.) symbolize the negative forces in the microcosmos. The sides of the horn goblet, which was carved by Nikolaus Pfaff, are enlivened by snakes, lizards and insects. Healing powers were attributed to the horn itself, the adder's tongue and also to the sculpted branches of coral around the stem and body of the goblet. The unknown goldsmith belonged to the tradition of the Nuremberg masters.   R. D.

EWER MADE OF HALF A SEYCHELLES NUT
Anton Schweinberger
(Augsburg mid-16th century – 1603 Prague)
Prague
1602
Seychelles nut (Lodoicea Maledivia),
Silver, partly gilt; H 38.5 cm
Inv. No. 6872

This ewer is a masterpiece of Prague goldsmith work from the time of Emperor Rudolph II. Schweinberger, who had been employed at the court in Prague since 1587, greatly surpassed what was usually produced when accomplishing

the conventional task of mounting a rare natural object. The nut was at that time found among flotsam at the Maldives and was regarded as a fruit of the sea, which is why the work abounds in motifs from the marine world. Schweinberger inscribed his sculptural conception within a rhombus, whose diagonals run through the horizontals provided by the edge of the nut and through the verticals of the side clasps and the axis of the vessel. The changes from one direction to another are effected in smooth and flowing transitions. The vessel is borne by two tritons sitting back to back at the base; their craning heads and outstretched arms lead into the horizontals of the

BEZOAR GOBLET
Jan Vermeyen
(Brussels, before 1559–1606 Prague)
Prague
c. 1600
Oriental bezoar, enamelled gold; H 14.5 cm
Inv. No. 3259

Bezoars are stones found in the stomach of the Asiatic bezoar goat or of the South American Lama. The term comes from the Persian *(bâdsahr* = antidote to poison) and indicates that the bezoar was considered a highly effective medicine for many illnesses. The oriental bezoar sometimes cost ten times more than gold. As it was supposed to neutralize poison in drink, Rudolph II, who in later life was afraid of being poisoned, had this bezoar hollowed out and made into a precious goblet by his court jeweller. The costliness of the stone as well as the imperial status of the owner demanded the highest artistic excellence. The ornamentation in gold enamel symmetrically laid out along two axes is one of Vermeyen's finest works.   R. D.

MOSS-AGATE BOWL
Ottavio Miseroni
(Milan 1567–1624 Prague)
Prague, c. 1600
Moss-agate; setting: gold enamelled; H 17.1 cm,
W 18 cm, L 14 cm
Inv. No. 1987

The vessel and the figure of the triton are made out of one piece of moss-agate, and yet they are clearly separated from each other. Ottavio Miseroni was guided with great subtlety solely by the veining of the stone. The head and bust of the triton grow almost without transition from the rim of the cup. On the outside his complete figure is seen with his fin-like arms and fish-tailed legs clasping the cup. Broad scrolls are laid across his arms as if to shackle him. The metamorphosis between the sea dweller and the cup seems to be held in suspense. Ottavio Miseroni, who had been working in Prague from 1588 onwards, was still following the tradition of his Milanese workshop, but had nevertheless already fully developed his own personal style. The setting is by Jan Vermeyen.   R. D.

boat-shaped body of the ewer. The dynamics of this is complemented by the vivid group on the lid with Neptune, whose trident is missing, riding a seahorse, while the istricate scrolls and curves of the spout and handle maintain the balance in the other two corners of the rhombus. The effect of heterogeneity is heightened by the alternating use of gold and silver for the surfaces, and this also provides the whole with an element of clarity when the line between abstraction and objectification becomes blurred. As for example in the curving handle, the back of which suddenly transforms into a crouching figure whose fin-like arms reach round to the shoulder of the vessel.

Schweinberger has achieved a work which possesses an inner monumentality, has created a memorial to Neptune. This ewer, which he signed on the underside of the base with his full name, is the only surviving work which can be ascribed to him with certainty and it was also the last piece which he completed. With its high artistic claims, this "mount" left the domain of what is usually understood under the decorative arts far behind and the Imperial *Kunstkammer* received what was a work of art in its own right. The subtle bas-reliefs on the nut, which represent gods and goddesses of the sea, were executed by the court wood-carver Nikolaus Pfaff.   R. D.

PRASEM BOWL
Jan Vermeyen
(Brussels, before 1559–1606 Prague)
Prague
c. 1600/05
Prasem, gold, partially enamelled, garnets, citrine,
amethyst, hyacinthe; H 23.5 cm, Diam. 17.6 cm
Inv. No. 1918

In the case of this ornamental vessel first place
must be given to the goldsmith whose design
must have served as a model for the stone-cutter.
This cup is therefore unique among those cut

from semi-precious stones. Only the extremely
thin cutting of the stone (1.2–2 mm) indicates
Ottavio Miseroni's collaboration. The richly decorated lid composed of heart shaped, slightly
arched plaques shows how much the stone
cutter's work was subordinated to the goldsmith's. The knob of the lid is formed by a facetted
citrine. The numerous garnets which are even set
in gold enamel bands on the inside of the cup,
make it certain that the object originated in
Prague. This is also proved by the details of the
gold enamel work which denote the hand of
Vermeyen.   R. D.

MADONNA WITH CHILD
Alessandro Masnago (cameo)
(working in Milan at the end of 16ᵗʰ and 1ˢᵗ quarter of 17ᵗʰ century)
Jan Vermeyen (setting)
(Brussels, before 1559–1606 Prague)
Brussels
c. 1602
Cameo: agate; setting: gold enamelled;
H 5.5 cm, W 5.5 cm
Inv. No. XII 815

As if by a miracle of nature the shape of the madonna emerges from the cloudy coloured agate. The heavenly apparition on the one hand gives the impression of having been hidden in the stone from the beginning, while on the other hand it is just in a process of materializing. The natural material appears self-creating, the artist's hand merely setting the figure free for the eye to behold. Gem cutter Masnago who mainly worked for Rudolph II and many of whose works are preserved in the Vienna collection, was famous for his sensitivity in using the veining of agate which resulted in this striking identity of nature and figurative form. This cameo is already mentioned in Morigia's *Nobilità di Milano* of 1595 as one of Masnago's works. The precious setting is by Jan Vermeyen. R. D.

CERES
Ottavio Miseroni
(Milan 1567 – 1624 Prague)
Prague, c. 1601/05
Agates, jasper, chalcedony; setting: gold enamelled; H 8.2 cm, W 6.6 cm
Inv. No. XII 29

The figurative relief composed of hardstones (*commesso*) in the manner of a cameo is considered an invention of Ottavio Miseroni. He was probably inspired by the *Pietre-dure*-inlay work of the Castrucci workshop in Prague. This new technique made Miseroni independent of the natural coloured veining of the stone and achieved new naturalistic material and pictorial effects. The pink agate of the flesh contrasts with the jasper of the hair and the speckled agate of the robe and the wreath of wheat ears on Ceres' head. The relief bust is set on translucent chalcedony with a dark underlay. This object was probably one of the first made by Ottavio Miseroni in this new technique. This is also confirmed by the setting by Jan Vermeyen which must be dated before 1606. R. D.

ORNAMENTAL VESSEL
South German
2nd half of 17th century
Horn of rhinoceros, ivory, emeralds, silver gilt,
partially enamelled; H 45.3 cm, W 41.8 cm
Inv. No. 3689

This peculiar vessel composed of two different
natural items reminds one of Chinese models.
The stem rises on a base formed by stags,
hounds and a wild boar locked in combat, carved
in horn of rhinoceros in shallow relief. The stem of
ivory is built by the figures of a couple of lovers
balancing the horn of a rhinoceros on their heads.
The flat lid of the vessel is decorated with a group
of ivory figures. The ladies' necklaces and
bracelets are set with small emeralds. The combination of ivory and rhinoceros horn strikes one as
rather strange, as the rhino was considered
thearch-enemy of the elephant.   R. B.

TANKARD WITH LID DECORATED WITH
BACCHANTIC SCENE
Circle of Georg Petel
Andreas I Wickert (setting)
(Augsburg 1600 – 1661 Augsburg)
Augsburg
c. 1625/30
Ivory, silver gilt; H 38 cm
Inv. No. 4519

This ivory vessel narrowing towards the top
represents a bacchanalian scene. Within the
deeply cut relief numerous freestanding parts are
included. The drunken Silenus is supported by a
female satyre with hoofed feet and a satyr wearing
a cap in the shape of a lion's head. A young satyr
dances on the lid, squeezing grape juice into his
mouth. The striking design of the tankard probably
reproduces a lost masterpiece by Georg Petel,
which was possibly executed after a design by
Rubens. Several motifs can be traced to paintings
by Rubens. The Viennese replica itself is of such
high quality that for a long time it was considered
to be a work of Petel himself.   S. K.

THE SCOURGING OF CHRIST
Alessandro Algardi
(Bologna 1598 – 1654 Rome)
Rome
c. 1635/40
Bronze, fire gilt, agates, lapislazuli, marble;
H 44 cm, W 49 cm
Inv. No. D 187

This group belongs to the category of private objects of meditation. Presumably it came to the Viennese court as a papal gift. Here it was mentioned in an inventory of 1758 of the Eccesiastical Treasury with a note to the effect that it was the work of Algardi. Algardi's creation was probably executed in the late 1630s and was widely copied. More than thirty preserved replicas and variants testify to this. In one of the variants of which the Vienna Treasury also owns a copy, the movement of the scourgers is less dramatic. François du Quesnoy is considered as possibly responsible for this latter variant.   M. L.-J.

MARTYRDOM OF ST. SEBASTIAN ▽
Johann Caspar Schenck?
(Constance 1630 – 1674 Vienna)
Constance?
1655
Ivory, velvet; H 54 cm, W 80 cm
Inv. No. 3654

When the Christianized Roman soldier Sebastian refused to continue worshipping the pagan gods, he was sentenced to be pierced by arrows and to suffer an agonizing martyrdom. The naked saint is shown tied to a tree, two of his companions already dead at his feet. Two guards aim at him with their arrows, while two angels floating down from heaven hold out a martyr's wreath and palm promising him eternal life. This superbly cut relief, probably by Johann Caspar Schenck, later appointed "Court bone carver", achieves a dramatic rendering of the scene by the violent movement imposed on single elements.   S. K.

ECSTASY OF ST. TERESA
Tommaso Amantini
(Urbania ? – after 1675 Urbania?)
c. 1660/70
Terracotta; H 63 cm, W 32 cm
Inv. No. 7513

In front of her prie-dieu bench the saint collapses into the arms of two angels, of whom the one on the left is driving an arrow (now broken off) into her breast. The dove of the Holy Ghost shines from above, breaking through the clouds between two angels and a cherub. On the lower front edge of the relief there is the signature *TOMAS AMANTINUS URBANIUM F.* Amantini, a sculptor and master potter from Urbania, was a pupil of Ercole Ferrata's in Rome and through him familiar with the work of Algardi and Bernini. That explains why this relief is a free variant of Bernini's famous marble group (1647–1652) representing the same scene in the Capella Cornaro in Santa Maria della Vittoria in Rome.   M. L.-J.

KING DAVID
Leonard Kern
(Forchtenberg 1588 – 1662 Schwäbisch-Hall)
Schwäbisch-Hall
c. 1620/25
Ivory; H 27.4 cm
Inv. No. 4573

King David is clad as a Roman military leader, with breast plate, short tunic, cuisses and a draped mantle. On the other hand, his crown, decorated with lilies, reminds one of traditional Gothic insignia. The biblical singer strums a harp as David is believed to be the author of the psalms and is therefore considered the patron of poets and musicians. His massive athletic body charmingly contrasts with the delicate movement of the hands. Leonhard Kern's masterly skill in carving combines a superb understanding of human anatomy with a broad, almost cubic concept, to achieve a work of timeless classicism.   S. K.

SATYR AND THE NYMPH CORISCA
Adam Lenckhardt
(Würzburg 1610 – 1661 Vienna)
Vienna
c. 1639
Ivory; H 22.7 cm (without base)
Inv. No. 4564

In Giovanni Battista Guarini's bucolic melodrama *Il Pastor Fido* ("The Faithful Shepherd", Act II, scene VI) the satyr ambushes the nymph Corisca in order to revenge himself for the faithlessness of his former love. Grabbing her hair, he threatens vengeance, but she manages to flee, leaving her wig behind. The surprised, rejected suitor is confronted with the disillusion as to her beautiful hair. Adam Lenckhardt reproduced the turbulent scene from the melodrama (originally staged in Turin in 1585 and soon popular all over Europe) as a true cabinet piece. The grotesque subject is treated almost as a caricature, which is also reflected in the daring balancing of the figures and the diverging lines of the composition.   S. K.

JOHN THE BAPTIST PREACHING
Georg Schweigger
(Nuremberg 1613 – 1690 Nuremberg)
Nuremberg, 1645
Stone from Kehlheim/Germany; H 20 cm, W 14 cm
Inv. No. 4376

In his *Teutsche Academie* of 1675 Sandrart describes an auction of Schweigger's works in 1642 and notes that he first saw these works in Amsterdam. There were two stone plaques about a foot high depicting the birth of John the Baptist, which he described as minutely and cleverly carved (*so zierlich/wol und fleissig vorgestellet*). Sandrart ends his description by saying that the crowd of admirers drove the prices up to 300 and 400 guilders. The relief depicted here is monogrammed and fully signed on the back, and dated 1645. The work is an example of the Dürer revival of the 17th century. Dürer was considered the greatest and most universal of German artists. The story goes that the legendary Dürer sculpture disappeared in the princely treasuries and that its artistic perfection was never surpassed. What remained, however, was the permanent connection between the followers of Dürer and the inspiring milieu of the princely collections, with Georg Schweigger as its main exponent. He not only uses single figures from Dürer's graphic work such as the splendid mercenary in the forefront but also has Dürer himself (placed behind the mercenary) listening to the sermon of John the Baptist.   H. T.

◁ GLORIA MARIAE
Matthias Loth?
Munich
Early 18th century ?
Ivory; H 29.8 cm, W 20.8 cm
Inv. No. 3658

The Madonna with child is enthroned among the clouds. Angels carry her in her throne of clouds and hold an imperial crown above her head. This composition is modelled on designs produced in Munich around 1600 in the circle of the Court painters Christoph Schwarz and Peter Candid. The figure of the Madonna was widely copied in pictures, plaques and silver reliefs. But this ivory carving was executed much later. The bulging voluminosity of the partially almost free-standing figures and the occasional ample forms combine with small-sized draperies having sharp angles. Master Matthias Loth has been suggested as the author of similar reliefs.   S. K.

LOCKET
Henry Toutin
(Châteaudun 1614–after 1683 Paris)
Paris
c. 1643
Gold enamelled; H 7.8 cm, W 6.3 cm
Inv. No. 1590

A profusion of coloured flowers is painted in delicate enamels on a white background on both sides of this locket. Henry Toutin belonged to a Parisian family of goldsmiths and enamellists. Some of them brought this technique to such perfection that they were able to paint on a white enamel surface with opaque colours as if on paper. The inside of the locket contains two miniature paintings on parchment. One of them represents Anna of Austria, Queen of France, the other her son Louis, later Louis XIV of France, at the age of about five.   R. B.

GOBLET WITH LID
Georg Burrer
(working in Stuttgart 1597/98–1627)
Stuttgart
1616
Ivory; H 37.4 cm
Inv. No. 4681

Turned ivories executed on a highly perfected lathe were above all ingeniously conceived masterpieces of micro-technique and not intended for any practical purpose. The turners developed the greatest dexterity in producing intricate gadgets. The goblet depicted here shows very fine, almost transparent, open-work décor, a twelvefoil curved cup, and three independently movable open work polygons on top of the lid. In their centre, a barbed sphere is placed. The patrons who commissioned such works were frequently so fascinated by their intricacy that they wished to be instructed in ivory turning themselves. Several of the lathes used by princely owners are still preserved today.   R. B.

217

FIGHT WITH A DRAGON
Daniel Neuberger
(Augsburg 1621–1680 Ratisbon)
Vienna
1651/52
Coloured wax on glass; H 14 cm, W 15.8 cm
Inv. No. 3087

Two horsemen attack a dragon with long spears while a fallen warrior pierces his neck with a spear from below. White wax is used only for the landscape and for the harnesses and saddles of the horses, pink wax on a background of dark green glass being used for the figures. They stand out clearly and are placed in front of the background of trees and rocks which are executed in shallow relief. The whole work is of great delicacy and carved with a stone cutter's precision. Daniel Neuberger was the most prominent member of an Augsburg family specializing in wax craftsmanship. Between 1651 and 1663 he worked in Vienna for Emperor Ferdinand III. It was here that he also executed his famous panel composed of 60 small wax reliefs depicting stories from Ovid's *Metamorphoses* (Inv. No. 2460). R. B.

GIULIA ALBANI DEGLI ABATI OLIVIERI
Camillo Rusconi
(Milan 1658–1728 Rome)
Rome
c. 1719
Marble; H 96 cm
Inv. No. 9914

Giulia Albani degli Abati Olivieri (1630–1718) was the aunt of Pope Clement XI (Albani). Distinguished by great piety and talent as a writer, she was responsible for his upbringing and therefore influenced his later development. After her death, the Pope, who was very devoted to her, commissioned the most important Roman sculptor of the time, Camillo Rusconi, to make this portrait for her tomb which he had ordered to be made in San Domenico in Pesaro. The half-length figure is a masterpiece of virtuoso chiselling as well as of psychological insight and physiognomical characterisation. Giulia Albani is portrayed as a widow, in prayer as if she were hearing Mass in the family chapel. M. L.-J.

PHAETON SCORCHING THE EARTH ▷
Johann Ignaz Bendl
(working in Bohemia and Vienna, d. c. 1730)
Vienna
c. 1684
Ivory; H 14 cm, W 23.8 cm
Inv. No. 3782

At the left in the background, Phaeton crosses the heavens in his father's horse-drawn sun chariot. The youth had solicited the loan of the sun god's chariot for one day, but was unable to control it.

BATTLE OF THE AMAZONS
Ignaz Elhafen
(Innsbruck 1658–1715 Düsseldorf)
Vienna, c. 1680/85
Light cedar wood; H 12.8 cm, W 19.7 cm
Inv. No. 3932

This relief is based on an engraving by the copper engraver Antonio Tempesta working in Rome. The scene represented is one of the twelve deeds of Hercules: his battle against the warlike Amazons, in which Hyppolita, Queen of the Amazons, was killed. On the right side of the relief, Hercules, clad in a lion's skin, is shown fighting with a club in his raised right hand. On the left, an Amazon – probably the unhappy Queen – is falling off her horse and being caught by two of her companions. Ignaz Elhafen shows great skill in the detailed execution of the densely crowded scene, the figures of which stand out like statues.
S. K.

He came too close to earth. In an unparalleled heatwave, all the rivers dried up and the earth caught fire. Finally, Zeus hurled Phaeton out of the chariot by means of a lightning bolt. In the foreground a descending godly figure pours water into a shell in order to dispense it to thirsting mankind. This relief is part of a series of twelve panels representing mythological scenes. One of them carries the signature *IGNATI BENDL F(ECIT) 1684*. This skilfully carved work is meant to be lit up from behind in order to appear "illumined by the sun's rays". S. K.

TANKARD WITH LID DECORATED WITH HUNTING AND FISHING SCENES
Monogrammist "BG"
(working in Vienna? before 1662 – after 1680?)
Vienna?
3rd quarter of 17th century
Ivory; H 29.8 cm
Inv. No. 4472

This masterpiece of virtuoso ivory carving was never intended for practical use. Almost the entire surface of the vessel with its hunting and fishing scenes is modelled on Dutch engravings from the late 16th to the middle of the 17th century. Even the delicate handle and spout show decorative elements referring to hunting and fishing. The vessel is crowned with putti riding on dolphins. The artist was no doubt working in Vienna, but his monogram *BG* has not yet been identified. His works are characterized by a clear division of figurative and ornamental friezes as well as by its skilful combination of shallow reliefs, high reliefs and numerous sculptural carvings. S. K.

APOLLO AND DAPHNIS
Jacob Auer
(Haimingersberg/Tyrol, c. 1645–1706 Grins/
Tyrol)
Vienna
after 1680/85
Ivory; H 43.9 cm
Inv. No. 4537

In his *Metamorphoses* Ovid tells the story of the
nymph Daphnis who escaped the attentions of
Apollo by imploring the goddess Diana to change
her into a laurel tree. This favourite theme of the
Baroque period found its most famous representation in Bernini's life-size marble group. The
superb ivory carving by the Tyrolese master
craftsman Jacob Auer is modelled on Bernini's
sculpture. Apollo has almost achieved his aim
when his beloved disappears all of a sudden. The
two entwined figures are meant to be looked at
from all angles. Fragile postures and skilfull drapery heighten the effect of movement in this piece
of virtuoso carving.   S. K.

**ALLEGORY OF THE ELEMENTS WATER AND
AIR**
Matthias Steinl
(Mattsee/Salzburg? c. 1644–1727 Vienna)
Vienna
c. 1688–1690
Walrus tusk; H 43.9 cm
Inv. No. 4533

On a base of shells, dolphins and sea creatures,
three entwined sea gods rise up: a triton blowing
into a horn shaped shell, an almost naked young
man carrying a fish on his back, and an equally
naked woman holding a shell aloft. Under a
flowing ribbon a putto approaches from above and
reaches for the shell. This composition represents
the elements water and air which meet in the crest
of a foaming wave. The rich composition of "one
of the most beautiful examples of ivory carving" is
incomparably fitted into the narrow dimensions of
the walrus tusk.   S. K.

KING JOSEPH I ON HORSEBACK
Matthias Steinl
(Mattsee/Salzburg ? c. 1644–1727 Vienna)
Vienna
1693
Ivory: H 70.8 cm (including base)
Inv. No. 4663

This equestrian statue of the fifteen year-old Joseph I forms part of an allegorical double monument. The counterpart represents a similar statue of his father, Emperor Leopold I. The occasion for this commission was probably the election and coronation of Joseph I as Emperor of the Holy Roman Empire on March 4th, 1690 and the subsequent triumphal return of the Imperial family to Vienna. Emperor Leopold I and his successor (after 1705) represent the present and the future of the resurgent Habsburg dynasty. Joseph I is wearing a cuirass over a lace-edged vest. The cuirass is decorated with the Imperial coat of arms, the double eagle, with the initials J I. The Hungarian and Bohemian coats of arms decorate the left and right pistol holsters respectively. Beneath the rearing horse lies the fallen allegory of *Furor* (raging madness) vanquished by the virtues and powers of the young king, which are symbolized by the attributes of snakes, torch and shackles locked to his right upper arm. The reclining figure with its Turkish arrows trodden on by the horse's right rear hoof, is not only to be taken as an acolyte of War but also symbolizes the powers of evil in general. In front of the galloping horseman with flowing cape, the foe withdraws his hand in fear. In this work, composed of several pieces of ivory joined together, Steinl achieved the peak of his art as a carver.   S. K.

221

TABLE CENTRE-PIECE BELONGING TO DUKE KARL ALEXANDER OF LORRAINE
Pieter Jozef Fonson
(Mons 1713–1799 Brussels)
Brussels
1755 (additions 1770 and 1794)
Gold, porcelain; H 54.5 cm, W 46 cm, L 63.2 cm
Inv. Nos. 1268–1280

The gluttonous brother-in-law of Maria Theresa, Duke Karl Alexander of Lorraine, owned wonderful tableware. Only four candelabras, two sauceboats and the *epergne* reproduced here have been preserved from his large golden table service. On a base in the shape of a tray an open work basket is placed as a central piece, supported by four candelabras. Out of the basket sprout the most delicate porcelain flowers, which, however, are not original. Below several small Chinese porcelain figures and around this centre group are arranged two pairs of porcelain oil and vinegar jugs set in gold, two golden sugar shakers and four little porcelain bowls with lids. These last items are dated 1794 and bear the mark of the Vienna Augarten manufacture. Jakob Frans Van der Donck (Brussels 1725–1801 Brussels) was commissioned as early as 1770 with the extension and remodelling of this set. In carrying out his work he re-used older parts of the *epergne*. Except for the tablet dated and signed by Fonson to the left and right of the Duke's coat of arms, we are not able to establish what other parts of the original work by Fonson are still preserved in this *epergne*.   B. D.

ONE OF THE HESPERIDES DECEIVING THE DRAGON LADON ▽
„Furienmeister" (master of the furies)
South German (Salzburg ?)
1st quarter of 17th century
Ivory; H 30.4 cm
Inv. No. 4559

In Greek mythology there is a striking parallel to the paradise motif of the Old Testament. On the western shore of the great ocean in the middle of a garden, the Hesperides, daughters of Night, are supposed to guard a large tree bearing golden apples which bestow immortality and eternal youth. The immortal dragon-serpent Ladon is designated as guardian of the tree. The "master of the furies" with this group probably depicts that episode of the twelve labours of Hercules in which the Hesperides put the dragon to sleep in order to be able to present the hero with apples. The young girl feeds it with golden apples (Vergil, *Aeneid* IV/484), swinging a magic wand above its head.   S. K.

FURY
"Furienmeister" (master of the furies)
South German (Salzburg ?)
1st quarter of 17th century
Ivory: H 37.4 cm
Inv. No. 3727

Due to this figurine, the unknown ivory carver was given the name "master of the furies". This name likewise describes all the characteristics of his style. He combines whirling movement with over-expressive figurative representation. The fury reaching out into space is wildly expressive, with its elongated sinewy proportions, dramatically flowing drapery, and deeply carved details. So far, it has not been possible to establish the exact location of the remarkable artist's workshop in which the figure was made. This eminent artist probably worked in the Salzburg area and occasionally in Northern Italy.   S. K.

SERVICE
Anton Matthias Domanek
(Vienna 1713–1779 Vienna)
Vienna
c. 1750
Gold, ebony, porcelain
Inv. No. 1197 ff

In a post-scriptum dated January 16th, 1781, the Treasury inventory of 1773 indicates the reception of a boudoir set belonging to Her late Majesty, the Empress Maria Theresa, who had died on November 29th, 1780. This set consists of about 70 pieces of pure gold, which belong to two matching sets for different uses. One part is a breakfast service, and the other a washing set. The illustration above shows the tea-pot, a table stove and a kettle for water, a chocolate pot, a chocolate cup made of Meissen porcelain with golden holder, a sugar bowl on a tablet, a tea cup of Chinese porcelain, a spatula, and a spoon. The washing set is composed of a mirror, a basin and ewer, a candlestick, powder-boxes, rock crystal phials set in gold, a tooth brush, and razors, as well as other utensils. The existence of the razors indicates that the washing set belonged to Maria Theresa's husband, the Emperor Franz I. This dual set, with its formal elegance and perfect execution, may be considered one of the most remarkable examples of its kind, and one of the most outstanding achievements of the art of the Viennese goldsmiths in the 18th century.   R. B.

◁ **ARCHDUCHESS MARIE ANTOINETTE, DAUPHINE DE FRANCE**
Jean Baptiste Lemoyne II
(Paris 1704–1778 Paris)
Paris, 1771
Marble; H 76.5 cm
Inv. No. 5478

Marie Antoinette is depicted in the year of her marriage at the age of 15. As wife of the French dauphin the later queen carried the traditional title *dauphine*. This marble bust was commissioned by Marie Antoinette's father-in-law King Louis XV as a present to her mother Empress Maria Theresa. Lemoyne, Court sculptor to the King, worked at the bust for over a year before he was able to present it in Versailles on September 15th, 1771. Louis XV and the art critics of the day celebrated the bust as the most important work of the aged artist. The graceful, elegant fluidity of the lines and the vivid physical likeness achieved inspite of intended idealisation make this sculpture a perfect example of the aristocratic taste of that period.

S. K.

TABLE DECORATION IN THE SHAPE OF A DRAGON
Milan
c. 1650
Rock crystal; setting: silver gilt; relief tendril: gold enamelled; H 48.2 cm, B 33.8 cm, L 56.4 cm
Inv. No. 2331

This winged and scaled dragon presents itself in the shape of a lion, its tail raised up high, ending in a tassel. With its front claws the dragon clasps a shell. The entire fabled beast is hollowed out to the last curve of its tail. With its head raised in furor, the grotesque lionized dragon crouches on a dirigible vehicle in the shape of a heraldic lily. The crystal body of the animal was conceived as a table fountain. A drink could be poured into the blossom-like opening of the tail-tassel. The liquid then would gush into a shell through nozzles in the animals' breast.

H. T.

ORNAMENTAL VASE MADE OF CITRINE
Dionysio Miseroni
(Prague 1607 ? –1661 Prague)
Prague
1647/48
Citrine; flowers made of agate, jasper, chalcedony, rock crystal; setting: gold enamelled;
H 26 cm (without flowers)
Inv. No. 1330

GOBLET OF SMOKED QUARTZ WITH LID
Prague
1648/49
Smoked quartz; setting: silver gilt, *basse taille*
enamel; H 30 cm
Inv. No. 1339

◁ **ROCK CRYSTAL GOBLET WITH LID**
Prague
c. 1655
Rock crystal; setting: silver gilt, *basse taille* enamel; H 47.5 cm
Inv. No. 2246

In the spring of 1623 the ageing Ottavio Miseroni urged the Emperor to engage his son Dionysio who was as good a glyptographer as he himself as a paid assistant. After the death of his father in 1624 Dionysio took over his father's studio and even surpassed him in fame. In his cut vessels the Prague school of hardstone carving achieved its final apogee, as his son Ferdinand Eusebio (d. 1684) was not able to reach his father's outstanding rank. Dionysio in his vessels liked to follow the oblong, angular crystalline form. The slightly conical monolithic citrine vase (left) is based on a regular hexagon the ledges of which are decorated with hermae executed in relief. Two opposite hermae of a more strongly cut form have been topped by goldsmith's work, two heads of satyres fitted with fragile handles in the shape of sirens. Miseroni was paid 6000 guilders for this piece. The tulips, roses and bell flowers on stems of painted silver were executed by the Imperial gem-cutter Paul Pertz. The concept of a vase with flowers assembled from precious and semi-precious stones goes back to Milan models.
The smoked quartz goblet (centre) which was produced immediately after the citrine vase, is also formed on a hexagonal base. All sides are decorated with straight flutes. The yellowish or brown-hued quartz usually is processed like opaque stone, i.e. it was deeply cut with strong profiles, as the colour changes according to the thickness of the side.
When carving rock crystal Dionysio still used the tendril and foliage *intagli* in the Italian manner in which the frosted carving stands out against the polished surface of the crystal. The mighty vase (right) is cut in twelve facettes which turn concave on base and lid and are bent in an obtuse angle. The tendrils group around two main axes marked by the Imperial eagle and the Austrian *Bindenschild* coat of arms. Thus, Dionysio Miseroni applied three variants of décor in order to enhance the individual character of the three different shades of quartz stone.   R. D.

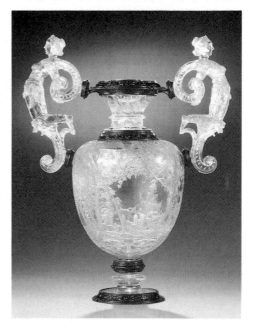

DOUBLE-HANDLED ORNAMENTAL VASE
Milan
1st half of 17th century
Rock crystal; setting: silver gilt; superimposed garland: enamelled gold; H 54.4 cm
Inv. No. 1549

The dominant feature of this amphora-shaped vessel are its two grandiose ample sculpted handles. The ornamental volutes of the handles in a subtle metamorphosis change into the bodies of two female figures whose heads and limbs stand out freely. The retracted leg of each figure is supported by a curled tendril which leads it back to the spiral form of the handle. The massive, proto-Baroque appearance of this ornamental vase that is best recognized in its contours, corresponds to the deeply cut hunting frieze of large figures on the body of the vessel. The intention was to play upon the contrast between the opaque and transparently cut sections.   H. T.

BRATINA
Moscow
before 1637
Gold, partially enamelled, rubies, sapphires,
emeralds, pearls; H 27 cm
Inv. No. 1114

This richly enamelled covered vessel set with
pearls and precious stones is a Russian friendship
cup. These cups were used for taking a welcome
drink or were placed on a grave, filled with *syta*,
i. e. honey dissolved in water. This *bratina* was
one of the gifts sent by Tsar Michael Feodorovich
of Russia on the occasion of the marriage of the
Polish King Ladislaus IV to the Archduchess
Caecilia Renata of Austria in 1637. Under the rim
there is an enamelled Russian inscription clearly
setting out the name and full title of the donor. The
lid is crowned by the Polish white eagle with the
king's monogram.   R. B.

ROCK CRYSTAL PYRAMID ▷
Dionysio Miseroni
(Prague 1607 – 1661 Prague)
Hanns Reinhardt Taravell (mounting)
Prague
1651/53
Silver gilt; appliqués: gold enamelled;
H 115.4 cm
Inv. Nos. 2251–2254
(Text see opposite page, below)

EMPEROR LEOPOLD I
Paul Strudel
(Cles/Tyrol? 1648 – 1708 Vienna)
Vienna
1695
Marble from Laas; H 86 cm
Inv. No. 5458

This work belongs to a series of six portrait busts of the various Habsburg monarchs living around 1695 and their male offspring. The series was commissioned by Elector Johann Wilhelm of the Palatinate-Neuburg, brother-in-law of Emperor Leopold I, in order to set up a monument to the Austrian monarchy and its dynastic connections at his Düsseldorf residence. On 27th August, 1695 Leopold I inspected this series executed by the Court sculptor Strudel. He was so pleased that all the busts remained in Vienna. The august appearance, the long wig and crowning laurel wreath, as well as the skilful drapery of the bust idealize the irregularity of Leopold I's features and make this into an impressive regal portrait. S. K.

ARCHDUKE LEOPOLD WILHELM
François Dieussart
(Arquinghem/Belgium c. 1600 – 1661 London?)
Brussels, 1656
Marble; H 72 cm
Inv. No. 8933

This half-length marble figure represents Archduke Leopold Wilhelm (1614–1662) in his 42nd year. The Governor of the Spanish Low Countries is wearing a suit of armour decorated with rivets and covered with a richly draped sash proclaiming his station. In his slightly raised right hand he holds a marshal's baton, while his left hand is laid on the cross of the Grandmaster of the Teutonic Order. This official portrait convinces through its stately posture and the energetic facial expression of the Archduke. By the subtle counterbalance between the grasp of the right hand and the sensitive relaxed pose of the left, the sculptor has sought to highlight Leopold Wilhelm's real historical importance as patron of the arts, art collector, and one of the founding fathers of the Vienna Gallery. S. K.

◁ This so-called pyramid is Dionysio's most perfect masterpiece. The massive form of the largest vase rises from the hexagonal base of the pyramid almost in the shape of a hexafoil. Scaled friezes below the hermae heads frame two decorative sides alternately ornamented with vine leaves and grapes. On the main vase stand four smaller cylindric vases crowned by a lid with a double eagle. The master craftsman cut all the

smaller vessels of the pyramid out of the largest vase at the base. In executing this work, the smallest vessel at the top was cut first, being followed by each of the larger vessels in turn. This masterpiece of technique became a true *mirabilium* of the Vienna Treasury and owes its unusual form to the artistic virtuoso attitude of the master artisan. Significantly, it is his only signed and dated work. R. D.

THE SEVEN DEADLY SINS: AVARICE
Pieter Coecke van Aelst (design)
(Aelst 1502–1550 Brussels)
Willem de Pannemaker (weaver)
(documented 1539–1580)
Brussels
c. 1555
Wool, silk, gold and silver threads; H 460 cm,
W 785 cm
Inv. No. T XXXV/4

The series of the Seven Deadly Sins is one of the
most beautiful of Brussels tapestries from the
middle of the 16th century. It has a very complex
content: ideas taken from mediaeval catalogues
of the vices mixed with animal symbolism,
humanistic concepts and antique mythology. The
personified sins issue from hell in a triumphal
procession, accompanied by historical and biblical
personages who were known for this specific sin.
In the case of Pygmalion, shown representing
avarice, there is an amalgamation of two persons
of the same name. The brother of Queen Dido of
Carthage murdered his brother-in-law Sichaeus
out of greed; yet the figure carried by a horseman
points to Pygmalion who fell in love with a statue
which later on was brought to life by Venus.   R. B.

THE TWELF MONTHS: FEBRUARY
Cornelis de Ronde (weaver)
(d. 1569)
Brussels
Mid-16th century
Wool, silk, gold and silver threads; H 430 cm,
W 470 cm
Inv. No. T XI/2

Symbolical representations of the months, known
since antiquity, were particularly popular ever-
since. The idea of placing each month under the
patronage of a god was taken from the Romans.
On this tapestry the god is Neptune, with the
zodiacal sign of Pisces dominating February.
From Roman times onwards, characteristic countryman's labours of the various seasons of the
year were used to illustrate the months. Pruning
vines and cutting trees are typical tasks for
February. Behind Neptune and in the small landscapes on both sides spatial depth provides a
contrasting tension with the flat red backdrop
including a wealth of grotesque animals and
foliage.   R. B.

THE TRIONFI OF PETRARCH: DEATH TRIUMPHING OVER CHASTITY

French
Early 16th century
Wool, silk; H 414 cm, W 542 cm
Inv. No. T CII/3

The three symbolical figures of death, the goddesses of fate – namely Clotho, the Spinner, Lachesis, the Distributor of the thread of life, and Atropos, who severs the thread – riding in a wagon drawn by oxen crush fallen Chastity. Pandora, leading the procession, has opened her box, allowing dragon-like monsters to escape. These represent disease and calamity. The transition between two stylistic epochs is clearly visible in this tapestry. The flat *millefleur* background is reminiscent of the late Gothic period, yet the upper part of the composition with its broad landscape perspective, is characteristic of the Renaissance. This tapestry is one of a series of six illustrating the songs of Petrarch's *Trionfi*.

R. B.

MYTHOLOGICAL-ALLEGORICAL SCENES: DEATH OF ADONIS
Rosso Florentino (design)
(Florence 1494 – 1540 Fontainebleau)
Jean and Pierre Le Bries (weavers)
Fontainebleau
1540–1550
Wool, silk, gold and silver threads; H 330 cm, W 640 cm
Inv. No. T CV/2

Aphrodite, goddess of love and beauty, is in love with the beautiful youth Adonis. When he is killed by a wild boar while hunting, the goddess is inconsolable and pleads with Persephone, wife of the god of the underworld that Adonis should spend six months of the year on earth. This tapestry represents the lament for the dead youth. In this six-piece series we see a faithful reproduction of the south side of the great gallery of the Fontainebleau Palace, where the tapestries were executed for King François I of France. When the composition was transposed to the tapestry all the decorative elements of the wall, complete with cornices, stucco figures, frescoes and panelled ceiling, were brought in.   R. B.

SCENES FROM THE LIFE OF ALEXANDER THE GREAT: ALEXANDER AND THE PERSIAN QUEENS
Charles Le Brun (design)
Paris 1619 – 1690 Paris)
Gobelin manufacture Paris
1687/88
Wool, silk, gold and silver threads; H 490 cm, W 720 cm
Inv. No. T V/7

Against the background of the dark blue tent there are the Persian Queens and their retinue, kneeling and begging for mercy. In front of them are Alexander and his friend Hephaestion, clad in a bright red mantle. The scene represented took place after the Battle of Issus in 333 B. C. Even in his lifetime, writers showed interest in the biography of the great Marcedonian leader. A legendary conception of Alexander emerged, which lasted from late antiquity to Renaissance times and became widely known in the form of the saga of Alexander. This richly coloured tapestry is a good example of how in the late 17th century weavers tried to copy the pictorial character of paintings by using numerous different shades of colours in tapestry weaving. This resulted in a diminished interest in tapestries a century later.   R. B.

TUNIS CAMPAIGN OF EMPEROR CHARLES V: BATTLE IN THE RUINS OF CARTHAGE
Jan Cornelisz. Vermeyen (design)
(Beverwijck by Haarlem 1490/95 – 1559 Brussels)
Judocus de Vos (weaver)
(active 1700–1725)
Brussels
1712–1721
Wool, silk, gold and silver threads; H 520 cm, W 860 cm
Inv. No. T X/9

Based on 16th century designs, the tapestry is part of a ten-part series woven in the 18th century, on commission from Emperor Karl VI. In 1535, the painter Vermeyen accompanied Emperor Charles V on his Tunis Campaign to record the event. This accounts for the topographically precise reproduction of the military theater of operation. Vermeyen, in 1546, then painted to size the cardboards that were to serve as weavers' patterns (also in the Museum). The first series of the tapestries was turned out between 1548 and 1554 in Brussels (presently in Madrid). The Vienna series, done some two hundred years later, differs in that its colouring is stronger and that in one tapestry there is a self-portrait of the weaver, de Vos.   R. B.

RIDING INSTRUCTIONS: CREATION OF THE HORSE
Jakob Jordaens (design)
(Antwerp 1593 – 1678 Antwerp)
Everard Leyniers (weaver)
(c. 1597–1680?)
Brussels
c. 1660
Wool, silk, sparing use of gold and silver threads; H 410 cm, W 521 cm
Inv. No. T XL/1

In a monumental back view, Neptune is seen as he (according to Vergil) creates the first horse, with a bold thrust of his trident in the ground. In one violent leap, the horse breaks out of the reeds. The god of the sea is standing on a floating shell, surrounded by dolphins and tritons. These heralds of the seas were mermen and are blowing on "buccina", or conch-horns. The oil painting from Jakob Jordaens used as a model is found in the Galleria Palatina in Palazzo Pitti in Florence.
                                            R. B.

THE PICTURE GALLERY

The Picture Gallery of the Kunsthistorische Museum owes its beginnings and its idiosyncrasies to a number of outstanding Habsburg collectors. Its character, that of a distinguished private collection belonging to a princely house, was already clearly defined by about 1800. It has remained such despite the drastic political changes which have occured since then, and in spite of the acquisitions made in the 19th and 20th centuries. To this day, the Vienna Picture Gallery has retained this character, both in content and layout, probably more so than any other European gallery formed under the patronage of a ruling dynasty.

Although greatly diversified and opulent, the collection as a whole is somewhat uneven; all periods are not equally represented. It has strengths unrivalled by any other Central European collection of paintings as well as very significant and even surprising gaps. Closely linked with the countries ruled by the Habsburg dynasty, the collection derives its specific character from the art of those regions. In terms of both quality and quantity the most important pictures come from Germany and the Southern Catholic Low Countries, from Northern Italy and from the Italian and Spanish centres of baroque painting (Bologna, Naples, Florence, Venice and Madrid). France, England, Holland (with very

notable exceptions) and the Italian City States of the later Middle Ages are hardly represented.

As "grands seigneurs", the Habsburgs loved "the perfect and the complete", and collected nothing that was still in a state of development. There are few works showing "early" phases of style, works still striving for inner perfection. There is nothing from the 13th and 14th centuries, almost nothing from the republican "Quattrocento", no "tormented souls", and few sketches. What the Habsburgs loved was mature style, even the "overmature": Venetian and Flemish art of the 16th and 17th centuries; the elaborate, perfect, even decorative piece. The emphasis on the portrait, which to a certain extent characterizes every princely gallery is especially evident in the Viennese painting collection. All the way through one might speak of a certain "top heaviness". Not the eccentric, but the judiciously contrived and the naturally elegant represent the Habsburg attitude. Indeed, the gallery itself was conceived as a decorative whole. The Habsburg taste was "pious" without ever actually falling into bigotry. All the great Habsburg collectors loved the Flemish primitives, Bruegel, the Venetians, Dürer and later on, Rubens and Van Dyck as well as the representative and decorative Italian Baroque. Whatever came after that was to fit into that

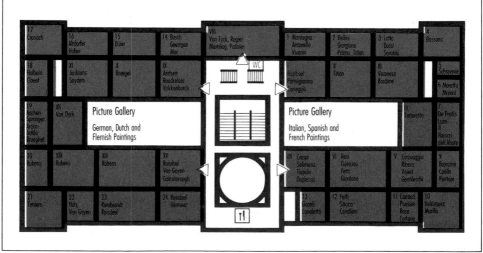

"family taste", one-sided though it may have been.

There are four major acquisition complexes associated with Habsburg princes and it is these that lend the Viennese collection its own character. Although most of Emperor Rudolph II's collection was scattered to the four winds, especially as a result of the Swedish plundering of Prague in 1648, important parts of it had found their way to Vienna after the Emperor's death in 1612 and thus remained in the possession of the Habsburgs.

These include the Bruegel collection that Rudolph had taken over from his brother, Ernst; the Dürer group, and the works of Rudolph's court painters in Prague. These paintings and a group of Italian Mannerist master works especially satisfied Rudolph's predilection for erotic subjects. Rudolph's collection must have been considered a heritage which imposed an obligation, and a theoretical starting point for all subsequent Habsburg patronage of the arts.

The actual founder of the Viennese painting collection as we know it today was Archduke Leopold Wilhelm (1614–1662), the brother of Emperor Ferdinand III. His purchases, made almost exclusively during his governorship in the Spanish Low Countries (1647–56) were facilitated by the collapse of the British monarchy and the confiscation and subsequent auction of some of the rich English aristocratic collections. Leopold Wilhelm's acquisitions had two objectives: one was to acquire a personal collection of some fourteen hundred paintings; the second, to replenish the stock of his Imperial brother, Ferdinand III, and replace losses from the Prague castle at the end of the Thirty Years War. Leopold Wilhelm's own collection, which centered on Northern Italian painting of the 16th century as well as Flemish works of the 15th to the 17th centuries, was transferred to Vienna in 1656.

The Archduke had his collection catalogued in 1659 in an extremely detailed inventory and displayed in the Stallburg, part of the Imperial palace in Vienna. In 1662, he left the collection to his nephew, Emperor Leopold I. In the 1720's, as a result of the overall reorganization of the Imperial art collections under Karl VI, many paintings from the Prague stock were brought to Vienna. There they were combined not only with Leopold Wilhelm's but also with those paintings acquired by Karl VI. They were all exhibited in the newly adapted Stallburg, in a baroque decorative system based on axial symmetry, analogous dimensions, and pyramidal arrangement. A painted inventory gives us a clear idea of what the Imperial gallery must have been like in the reign of Karl VI.

The new and outwardly splendid grouping must have seemed rigid and lacking in fresh possibilities soon after the installation. Supporting this supposition is the fact that Empress Maria Theresa and later on her son, Joseph II, began to build up the collection with large-scale Flemish and Italian altar paintings from dissolved churches and monasteries in the 1770's and 1780's. Gradually the scope of the Gallery shifted. Maria Theresa decided in 1776 to open the Imperial art collection to the public by putting it on display in the Upper Belvedere Palace in Vienna. This was completed in 1781. The paintings were ordered historically and the entire concept of presentation as well as the catalogue showed an enlightened approach to systematic representation and a clamouring for education.

The 19th century brought almost a complete stop to new acquisitions in the Imperial collection. During Napoleon's conquest of Vienna in 1809, sizeable losses to the Collection were incurred. Ironically enough, the 19th century saw the rise of the great national galleries of England and Germany. In the last quarter of the century, however, a new internal and external reorganization was made of all art in Habsburg possession and plans were drawn up for one central location to house it all. This new building, the Kunsthistorische Museum, was opened to the public in 1891.

The recently established new discipline, art history, led, in 1883, to the publication of the monumental Jahrbuch der Kunsthistorischen Sammlungen des Allerhöchsten Kaiserhauses (Yearbook of the Art History Collection of the Most High Imperial House). A new catalogue of the painting collection with 1,734 entries was edited at the same time.

Acquisition activity was first renewed in the present century; despite serious financial difficulties it was particularly successful under the direction of the great scholar Gustav Glück. However, instead of venturing into wholly new fields, the emphasis lay upon further consolidation of the traditional interests, namely in those artistic periods and areas from which the most significant paintings of the collection had originated.

W. P.

EMPEROR SIGISMUND
Antonio di Puccio Pisano, called Pisanello
(Pisa c. 1395–1455 Rome?)
c. 1433
Parchment/wood; H 64 cm, W 49 cm
Inv. No. 2630

The (for the 15th century) unusually large format of this painting and the grandly austere formation of the head and chest, along with a graphic world of finely worked detail in the face, hair and fur produce a stylistic blend of elements from both the Late Gothic and the just dawning Early Renaissance. This blend was characteristic of the work done in Northern Italy by Pisanello. Sigismund he painted during the latter's stay in Italy from 1431 to 1433. Sigismund (1386–1437) was the last ruling Luxembourg Emperor and lived in Prague. The likeness was a landmark along the artistic path to Renaissance portraiture in its monumental scale and its attempt to maintain a close hold on reality. M. H.

HIERONYMUS ALTAR ▷
Antonio Vivarini
(Murano c. 1415–c. 1486 Venice)
1441
Wood; H 235 cm, W 157 cm
Inv. No. 6813–18

Painted in 1441 for the Venetian church of S. Stefano, the altar follows the late mediaeval polyptych form of Italy. Each saint is confined in a separate frame and they are arranged in a series adjacent to and above each other. The use of the, for 1441 already antiquated, gold background corresponds to the two-dimensional treatment as a whole. Caught between Gothic and Renaissance, Vivarini grapples with three-dimensional corporeality. On the other hand, the conservatism of Vivarini's studio returns to the gothic form in the (almost entirely original) carved frame. M. H.

ST. SEBASTIAN
Andrea Mantegna
(Isola di Carturo 1430/31–1506 Mantua)
c. 1457/59
Wood; H 68 cm, W 30 cm
Inv. No. 301

Mantegna, himself the central figure in the Northern Italian Early Renaissance, set the tone for its
development both in practice and in theory.
Mantegna considered Greek and Roman art his
ideal in the realistic presentation of space and
figures. The Roman martyr, St. Sebastian, almost
resembles a stone sculpture here and we experience first-hand the rounded body contours
achieved in the distinct moulding of the figure.
The background stretches forever behind the
figure and is enriched with fragments of ancient
architecture. Mantegna's signature on the column
of the Triumphal Arch is done in Greek, one more
evidence of his intense knowledge of the Ancient
World.   M. H.

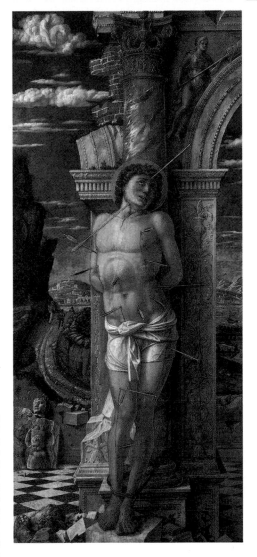

CHRIST'S BODY HELD BY ANGELS ▽
Cosmè Tura
(Ferrara c. 1430–1495 Ferrara)
c. 1460/70
Wood; H 44.5 cm, W 86 cm
Inv. No. 1867

Cosmè Tura's highly individual work shows traces
of Mantegna's preference for antiquity. (He and
Mantegna studied together under Squarcione in
Padua.) But even stronger is the influence of Late
Gothic painting from the North, known to Tura
from graphic reproductions and contact with
Rogier van der Weyden, who had found favour in
1449 in Ferrara. Conceived as a lunette in the
altar, the panel – a *pietà* with angels – captures
our attention by its overwhelming intensity, an
intensity that does not flinch from facial grimaces.
Cold metallic colour and agitated linear effects
heighten the excitement. The letters of the ornamental signature have been purposely rear-
ranged, reflecting refined society's partiality towards cryptic inscriptions.   M. H.

TABERNACLE DOOR
Gentile Bellini
(Venice c. 1431–1507 Venice)
1472/73
Wood; H 102.5 cm, W 37 cm
Inv. No. 9109

In 1472, the *Scuola della Carità,* one of Venice's six great brotherhoods, received as a bequest from Cardinal Bessarion a reliquary containing parts of the Cross. The reliquary was originally from the Cardinal's native land, Byzantium. In the same year Gentile Bellini (brother of the more famous Giovanni Bellini) was commissioned to paint the door of the reliquary's wooden tabernacle housing. This panel reproduces in minute detail and in its original size the reliquary behind it. (The reliquary itself is still where it always had been in the *Scuola,* now the Venice Academy of Fine Arts.) In addition, Bellini painted the Cardinal and two brothers, kneeling, as donors. They are greatly reduced in proportion due to spatial restrictions. M. H.

MADONNA WITH THE SAINTS NICHOLAS OF BARI, ANASTASIA, URSULA AND DOMINIC
Antonello da Messina
(Messina c. 1430–1497 Messina)
1475/76
Wood; H 115 cm, W 133 cm
Inv. No. 2574

It was at the Neapolitan court of the Anjou Kings that Antonello came in contact with Franco-Flemish art and the new technique of oil painting. Before that, oil painting was unknown in Italy, only tempera had been used. With this altarpiece for the Church of S. Cassiano in Venice, Antonello introduced oil technique to northern Italy. What is today just a fragment was originally a high, rectangular panel with eight saints painted full-length in a church interior on either side of the Madonna and grouped in a *Sacra Conversazione*. The new oil painting technique with its possibilities for light and shadow lifted the hardness out of the modelling of plastic forms. In addition, the subtly applied colours better rendered the image of material substance. The *Pala of S. Cassiano* was admired not only by Antonello's contemporaries; its lasting influence on Venetian painting reached from Bellini all the way to Titian.

M. H.

BAPTISM OF CHRIST
Pietro Vanucci, called Perugino
(Città della Pieve/Perugia c. 1450–1523 Fontignano/Perugia)
c. 1500
Wood; H 30 cm, W 23.3 cm
Inv. No. 139

For modern tastes Perugino's work seems to represent the epitome of a (now strangely foreign) cloying and "nazarene" piety. His characters all look alike; they seem genderless and move as isolated figures through translucent landscapes or airy architectural backdrops. Their tenderness is bridled and they show no great emotion. This criticism of Perugino could be especially applied to the last twenty years of his career. The spareness of these late compositions through overuse of rows and symmetry eventually becomes purely schematic. The small *Baptism,* however, is based on one of the most inspired compositional ideas of his best years, from the multi-figured frescoe in the Sistine Chapel in Rome (c. 1482). Around 1500 Raphael came to Perugino's studio. No matter how different the two painters were, Raphael surely was struck by Perugino's Umbrian landscapes, as may be surmised from a look at Raphael's *Madonna in the Meadow,* painted five years later. W. P.

MADONNA IN THE MEADOW ▷
Raphael
(Urbino 1483–1520 Rome)
1505 or 1506
Wood; H 113 cm, W 88.5 cm
Inv. No. 175

Within the short span we call the High Renaissance, Raphael's *Madonna in the Meadow* is the classic example of a geometric composition based on a triangle or, more exactly, a pyramid. Within this confinement, we find a spirited yet harmonious treatment of the figures. It is full of parallel and contrapunctal relationships. Beyond that, the wide green landscape, turning blue in the distance, and the softly curving hills combine to unite all the various elements into a balanced whole. The group of figures is at one and the same time ordered and lively, a new and unusual combination of contrasting elements, complete in itself without any extraneous factors. At the time of this painting, Raphael had been influenced greatly by Leonardo da Vinci (30 years his elder) and had avidly followed Leonardo's formal experiments with Madonna compositions. Above all, the organic linking of psychic and physical motifs, of action and reaction, create a suspended unity of both formal and programmatic elements. "Only the purest beauty of woman and child can evoke thoughts of the supernatural. After one and a half millennia, arts has finally reached the point where the figures alone, without any additions, seem eternal and divine" (Jacob Burckhardt). W. P.

THE SCENE OF CHRIST IN THE TEMPLE
Baccio della Porta, called Fra Bartolomeo
(Florence 1475–1517 Florence)
1516
Wood; H 156 cm, W 159 cm
Inv. No. 207

The Florentine Renaissance may be said to have reached a high point in the work of Fra Bartolomeo. His numerous altar paintings (all of them of monumental impact) show his attempt to blend the ideal of human dignity with the concept of divine order and perfection. In his compositions his logic is consistent, the structure is symmetric and tectonic. Festive solemnity and restraint connect the figures, all of them in majestic robes. In keeping with the deep, universal significance of what is happening, a strong feeling of timelessness pervades the moment as the Elder, Simon, recognises the child he has taken into his arms as the Saviour of the World and the herald of a new age. He turns to Mary and prophesises her future sufferings. *The Scene in the Temple* was painted for an altar in San Marco in Florence, the church of the Dominicans to whose order the painter himself belonged.

G. H.

MOURNING OF CHRIST
Andrea d'Agnolo, called Andrea del Sarto
(Florence 1486–1530 Florence)
c. 1519/20
Wood; H 99 cm, W 120 cm
Inv. No. 201

Andrea del Sarto superseded his roots in the Florentine High Renaissance, going beyond the Renaissance principle of tranquillity and balance and on to the expression of a more discarded sensibility. Of all his works, this *pietà* is one of the most forceful. With an almost aggressive use of pathos, he intensified the physical and psychical presence of the bereaved, bringing them in close contact with the observer. Although Sarto adhered to the demand of immaculate beauty and classical composition, his *Mourning* portrays impassioned grief and spiritual strife. The expressive quality of the drastic emotional display, the restriction of space and above all the bold reduction in the size of Christ's body – all these new initiatives suggest the approach of Mannerism.

G. H.

JUPITER AND IO ▷
Antonio Allegri, called Correggio
(Correggio 1489/94–1534 Correggio)
c. 1530
Canvas; H 163.5 cm, W 74 cm
Inv. No. 274

ABDUCTION OF GANYMEDE ▷
Antonio Allegri, called Corregio
c, 1530
Canvas; H 163.5 cm, W 74 cm
Inv. No. 276

Inspired by the ancient poetry of Ovid's Metamorphoses, Correggio chose Jupiter's

liaisons as his subject matter for paintings in the chambers of the ducal palace in Mantua. One of these is a picture of the beautiful nymph, Io, wondrously captivated in the embrace of the god. Barely visible, Jupiter's countenance and hand shimmer tenderly through the grey mist he created to still the fleeing footsteps of the shy nymph. The nuances of colour, the mild light and the bright shadows imperceptibly work together to mould and play about the supine, almost melting body of the nymph. Even the clouds seem tangible. In the figure of Io, in the sensitive sensuality of her surrender and rapture, Correggio has not only created a nude of unsurpassed charm and subtle eroticism, he has also brought out the deeper meaning of the myth – that of the bond of the living and non-living in nature – and created his own rare poetry.

The picture of the shepherd boy, Ganymede, abducted and taken to Olympus by the father of the gods (in the guise of an eagle), was intended for the same setting as the painting of the nymph, Io. Correggio makes skillful use of the narrow format, employing both movement and foreshortening with elan, giving the impression of weightless soaring through free, airy space. His art of sensual suggestion points toward the illusion painting of the baroque era, of which it may be said he was the forerunner.

G. H.

SELF-PORTRAIT IN A CONVEX MIRROR
Francesco Mazzola, called Parmigianino
(Parma 1503–1540 Casalmaggiore)
c. 1523/24
Segment of a wooden sphere; Diam. 24.4 cm
Inv. No. 286

As his name implies, the painter of this small round portrait came from the Emilian city of Parma. His portrait belongs to the most famous and unusual paintings of the then nascent Mannerism. At the age of 21 – "as lovely as an angel" (this, the description of his renowned features) – the young prodigy elegantly dressed in fur, used the distortions of a convex mirror to bring his hand boldly into the proper light – his hand that "knew how to paint and draw so excellently". Parmigianino's intelligent head rests in the centre of the curved reflection; proud of his brilliant idea, he directs his derogatory gaze Into the mirror. To make the game of confusion "Picture or Mirror" complete, he paints the whole, not on a flat panel, but on a convex piece of wood. With this master-piece he hoped to win the favour of Pope Clemens VII for further commissions.   G. H.

PORTRAIT OF A MAN
(Condottiere Malatesta Baglione?)
Francesco Mazzola, called Parmigianino
(Parma 1503–1540 Casalmaggiore)
c. 1525/30
Wood; H 117 cm, W 98 cm
Inv. No. 277

The portrait of this imposing man is one of early Mannerism's most impressive. The character with the small head seems threateningly close. This may be represent the famous Florentine military leader as suggested by two halberds flanking him – emblematic of his active field service. It is not so much the ideal of perfect balance or the harmony between the man and the space around him, as it is the tension and ambivalence that give the (supposed) Condottiere his fascinating grandeur. Parmigianino depicts the discrepancies and unpredictability of mankind within a brilliantly organized design, bringing together dissonant spatial impressions, as well as contrasts between sensual substance and brusque coldness, or physical presence and melancholy gloom.   G. H.

THE CONVERSION OF ST. PAUL
Francesco Mazzola, called Parmigianino
(Parma 1503–1540 Casalmaggiore)
c. 1527/28
Canvas; H 117.5 cm, W 128.5 cm
Inv. No. 2035

Parmigianino's religious works express ecstatic and visionary content with a heretofore unknown subtlety. In illustrating miraculous events, this innovative artist was more concerned with the suggestion of subjective-psychical feeling than with a true-to-life rendering of reality. Enigmatic light effects and arbitrary perspective, distortion to the point of deformity, all these heighten the expression of spiritual agitation in the face of heavenly enlightenment and inner conversion. With a bold change of proportions, Parmigianino makes the rearing horse into the main figure and focus of tension. Sudden brightness and God's voice from the clouds have made the horse shy and throw its rider, who from then on not only refuses to persecute the Christians; he becomes an ardent champion of their faith.   G. H.

245

BOW-CARVING AMOR ▽
Francesco Mazzola, called Parmigianino
(Parma 1503–1540 Casalmaggiore)
c. 1533/34
Wood; H 135 cm, W 65.3 cm
Inv. No. 275

This painting displays eroticism and frivolity more frankly and explicitly than any of Parmigianino's other works. Amor is portrayed life-sized and close enough to touch. His glance is provocative while innocently coquettish as he carves his new bow. He has it steadied on top of two tomes, over whose wisdom he seems to be gloating. Between his legs we see the antics of two putti, or cherubs. The little girl is pulling back from touching the love god for fear of his fire. The interplay between cryptic content and open provocation made this carefully calculated picture the very embodiment

of a collector's item for that period. Parmigianino had hit exactly upon the tastes of an elite public of connoisseurs.   G. H.

HOLY FAMILY WITH ANNA AND THE YOUNG JOHN THE BAPTIST
Agnolo di Cosimo, called Bronzino
(Monticelli/Florence 1503–1572 Florence)
c. 1545/46
Wood; H 124.5 cm, W 99.6 cm
Inv. No. 183

Bronzino gave his *Holy Family* (a masterpiece of Florentine Mannerism) the tactile illusion of stone sculpture, as if painting and sculpture were in competition with one another. No other painter carried the interplay between nature and artificiality to such an extreme. This was a much beloved artistic device at that time and Bronzino brought it to the point of near abstraction. He conformed in the utmost to the Florentine precept that the best of art was to be found in clear drawing and precisely defined form. The painting's unreal beauty arises out of the tension between tender emotion and marble-like coldness, familiar intimacy and strict symmetry, softly flowing movement and rigid formalisation. The panel is bathed in sallow light, creating a sinister atmosphere. Bronzino's sophisticated art reflected the taste of the aesthetically cultivated connoisseurs belonging to Florence's patrician society.
                                                                                    G. H.

YOUNG WOMAN AT HER TOILETTE
Giovanni Bellini
(Venice c. 1433–1516 Venice)
1515
Wood; H 62 cm, W 79 cm
Inv. No. 97

This late work of Bellini's is one of his few secular paintings and was done towards the end of his life. The choice of such an unusual motif (for him) – a nude – discloses the tastes of the coming generation of painters, especially those of his two great students, Giorgione and Titian. Bellini was mainly devoted to the – very Venetian – attempt at using the medium of colour to create an atmosphere of unity between interior and exterior spaces as well as between figure and landscape. Looking closely, we see all the colours of the main motive condensed in the carpet and repeated in the background landscape. M. H.

YOUNG WOMAN ("LAURA")
Giorgio da Castelfranco, called Giorgione
(Castelfranco Veneto c. 1477–1510 Venice)
1506
Canvas; H 41 cm, W 33.6 cm
Inv. No. 31

Giorgione's bust of a young, partially robed woman (possibly a courtesan) in a fur-collared cloak is one of his few works to be certified by an inscription and date on the back. The laurel branch *(lauro)* in the background may be a clue to the identity of the portrayed. It may also be a reference to the art of poetry. Laurel was often found in Venetian double portraits of courting or married couples, symbolizing (hoped-for) fidelity and chastity. It could be that "Laura" is a companion piece to a portrait of "Mr. Giacomo" who is named on the reverse side as the patron. This painting served as a prototype for later courtesan portraits in Venetian art (Titian, Palma, Bordone). The effect of Giorgione's typically shaded palette together with the flowing transitions between colours is heightened by the sensual appeal of the soft fur against the fair skin. C. Z.

THREE PHILOSOPHERS
Giorgio da Castelfranco, called Giorgione
(Castelfranco Veneto c. 1477–1510 Venice)
c. 1508/09
Canvas; H 123.8 cm, W 144.5 cm
Inv. No. 111

As little as is known about Giorgione's life, it is clear that his influence on the art of Venice in the early 16th century was decisive. Giorgione was born about 1477 in the province of Venetia and moved into the city at the turn of the century, like almost all the great painters there, to work and study with Giovanni Bellini. Giorgione died of the pest at the age of thirty.

From the few authenticated works of his (they may be counted on the fingers of both hands), the Viennese Collection possesses two: the portrait "Laura" and the Three Philosophers. Much speculating has been done about the actual meaning of the Three Philosophers. Whether or not it is about three stages of man's life, or three different philosophical (or mathematical) schools, or the three Magi remains unexplained. The reason for this enigma ist that the theme was made to order for an exclusive patron and only known to him, his friends and the painter. Even the original title, certified in 1525, Three Philosophers in a Landscape . . . with That Wonderfully Painted Rock, indicates the new and unusual in Giorgione's work. For the first time, landscape attains the same importance as the human figure. Unprecedented was also the way his painting methods were concentrated on colour effect. Giorgione created an illusion of airiness and atmosphere in his landscapes by using warm, delicately shaded colours over relatively large areas and by letting one hue flow into another similar one. Instead of the geometrically constructed central perspective, he employed the visual experience of an aerial perspective and its sfumato, suggesting the spatial depths by colours and contours that melt into the distance. The novelty and intensity of Giorgione's expressive media – colour, light and atmosphere – fascinated his Venetian contemporaries and "Giorgionism" made itself felt in the art of his successors long after his death.   M. H.

NYMPHS BATHING
Jacopo Negretti, called Palma Vecchio
(Serina/Bergamo c. 1480–1528 Venice)
c. 1525
Canvas/wood; H 77.5 cm, W 124 cm
Inv. No. 6803

With *Nymphs Bathing*, Palma (while ostensibly painting mythological figures) picked up on an appealing theme that had been popular in Venetian painting ever since Giorgione. He used female nudes in front of the backdrop of landscape scenery to evoke a sense of the wondrous unity of man and nature. The many poses of the nymphs he borrowed from ancient Greek and Roman sculpture and from his Mannerist contemporaries (like Rosso Fiorentino and Giulio Romano) whose work he knew from etchings that had been passed around. From his home of

Bergamo, Palma took the light pastel shades and turned them to advantage against the more brownish palette of Venice.

M. H.

MARY WITH THE CHILD AND SAINTS ▽
Jacopo Negretti, called Palma Vecchio
(Serina/Bergamo c. 1480–1528 Venice)
c. 1520/25
Wood; H 133 cm, W 198 cm
Inv. No. 60

Palma, documented as having been in Venice after 1510, was close to the circle of Giovanni Bellini and Titian. His favorite themes, other than

half-length female figures, were above all settings of *Sacra Conversazione*, as seen in this devotional painting. Palma seizes upon one of Bellini's ideas when he sets the group of saints around the Madonna within a landscape instead of within a church. His own innovation came with presenting the characters in full size and in relaxed "human-like" poses, so that what had always been a strict and hierarchically ordained scene achieved an intimate, almost secular quality.

M. H.

VIOLANTE
Titian
(Pieve di Cadore c. 1488–1576 Venice)
c. 1515/18
Wood; H 64.5 cm, W 50.8 cm
Inv. No. 65

Titian's portrait of *Violante* is definitely one of the so-called *Bella*-Portraits, a speciality of Venetian painters in the first half of the 16th century. The idea behind the courtesan portrait was the idealized presentation of a fashionable beauty. She is brought right up before the eyes of the observer. To capture the clear sparkling splendour of this woman, Titian chose a colour scheme of yellow, blue and pink, a scheme that is echoed, although subtly condensed, in the pansy *(viola)* of her decolleté. At the same time he used refined brushwork, here finely drawn and there broadly flourishing, to reproduce the surface effects of the hair, skin and fabric. The combination of a generalised ideal of beauty with this almost physical tangibility is responsible for the enormous appeal of the painting. The portrait bore earlier the appropriate name of *la bella gatta* (the beautiful cat). M. H.

MADONNA OF THE CHERRIES
Titian
(Pieve di Cadore c. 1488–1576 Venice)
c. 1516/18
Wood; H 81 cm, W 99.5 cm
Inv. No. 118

In the *Madonna of the Cherries*, Titian uses the same triangular motif as in the *Gypsy Madonna* (painted only a few years before). In so doing, he encloses the Madonna, the Infant Jesus and the young John the Baptist in one large, self-contained form. In addition, he ventures to make the composition more dynamic; the figures relate to each other actively, through motion and visual contact, thereby creating additional room in which to move. (The two holy fathers, Joseph and Zacharias, were added later, after the painting had been completed, possibly at the patron's wish.

Their addition in no way however affects the compact figure grouping in the centre.) M. H.

BRAVO
Titian
(Pieve di Cadore c. 1488–1576 Venice)
c. 1520
Canvas; H 77 cm, W 66.5 cm
Inv. No. 64

This celebrated painting captures our immediate interest in two ways: first, the dark drama of the assault scene *(Bravo* was the name of a hired assassin) and secondly, the whole nebulous situation, whose beginning and end remain shrouded in mystery. Within the closest of quarters, the first instant of attack becomes condensed into a counterrotating play of arms and heads. Out of this confusion of gestures, colour contrasts elucidate the different roles of the protagonists: aggressive red and black for the attacker; soft blue and green for the surprised youth. Titian's authorship is clear not only in the scene's pointed tension, but also in the subtle distinctions within his paint. Thus, the figure of *Bravo* has been executed vigorously and pastose with meaningful light effects. His domination of the foreground contrasts strongly with the fine and lustrous painting of the youth, who is imbued with a Giorgione-like *sfumato*. M. H.

◁ **GYPSY MADONNA**
Titian
(Pieve di Cadore c. 1488–1576 Venice)
c. 1510
Wood; H 65.8 cm, W 83.5 cm
Inv. No. 95

The devotional picture of the *Gypsy Madonna* – so named because of her unusually dark appearance – is one of Titian's earliest works. The influence of the structural principles of his teacher, Bellini, and his colleague, Giorgione, is reflected in the harmonious autonomy of the composition's construction: the wellbalanced triangular form of the two figures, the choice of complementary colour schemes (each colour enhancing the other) and the dream-like atmosphere between the figures and the landscape on the one hand and the foreground and the background on the other. The equally generous but subtle brushwork immediately set Titian apart from his contemporaries. He moulded the fullness and volume of his subjects with the finest nuances and shadings of colour, giving them a visually fascinating surface beauty.

M. H.

PORTRAIT OF A YOUTH AGAINST A WHITE CURTAIN
Lorenzo Lotto
(Venice 1480–1556 Loreto)
c. 1508
Wood; H 42.3 cm, W 35.5 cm
Inv. No. 214

Lotto's early paintings show the influence of his teacher, Bellini, in the strict construction and the well-emphasized use of light. The extreme precision of Lotto's surface realism shows the inspiration he got from Northern painters, above all Dürer, who had been in Venice at the turn of the century. Unlike the idealized portraits of the High Renaissance, Lotto's portraits strive for exact visual rendering, of even psychical moments. In order to capture the individual character, the inner essence of the portrayed, Lotto employed an encoded language, whose meaning, now lost to us, was once only known to the patron who had commissioned the painting. The small oil lamp glimpsed through a gap in the curtain is one of these symbolic comments.   M. H.

PORTRAIT OF A GOLDSMITH IN THREE VIEWS ▽
Lorenzo Lotto
(Venice 1480–1556 Loreto)
c. 1525/35
Canvas; H 52 cm, W 79 cm
Inv. No. 92

As unusual at first glance as this portrait with three heads may be, its explanation is simple enough. It was an attempt at providing a view of the sitter from all sides within the medium of painting. The moving force behind the painting goes back to the 16th century argument between painters and sculptors, the *paragone* as to who could better present three-dimensionality. Lotto solved the problem with three different simultaneous views of one and the same person. Since the man is holding a box of rings, it seems appropriate to assume that he was Lotto's close friend, the goldsmith Bartolomeo Carpan of Treviso. Carpan's own artistic nature would have been intrigued by the combination of theory and practice in this clever concept.   M. H.

MARY WITH CHILD AND THE SAINTS CATHERINE AND JAMES THE ELDER
Lorenzo Lotto
(Venice 1480–1556 Loreto)
c. 1527/1533
Canvas; H 113.5 cm, W 152 cm
Inv. No. 101

Lotto, of the same generation as Giorgione and Titian like them had his beginnings within the group around Bellini in Venice. A loner, personally as well as artistically, he remained outside the official Venetian art world, moving constantly between Venice (his home), Treviso and Bergamo as well as the marks (Ancona, Recanati and Loreto), taking inspiration from all these different art scenes. His work showed little of the classicism and idealism of the High Renaissance. He tended more towards the strange and unusual, finding compact and highly individual solutions within his own quite subjectively-coloured views. In this devotional picture, Lotto returned to the

Sacra Conversazione, a favourite motif of Venetian painting ever since Antonello's *Pala di S. Cassiano.* (The *Sacra Conversazione* presents an intimate group of saints gathered around the Madonna). Lotto breaks here (as also in his mature portraits) with the traditional hierarchical ordering of the figures. Partially out of his own preference for relaxed, true-to-life bearing in his characters, Lotto has Mary blending in with the other figures and the landscape, instead of being enthroned in a prominent position. She is restrained by her gesture, glance and pose. The compact relationship of the figures and nature is mysteriously enlivened by the constant changes between light and dark. The whole atmosphere becomes very lyric, bringing the human and the heavenly, as well as inner contemplation and external agitation together in one suggestive whole. Lotto's colouring, a surprising departure from the Venetian school, shows the influence of the colour school of Bergamo where he lived for ten years. M. H.

GIRL IN A FUR
Titian
(Pieve di Cadore c. 1488–1576 Venice)
c. 1535
Canvas; H 95 cm, W 63 cm
Inv. No. 89

The lovely young woman captured here by Titian, with her fur cloak coquettishly in disarray, was painted by him several times, both nude and clothed, but always for the Duke of Urbino. The tendency of the mature Titian to monumentalize, even within such an intimate motif, led him into large-format work. Face, bust and body were elevated beyond reality. Far removed from his multi-coloured earlier paintings, Titian here limits his colouring to only a few related hues. Not only that, he joins the material diversity of the surfaces (hair, fur, jewels) with the staggered light and dark zones and creates an artistic unit out of them by the use of all-brown tones.   M. H.

BENEDETTO VARCHI
Titian
(Pieve di Cadore c. 1488–1576 Venice)
c. 1540
Canvas; H 117 cm, W 91 cm
Inv. No. 91

With his sparing and yet impressive use of stately gestures and outer show, Titian spoke directly to the vaunted self-consistency of the 16th century aristocracy. The aura of formal restraint and self-assured dignity reflected in the ambience and pose in the portrait of *Benedetto Varchi* served as Titian's general framework for revealing individual features. In this particular case, Varchi's both pensive and alert expression discloses his intellectual prowess. Benedetto Varchi (1503–1567), although essentially scholarly and art-minded, spent fifteen years in political exile in, among other places, Venice. He had been forced to leave Florence in the wake of tensions during the Medici rise to power.   M. H.

ECCE HOMO
Titian
(Pieve di Cadore c. 1488–1576 Venice)
1543
Canvas; H 242 cm, W 361 cm
Inv. No. 73

During the 1640's, the compositional principles of Mannerism can be found in Titian's work. The painting, *"Ecce Homo"* (dated 1643) comes from this brief period. Influenced by Michelangelo and his circle in Florence and Rome, Titian assumes their predilection for asymmetric composition. The treatment advances rapidly from lower right to upper left and the main figure of Christ is found, amazingly enough, not in the centre as was customary, but at the outermost edge of the canvas. Additional Mannerist devices may be seen here in the vigorous movement motifs and the uneven use of colour, sometimes dull and then again aggressive. The painting was con-

ceived for the city palace (on the Grand Canal) of the Flemish businessman, Giovanni d'Anna (actually, van Haanen). This explains the theme of the picture, a theme rarely found in Italy but highly regarded in the North. Depicted is the dramatic and portentous scene (John 19:4–16) in which Pontius Pilate, the Roman procurator of Jerusalem, leads Christ, after his questioning and scourging, before the masses and says "Ecce homo!" (Behold the man!) and offers his release. The masses however demand his crucifixion. Within the pictorial setting of the ancient Roman Empire, Titian mixes time periods together by introducing the current Habsburg Imperial House into the scene. (He had been their titled court painter since 1533.) The double eagle on the shield and next to it the addition to the signature of *eques ces(aris)* – imperial knight – these were homage paid by Titian to his Habsburg sovereigns.

M. H.

ELECTOR JOHN FREDERICK OF SAXONY
Titian
(Pieve di Cadore c. 1488–1576 Venice)
1550/51
Canvas; H 103.5 cm, W 83 cm
Inv. No. 100

On the occasion of his victory over the protestants at Muehlberg in 1547, Emperor Charles V had not only himself and members of his court painted but also his most prominent opponent, Elector John Frederick of Saxony (1503–1554). For five years after his defeat, the Elector was kept in custody in Augsburg (where the portrait was also painted). Titian was then at the peak of his work in portraiture. His keen psychological insight and his artistic use of concentration and condensation eliminating any embellishing detail focussed on the idiosyncratic bearing and the special cast of the Elector's features. His almost monstrous corporeality, his wary, brooding stillness and his remote pride seem transcendent of time but also unbelievably present.   M. H.

JACOPO STRADA
Titian
(Pieve di Cadore c. 1488–1576 Venice)
1567/68
Canvas; H 125 cm, W 95 cm
Inv. No. 81

Jacopo Strada (Mantua 1515–1588 Vienna) was a true "Renaissance Man" – painter, architect, goldsmith, inventor (of machines), numismatist, linguist, art collector and dealer. Above all, he was the Imperial *antiquarius* in service to the Habsburgs. At the peak of his ambitious career he let himself be painted by none other than the portrait-ist of Kings and Popes – Titian – with whom he had had business dealings. Titian captured the impressive diversity and animation of Strada in an extremely lively "career portrait", showing Strada "in action". The painting bears all the trademarks of Titian's later style of painting in which exceed-ingly broad, pastose brush strokes are used to create more a sense of light and dark than of volume and plasticity.   M. H.

NYMPH AND SHEPHERD ▷
Titian
(Pieve di Cadore c. 1488–1576 Venice)
c. 1570/75
Canvas; H 149.6 cm, W 187 cm
Inv. No. 1825
(Text see right side, on the top)

Nymph and Shepherd belongs to the few works of Titian's last period. In spite of its pompous format this last of his "poesies" or "fables", as he called them, was not commissioned. Titian painted it for himself without having to bow to anyone else's tastes. It is unclear whether he was following a particular mythological theme, like perhaps Daphnis and Chloe. More important to him than any specific narrative was a general concept of figures bound together in a mysterious and suggestive landscape – a concept that he had explored in some of his early works, while still under Giorgione's influence. After sixty years, however, with all the complex painting experience that a long life in art brings, Titian's artistic transposition took on another aspect: Now all that mattered to him was the outward appearance of content expressed through colour. He abandoned the clear line, the boldly outlined and plastically moulded form. He loosened up the smoothly closed picture surface so that only a few patches of light penetrate the dark glittering of the air. He was the first to make this device palpable. Thus, from both the raw and the subtle blending of his excessively broad brushstrokes (it is said he even used his fingers), a vision slowly emerges, turning the entire canvas into a solely visual impression. It is a splendid vision of man and nature merging into a cosmic unity. The enormous spectrum of artistic possibilities that Titian had at his command in the use of colour and brushwork was pithily described by Titian's contemporary, Vasari, the Florentine painter and art critic. Although he was not charitably inclined towards Titian, he wrote of his work that "the early (pictures) have been executed with delicacy and great care so that they may be seen at close quarters or from afar; the last ones are coarse and spotty, thrown on the canvas so that only from a distance do they seem complete". The wisdom of age kept Titian from turning his last works into mere images of reality. They approach reality, but they go beyond it to become purely visual sensations.

M. H.

ALLEGORY
Paris Bordone
(Treviso 1500–1571 Venice)
c. 1560
Canvas; H 111.5 cm, W 174.5 cm
Inv. No. 120

The painting of a pair of lovers dressed as Mars and Venus – crowned by a spirit with myrtle wreaths and accompanied by Cupid, the god of love – belongs to a series of love or wedding allegories that Bordone painted as variations on this inexhaustible theme. A student of Titian, Bordone turned in his mature period to the colour and form preferences of middle Italian Mannerism. This is evident in the garish, cool and somehow artificial colouring, the monumental figures and the unstable structure of the composition. Bordone's Venetian heritage shows through as well, in the free and open brushwork and an almost blotchy application of colour.   M. H.

HOLY FAMILY WITH ST. CATHERINE AND THE YOUNG JOHN THE BAPTIST
Andrea Meldolla, called Schiavone
(Skradin 1510/15–1563 Venice)
c. 1552
Canvas; H 95 cm, W 118 cm
Inv. No. 325

This presentation of a *Sacra Conversazione* (a gathering of saints) is firmly entrenched in Venetian tastes and takes place in a landscape full of atmospheric effects. The rich nuances of the colouring and the boldly generous brushstrokes – concerned more with pictorial appearances than with precisely drawn form – show Schiavone (originally from Dalmatia) strongly anchored in the Venetian tradition. Like most of his mid-century Venetian contemporaries, Schiavone borrowed heavily from Roman and Florentine Mannerism. This is especially evident in the soft, flexible Parmigianino-like elegance of the figures. Middle Italian sense of form joins up with the painting school of Venice to become an appealing variation on the Mannerist movement.

M. H.

BELSHAZZAR'S FEAST
Tintoretto
(Venice 1518–1594 Venice)
c. 1543/44
Wood; H 29 cm, W 156 cm
Inv. No. 3829

This depiction of the King's feast where the ruin of the King of Babylon is being prophesied by the handwriting on the wall (with the words *mene, mene, tekel and upharsin) is one of six wooden panels, all the same size, with scenes from the Old Testament. Their unusual format indicates their use on furniture. Just such cassoni deco-*

LORENZO SORANZO
Tintoretto
(Venice 1518–1594 Venice)
1553
Canvas; H 116 cm, W 100 cm
Inv. No. 308

Some of Tintoretto's most impressive portraits are far removed from the idealized and formal concepts of the High Renaissance. Tintoretto was concerned, from a moral and psychological standpoint, with working out the individual and subjective features of the portrayed, free of any social context. For that reason, the portrait of *Lorenzo Soranzo,* a Venetian patrician and member of the Council, shows no evidence of rank or position. Outside of the date on the balustrade, only his age – 35 – and his initials are given. The pointedly "unofficial" slackness of his pose, the almost mystical illumination of the face and hands out of impenetrable darkness, the clearly expressed spirituality – all these were designed to show Soranzo, the man, removed from the usual social trappings. M. H.

SEBASTIANO VENIER
Tintoretto
(Venice 1518–1594 Venice)
c. 1571/72
Canvas; H 104.5 cm, W 83.5 cm
Inv. No. 32

In officially commissioned portraits as painter to the Venetian Republic, Tintoretto was expected to emphasize the elements of pomp and circumstance. Sebastiano Venier (1468–1578), descendant of one of the old patrician families of Venice, was Captain-General of the Venetian fleet at the naval battle of Lepanto in 1571. This portrait was commissioned on the decisive victory of the allied fleets of Spain, Venice and the Holy See over Turkish forces. Venier, in the traditional pose of an admiral, in armour, baton in hand, is shown in front of the battle scene. M. H.

rated the fronts of chests, cabinets or organ balustrades in the 15th and 16th centuries. Occasionally they were set into wooden wall paneling. The flowing, sketch-like manner of painting, that, almost like a watercolour, lets the lighter background show through, was often used by furniture painters because it could be produced quickly. In spite of their seemingly improvised nature, Tintoretto's panels, even the earliest, show an attempt at carefully constructed composition. The panels are full of richly moving figures populating rapidly receding architectural backgrounds and landscapes.

M. H.

ST. JEROME
Tintoretto
(Venice 1518–1594 Venice)
c. 1571/75
Canvas; H 143.5 cm, W 103 cm
Inv. No. 46

Tintoretto's constantly new modifications in form, colour and perspective come together in his late work, *St. Jerome,* in a violent distortion of the human figure. The figure is taken almost to the farthest extremes of anatomical possibility. The Saint is presented life-sized at the foremost edge of the picture, but terribly bent as if his monumental body cannot find enough space. The vivid prominence of the penitent church father is also emphasized by the colouring. The sallow but strongly modelling light of the Saint contrasts with the dark landscape only hinted at with a few brushstrokes. St. Jerome is surrounded by his attributes: the biblical translation, the cardinal's hat and the tame lion.   M. H.

THE FLAGELLATION OF CHRIST ▷
Tintoretto
(Venice 1518–1594 Venice)
c. 1585/90
Canvas; H 118.3 cm, W 106 cm
Inv. No. 6451

In the last years of his life, Tintoretto concentrated on painting nocturnal pieces full of mystic expression. Colouring, corporeality and spaciousness undergo a reduction almost to the point of negation. Out of the darkness, the figures become illuminated almost like spirits, only hinted at with a few generous brushstrokes of spectral, flickering light – more vision than reality. This passion scene of the scourging of Christ assumes a mystically expressive quality that the aging Tintoretto must have seen as the only possible way to communicate the mysteries of faith.   M. H.

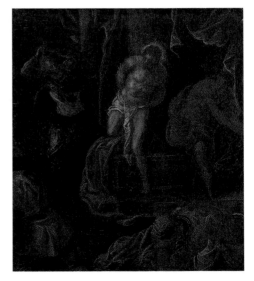

SUSANNA AND THE ELDERS
Tintoretto
(Venice 1518–1594 Venice)
c. 1555/56
Canvas; H 146.6 cm, W 193.6 cm
Inv. No. 1530

Tintoretto's *Susanna and the Elders* can be considered as one of the major works of Venetian Mannerism, a specific variant in the synthesis between the Roman-Florentine sense of form and the Venetian painting tradition. Tintoretto, as its founder and leading exponent, employed foremost a masterfully vigorous expansion of body, space, motion and light to awaken admiration, wonder and astonishment in his observer. Mannerist devices like exaggeration, distortion and the play of opposites give as common a subject as *Susanna and the Elders* a new note of irritating challenge and all the threatening feeling of a trap door. These actually fit the Old Testament story well (Daniel 13) of how Susanna is surprised at her bath by two intruders in her bower. When she spurns them, the men take revenge and accuse her wrongfully to her husband. Only the judgement of the wise prophet Daniel frees Susanna from the death sentence incurred on grounds of adultery. The tension inherent in the moment of the bath scene is depicted and concentrated in the sharp contrasts: between light and dark, extreme nearness and cavernous distance (Venice in the upper left-hand corner!), dazzling feminine beauty and caricatured male ugliness, supposed safety and approaching peril. These formal violations and antitheses do not come crudely undisguised to the light of day. Instead, they are transformed by the magic of Venetian painting with its subtle greenish-brownish hues and its emphasis on landscape and atmospheric elements to a moment held at bay, like the calm before the storm. Only a second glance at all the carefully laid out narrative and symbolic details discloses the unexpected and stunning connection between beauty and terror, a connection out of which this painting derives its many-faceted expressiveness.   M. H.

THE ANOINTMENT OF DAVID
Veronese
(Verona 1528–1588 Venice)
c. 1555
Canvas; H 173 cm, W 364 cm
Inv. No. 40

Veronese's mastery of broadly conceived pageantry within the subject matter of his paintings can best be appreciated in his large-format works. In this Old Testament scene, the prophet, Samuel, acting on God's command, anoints the shepherd boy, David, as the future King of Israel. In Veronese's rich compositions, there are never isolated main figures grouped around a central theme; rather, a group of individuals stretches almost like a relief across the entire surface of the picture, connected to each other by movements and colours. Framing the action like curtains on either side, are landscape scenes of antique ruins as well as buildings in the style of Veronese's contemporary, Palladio. M. H.

THE RAISING OF THE YOUTH OF NAIN
Veronese
(Verona 1528–1588 Venice)
1565/70
Canvas; H 102 cm, W 136 cm
Inv. No. 52

In Veronese's mature period, his paintings assume a radiant brightness of colouring that had been unknown in Venice until then. Out of this productive period comes the scene of Christ's raising the youth from the dead. The shimmering jewel-like colours of the garments contrast with each other and glow before the cool backdrop of the sky and architecture, giving the treatment a worldly and festive effect. The moment of surprise, done in the best Mannerist fashion, comes when Veronese moves the main character (the youth) into the lower left corner of the painting. Only half of him is visible. The grateful mother, on the other hand, is right in the middle of the composition. With the clever use of a scenic excerpt, where figures and buildings are arbitrarily cut off, Veronese created the illusion that the observer is actually witnessing the event. M. H.

JUDITH WITH THE HEAD OF HOLOFERNES
Veronese
(Verona 1528–1588 Venice)
c. 1583/85
Canvas; H 111 cm, W 100.5 cm
Inv. No. 34

Even the gloomy story of *Judith* with the decapitated head of Holofernes becomes, in Veronese's treatment, a decorative and festive event. The radiant colouring and the worldly beauty of the heroine allow the gruesome deed to be overlooked although it is actually present. Only at second glance does the head of Holofernes appear, like a foreign body in Judith's hands. It belongs more to the dark sphere of the surroundings than to her bright figure. Exactly this contrast – between light and dark, beauty and terror – marks the fascination of Mannerism in this painting. The Old Testament relates how Judith, to save the Jewish people from destruction at the hands of the Assyrians, wins the trust of their general, Holofernes, and beheads him in his sleep. With this trophy, she brings the enemy to retreat. M. H.

LUCRETIA
Veronese
(Verona 1528–1588 Venice)
c. 1580/83
Canvas; H 109 cm; W 90.5 cm
Inv. No. 1561

This picture of the Roman heroine, *Lucretia,* is a counterpart to the biblical *Judith* in that both deeds are among those always cited as great examples of feminine heroism. Lucretia killed herself because she had been raped by the King's son, Tarquinius. Before that, however, she swore revenge, so that the guilty one would pay with his life, his father lose the throne and the Roman republic be called up. Veronese indicates the moment of suicide in a stage-like setting. Through the arrangement of figure and drapery we have a fascinating presentation of the heroine. Only the shadows of grief on her face and the dagger, which looks like a piece of jewellery, give away what has just happened. The strange and garish but dull colouring – the purple of the blood runs like a leit-motiv throughout – gives the basically morbid tone of the scene a refined camouflage. M. H.

ADORATION OF THE MAGI
Veronese
(Verona 1528–1588)
c. 1580
Canvas; H 117 cm, W 174 cm
Inv. No. 1515

In Veronese's late period there is a loosening of his earlier broad, stage-like compositions. Where formerly the action took place in a complicated and many faceted "frieze", this late version of the *Adoration of the Magi* consists of only a few figures, whose confined movements orient us to the main character (the Infant Jesus) in the center of the painting. Characteristic for Veronese's late style is also the unfolding of a dusky atmosphere. Coming from the landscape in the background, it seems to devour the power of light in the colours and give a melancholy tinge to the festive encounter of the three Magi with the Divine Child.

M. H.

HERCULES, DEIANEIRA AND NESSUS
Veronese
(Verona 1528–1588 Venice)
c. 1586
Canvas; H 68 cm, W 53 cm
Inv. No. 1525

Although Veronese was truly an "urban" painter, he became more and more concerned in his later years with a concept that had been a tradition in Venice ever since Giorgione: the merging of figure and landscape into a poetic and atmospheric idyll. In this small picture (a companion piece to *Venus and Adonis*), the abduction of Hercules' wife, Deianeira, by the centaur Nessus and the subsequent chase is actually secondary. The story is more a point of departure, an excuse to explore the tie between man and the mysterious realm of nature. Veronese's late style may be clearly seen in the darker "autumnal" colours (compared to earlier) and the overall loose, open brushstrokes lying over the picture like a fine mesh.

M. H.

HAGAR AND ISHMAEL IN THE DESERT
Veronese
(Verona 1528–1588 Venice)
c. 1585
Canvas; H 140 cm, W 282 cm
Inv. No. 3673

Out of a series of originally ten and now only seven frieze-like paintings of scenes from the Old and New Testaments (works of Veronese's late period), *Hagar and Ishmael* is one of the most impressive. Veronese's colouring is built on a sonorous chord of orange and green. The stage-like gesture language between the figures, and the landscape full of atmospheric effects, convey a great deal of moving expressiveness within this scene of desperation and deliverance. Described is the Old Testament episode where Abraham's secondary wife, Hagar, and their son, Ishmael, are in flight because of the jealousy of Abraham's wife, Sarah. As they are about to die of thirst, a messenger of God sends them a spring of water, turning the spot where they are into a fertile oasis for them to live in. M. H.

ADORATION OF THE MAGI
Jacopo da Ponte, called Jacopo Bassano
(Bassano c. 1515–1592 Bassano)
c. 1560/65
Canvas; H 92.3 cm, W 117.5 cm
Inv. No. 361

Although Jacopo Bassano, after studies in Venice, went back home to take over the family workshop in the provincial town of Bassano, he managed to keep abreast of all the latest trends in the art world. The *Adoration of the Magi,* a work from his mature period, bears all the traits of his particular variant of Mannerism. The figures, nearly abstract elements in an ever-changing play of diagonal lines, the refined contiguity of bold simplification and realistic detail drawing, the use of clashing, cold and acid colours – all these lend the familiar scene a willfully original tone, a tone that exactly expressed the Mannerist propensity for the unusual and the striking. M. H.

AUTUMN
Francesco da Ponte, called Francesco Bassano
(Bassano 1549–1592 Venice)
c. 1576
Canvas; H 75.5 cm, W 109 cm
Inv. No. 4304

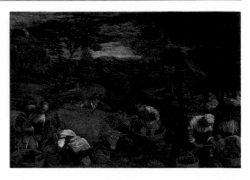

It is true that most of Francesco's paintings can be traced back to the ideas of his father, Jacopo. Nevertheless, Francesco was decisively influential in the development of the Bassano workshop style because he set almost every theme, whether religious, mythological or allegorical, in a rustically contemporary setting and decor. In the three pictures of *Spring, Summer* and *Autumn* – originally belonging to a larger seasonal series – Francesco illustrated the time of year by showing the corresponding country activity for that season. He displays an attention to detail (see the figures and equipment in the foreground) that shows what an acute observer of everyday life he was.

To the vast, darkly romantic background landscape, he adds, in decidedly sketchy form, scenes from the Old Testament (Expulsion from Paradise, Abraham sacrificing Isaac, and Moses receiving the Ten Commandments). These ephemeral episodes make a remarkable contrast to the robust reality of the farm scene.   M. H.

JUPITER AND MERCURY
Dosso Dossi
(Ferrara 1489–1542 Ferrara)
1529
Canvas; H 112 cm, W 150 cm
Inv. No. 9110

Since Ferrara bordered on two different painting traditions, Dosso was as influenced by the magic of Venetian colouring and atmosphere as he was by the impressions left by Raphael, Michelangelo and antiquity. This picture of Jupiter, the supreme god, seated on clouds and painting butterflies while Mercury protects him from being disturbed

is based on antique mythology. Beyond this basic content, the painting shows the pleasure that humanist artists and their patrons had in ingenious encodings. For instance, Jupiter at the canvas is portrayed as an artist, in which case the painting could be considered an allegory of art. Not only that, Dosso could have painted himself as the artist. This theory gains substance if the figures are seen as representing the planets, Jupiter and Mercury, and the constellation of the Virgin; they – together with the year of Dosso's birth and the year the painting was completed (1529) – could add up to an astrological self-portrait of Dosso.   M. H.

ST. JUSTINA, VENERATED BY A PATRON
Alessandro Bonvicino, called Moretto da Brescia
(Brescia c. 1498–1554 Brescia)
c. 1530
Canvas; H 200 cm, W 139 cm
Inv. No. 61

Moretto created, with this painting, one of the major works of the Northern Italian High Renaissance. Seldom has the union between a religious subject and the figure of a patron been brought to such a self-contained yet intimate whole. The feeling of a pastoral love scene emanates from what is essentially a devotional picture. Portrayed is St. Justina, in all of Northern Italy revered as the patron saint of Padua, with her attributes, the martyr's palm and the unicorn. Moretto merges the legendary figure of a sorcerer who was converted by Justina, into the donor of the painting. He gazes up at the Saint with an enraptured reverence that seems to have affected even the unicorn. This dream-like, elegiac mood binds the figures closely together and can be traced back to the influence of Venetian "Georgionism". In no way, however, does Moretto deny his awareness of the Roman High Renaissance. The influence of Raphael's monumental expression of form is clearly evident in the statuesque, suspended form of the beautiful saint.   M. H.

ADORATION OF THE MAGI
Francesco da Ponte, called Francesco Bassano
(Bassano 1549–1592 Venice)
c. 1588/90
Canvas; H 304 cm, W 178 cm
Inv. No. 5801

Since certain paintings of Jacopo Bassano, like the *Adoration of the Magi,* enjoyed great popularity, they were taken into the thematic repertoire of his workshop and used again and again by him and his sons with few or many alternations. This altar painting from Francesco, the eldest son of Jacopo, is one of these "free" repetitions. All that Francesco retained from the father's painting were the types of figures and their characteristic diagonal bearing. These were set into a contemporary and rustic setting. Brimming over with everyday accoutrements seen in great realism, the biblical scene gets a stamp of popular matter-of-factness typical of the Bassano workshop of the late 16th century, and anticipating the baroque taste for "genre-painting".   M. H.

PORTRAIT OF A YOUNG LADY
Alessandro Bonvicino, called Moretto da Brescia
(Brescia around 1498–1554 Brescia)
c. 1540
Canvas; H 101 cm, W 82 cm
Inv. No. 1914

Moretto found himself, like most northern Italian painters, caught between two artistic spheres, both of which contributed to his own development of an innovative and appealing portrait style. The basis of his female portraits, notable for their tranquil display of opulent "fashionable" beauty, is found on the one hand in the Venetian *Bella*-Portraits – those idealized, well-known presentations of lovely young women. Even the pensive facial expression may be traced back to the dreamy atmosphere of "Giorgionism". On the other hand, Moretto's Lombard sense of reality, in its sobriety and keen observation, manifests itself in the directness of the presentation. Also, the Brescian tradition with its gleaming colouring of silvery pastels gives the portrait sharpness and precision. M. H.

THE SCULPTOR, ALESSANDRO VITTORIA
Giovanni Battista Moroni
(Albino/Bergamo 1520/24–1578 Bergamo)
1552
Canvas; H 87.5 cm, W 70 cm
Inv. No. 78

Moroni, with his own objectivity and precision in portraiture, brought northern Italian portraiture to a height and autonomy that gave impulse not only to his great contemporaries, like Titian, but even later to Caravaggio and Van Dyck. The portrait of the most significant 16th century Venetian sculptor, Alessandro Vittoria (1525–1608) is a "career portrait". It affords us a quick snapshot look at his daily life and a terse statement of his personal and artistic abilities. In working clothes, sleeves rolled up, Vittoria holds up the torso of an antique statue for our inspection, as if offering comment on his own work. In spite or even because of the frugality of the gesture in the portrait, and in keeping with the sparing colouring, Vittoria has a force of conviction and intense closeness that seems to negate any distance between him and the observer. M. H.

INFANTE DON CARLOS ▽
Alonso Sánchez Coello
(Alqueria Blanca/Valencia 1531/32–1588 Madrid)
1564
Canvas; H 186 cm, W 82.5 cm
Inv. No. 3235

Don Carlos (1545–1568), eldest son of Philip II of Spain, was severely handicapped physically as well as mentally. His unstable character, given to violent outbursts of anger, brought the prince in conflict with his father, who felt he could not trust the prince's political plans. He had Carlos put under custody in 1568, during which year he died of fever. In any case, the historical personage of Carlos forbids the kind of hero worship we have in Schiller's drama and Verdi's opera. The portrait was intended to engender interest in Don Carlos as a bridegroom at the Viennese Court: Marriage plans were being drawn up in 1564 for Carlos and his cousin, Anna, daughter of Maximilian II. According to court etiquette, there is an officially required distance of the model. Along with that, the vacuity of the ambience, the physical stiffness of the figure and the sober and dry execution of the painting allow the observer no possible sensual identification.   W. P.

ALLEGORY OF VANITAS
Antonio de Pereda
(Valladolid 1611–1678 Madrid)
c. 1634
Canvas; H 139.5 cm, W 174 cm
Inv. No. 771

Pereda, as a young artist at court, was commissioned along with the elite among Spanish painters to decorate the Salon de Reinos in Buen Retiro Palace in Madrid with pictures of Spanish history. The *Allegory of Vanitas*, from this time, also seems to have been a court commission, judging from the cameo bearing a portrait of Emperor Charles V, which the winged spirit is holding in its left hand while pointing with the right to the globe, an allusion to the world dominion of the *Casa de Austria*. These references are reinforced by the antique medal of Augustus, indicating a connection with the Roman Empire, or, as the case may be, emphasizing the continuity of its rulership. Objects alluding to wealth, power and glory strewn about on the velvet-covered pedestal (on the right) are contrasted with the symbols of transiency on the broad table opposite. There, time, fortune, military glory, beauty and science are all represented. All is vain: *nil omne* is written between the hour glass and the skull.   W. P.

INFANTA MARGARITA TERESA IN A PINK GOWN
Diego Rodriguez de Silva y Velázquez
(Seville 1599–1660 Madrid)
1653/54
Canvas; H 128.5 cm, W 100 cm
Inv. No. 321

Ever since Emperor Charles V split the Habsburg countries that he had inherited from his grandfather (Maximilian I) with his brother, Ferdinand I, the *Casa de Austria* was divided into a Spanish line and an Austrian line. The close dynastic connection between the Madrid and Viennese Courts was constantly being renewed through marriages. As a result, the Vienna Picture Gallery can boast the famed Infanta portraits of the Spanish court painter, Velázquez. King Philip IV of Spain (1605–1665), son of Philip III and Archduchess Margarete of Austria, was widowed and, after the premature death of the Infante Balthasar Carlos, without an heir to the throne. In 1649, he entered into a second marriage, this time with his niece, the 14-year-old Archduchess Maria Anna of Austria (1635–1696), daughter of Ferdinand III and previously engaged to Philip's son Balthasar Carlos. The first-born child to this marriage was the Infanta Margarita Teresa, who was promised at an early age to her cousin and uncle, the future Emperor Leopold I. Before the wedding took place in 1666, the Madrid Court sent portraits of the Infanta at regular intervals to Vienna, so that the Picture Gallery possesses three portraits of the princess, all at different ages. In the first portrait, *Infanta in a Pink Gown,* the princess is two or three years old. Here, Velázquez followed the formal, conventional etiquette (dating from the 16th century) of official court portraits in the picture's format, the pose of the portrayed and the characterisation of the ambience (drapery and table). In appealing contrast is the richness of the painting's execution and colouring. The free-flowing brushstrokes are reminiscent of the great Venetians of the 16th century. The brushwork differentiates masterfully between broad colour expanses and superimposed dabs of colour. C. Z.

INFANTA MARGARITA TERESA IN A BLUE DRESS
Diego Rodriguez de Silva y Velázquez
(Seville 1599–1660 Madrid)
1659
Canvas; H 127 cm, W 107 cm
Inv. No. 2130

One year before his death, Velázquez painted the portrait, *Infanta Margarita Teresa in a Blue Dress.* The composition, now cut down at the top, is dominated by the overwhelming silver-blue skirt. It was representative of 17th century Spanish fashion and was originally cone-shaped, but took on its extreme breadth through wiring. Not only the colouring is responsible for the picture's liveliness; the artist's own differentiating way of painting is equally as important, permitting the observer to grasp the physical form of the princess only from afar. The thin, glazed colour applied to the head and hands becomes vigorously pastose in the splendid sleeves. The skin of the eight-year-old princess provides a gentle contrast to the cool, metallically shining gown and to the brownish, only partially completed background.

C. Z.

◁ **INFANTE PHILIP PROSPER**
Diego Rodriguez de Silva y Velázquez
(Seville 1599–1660 Madrid)
1659
Canvas; H 128.5 cm, W 99.5 cm
Inv. No. 319
(Text see page 272)

In the same year as the portrait, *Infanta Margarita Teresa in a Blue Dress,* Velázquez painted the Portrait of the *Infante Philip Prosper* (1657–1661). One of Velázquez' last works, it was sent at once to the Imperial Court in Vienna. It shows, shortly before his death, the two-year-old brother of the Infanta, in whom – as the only heir to the crown – all the hopes of the Spanish Habsburgs had been placed. In the traditional court portrait pose, the child rests one hand on the back of a small red velvet chair, containing a dainty little dog. The sickly prince wears a white smock over his "official" red gown; the smock is decorated with tiny bells and lucky amulets. The portrait's colouring is derived from the use of highly varied red and white tones. It is an impressive witness to the rich inventiveness and especially the psychological sensitivity of the mature Velázquez.   C. Z.

THE FAMILY OF THE ARTIST
Juan Bautista del Mazo
(Beteta/Cuenca 1612/16–1667 Madrid)
1664/65
Canvas; H 148 cm, W 174 cm
Inv. No. 320

Depicted is the family of Juan Bautista del Mazo, painter to the Spanish court as well as Velázquez' son-in-law and successor. On the left, in dark clothing, are his children by his first marriage; on the right, his second wife with their four children. In the middle of the painting, hanging on the wall, is a portrait of King Philip IV of Spain done in the style of Velázquez. Not yet satisfactorily identified is the atelier scene in the background where we see a painter (Velázquez? Mazo?) standing before a likeness of the Infanta Margarita Teresa and, next to the painter, a woman with a child running to her. Mazo's entire set-up including the royal portrait in the middle is derived from Velázquez' *Meninas,* the famous royal family portrait in the Prado. Mazo is here paying subtle hommage to the greatest of all Spanish painters with the wealth of all these allusions, found in Velázquez' family court portrait and here within Mazo's own private sphere.   W. P.

ST. MICHAEL
Bartolomé Esteban Murillo
(Seville 1617/18–1682 Seville)
Canvas; H 169.5 cm, W 110.3 cm
Inv. No. 9821

Murillo stood at the peak of his artistic fame when he created a series of paintings for the Capuchin Church of his home town, Seville. One of the series was the *St. Michael* seen here. The picture of the heavenly warrior in his wind-swept mantel was painted to be seen from below. It was to have

LAMENTATION OF CHRIST
Annibale Carracci
(Bologna 1560–1609 Rome)
c. 1603/04
Copper; H 41 cm, W 60.8 cm
Inv. No. 230

In the mid–1580's in Bologna, Annibale, together with his brother, Agostino, and his cousin, Ludovico Carracci, founded an art academy. The goal of the school was to establish Nature once again as the point of departure throughout the realm of art, requiring the students at the academy to adhere closely to Nature in their drawing. The conceptual mentors of this endeavour were the great Venetians, Titian, Tintoretto and Veronese, because of their having cherished and preserved Nature in art.

When, in 1595, Annibale was called to Rome to paint the gallery of the Farnese family palace, his work came under the influence of antiquity as well as of the work of Raphael and Michelangelo and gradually changed in the sense of Roman *gravitas*. The path he took – approaching classical stringency – is evident in this small *Pietà*. It was created only shortly before Annibale fell mentally ill. Asceticism, spareness, complete agreement of content and formal effect, a repression of colour into almost monochromism – all these lend the small composition heroic dimensions. W. P.

DAVID WITH THE HEAD OF GOLIATH
Michelangelo Merisi da Caravaggio
(Milan 1571–1610 Port' Ercole)
1606/07
Wood; H 90.5 cm, W 116 cm
Inv. No. 125

Caravaggio's Viennese *David* has caused controversy in art literature. Possibly because Caravaggio used wood for the picture (unusual for him), the surface seems smoother, more „polished" than we are accustomed to from his canvasses. Nevertheless, one senses the stylistic proximity to the *Madonna of the Rosary* and other Neapolitan works of the master. Caravaggio's concept of the unequal battle between the boy, David, and the gigantic Philistine, Goliath (1 Samuel 17:41–51) is emblematic and his interpretation is intensely personal. We see no radiant conqueror over evil, but rather a melancholy victor who seems to be contemplating himself and his victim. W. P.

been placed high up above the entry to the choir. Murillo treated this popular subject (the triumph of faith over heresy) as a sensitive dialogue: not only the triumph of the angel over his opponent, but also the victory of light over the darkness into which the youthful soldier of God has descended. With his usual airy way of painting, Murillo has removed every sign of heaviness from the fight. He envelops the events in a soft, coloured mist, in sensuality and intimacy and imbues the angel with that gentle charm that is all too characteristic of his art and certainly the key to his popularity. G. H.

◁ **MADONNA OF THE ROSARY**
Michelangelo Merisi da Caravaggio
(Milan 1571–1610 Port' Ercole)
1606/07
Canvas; H 364 cm, W 249 cm
Inv. No. 147

Caravaggio was a revolutionary – in his turbulent and violent life as well as in his art. In opposition, intentional opposition, to by-gone epochs, he used the overwhelming presence of the *personae* in his paintings to achieve the requisite (during the Counterreformation) intense effect on the viewer. His particular artistic devices were the vehement chiaroscuro contrasts, providing figures and objects with a sharp, never-before-beheld physical presence, and a rendering of the observed that approached veracity. This realism, as trivial as it may have seemed to Caravaggio's critics is actually derived from the spiritualism of a subtle understanding of art.

The enthroned Madonna advises St. Dominic to distribute rosaries among the people who are crowded about the Saint. Taking part in this supernatural-natural event are not just those found within the picture itself. The observer is drawn into the action as well, through the directional gesture of St. Peter Martyr on the right and through the invitation of the donor (on the left) to take cover under the protective mantel of St. Dominic. While the (painted) worshippers see only the Saint, the faithful viewer standing in front of this painting experiences within earthly reality the tangible results of supernatural grace: he is drawn towards Christ, the Redeemer – standing exactly in the picture's central axis – and the interceding Mary and Dominic.

Exact details of the provenance of the painting, the donor and its first intended location are still unknown. The picture was probably executed in Naples, only to be given to the Dominican Church in Antwerp by a group of artists, including Rubens and Jan Brueghel, around 1620. It was acquired by Emperor Joseph II in 1781.   W. P.

AGONY IN THE GARDEN
Giovanni Battista Caracciolo, called
Battistello
(Naples 1578–1635 Naples)
c. 1615/17
Canvas; H 148 cm, W 124 cm
Inv. No. F 17

Caracciolo, the most eminent of Caravaggio's followers in Naples, combines a literal interpretation of the biblical account of the fearful prayer of Christ on the Mount of Olives and the comforting appearance of the angel with an intense appeal to the beholder to meditate on the Passion of Christ. Christ's hands folded over one another and his narrowed eyes allude to the "Man of Sorrows". The painting's significance is found in the combination of static representation along with narrative depiction, a combination that, ever since the Counterreformation, was the offspring of the clearly defined relationship between the subject of a picture and the viewer. Also proscribed was the emotional impact on the worshipper. On the other hand, the sharply dramatic use of light and dark, the comparatively cool colouring and the opaque, porcelain body surfaces give this early work of Caracciolo a particular austerity.   W. P.

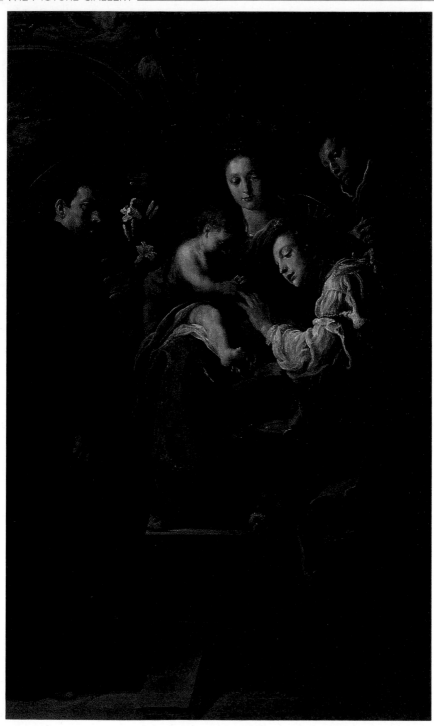

THE MYSTICAL BETROTHAL OF ST. CATHERINE AND SS DOMINIC AND PETER MARTYR
Domenico Fetti
(Rome c. 1588/90–1623 Venice)
c. 1613/14
Canvas; H 229.5 cm, W 140.5 cm
Inv. No. 167

In the space of only a few months in Venice, Fetti gave the Venetian seicento school new impulse. The altar painting, *The Mystical Betrothal of Saint Catherine* probably was done on commission of the Dominicans. It describes the vision of St. Catherine of Alexandria, a royal princess of Cyprus, who died a martyr's death at the hands of Emperor Maxentius. A late mediaeval legend has the Christ Child appearing to St. Catherine in her dream. He, in return, slips an engagement ring on her finger. In Fetti's painting, the Madonna is enthroned before a dark green drapery. She is flanked by St. Dominic on the left (with a star on his forehead and white lilies symbolic of purity to his left) and St. Peter Martyr on the right (recognizable by the hatchet in his head). The fragmentary wheel and the book lying on the floor relate to Catherine's martyrdom as well as her learnedness. Fetti's painterly technique extends from rather solid parts (faces) to the masterly unfolding in the flow of his brushwork (especially noteworthy in the white sleeve). The unearthly atmosphere of the picture – in keeping with the mystical, visionary subject – is achieved in a number of ways: the spatial aspect being left so unclear (on purpose), the sallow lighting, the lack of substance to the figures, the reduced colour spectrum and the particular chiaroscuro painting that was Fetti's specialty. Compared to Caravaggio whose direct lighting acts as a strong modelling factor on the figures, Fetti's diffuse shimmer of light barely achieves any kind of modelling at all, much less making us aware of another source of light.   C. Z.

RETURN OF THE PRODIGAL SON
Domenico Fetti
(Rome c. 1588/90–1623 Venice)
c. 1620/23
Wood; H 61 cm, W 44.5 cm
Inv. No. 9799

Characteristic of Fetti's late period are the fourteen parables from the Bible, some of which he repeated several times. They straight-forwardly illustrate the Christian truths that Christ himself had illustrated with examples taken out of daily life. Fetti retells the parables using true-to-life observations and genre-like scenes of everyday life, as seen here in the *Return of the Prodigal Son,* in which the father joyfully embraces his first exiled and then penitently returned son (Luke 15: 11—24). Fetti's use of the palace backdrop in the style of Palladio is reminiscent of the Venetian tradition (Veronese).   C. Z.

SUSANNA AND THE ELDERS
Jacopo Chimenti, called da Empoli
(Florence c. 1551–1640 Florence)
1600
Canvas; H 229 cm, W 172 cm
Inv. No. 1518

As related in the Bible, Susanna had retired to bathe in the privacy of her garden. Two men were lying in wait there and tried to seduce her. Susanna repelled them, however, and went down in history as a heroine of great chastity and faith in God. Empoli's *Susanna* is one of the very few paintings on this theme where the virtuous Susanna is shown clothed, still making preparations for her bath. Always concerned with dignified tranquillity in his pictures, the Florentine painter approaches the gripping story not as a drama but as a peaceful idyll. Blending domestic intimacy with aristocratic refinement, Empoli creates an introspective scene out of the elegant figures at the fountain. He almost conceals the lustful elders from view by matching their colouring with that of the park backdrop.   G. H.

ARCHDUCHESS CLAUDIA FELICITAS
Carlo Dolci
(Florence 1616–1668 Florence)
1672
Canvas; H 90.5 cm, W 69.5 cm
Inc. No. 3352

Close family ties between Austria and Florence, in particular the marriage of two successive Habsburg generations (the Tyrolean line) with Medici princesses, not only brought innumerable art works northward across the Alps. It also brought artists to Innsbruck where court portraiture eventually came to be more Florentine than anything else. Carlo Dolci was summoned specifically to portray the nineteen-year-old Archduchess, a Medici on the maternal side. She was destined to become the second wife of Emperor Leopold I a year later. Dolci was mainly known for his brilliant and precious devotional paintings. Here, he created a likeness of striking stillness and suppressed, sensual appeal. Precisely defined forms with smooth surfaces, especially the refined colouring — the sallow blue-green together with the paleness of the face framed in dark hair — all these lend the imperial bride a melancholy charm, a dreamy elegance that is characteristic of many Florentine paintings of this period.   G. H.

CHRIST APPEARING TO THE APOSTLES PETER AND PAUL
Giovanni Battista Crespi, called Cerano
(Busto Arsizio 1567/70–1632 Milan)
c. 1626/28
Canvas; H 274 cm, W 184 cm
Inv. No. 273

The demands on painting made by the Counter-reformation in Lombardy (closely supervised by the bishops from the House of Borromeo) were threefold: the representation of religious fervour; the realistic relating of biblical events in story-telling pictures designed to make them utterly believable; and, thirdly, the depiction of visions so as to arouse the emotions and serve as dogmatic lessons. In this late work, which Cerano did for the Church of S. Pietro dei Pellegrini in Milan (one of many paintings and architectural designs he was to do for the Borromeo), Christ appears twice, transfigured and "un-materialised". Within the typical form of an altar painting, he may be seen in the foreground accompanied by the two apostles along with their canonical attributes. The vision is unique in its colouring. Then, again, way in the background, Christ appears with the church's patron saint who asks him the famous question, while fleeing from Roman imprisonment, "Domine, quo vadis". W. P.

REST ON THE FLIGHT TO EGYPT
Orazio Gentileschi
(Pisa 1563–1639 London)
c. 1626/28
Canvas; H 138.5 cm, W 216 cm
Inv. No. 180

Gentileschi, the friend and early follower of Caravaggio, ended his many-sided career in England where he had been appointed court painter in 1626. Gentileschi painted this Viennese version of an often repeated theme for the Duke of Buckingham, who was murdered in 1628. Idiosyncratic for Gentileschi are the Tuscan's own precise draughtsmanship, the bright colouring derived from the work of Caravaggio before 1600 and the delicacy of the nuances between colours, wonderfully effective in the drapery and hair. Caravaggio's powerful influence is especially evident in the concept of the painting: the "natural" realism of a family in flight is reflected in the nursing mother and the exhausted father who regardless of decorum has stretched out on the travelling packs to sleep. The "technical" influence is evident of course in the lighting and the rendering of the background wall. The almost formal attire of the Madonna and her elegant accessories are directly opposed to the "normalcy" of the ambience, the sort of contrast running throughout Gentileschi's entire career.

W. P.

THE RETURN OF THE PRODIGAL SON
Giovanni Francesco Barbieri,
called Il Guercino
(Cento 1591–1666 Bologna)
c. 1619
Canvas; H 107 cm, W 143.5 cm
Inv. No. 253

The scene illustrates Jesus' parable of God's forgiveness to repentant sinners (Luke 15:11–32). The younger of two sons leaves his father's house and squanders his inheritance. Poor and suffering, he decides to return to his father who receives him with forgiveness and clothes him anew. The picture, painted for the papal legate in Ferrara, Jacopo Serra, is a brilliant example of Guercino's early work. It derives much from Ludovico, one member of the Carracci family who remained in Bologna. The spontaneously inventive and often asymmetrical composition with overlapping figures, the restless, "smeared" light fragmenting the body forms and the deep, dark colouring are all trademarks of a style that was to become quietly evened out and more representative of classicism after Guercino's stay in Rome (1621/23).   W. P.

THE MADONNA APPEARING TO ST. JAMES
AND ST. ANTHONY ABBOT
Giovanni Lanfranco
(Parma 1582–1647 Rome)
c. 1624
Canvas; H 220 cm, W 127.5 cm
Inv. No. 223

The boldness and progressiveness of Lanfranco's painting stems from the full use of two systems of perspective. The painterly illusion of the image survives despite the qualities of asymmetry, imbalance, distortion of size and proportion. The Madonna, seen from a greater distance, is especially small in comparison to both the huge St. James who fills almost the entire canvas, and the disproportionately large child she holds. Via the strong diagonal composition, restless lighting, robust and rapid brushwork a sense of emotion, drama and pathos are conveyed to the viewer.
                                                  W. P.

CONQUEST OF JERUSALEM BY EMPEROR
TITUS ▷
Nicolas Poussin
(Les Andelys 1594–1665 Rome)
1638
Canvas; H 148 cm, W 199 cm
Inv. No. 1556

The subject is taken from the *Jewish War* of Flavius Josephus. Riding on his dapple grey, Titus, the son of the reigning Roman Emperor, sees with horrow how — against his express will — the Old Testament prophesy of the destruction of the Temple of Solomon comes true. The chaos of the dramatic plot is set by Poussin within a well-

THE RETURN OF ASTRAEA
Salvator Rosa
(Naples 1615–1673 Rome)
c. 1640/45
Canvas; H 138 cm, W 209 cm
Inv. No. 1613

The virgin Astraea, goddess of justice, appears on the clouds with a lion and presents the surprised country folk with her attributes of sword and scale. Rosa took this announcement of the Return of the Golden Age of peace and justice from Vergil. In the *Georgics,* Vergil describes how Astraea as the last of the gods to leave the decimated earth lived among the upright and peaceful country people.

In the Fourth Eclogue, he recounts the dawning of the new and august Golden Age, as prophesied by the virgin. Part of the purpose of the painting was to extoll the Medici regime; they had long used the traditional myth of the Golden Age as justification for their power and had ordered this painting during Rosa's sojourn in Florence. One other motivation for the commission may have been the desire for peace at the end of the Thirty Years War. Rosa, who was also author of a passionate anti-war poem will have been more than eager to have set his learned fantasy in service to the task before him, bringing the dialectic of idyll and the horrors of war together in a poetic, almost playful approach. W. P.

ordered framework. In its rigorous form, in the spatial clarity where everything has its proper place, this work is witness to the decisive turn that Poussin made towards strict classicism, relief-like composition, and sober colouring, as well as towards a precise definition of the figure within space. The painting was commissioned by the Cardinal Francesco Barberini, who presented the work to Emperor Ferdinand III on behalf of his uncle, Pope Urban VIII. Was it intended as praise for the victory of Ferdinand over the Protestants at Nördlingen (1634) or as criticism over the conquest and plundering of Mantua by Imperial troops (1627)? W. P.

BAPTISM OF CHRIST
Guido Reni
(Bologna 1575–1642 Bologna)
c. 1622/23
Canvas; H 263.5 cm, W 186.5 cm
Inv. No. 222

The *Baptism of Christ* makes us receptive to the virtues of this master who constantly strove to meet the ideals of beauty. An artistic watershed, the painting offers a masterful solution to the tensions of composition, colour and psychological oppositions. The masculine dark, active John is contrasted with the humbly tender, fair-skinned Christ. The exchange of glances between the two finds an echo in the two angels in the middle. The "colourless" figures in the foreground contrast with the radiantly colourful angels behind them (the festive sensuousness of it all!). Rising out of Venetian-Carraccesque colouring, the Baptism is in the tradition of the Bolognese School. Already, however, in the cool, silvery light of the foreground we see the beginnings of the light tones of Reni's late period.   W. P.

ST. JEROME
Guido Reni
(Bologna 1575–1642 Bologna)
c. 1635
Canvas; H 278 cm, W 238 cm
Inv. No. 9124

"Imitating" the Evangelist St. Matthew, Saint Jerome (inspired by his angel) is working on the translation of the Bible into Latin. Reni's late work is distinctive above all for its bright silvery light against which the strong colours glow even more intensively. The conflicts in Reni's art revolve around naturalness vs. artificiality, virtuosity vs. simplicity, grace vs. depth, superficiality vs. seriousness, elegance vs. moral standards, light vs. matter. They are convincingly resolved through Reni's characteristic use of a well-conceived diagonal composition, the lively but piercingly precise contours, the rich inner drawing culminating in the "landscape of wrinkled skin" of the Saint, and the control over the ever-changing interplay between form and its foil.   W. P.

RETURN OF HAGAR
Pietro Berettini, called da Cortona
(Cortona 1596–1669 Rome)
c. 1637
Canvas; H 123.5 cm, W 99 cm
Inv. No. 153

Hagar, pregnant with Abraham's child, has sought to escape the jealousy of Abraham's wife, Sarah. The angel of the Lord has commanded her to return and reassume her yoke. Abraham greets the humble Hagar and appears to want to act as an intermediary for the two women. Cortona's career, as painter, architect and art theoretician, was along with that of Bernini the most comprehensive of the Roman High Baroque. He completed the enormous illusionistic ceiling painting for the salon of the Palazzo Barberini in Rome before being summoned to Florence for frescoes in the Palazzo Pitti. Here are the closest parallels to *The Return of Hagar,* especially in the treatment of the landscape. In general, the figures themselves follow the canons of draped figures of the antique, of Raphael and of Annibale Carracci; there is, however, more energy and variety in their movement, expression of the elevated sense of life permeating that epoch.   W. P.

INCREDULITY OF ST. THOMAS
Mattia Preti
(Taverna/Calabria 1613–1699 Malta)
c. 1660/65
Canvas; H 187 cm, W 145.5 cm
Inv. No. 259

The painting is not only a dramatic depiction, it is also an appeal to the faithful beholder to examine Christ's stigmata and convince himself (like the doubting apostle Thomas and the others) of Christ's resurrection. In a typical baroque manner, static, iconic elements are combined with the labile narrative. Christ, painted frontally, with his eyes fixed on the viewer and the banner of resurrection on his shoulder, presents his wounds (much as in a devotional painting). He is the axis of a drawn-out diagonal composition; the side sections are peopled with dramatically moving half-figures cut off at the edge of the picture. The restless light, reinforcing the dramatic impetus, dilutes the painting's dogmatic, "catechismic" purpose.   W. P.

LUTE PLAYER
Bernardo Strozzi, called Il Capuccino
(Genoa 1581–1644 Venice)
c. 1640/44
Canvas; H 92 cm, W 76 cm
Inv. No. 1612

Strozzi, a Capuchin father in Genoa and later a cleric in Venice, incorporated many diversified stylistic trends into his art. Here, he creates an especially poetic version of a theme that had been popular in early 16th century Venetian art as well as with Caravaggio and his followers: the lute player in tuning his instrument is so detached from reality that he seems to be attuning himself as well. Strozzi's brushstroke became looser and freer in his later period, sometimes extremely pastose, even "spotty" or dabbed, while at other times especially finely shaded, airy and soft. W. P.

GALATEA AND POLYPHEMUS
Domenico Fetti
(Rome c. 1588/90–1623 Venice)
c. 1620/23
Wood; H 41 cm, W 97 cm
Inv. No. 172

The small-format pictures on mythological or biblical subjects done in the last months of Fetti's life, in Venice, range among the most original of his creations. *Galatea and Polyphemus* may have been intended for a wall-panel or furniture façade, along with *Andromeda and Perseus* (Inv. No. 7722) and *Hero and Leander* (Inv. No. 160). The

painting relates the tragic ending of a love story. The sea goddess, Galatea, loveliest of Nereus' fifty enchanting daughters, flees in desperation in her cockle-shell chariot drawn by dolphins. She is escaping the wrath of the horrid, one-eyed Cyclops, Polyphemus, who, in the glow of his love for Galatea, has just killed her lover, Acis, in a fit of passionate jealousy by hurling a huge boulder down on him. The poetic, fairy-tale setting of the picture is evoked in rich painterly devices, especially in the shimmering colour tones of the heavens and the water. They seem to dissolve in atmospheric light.

C. Z.

THE PROPHET ELIAS AND THE WIDOW OF ZAREPHATH
Bernardo Strozzi, called il Capuccino
(Genoa 1581 – 1644 Venice)
Late work
Canvas; H 106 cm, W 138 cm
Inv. No. 258

Two moments from the story of the prophet Elias' visit to the widow of famine-plagued Zarephath (1 Kings 17:9 ff.) are joined here in an unusual way in that the observer is forced to take an unusual position. In response to Elias' initial plea for water, the widow's son, his countenance full of devotion and awe, offers the prophet a bowl. At the same time, although in the biblical story it comes afterwards, the viewer is witness (his eye is at the level of the tabletop and falls on the "barrel of meal" and the "cruse of oil") to the prophetic promise. Elias, with one generous gesture of his open hand, relieves all the fears of the afflicted widow. He assures her that she will never find herself without meal or oil again. In the same way that the widow and her son regard the ageing prophet with faith, so is it intended that the viewer looks up to the three biblical figures. On the other hand, the massive physical presence of the figures brings them into the beholder's space.

W. P.

ADORATION OF THE MAGI
Bernardo Cavallino
(Naples 1616 – 1656 Naples)
c. 1640
Canvas; H 101.5 cm, W 127 cm
Inv. No. 6764

Cavallino is the only one of the sometimes grandiloquent Neapolitans who knew how to evoke a sense of fable, the lyric feeling of a smile or of gentle grief. His painterly refinement (the epitome of a polished cabinet painting for the connoisseur) is never ostentatious or loud. It remains extremely and consistently sensitive. In his pictures are often found scenes in which the protagonists, or some observer of the event, react with tenderness and sympathy towards one another. Still valid for the comparatively early *Adoration of the Magi,* is the characterization of style as given by the Neapolitan art historian, Bernardo De Dominici in 1742/43: "His style is beautiful and erudite, meaningful yet decorative. Tenderness, grace and delicacy combined with the strong, deep chiaroscuro, the result of a single light source, serve to highlight the dramatic focus of the painting."

W. P.

GIDEON REVIEWS HIS TROOPS
Johann Heinrich Schönfeld
(Biberach 1609 – 1683/84 Augsburg)
c. 1640/45
Canvas; H 99 cm, W 179 cm
Inv. No. 1143

Schönfeld's style is seen here in an idiosyncratic mixture. His northern education, his involvement with the French engraver Callot, and his contact with his Neapolitan contemporaries, Micco Spadaro and Cavallino, are evident in the mannered, elegant grouping of his figures. Combined with this are the Roman-Classical architectural ruins, like the Colosseum in the background to the right. The entire picture is bathed in an unreal bluish light as if the Old Testament were a mediaeval fairy tale. The Swabian Schönfeld worked in Naples from the second half of the 1630's until 1649. From 1633 on, he had been part of the circle of French and Dutch painters around Poussin and Claude Lorrain in Rome. The theme of the painting is taken from the Book of Judges (7:5 ff) and relates the episode from Gideon's war with the Midianites. He was faced with too many volunteers in his army. God bade Gideon select only those who "lap of the water (of the Jordan) with their tongues, as a dog laps".   W. P.

THE ARCHANGEL MICHAEL FORCES THE FAITHLESS ANGELS INTO THE ABYSS
Luca Giordano
(Naples 1634 – 1705 Naples)
c. 1655
Canvas; H 419 cm, W 283 cm
Inv. No. 350

The works of Luca Giordano, notable for their extraordinary breadth, unusually fertile conceptions and individual style, mark the closing of High Baroque decorative art. At the same time, especially with regard to his interest in colouristic problems, Giordano's work stands at the threshold of 18th century Italian painting. This altarpiece was donated to the Minoritenkirche in Vienna by the Patalotti family and is documented as having been part of the Imperial gallery since 1796. The altar is from Giordano's early period as is evidenced by the influence of Ribera's *verismo* expressed in the desperately screaming, distorted faces of the vanquished demons. The neo-Venetian palette of Ribera is seen as well in the refined colouring of Michael's drapery. Nevertheless, behind the Archangel's elegant and weightless flight one senses the classical influence of Guido Reni's *St. Michael* in S. Maria della Concezione in Rome.   W. P.

◁ **DESCENT FROM THE CROSS**
Francesco Solimena
(Canale di Serino/Avellino 1657 – 1747 Barra/ Naples)
1730/31
Canvas; H 398 cm, W 223 cm
Inv. No. 3507

Under Austrian rule in Naples (1707–34), the city's most important artists worked for the Austrian aristocracy, for the Imperial Court and for Prince Eugene of Savoy. For the latter, Francesco Solimena created a *Resurrection of Christ* which has remained *in situ* and the *Descent from the Cross*, both for the palace chapel of the Upper Belvedere in Vienna. One begins to realize why Solimena must have been one of the most influential artists and teachers of the Middle European Rococo painters. He applied a decorative play of light and shadow based on securely applied colour accents to the heavy, dusky and expressive style of the Neapolitan 17th century. In contrast to Luca Giordano's visionary, fantastic style and open brushwork, Solimena's compositions retain a firm structure that in spite of baroque movement presents the figures with unremitting plasticity and tempered expressiveness.   W. P.

EMPEROR KARL VI AND COUNT GUNDAKER ALTHANN
Francesco Solimena
(Canale di Serino/Avellino 1657 – 1747 Barra/ Naples)
1728
Canvas; H 309 cm, W 284 cm
Inv. No. 1601
(Text see page 288)

Karl VI decided to concentrate the paintings in Habsburg possession, at that time divided between many different castles as well as Prague and Vienna, so that they could all be displayed in the Stallburg in Vienna. As a final step the Emperor had produced a miniature inventory in three volumes. He engaged Francesco Solimena, the leader of the Neapolitan school, to paint the scene of the dedication of that inventory. In this showpiece of Baroque panegyric Count Gundaker Althann, the Imperial minister of buildings, presents the Emperor with the inventory of the collection. Karl VI's devotion and feeling for art is proclaimed by Fama. Although Naples at that time belonged to the Austrian monarchy and likenesses of those portrayed would surely have been available, Solimena did not paint the portraits himself. Johann Gottfried Auerbach, painter to the court in Vienna, completed them over the already finished, unportrait-like, dynamically interrelated heads. In all probability, the iconic faces of Auerbach were an attempt to satisfy the court's desire for stately conformity.

W. P.

THE DEATH OF CLEOPATRA
Guido Cagnacci
(San Arcangelo di Romagna 1601 – 1663 Vienna)
1659/63
Canvas; H 140 cm, W 159.5 cm
Inv. No. 260

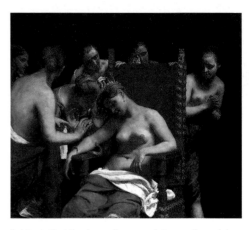

Cleopatra VII (51–30 B. C.), the last Queen of Egypt, killed herself with the venomous bite of an asp in order to avoid the indignity of being led through Rome in the triumphal parade of Octavianus Augustus. Cagnacci, painter to the Viennese Court, never forgot his artistic education in the circle around Guido Reni nor his indebtedness to Caravaggio and his followers, above all Orazio Gentileschi. He attempted a synthesis of both stylistic concepts in this masterpiece of Bolognese baroque painting. The sharply rendered realism of the weeping servants' body language in all its excitement contrasts with the classically reclining Cleopatra, who is sovereignly tranquil. The figures are bathed in Correggesque light, so that the hues flow one into another giving the scene a highly sensual character.

W. P.

THE CENTAUR CHIRON TEACHING ACHILLES TO DRAW THE BOW ▷
Giuseppe Maria Crespi
(Bologna 1665 – 1747 Bologna)
c. 1695
Canvas; H 126 cm, W 124 cm
Inv. No. 270

Achilles' mother, Thetis, placed her son in the care of Chiron for his education. Accordingly, books and instruments for astronomical teaching lie strewn upon the floor. Contemporary sources were quick to report (partly critical) that Crespi wanted to represent Chiron in the act of giving Achilles a kick with his hoof in return for an off-target shot. Prince Eugene of Savoy commissioned Crespi to paint this, as well as four other Bolognese paintings for his city palace in the Himmelpfortgasse in Vienna. During the 1720's the *Achilles* and its counterpart, Crespi's *Aeneas, Sibyl and Charon,* were placed above the doors in the Prince's State Bed Room. The great painting tradition of the Bolognese school culminated again in Crespi. "The clarity of his compositional thinking" speaks for the Bolognese roots. On the other hand, he represents "the beginning of a new era in the evolution of a painting style from a more graphic conception to a more painterly one" (Heinz).

W. P.

THE DEATH OF THE CONSUL L. J. BRUTUS
Giovanni Battista Tiepolo
(Venice 1696 – 1770 Madrid)
c. 1728/30
Canvas; H 383 cm, W 182 cm
Inv. No. 6798

During the late 1720's Tiepolo painted a ten-part cycle of canvasses for the Main Hall of the Palazzo Dolfin near S. Pantalon in Venice. The paintings centre around the heroic events in Livy's accounts of Roman history. Shown here is the death of L. J. Brutus, the first Roman consul. In battles between Rome and the Etruscans, Brutus died while engaged in hand-to-hand combat with the son of the last Etruscan king, Aruns, who also died. Seen from the deplorable political and military situation in 18th century Venice, it may seem ambiguous that the Venetian aristocracy would glorify the virtues of the Roman Republic. In any case, Tiepolo's gigantic, stormy and dramatic pictures must have had an overwhelming effect with their powerful contrasts, their glistening colour and the strong, life-like plasticity.
W. P.

MIRACLE OF A DOMINICAN SAINT
Francesco Guardi
(Venice 1712–1793 Venice)
1763
Canvas; H 122 cm, W 172 cm
Inv. No. 6811

Painted for the chapel of St. Dominic in the Church of S. Pietro Martire on Murano, the painting gives an account of the miraculous deeds of a Dominican monk who saves himself and, standing on the water, all the others with him from drowning after the bridge they were on collapsed. Palely lit, as if hit by lightning, the event is full of fluctuating contours and hazy boundaries between land, water and air. The expression in the spasmodic brushstrokes with which Guardi releases physical form into apparitions of pure colour and atmosphere creates a sense more of vision than reality. In spite of the drama depicted, the scene has a tinge of the frivolous rococo, due to the bizarre bend of the contours and the pastel colouring.

M. H.

PHILIPP WENZEL COUNT SINZENDORF
Hyacinthe Rigaud
(Perpignan 1659–1743 Paris)
1728
Canvas; H 166 cm, W 132 cm
Inv. No. 9010

The diplomat, portrayed in the official robes of the Order of the Golden Fleece, had taken part in the negotiations of 1728 at the Conference of Soissons, where Rigaud, originator of the French court portrait under Louis XIV, painted him. Sinzendorf (1671–1742) was the son of the infamous President of the Court Chamber, Georg Ludwig Sinzendorf, who was exiled after his embezzlement of large sums of money intended for the Imperial army. His son, nevertheless, succeeded in making a successful career: as Imperial Court Councillor, Envoy to France, Authorized Representative of the Emperor in the Netherlands and Chief Privy Councillor and Director of the Oriental Trade Company. Brazenly "loud" symbols of stately power are found in that particular French concept of portraiture. The enlarged physical presence and dynamism of the portrayed follows from the tremendous movement in the drapery. W. P.

EMPEROR JOSEPH II WITH GRANDDUKE PIETRO LEOPOLDO OF TUSCANY
Pompeo Batoni
(Lucca 1708–1787 Rome)
1769
Canvas; H 173 cm, W 122 cm
Inv. No. 1628

Aristocrats on their *Grand Tour* generally had themselves portrayed in Rome by Pompeo Batoni. This double portrait (in its original frame) shows Joseph II (1741–1791, Emperor 1765), the eldest son of Maria Theresa, and his brother Pietro Leopoldo (1747–1792, Grandduke of Tuscany 1765, Emperor 1790). The portrait, done on the occasion of the brothers' reunion in Rome, reflects the neo-classical portrait concept of the artist as well as the maxims of the Enlightenment, as shown by Montesquieu's *L'esprit des lois* on the table. The simple composition although free of pomp and splendour, nevertheless shows the rank and dignity of these two enlightened rulers. At the same time, the ambience, with its reference to Rome, renders both princes as cultivated travellers to Italy.   C. Z.

CHRISTOPH WILLIBALD VON GLUCK
Josèphe-Sifrède Duplessis
(Carpentras 1725–1802 Versailles)
1775 ·
Canvas; H 99.5 cm, W 80.5 cm
Inv. No. 1795

Christoph Willibald von Gluck (1714–1787), the great reformer of the opera (in the direction of dramatic music theater), enjoyed, in the mid-70's in Paris, his most unequivocal successes: in 1774, the performance of *Iphigenie en Aulide* and the French version of *Orpheus*, and in 1776, *Alceste*. Member of the Academie in Paris from 1774 on, Duplessis also stood at the peak of his career. He presents the composer wigged and "in action" at the harpsichord, as if he were at work. At the same time, he created the most convincing musician's portrait in history. The face is in itself plain and pockmarked with large eyes directed upwards, the left hand expectantly raised. The expression catches Gluck in a moment of musical inspiration. Rare enough it was that an official portrait emanated such soulfulness, emotion and enthusiasm.   W. P.

MADONNA WITH CHILD AND TWO ANGELS
Anton Raphael Mengs
(Aussig 1728–1779 Rome)
c. 1770/73
Wood; H 112 cm, W 86 cm
Inv. No. 126

Only in the last decades have we once again found aesthetic access to Mengs' paintings. In his own time he was one of the most highly regarded and sought after artists in Europa. Whether in Rome, Dresden or Madrid, he was celebrated everywhere as the new Raphael, as the conqueror of bad baroque taste and as reformer of painting in the spirit of antiquity (filtered by Winckelmann) and the High Renaissance. Actually, Mengs' inspiration flowed from many different sources. His neo-classicism, at times toned down, is nonetheless more sensuous and more artistic than that of his "classical" mentors. The Viennese Madonna was executed shortly after Mengs' first sojourn at the Court of Madrid where he worked with, among others, Tiepolo, on paintings in the royal palace. The Madonna is less influenced by Raphael than by Carlo Maratta who created this type of work. Maratta's Madonnas however are more severe, more heavily outlined and more majestic. He would never have wrapped his figures in the soft atmospheric *sfumato* that Mengs, in his admiration for Correggio, did. W. P.

ARCHDUCHESS MARIE CHRISTINE
Johann Zoffany
(Frankfurt am Main 1733–1810 Strand-on-the-Green)
1776
Canvas; H 131 cm, W 94 cm
Inv. No. 1809

Zoffany was successful as a portrait painter in the court milieu because of his gifted ability to reproduce likeness within an ideal setting of conflict-free serenity. He was also admired for his ability to heighten the costly appearance of fabric. He overemphasized the surfaces, presenting them as most sumptuous and precious. During the mid-70's, he resided in Florence, where he was given a commission by Empress Maria Theresa not only for the large painting of her son's family, that of the Grandduke Leopold of Tuscany, but also for the portrait of her favourite daughter, Marie-Christine. The latter was at that time in Italy on an art tour of several months duration with her husband, Duke Albrecht of Saxony-Teschen. At the end of their journey they took possession of the collection of prints and drawings that Albrecht had ordered and which were to form the basic stock of the Albertina in Vienna. K. S.

VIENNA, VIEWED FROM THE BELVEDERE PALACE
Bernardo Bellotto, called Canaletto
(Venice 1721–1780 Warsaw)
1758/61
Canvas; H 136 cm, W 214 cm
Inv. No. 1669

In connection with the growing number of travellers on their *Grand Tour,* there developed in 18th century Venice a special form of landscape painting, that concerned itself with the exact topographical reproduction of urban panoramas. One of its main representatives was Bernardo Bellotto, nephew and pupil of Antonio Canal, both of whom were called Canaletto. As a sought-after specialist in this area, Bellotto worked at the princely courts of Dresden, Vienna, Munich and Warsaw, thereby spreading the idea of *veduta* painting far beyond Venice alone. The view of Vienna from the Belvedere Palace is one of a series of thirteen views of Vienna and Imperial palaces painted by Bellotto between 1758 and 1761 for Maria Theresa. The Belvedere Palace, on a slight rise south of Vienna, affords a panorama of the city all the way to the hills of the Vienna Woods. The perspective construction unfolds between the gardens of both the Schwarzenberg Palace and the Belvedere itself in the foreground to a row of stately baroque palaces and churches in the middle focal plane of the painting. These buildings are evidence of the active construction "boom" in Vienna after the Second Turkish siege in 1683. The monumental domes of St. Charles Borromeo (left) and the Salesianer Monastery (right) frame the picture and carry the composition. Within this structure may be seen the garden palace of the Schwarzenberg and the Lower Belvedere with its orangerie. Surrounded by fortification walls and dominated by the spire of St. Stephen's Cathedral, the inner city lies behind the tract of glacis. Its skyline of roofs, towers and domes is extremely dynamic. In spite of the amazing topographical precision and attention to detail, Bellotto has taken liberty with the perspective. In order that the composition be more compact, he has reduced the distance between the two domed churches. The painting derives its special appeal from the effectively constructed perspectives, the fine workmanship and the carefully chosen light setting. The allée trees and the figures cast long shadows in the warm light of the sunset. The light also turns the façades, roofs and houses into interchanging colour zones.   C. Z.

293

FREYUNG SQUARE IN VIENNA, VIEWED FROM THE SOUTHEAST
Bernardo Bellotto, called Canaletto
(Venice 1721–1780 Warsaw)
1758/61
Canvas; H 116 cm, W 152 cm
Inv. No. 1654

The painting is one of a series of six views of the inner city of Vienna. In each case, Bellotto chose either a large square or square-like boulevard, but in either case dominated by a baroque church or place. These paintings are of smaller format than the *vedute* of the Imperial palaces in and around Vienna. Resembling a stage with genre-like decorative figures, the view of the market on the Freyung ends at the massive Schottenkirche. From the buildings, those on the left, the Harrach and Kaunitz Palaces, stand out. The artistic effect lies not only in chiaroscuro contrasts and the effective use of large shadowed areas, but also in the cool colouring with its basically olive-green tone. C. Z.

IMPERIAL SUMMER RESIDENCE, SCHÖNBRUNN: COURT FAÇADE
Bernardo Bellotto, called Canaletto
(Venice 1721–1780 Warsaw)
1758/61
Canvas; H 135 cm, W 235 cm
Inv. No. 1666

The stately palace *veduta* gives in panoramic view the entire inner lay-out of Schönbrunn, with the main building, the side pavilions and the court of honour. The painting was done after Maria Theresa had completed the massive rebuilding and expansion of her summer residence. This precisely drawn view was achieved with the help of a *camera obscura*, a simple aperture camera. It is the only painting in the Vienna series that is about an actual historical event: On August 16, 1759, Maria Theresa, on the balcony of the Beletage, was awaiting the arrival of her Special Envoy, Count Josef Kinsky, to bring her news of the victory of the allied Russo-Austrian army over Friedrich the Great at Kunersdorf. C. Z.

SMALL ALTARPIECE: THE ANNUNCIATION, THE MYSTIC MARRIAGE OF ST. CATHERINE
Master of Heiligenkreuz
(active in France, c. 1395–1420)
c. 1410
Wood; each panel H 72 cm, W 43.5 cm
Inv. Nos. 6523, 6524

This diptych is by an unknown painter whose name derives from the monastery of Heiligenkreuz near Vienna, where the altarpiece comes from. It shows on the left side the *Annunciation to Mary,* and on the right side the *Mystic Marriage of St. Catherine.* The exteriors depict individual figures of the Virgin and St. Dorothea. The decorative aspects of the picture, with its long, narrow figures clad in brightly coloured swinging garments, and standing in architectural motifs untrue to scale, against a golden background, suggests that the altarpiece belongs to the „International Style" of about 1400. Its cosmopolitan

character is typical for this elegant, courtly painting which bears the elements of French as well as of Bohemian and German art. K. S.

THE COURT JESTER GONELLA
Jean Fouquet
(Tours 1415/20–1481 Tours)
c. 1440–1445
Wood; H 36.5 cm, W 26 cm
Inv. No. 1840

Despite its description as a portrait of *The Court Jester Gonella* in the inventory of Archduke Leopold Wilhelm's collection, this portrait of a wily old man remains a mystery. His arms tightly folded, his head tilted to one side, he seems to be squeezed into the picture. The precision of Jan van Eyck's portrait art is the basis for the minutely detailed reproduction of a face complete with wrinkles, stubble and reddened eyes. At the same time, a type is created; the fool acting the part of a simple peasant who can amuse the court with crude jokes or rough wisdom. The colourful stripes of his jester's coat display a composition scheme that is unusual in Early Netherlandish painting; this and the formation of the bulging plasticity of his form can be found in Jean Fouquet's work. The French painter portrayed Gonella, famous court jester of the time and in the service of Niccolò d'Este, when he stayed in Ferrara on his way to Rome. K. S.

CARDINAL NICCOLÒ ALBERGATI
Jan van Eyck
(Maaseyck c. 1390–1441 Bruges)
c. 1435
Wood; H 34.1 cm, W 27.3 cm
Inv. No. 975

Jan van Eyck is considered one of the founders and leading masters of Early Netherlandish panel painting. His portrait shows the Cardinal Niccolò Albergati, Head of the Carthusian Order who travelled on a pontifical mission to the courts of England, France and Burgundy for peace negotiations to end the Hundred Years War between England and France. Jan van Eyck, court painter to Duke Philip the Good of Burgundy, made a silverpoint sketch in one portrait sitting (today in Dresden) as a preparatory drawing for this painting. Despite the realistic, carefully observed traces of age in the old man's face, the portrait radiates dignified repose.   C. Z.

TRIPTYCH: THE CRUCIFIXION
Rogier van der Weyden
(Tournai 1399/1400 – 1464 Brussels)
c. 1440
Wood; centre panel H 96 cm, W 69 cm; wings: each H 101 cm, W 35 cm
Inv. No. 901

Besides Jan van Eyck, Rogier van der Weyden was, already in his lifetime, considered the greatest Flemish painter. As the inventor of impressive motifs he is even thought to be the more important in the development of late Gothic panel painting. On three panels of a winged altarpiece he represents the *Crucifixion* of Christ restricted to the most important figures, the Virgin and St. John beneath the cross. The donor couple are shown of equal rank. St. Mary Magdalene and St. Veronica can be seen on the wings. All three panels show one and the same landscape background, and are separated only by a narrow frame, painted as a simulated framing on the wings. Rogier's style is full of expressive fervour, the intensity of feeling mounting from quiet mourning to dramatic outburst. This is displayed not only in the bodies shaken by grief but also in the garments which seem to move in a storm, and in the deeply creased, broken folds.   K. S.

DIPTYCH: THE FALL OF MAN AND THE LAMENTATION
Hugo van der Goes
(Ghent ca. 1440 – 1482 Rode Klooster near Brussels)
c. 1470/75
Wood; H 32.3 cm, W 21.9 cm and H 34.4 cm, W 22.8 cm, resp.
Inv. No. 945, 5822

Hugo van der Goes combined two paintings widely differing in subject matter and style in this diptych. On the left is the *Fall of Man*, painted within the tradition and style of Jan van Eyck, the founder of Early Netherlandish painting. In this representation of the Temptation, leading to the Fall from Grace presented within a vast landscape, Adam and Eve are tempted by the Serpent in the form of a large lizard with a woman's head. Minute, almost microscopic observation of trees and flowering plants, as well as the exacting depiction of light effects, such as the points of sunlight reflecting off of individual leaves, fall entirely within the tradition established by van Eyck. The nude Adam and Eve likewise recall van Eyck's studies from the nude for the Ghent altarpiece.

In contrast to the very Eyckian *Fall of Man*, the right half of the diptych, the *Lamentation*, encapsulates the expressive tradition of Rogier van der Weyden. The emotional intensity of the moment controls all of the figures in the image. The passionate reaction of John the Evangelist and Mary responding to the dead Christ resonates in the animated patterns of broken, fluttering drapery folds.

The extreme stylistic contrast between the two panels is underlined by the differences between the lush paradise garden presented in the *Fall of Man* and the barren, desert-like hill of Golgotha in the *Lamentation*. This contrast corresponds to the meaning of the diptych as a whole, man's salvation after his Fall from grace is achieved through the sacrifice and crucifixion of Christ.

This early work by Hugo van der Goes demonstrates the tensions ruling both his life and his artistic productions. Emotionally disturbed and frustrated by unattainable artistic goals, he retired to a monastery.

A *St. Genevieve*, painted in grisaille (to give the illusion of a figure sculpted in marble within a niche) was originally attached to the outside of this small folding altarpiece. This panel has been removed from the diptych and is exhibited separately in the museum.

K. S.

297

LEGEND OF THE RELICS OF ST. JOHN THE BAPTIST
Geertgen tot Sint Jans
(Leyden ? c . 1460/65 – c. 1490/95 Haarlem)
after 1484
Wood; H 172 cm, W 139 cm
Inv. No. 993

Geertgen tot Sint Jans, active in Haarlem in the 15th century, was at that time the foremost master of Dutch painting. *The Legend of the Relics of St. John the Baptist* is a fragment of Geertgen's major work, the High Altar of the Order of St. John at Haarlem, which was destroyed during the 1573 siege of Haarlem. This panel, along with the *Lamentation* (also in the Kunsthistorische Museum) originally formed the front and back sides of a single wing of this altarpiece. Geertgen painted it for the chapel of the Knights of St. John soon after 1484 as a result of the return of the relics of St. John the Baptist to the Order of the Knights by the Turkish Sultan in that year. Within a unified narrative landscape Geertgen presents several events from the legend of the relics. In the background he depicts the separate burials of St. John's Head and Body. In the foreground the later exhumation and burning of the remains of St. John ordered by Emperor Julian Apostate in 362 as well as the 13th century rediscovery of the unburned relics and their delivery to the Order of the Knights of St. John at the castle of St. Jean d'Acre. Geertgen unifies the chronologically disparate events presented in the painting through the innovative use of group portraits of his patrons, the late 15th century Haarlem Knights of St. John. Thus, Geertgen created the earliest

CHRIST CARRYING THE CROSS ▽
Hieronymus Bosch
(Hertogenbosch c. 1450 – 1516 Hertogenbosch)
c. 1480/90
Wood; H 57 cm, W 32 cm
Inv. No. 6429

Among the Early Netherlandish painters Bosch, who worked in Northern Brabant, was unique. His symbolic interpretation of themes is strikingly different from his contemporaries. This panel, painted on both sides, at one time formed the left wing of a small, now lost altarpiece. Two separate, though narratively connected events are depicted

example of group portraiture, which subsequently reached its height in the 17th century Dutch tradition exemplified by Rembrandt and Frans Hals.   C. Z.

on the interior side of the panel. Christ is presented in the upper portion carrying the cross; bent down by its weight, he is pushed onward towards Gethsemane in the midst of a dense crowd of onlookers. Below the parable of the good and bad thieves is to be seen. The good thief, on the right, seeks absolution for his sins through confession, while the bad thief, on the left, howls and awaits his execution. Bosch depicts *Christ Carrying the Cross* as a timeless event, set in his own age, presenting the viewer with a mirror of the world's wickedness. This is contrasted on the reverse with the innocent image of a child with a pinwheel and toddler's chair. K. S.

ALTARPIECE OF THE ARCHANGEL MICHAEL
Gerard David
(Oudewater c. 1460 – 1523 Bruges)
c. 1510
Wood; central panel: H 66 cm, W 53 cm; wings: each H 66 cm, W 22.5 cm
Inv. No. 4056

THE BAPTISM OF CHRIST
Joachim Patinier
(Bouvignes 1475/85 – 1524 Antwerp)
c. 1515
Wood; H 59.7 cm, W 76.3 cm
Inv. No. 981

In this painting the religious scene in the foreground and the broad landscape which surrounds it share an equal importance. Landscape itself was Patinier's favourite subject. Yet he none the less felt compelled to justify it through the inclusion of the *Baptism of Christ* in the foreground. The eye of the viewer is drawn as much to the bizarre rock formation in the middle distance, with the River Jordan circling round it, as it is to the figures depicted in the foreground. Despite the seemingly disparate themes of landscape and religious narrative, Patinier is able to unify them. The central rock formation occupies a spit of land which juts into the pictorial space from the left. This complex of land provides a narratively separate space for the Sermon of John the Baptist in the Wilderness. In the far distance the view widens into a panoramic landscape. The overall blue tone of this portion of the landscape depends upon Patinier's understanding use of aerial Perspective. K. S.

The central panel represents the Archangel Michael doing battle with the demons and on the wing panels are depictions of St. Jerome as Cardinal and St. Anthony of Padua. On the backs of the wings appear St. Sebastian and a female Saint accompanied by a boy. The Apocalypse (Rev. 12:7) relates the final battle of the angelic hosts, led by the Archangel Michael, against Satan and his angels; yet here the battle, which in the Creation story is also described as the fall of the rebel angels, is relegated to a secondary scene in the background to the right. The representation of the Archangel Michael as victor over the fallen angels is found in Early Netherlandish painting in a composition by Jan van Eyck. In this composition, the original of which has been lost, the demons are for the first time endowed with a sinister reality as devilish creations. Their number recalls the Seven Deadly Sins. K. S.

VIRGIN AND CHILD
Joos van Cleve
(Cleves? c. 1485–1540 Antwerp)
c. 1530
Wood; H 74.3 cm, W 56 cm
Inv. No. 836

At the beginning of the sixteenth century, the Early Netherlandish tradition of painting had reached an impasse and began to take its inspiration from the broader perspectives of the Italian Renaissance, thus opening up new avenues of development. This resulted in a charming fusion of these two traditions in terms of both form and content. Joos van Cleve was one of numerous artists working in Antwerp, the new economic and cultural centre of the Netherlands, who embellished their paintings with the new ornamental and architectural motifs. Van Cleve adhered faithfully to the traditional forms of composition but incorporated impulses from Northern Italian painting deriving from Leonardo da Vinci, the originator of *sfumato*, the soft, almost imperceptible transition from one colour to another. Here van Cleve employs this technique to resolve and blur the sharp contours, suffusing the picture with soft light.   K. S.

ST. THOMAS AND ST. MATTHEW ALTARPIECE
Bernaert van Orley
(Brussels 1488–1541 Brussels)
c. 1515
Wood; H 140 cm, W 180 cm
Inv. No. 992

In or around the year 1512, Bernaert van Orley was commissioned by the Guild of Masons and Carpenters to paint an altarpiece portraying scenes from the lives of the Apostles Thomas and Matthew — the patron saints of the Guild — for the church of Notre Dame du Sablon in Brussels. The altar's central panel (the two wings are in the Musées Royaux des Beaux Arts, Brussels) is divided into two parts by a richly decorated pillar. The left-hand half depicts the martyrdom of St. Thomas, run through with a sword by an Indian idolater, on the right St. Matthew is being summoned as an apostle. Both scenes take place beneath splendidly decorated, fanciful architectural canopies. The background contains further events from the saints' lives. The picture displays the characteristic feature of Netherlandish painting of the early sixteenth century: the fusion of the depiction of a wealth of minute detail and the formal richness with impulses from the Italian Renaissance which are especially noticeable in the architectural ornamentation.   C. Z.

THE PRESENTATION
Jan van Scorel
(Schoorl 1495–1562 Utrecht)
c. 1528/30
Wood; H 114 cm, W 85 cm
Inv. No. 6161

With the foundation of a humanist education, the young painter Jan van Scorel set out on a artistic journey through Germany and Italy, lasting several years. This journey reached its climax with his appointment as supervisor of the pontifical collection of antiquities by his countryman pope Hadrian VI. Trained in the works of classical antiquity and that of contemporary artists of the High Renaissance, he returned to the Netherlands as an expert on the presentation of Roman art. In his painting *The Presentation*, completed soon after his return, the Roman architectural characteristics reveal the student of Bramante's buildings. The lofty pillars in the forefront, the diagonal view into a series of rooms, closed in by coffered barrel-shaped vaults, gives the impression of an immensely high and wide room, where the figures are inserted like statues.   K. S.

ST. LUKE PAINTING THE VIRGIN
Jan Gossaert, called Mabuse
(Maubeuge c. 1478–1532 Middelburg)
c. 1520
Wood; H 109.6 cm, W 82 cm
Inv. No. 894

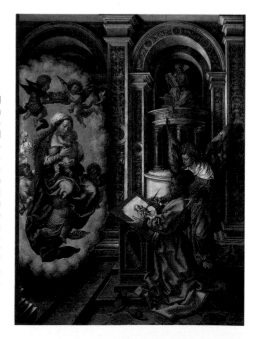

According to legend, the Evangelist Luke painted the Virgin Mary. The scene, frequently seen in Early Netherlandish painting often has the character of a real portrait sitting. Gossaert, who worked in Antwerp, breaks away from iconographic tradition by painting the Madonna as a vision, surrounded by light, clouds and angels. The Evangelist kneels before the heavenly apparition which he is drawing with the help of an angel. The cool monochrome of the vision is in distinct contrast to the brightly coloured figures of St. Luke and the Angel. Gossaert, who was in Italy in 1508/09, is one of the leading representatives of the Romanist style in the early 16th century. The richly decorated architecture points to the influence of the Italian Renaissance, whereas the realistic details and the brilliance of painting represent the Flemish tradition.   C. Z.

**LANDSCAPE WITH ST. JOHN THE BAPTIST
PREACHING**
Herri met de Bles
(Dinant c. 1510–c. 1555)
c. 1535/40
Wood; H 29 cm, W 39 cm
Inv. No. 1004

Herri met de Bles, working a generation later than Joachim Patinier, further developed the latter's model of landscape painting. He was perhaps a nephew of Joachim's, since "met de Bles" was merely a nickname, his real name being Patinier. Herri met de Bles executed a large number of small paintings in which the landscape dominates and the religious motif has been reduced to a group of tiny figures near the edge of the picture. These landscapes were not intended as realistic depictions. They are rather panoramas assembled from individual picturesque motifs, always following the same compositional idea. Almost like stage scenery ranged behind each other in diminishing perspective, the different colour zones succeed each other — first brown, then green, ochre and finally light blue. Herri met de Bles' small, miniaturistic pictures were much sought after as collector's pieces even during his own lifetime.   K. S.

VENUS AND MARS SURPRISED BY VULCAN
Maerten van Heemskerck
(Heemskerck 1498–1574 Haarlem)
c. 1540
Wood; H 96 cm, W 99 cm
Inv. No. 6395

Classical mythology relates that Venus, goddess of beauty and love, cheats her limping husband, the god of fire who spends his time in an underground smithy, with Mars, the god of war. Betrayed by Helios, the sun god who sees everything, the lovers are caught by Vulcan in a finely spun, nearly invisible metal net, and are exposed to the mockery of the other gods on Olympus. This picture, and *Vulcan giving Achilles' shield to Thetis* (also in the Kunsthistorische Museum), constitute the wings of a "mythological triptych" known as the *Vulcan Triptych*. The central panel (now in Prague) depicts Venus and Amor in Vulcan's smithy. Heemskerck used the form of an altarpiece for this profane theme in order to emphasize the moralizing aspect of the painting, namely that evil deeds will be discovered.   K. S.

ANTON PERRENOT DE GRANVELLA
Anthonis Mor
(Utrecht 1517/20–1576/77 Antwerp)
1549
Wood; H 107 cm, W 82 cm
Inv. No. 1035

In his portraits of courtiers, Mor personified the idealized political man, whose noble principles of princely virtue can be recognized even in an individual and often ugly physiognomy. He acquired his ability to make such portraits from his education in the Netherlandish painting tradition. He combined the sometimes soft, sometimes very precise drawing technique of this tradition with a sympathetic, psychological understanding of the sitter as well as with a striking sense of form. Early in his career, Mor met his later patron Granvella (1517–1586), son of the powerful chancellor of Charles V, who had known life at court from his earliest youth, and later became the leading Spanish politician in the Netherlands. He is shown here as prematurely aged at thirty-two, in the black garment of the scholar.   K. S

THE HOLY FAMILY
Martin Schongauer
(Colmar c. 1450–1491 Breisach)
c. 1480
Wood; H 26 cm, W 17 cm
Inv. No. 843

Martin Schongauer was the most famous German artist of the late 15th century prior to Albrecht Dürer. He was admired and imitated by his contemporaries particularly for his engravings owing to their variety of formal motifs and their technically precise execution. His small paintings, combining graphic characteristics with the colourful luminosity learned from the Early Netherlandish painting tradition, appeal particularly to the emotions of the viewer. In his *Holy Family* Schongauer gives the impression of quiet , happy family life, and lends to seemingly insignificant everyday objects – to the bundle of straw and grapes – a deeper meaning of Christian salvation.   K. S.

ADORATION OF THE TRINITY ▷
Albrecht Dürer
(Nuremberg 1471–1528 Nuremberg)
1511
Wood; H 135 cm, W 123.4 cm
Inv. No. 838

Matthäus Landauer, a Nuremberg patrician and the founder of the "Zwölfbrüderhaus", a home for twelve old and indigent citizens commissioned this painting from Dürer in 1508. The chapel for which the painting was intended was dedicated to the Trinity and All Saints and this determined the programme of the altarpiece. The painting presents the Holy Trinity in the company of All Saints and Christian believers in accordance with St. Augustine's conception of "The City of God" after the Last Judgement.
The Holy Trinity in the centre (God the Father enthroned on the rainbow with Christ on the cross and, above him, the dove of the Holy Ghost) is surrounded by concentric circles of worshippers. The innermost circle of winged angels' heads is followed by angels bearing instruments of the Passion. Beneath them on the right side are the patriarchs, prophets and kings of the Old Testament; prominent among them, Moses with the tablets of the commandments, King David as psalmist with harp and St. John the Baptist. Similarly, on the left, is found the group of holy virgins and martyrs, represented with their identifying attributes: St. Barbara with her chalice, St. Catherine with her wheel and sword, St. Dorothy with her basket of flowers and St. Agnes with her lamb. The Virgin Mary occupies a position parallel to that of St. John the Baptist. They thus fulfill their traditional intercessionary roles before Christ. In the bottom row, clearly divided into two groups, are the Christians who have passed judgement. They form a Christian community consisting of ecclesiastics on the left and laymen on the right. Matthäus Landauer, the donor, is found among the ecclesiastics, between the cardinal and the mendicant monk, wearing a fur trimmed coat. His son-in-law, Wilhelm Haller, is found on the right side, among the laymen, dressed as a knight in golden armour.
Within the panoramic landscape Dürer included his own self-portrait with an inscribed tablet. Dürer's absorption of Italian traditions and techniques is particularly important for this painting. He designed painting and frame (with the Last Judgement at the top) as a single unit following the Italian manner, instead of creating a mere Gothic triptych. The frame exhibited in the Gallery is a modern copy of the original in the Germanische Nationalmuseum in Nuremberg. The altarpiece shows the entire spectrum of scintillating colour that Dürer introduced to German painting, after having assimilated Venetian colouristic and painterly effects into his own painting techniques.   K. S.

PORTRAIT OF A YOUNG VENETIAN LADY
Albrecht Dürer
(Nuremberg 1471–1528 Nuremberg)
1505
Wood; H 32.5 cm, W 24.5 cm
Inv. No. 6440

Albrecht Dürer's main achievement in the development of German painting was to overcome the late Gothic style by introducing the principles of the Italian Renaissance to Germany. In 1505, during his second stay in Venice, he painted the portrait of an unknown *Young Venetian Lady*. It shows Dürer's newly won ability to dissolve hard contours with painterly softness. The austere graphic forms are changed to shining colours, the sharp outlines softened without losing the firm sureness of their drawing. The lady is wearing the Venetian fashion of the early 16th century. Her fair hair – the glory of Venetian women – is pinned up on the back and held by a net, with curls hanging down on each side of the face.   K. S.

THE MARTYRDOM OF THE TEN THOUSAND
Albrecht Dürer
(Nuremberg 1471–1528 Nuremberg)
1508
Canvas; H 99 cm, W 87 cm
Inv. No. 835

According to a legend of the Middle Ages, the Roman Emperors Hadrian and Antoninus sent an army on a campaign to Asia Minor. The soldiers converted to Christianity after angels appeared to them, promising victory. After their victory they were all martyred on Mount Ararat by King Sapor of Persia. They were crucified, stoned and thrust over rocks into thickets of thorns. The Elector Frederick the Wise of Saxony, who had a large collection of relics which were displayed annually until Martin Luther prohibited this practice, commissioned this painting from Dürer for the Collegiate Church in Wittenberg. In the centre of the picture one is struck by two men dressed in black – Dürer himself carrying a slip of paper with his signature on a cleft stick, and his recently deceased friend, the humanist Conrad Celtes. K. S.

306

VIRGIN AND CHILD WITH A PEAR
Albrecht Dürer
(Nuremberg 1471–1528 Nuremberg)
1512
Wood; H 49 cm, W 37 cm
Inv. No. 848

Of the many pictures that Dürer painted of the Virgin and Child – his most frequent subject – this is one of the best known. The picture is reduced to a few colours and large forms: the black background, the beautiful blue of the dress and the Madonna's light coloured veil which corresponds to the colour of her skin. The composition is limited to Mary's head which is bent over the Child, and the recumbent Child itself. Almost exaggerated in its distinctly moulded form and lively twisted position, the body of Christ is reminiscent of Italian prototypes as found in the works of Michelangelo and his contemporaries. In opposition to the classic form of the Christ Child the graphic realisation of the Virgin's veil suggests a dependance on late Gothic style.   K. S.

PORTRAIT OF JOHANN KLEBERGER
Albrecht Dürer
(Nuremberg 1471–1528 Nuremberg)
1526
Wood; H 37 cm, W 36.6 cm
Inv. No. 858

A strange portrait of a strange man: Johann Kleberger, of humble origin, left his native Nuremberg and returned years later as the owner of an immense fortune. In 1518 he married a daughter of the well known humanist Pirckheimer, a friend of Dürer's, against her father's will. For unknown reasons, Kleberger left her a short time later to settle in Lyon where as a benefactor he distributed his great wealth among the poor. Dürer painted this portrait eight years after Kleberger's disappearance as a memorial. Kleberger's absence is expressed in the form of the picture; the head, reminiscent of antique portrait medallions, is not meant as a relief but floats vaguely in space within the circular opening of a stone slab. In the corners we see Kleberger's shield and crest, the astrological sign of the lion, and the artist's signature. The marble-like background bears the inscription of Kleberger's name and age.   K. S.

PORTRAIT OF EMPEROR MAXIMILIAN I
Albrecht Dürer
(Nuremberg 1471–1528 Nuremberg)
1519
Wood; H 74 cm, W 61.5 cm
Inv. No. 825

By his marriage to Mary of Burgundy, Maximilian I, whose domain had been approximately that of present-day Austria, was the first Habsburg ruler able to expand his territories to Western Europe. He achieved his political aims not only by the use of modern warfare but also used the arts to justify his actions and to ensure his posthumous fame. Among the many painters, sculptors and engravers working for Maximilian I, Albrecht Dürer was the most important. In 1518 he portrayed the Emperor at the Imperial Diet at Augsburg in a chalk drawing which he used as draft for the portrait that was completed after the Emperor's death. In it, Maximilian is not wearing imperial robes but is shown as a plain nobleman in a fur-edged coat. Instead of the Imperial orb, he is holding a pomegranate as a symbol of power and wealth.   K. S.

EMPEROR MAXIMILIAN I WITH HIS FAMILY
Bernhard Strigel
(Memmingen c. 1460–1528 Memmingen)
1516
Wood; H 72.8 cm, W 60.4 cm
Inv. No. 832

This picture is an example of the way in which Maximilian used his family to carry out his political plans, and his desire to document his intentions in works of art. The picture shows Maximilian I, his first wife, Mary of Burgundy, who had died in 1482, and their family: their son Philip who had died in 1506, Philip's sons Charles and Ferdinand, as well as Maximilian's adopted son Ludwig, heir to the kingdoms of Hungary and Bohemia. Thus the picture refers to the double betrothal of 1515 in Vienna which sealed the union between the Habsburgs and the Magyar-Jagellon Royal Family. Johannes Cuspinian, humanist and counsellor of Maximilian I, who had taken part in the negotiations of 1515, received the panel, and commissioned Strigel to expand it to a representation of the Holy Kinship; on the reverse side, separated today, he had the main branch of the Holy Kin painted, and, on a second panel (now privately owned) his own family as another branch of the Holy Kinship.   K. S.

THE MADONNA HANDING THE CHILD A POMEGRANATE
Hans Holbein the Elder
(Augsburg c. 1465–1524 Isenheim)
c. 1510/12
Wood; H 42.2 cm, W 27 cm
Inv. No. 6503

Hans Holbein the Elder was active in the Southern German town of Augsburg when it was becoming prosperous as a centre of European trade and finance. As the most important late Gothic painter of Swabia he was himself responsible for its artistic supremacy. Belonging to the same generation as Albrecht Dürer, and following his example, Holbein achieved the transition from the Late Gothic to the Renaissance style of painting. The Kunsthistorische Museum possesses two works by Holbein. Neither of them would be imaginable without Netherlandish models. In the early panel depicted here, the motif of the two figures (the manner in which the Madonna hands the Child a pomegranate) goes back to Hans Memling. The sweeping lines delineating the form, the glowing colours and the almost tactile effect produced by the many small shining objects, by the jewellery, pearls and embroidery, are all further examples of the influence of Early Netherlandish painting. K. S.

CRUCIFIXION OF CHRIST
Lucas Cranach the Elder
(Kronach 1472 – 1553 Weimar)
c. 1500/01
Wood; H 58.5 cm, W 45 cm
Inv. No. 6905

The *Crucifixion of Christ* with numerous accompanying figures was one of the most frequently commissioned subjects in late Gothic painting. Especially in Southern Germany this image was increasingly loaded with bizarre or horrifying details which intensified the expressive force of the representation. The very earliest of his known works the *Crucifixion,* painted shortly after the young Cranach moved from Franconia to Vienna, shows Christ covered with blood and wounds, a rough cross made from a tree-trunk, grotesquely distorted and eccentrically dressed soldiers, all within a wild and rugged landscape. The whole, coarsely painted in intense colours, surpasses in expressiveness any earlier depiction of this subject. It was with this and other similar works from the same period that Cranach came to be regarded as one of the founders of the so-called Danube school. K. S.

JUDITH WITH THE HEAD OF HOLOFERNES
Lucas Cranach the Elder
(Kronach 1472–1553 Weimar)
c. 1530
Wood; H 87 cm, W 56 cm
Inv. No. 858

Cranach departed from the traditions of the Danube School and acquired his own unmistakable style shortly after his appointment as court painter to Frederick the Wise in Wittenberg in 1504. This mature style, which clearly differs from contemporary Mannerism, is marked by spatially compressed, flat compositions. Also typical is the use of strong colours which enhance the decorative effect of the painting. These stylistic traits are repeatedly found in a rather narrow repertoire of often repeated subjects; for instance, several versions of this representation of the Old Testament heroine Judith are still extant.

Judith, in order to save her country from the enemy general Holofernes, went to his camp in disguise, pretending to be a prostitute. He·fell for her ruse, and got drunk in his attempt to seduce her. She was then able to kill him by cutting off his head, and thereby saved her people. This version of the painting presents not only the essence of the biblical story, but is simultaneously also a portrait of an elegant lady of the Saxon court and a costume study. K. S.

STAG HUNT OF THE ELECTOR FREDERICK THE WISE
Lucas Cranach the Elder
(Kronach 1472–1553 Weimar)
1529
Wood; H 80 cm, W 114 cm
Inv. No. 3560

The duties of a court painter – a position Cranach occupied until he died in the service of the Elector of Saxony – was to provide the court with paintings in the widest sense of word. These were not only portraits of the princely family but also records of festive occasions.

The presentation of a vast slaughter at which countless stags were chased into the water to enable the court party to kill them more easily with their crossbows, records an event of thirty years earlier. Frederick the Wise and the Elector John the Steadfast as well as Emperor Maximilian I – seen in the foreground accompanied by keepers – had taken part in this hunt.

K. S.

THE THREE AGES OF MAN
Hans Baldung Grien
(Schwäbisch Gmünd c. 1485–1545 Strasbourg)
1509/10
Wood; H 48.2 cm, W 32.5 cm
Inv. No. 2636

Hans Baldung Grien received his artistic education primarily from Albrecht Dürer. He was also
influenced by the so-called Danube School, the
inspiration of which can be seen in the landscape
with the lichen-covered tree. Baldung here presents a symbolic interpretation of the ages of man
in the constant presence of death. The old woman
in the painting faces death resolutely, but tries in
vain to ward him off. The young woman, whose
smooth white body contrasts strongly with the half
decayed figure of death, takes no notice of him.
Instead, she regards herself in a mirror, a symbol
of the vanity and transiency of earthly existence.
The infant boy on the ground with his hobby-
horse embodies the first, immature stage of life.
He sees the world as yet indistinctly, through a
veil.   K. S.

ST. GEORGE AND THE DRAGON
Leonhard Beck
(Augsburg c. 1480–1542 Augsburg)
c. 1515
Wood; H 134.5 cm, W 116 cm
Inv. No. 5669

Leonhard Beck belonged to a group of artists in
the service of Emperor Maximilian I, including
among others Hans Burgkmair and Albrecht Altdorfer, who from around 1510 produced drawings
for woodcuts for the Emperor's numerous graphic
projects. The artistic quality of Beck's œuvre was
extremely uneven, but his portrayal of St. George
fighting the dragon is a masterpiece, towering
over his other works in its compositional de-
corativity and rich colouring. Beck renders the
mythic fight with the dragon as a mediaeval
legend in a forest landscape. The main subject is
framed on either side in the background by
scenes representing the preceding and subsequent events in the story.   K. S.

THE NATIVITY
Albrecht Altdorfer
(Regensburg c. 1480–1538 Regensburg)
c. 1520
Wood; H 44 cm, W 36 cm
Inv. No. 2716

The novelty of Altdorfer's style, and indeed of the entire Danube School, is characterized by the mixture of the intensely emotional and highly dramatic aspects of *The Nativity*. Also characteristic are the contrasts of decay and the growth of lush, overgrown nature. The supernatural aspects of light are used here by Altdorfer to emphasize the miracle of Christ's birth and the notion of Christ as the "Light of the World". Many of these ideas first appeared and were developed in mediaeval mystical and devotional literature. The setting of this nighttime *Nativity* is also important; the Holy Family rests outdoors, unprotected by shelter and surrounded by a fresh fall of snow. Music making angels are all around them; each emanates a glowing light that illuminates the darkness. Yet the lights from the angels are dimmed in comparison to the wonderful radiance of the newly-born Christ child. He illuminates the entire image: the ruin towering behind the family, the massive buttress and attached vault, as well as the buildings further in the distance.   K. S.

THE RESURRECTION OF CHRIST
Albrecht Altdorfer
(Regensburg c. 1480–1538 Regensburg)
1518
Wood; H 70 cm, W 37 cm
Inv. No. 6796

Two panels of the predella of Altdorfer's large *Altarpiece of St. Sebastian and the Passion of Christ,* one of the major works of the Danube School, are in this Gallery. The altarpiece was painted for the monastery of St. Florian in Upper Austria in 1518. The two panels in Vienna depict the final scenes of Christ's passion: the *Burial* and the *Resurrection*. Both paintings share a similar formal structure; an open landscape is seen beyond and through the opening of a dark grotto. Altdorfer's conception of the *Resurrection* is arresting in its nighttime setting. A light with the quality of a supernatural fire emanates from the body of Christ and illuminates the sombre clouds in the sky. This glistening light casts a red and yellow glow which colours the soldiers clustered, dazed and sleeping, around Christ's tomb.   K. S.

THE PAINTER HANS BURGKMAIR AND HIS WIFE ANNA
Laux (Lukas) Furtenagel
(Augsburg 1505 – after 1548 Augsburg)
1529
Wood; H 60 cm, W 52 cm
Inv. No. 924

Furtenagel's double portrait of a middle-aged couple in half-length functions as an allegory of death. The couple are identified by the scroll on the left of the painting as the Augsburg painter Hans Burgkmair and his wife Anna, née Allerlai. Before the small signature in the top right hand corner was discovered, this painting was thought to be painted by Burgkmair himself. It was not considered probable that an artist other than he could have painted such a tour-de-force in both form and subject matter. The wife holds a convex mirror in which two skulls are reflected. However, the couple do not look at the image in the mirror, but instead gaze steadily out of the picture at the viewer, for whom the ultimate message of the painting is intended. Inscribed on the mirror's edge is "Erken dich selbst" ("Know thyself"). The inscription above the pair "Sollche Gestalt unser baider was, im Spiegel aber nix dan das" ("Such faces we both once had; in the mirror, nought but this") suggests that Burgkmair and his wife are aware of their own mortality and calmly await death.   K. S.

THE HUMANIST JAKOB ZIEGLER
Wolf Huber
(Feldkirch? c. 1485–1553 Passau)
after 1544
Wood; H 58.5 cm, W 44.3 cm
Inv. No. 1942

Jakob Ziegler, (1470/71–1549) a humanist primarily known for his theological writings, was born in Landau on the Isar River. He studied at Ingolstadt, and worked in various other cities as a mathematician, geographer and astronomer before settling in Passau in 1544, at which time Wolf Huber was the painter to the episcopal court in that city. Huber here combines the painterly opulence of the Danube School, evidenced in the gleaming distances of the panoramic landscape, with the classical severity of a triangular composition. The name and origin of the artist are presented on an archaically inscribed tablet, like an epitaph. This, together with the transparent appearance of the head, suggests the possibility that Huber painted the portrait as a memorial to Ziegler after his death in 1549.   K. S.

JANE SEYMOUR, QUEEN OF ENGLAND
Hans Holbein the Younger
(Augsburg 1497–1543 London)
1536
Wood; H 65.4 cm, W 40.7 cm
Inv. No. 881

Holbein was appointed court painter to Henry VIII of England in 1536. His portrait of Jane Seymour was one of the first portraits he painted in that capacity. Jane Seymour, born in 1513, came to Henry's court in 1530 as a Lady-in-Waiting to Catherine of Aragon, Henry's first wife. She continued to serve in that position under Anne Boleyn and became Henry's third wife shortly after Anne's execution. Jane Seymour died in childbirth the year after her marriage, but was survived by her son Edward. Holbein's painfully accurate rendering of the precious materials of Jane Seymour's dress brings an archaic flatness to the portrait. This archaic quality, combined with the objective representation of the Queen's features is Holbein's approach to the idealized royal portrait whose effect is to widen and emphasize the distance betweeen the observer and the subject of the portrait.   K. S.

THE DUISBURG MERCHANT DIRCK TYBIS
Hans Holbein the Younger
(Augsburg 1497–1543 London)
1533
Wood; H 47.7 cm, W 34.8 cm
Inv. No. 903

Hans Holbein, along with Albrecht Dürer, was one of the few German artists able to transcend the confines of the artistic milieu of his native land and achieve international prestige. Holbein's initial training was in his father's workshop in Augsburg; he subsequently worked in Basle for some time, but ultimately settled in England. Active primarily as a portrait painter, during his first years there he captured the likeness of many of the German merchants living in London. These German merchants, including Dirck Tybis, lived at the Steelyard, a trading establishment founded by the Hanseatic League. The style of Holbein's portraits is characterized by a combination of monumental elements (despite the small format), with a masterly and uncompromisingly precise rendering of detail.   K. S.

DR. JOHN CHAMBERS, PHYSICIAN TO KING HENRY VIII
Hans Holbein the Younger
(Augsburg 1497–1543 London)
1543
Wood; H 58 cm, W 39.7 cm
Inv. No. 882

This painting of Dr. John Chambers, clergyman and personal physician to Henry VIII, was one of Holbein's last portrait commissions. The inscription in the background, having been added to the painting later, wrongly presents Dr. Chambers as 88 years old. In reality, he was 73 years old when Holbein painted this portrait as well as a large group portrait of all of Henry VIII's doctors. Holbein here achieves a culmination of his search for the combination of a simple, monumental form and the close perusal of physiognomic detail. The viewer's impression of the man Chambers is controlled by the way in which Holbein presents the visible effects of the ordeals of a long life in his set features and expression. K. S.

CHRISTOPH BAUMGARTNER
Christoph Amberger
(Augsburg c. 1500–1561/62 Augsburg)
1543
Wood; H 83 cm, W 62.5 cm
Inv. No. 889

The extant part of Amberger's extensive œuvre consists primarily of portraits commissioned by Emperor Charles V and South German patricians. In 1543, Amberger painted this portrait of the Nuremberg patrician Christoph Baumgartner in honour of the nobility conferred upon him at the Imperial Diet in that year. Amberger here captures the comfortable self-assurance of a successful man. He was able, like no other of the post-Dürer generation of German artists, to incorporate into his work aspects of the Venetian manner of painting. This is especially evident in his colour harmonies, painting technique and in the quiet, carefully composed formal arrangements of his portraits. In the portrait of Baumgartner, only the view through the open window to a distant landscape remains within the tradition of northern portrait painting. The rich colouristic effects and Amberger's extremely painterly style are closely connected to the Venetian tradition. K. S.

EMPEROR CHARLES V
Jakob Seisenegger
(Lower Austria 1505–1567 Linz)
1532
Canvas; H 203.5 cm, W 123 cm
Inv. No. A 114

Jakob Seisenegger, an Austrian painter, was appointed court painter to Ferdinand I in 1531. The next year, 1532, Seisenegger was sent by Ferdinand to Bologna to paint Ferdinand's brother, Charles V, who had been crowned Emperor in 1530. Seisenegger won international fame during his lifetime as well as art historical significance for his novel use of full-length portraits at a time when half-length representations were customary. He generally suppressed verisimilitude in his likenesses preferring instead to reproduce a few recognizable characteristic features within a generally noble and dignified representation. With this portrait of the Emperor Seisenegger created a prototype frequently imitated by later artists. (Titian used this painting as model for his own renowned representation of Charles V now in the Prado in Madrid.)   K. S.

KING CHARLES IX OF FRANCE
François Clouet
(Tours c. 1510/20–1572 Paris)
1569
Canvas; H 222 cm, W 115 cm
Inv. No. 752

François Clouet served as portrait painter to the French court after 1541. In his official likenesses, he unites exact portrait representation, worked out in advance with two-toned charcoal sketches, with the specific requirements for full-length court portraits as formulated by Anthonis Mor and Seisenegger for the Habsburgs. Archduke Ferdinand II who acted as a proxy for King Charles IX (1540–1574) on the occasion of his marriage to Archduchess Elisabeth, Ferdinand's niece, was presented with a series of most precious state gifts. Among these were the court chalice of Duke Philip the Good of Burgundy, Benvenuto Cellini's

THE PARABLE OF THE PRODIGAL SON
Master of the Prodigal Son
(active in Antwerp c. 1530–1560)
after 1550
Wood; H 128 cm, W 214.5 cm
Inv. No. 986

Painted by an anonymous artist known simply as the Master of the Prodigal Son, this picture illustrates the *Parable of the Prodigal Son* in various episodes (Luke, 15:11–32). In the foreground we see him dressed in rich garments sitting at a table with food and drink between two prostitutes. In the right half of the picture he is being driven out of the tavern, which, as the birdcage hanging up outside over the door indicates, is actually a brothel. To the left in the background, he is variously shown keeping pigs, sitting ruefully on a bridge and finally being welcomed back by his father. Through the broad depiction of the son's squandering of his fortune on women and gambling the painting becomes a morality picture, whose content corresponds to the morality tradition of 16th century popular literature.   C. Z.

famous salt cellar, and the Michael Chalice (now in the Collection of Sculpture), as well as probably this portrait. The King went down in history, sadly, for his part in the Huguenot Wars that reached their peak in 1572 with the Bartholomaeus Night where 30.000 Protestants from all over France were massacred.   K. S.

◁ STILL LIFE WITH CHRIST AT THE HOUSE OF MARY AND MARTHA
Pieter Aertsen
(Amsterdam 1508/09–1575 Amsterdam)
1552
Wood; H 60 cm, W 101.5 cm
Inv. No. 6927

In vivid colours and with painstaking differentiation of surfaces a plethora of objects is spread out before the viewer, the seemingly haphazard arrangement belying the careful composition. Earthly preparations for a feast are being made, the occasion for which – Jesus at the house of Mary and Martha – is shown in the background, painted in a sketch-like manner and in light, blended tones. The scene in the background represents the spiritual life, with Mary listening to the words of the Lord, while the industrious Martha scolds her for her idleness. And Jesus answered, "Martha, Martha, thou art careful and troubled about many things; but one thing is needful: and Mary hath chosen that good part, which shall not be taken away from her." (Luke, 10:38–42). K. S.

CHILDREN'S GAMES
Pieter Bruegel the Elder
(1525/30–1569 Brussels)
1560
Wood; H 118 cm, W 161 cm
Inv. No. 1017

The composition of this painting, with its steeply rising perspective of a town square strewn with numerous small figures, corresponds to that of other early paintings by Bruegel and gives expression to the idea of an encyclopaedic view of various actions linked by a unifying theme. Here we see 230 children absorbed in 90 different games, many of which are still played today. A number of modern interpretations have sought to endow the painting with deeper, latent meanings, seeing it as a moralizing allegory with the seeming pointlessness of the children's activity symbolizing the vanity, folly and even sinfulness of human action in general. However, this presupposes a deeply pessimistic view of the world on Bruegel's part instead of the manifest humanism that informs all his works.   K. S.

THE FIGHT BETWEEN CARNIVAL AND LENT
Pieter Bruegel the Elder
(1525/30–1569 Brussels)
1559
Wood; H 118 cm, W 164.5 cm
Inv. No. 1016

The title of this painting refers to the focal scene in the centre of the foreground which depicts the fight between Carnival and Lent as a jousting tournament between Prince Carnival and Dame Lent with their respective retinues. It had been performed as folk drama since the late Middle Ages, especially in the Shrove Tuesday processions of the Carnival brotherhoods. Bruegel further depicts various Flemish folk customs from the season between Twelfth Night and Easter, including pantomime and masquerade together with religious customs as the sum of numerous individual scenes in the common space of the market-place bound on two sides by the church and the inn. Thus, he vividly conveys the temporal sequence of the episodes by their spatial contiguity.   K. S.

THE TOWER OF BABEL
Pieter Bruegel the Elder
(1525/30−1569 Brussels)
Wood; H 114 cm, W 155 cm
Inv. No. 1026

The Book of Genesis tells of a great tower built by men not only from fear of a second Flood but above all "to make a name for themselves". God's punishment was the Babylonian confusion of tongues, with men unable to understand each other, the result being that the tower was never finished. Mediaeval interpretation of the Bible saw this myth as an allegory of the consequences of human pride. Bruegel underpins the moral significance with his realistic conception of the painting's subject (deriving from the sixteenth century's archaeological interest in the monuments of the Ancient World), whereby the extensive undertaking seems feasible, but demonstrates its fundamental impossibility. At a first glance the tower seems extremely solid with its broad base, the core a massive rock, its huge dimensions emphasized by the way it dwarfs the houses of the surrounding city and the swarming mass of tiny figures. On closer inspection however, one sees not only the lack of planning (complete and incomplete sections alike are juxtaposed even right at the base), but also the obviously unworkable concept of its design. Bruegel took his inspiration for the construction from the Colosseum in Rome. For Christians this had always been a symbol of ancient hubris as the site of early Christian persecution. Bruegel shows us the inner projection of the building with its rising barrel-vaulted galleries which all lead to the middle of the tower and are thus without function. A second contradiction becomes apparent: the multi-storey structure of the radial passages conflicts with the mounting helical ramps of the outer section. All the verticals are drawn in relation to the apparent horizontal plane of the ramps, with the result that the whole tower is crooked. The tower is deliberately portrayed as impossible and therefore unfinishable, but only reveals its secrets gradually, because the spectator is at first deceived by the many rational details of the construction based on classical Roman models and thus invested with their authority. Besides being a symbol of human pride, Bruegel's painting achieves a deeper significance as a parable of the ultimate failure of mere rationality.   K. S.

THE PROCESSION TO CALVARY
Pieter Bruegel the Elder
(1525/30−1569 Brussels)
1564
Wood; H 124 cm, W 170 cm
Inv. No. 1025

This painting reveals above all others Bruegel's indebtedness to the Early Netherlandish tradition. The compositional idea of depicting Christ carrying the Cross as a semi-circular procession of incidental scenes, set against a wide landscape crowded with figures goes back to Jan van Eyck, and was developed in many different versions well into the sixteenth century. In Bruegel's painting, the bible story is transported into the present, thereby not only giving it an immediacy for his contemporaries but simultaneously making a generally valid statement about human actions. The procession, hurried at beginning and end, comes to a halt where Christ falls under the weight of the Cross in the centre of the painting. A detailed scene next to this shows how Simon of Cyrene is forced to help him. In the foreground, as a remote, isolated group, we see the mourning women around Mary and John the Baptist.

K. S.

THE GLOOMY DAY
Pieter Bruegel the Elder
(1525/30−1569 Brussels)
1565
Wood; H 118 cm, W 163 cm
Inv. No. 1837

Bruegel's cycle of the seasons begins with *Gloomy Day,* portraying nature's transition from winter to its reawakening in spring. As in all the paintings belonging to the cycle, the eye is drawn into the distance from an elevated viewpoint on the edge of the village down to a rivermouth on the plain below, where winter catastrophes are wreaking havoc in the form of storms, breached dykes and floods. On the right, i. e. the side that leads into the rest of the series, peasants can be seen engaging in the typical seasonal activities of collecting wood, cutting willow switches and repairing walls. The children with paper crowns and waffles represent folk customs during this season.

K. S.

THE RETURN OF THE HERD
Pieter Bruegel the Elder
(1525/30–1569 Brussels)
1565
Wood; H 117 cm, W 159 cm
Inv. No. 1018

The cycle of six pictures painted in 1565, (three of the remaining five are in the Kunsthistorische Museum), which portray the progress of the seasons and the rustic activities associated with them, represent not only the peak of Bruegel's achievement as a painter but also the culmination of the calendar landscape, a tradition going back to classical antiquity. The cycle divides the year not into a rigid scheme of equal units or periods of months; each painting is rather dominated by the idea of a certain time of year, Bruegel keeping to the old division of the year into six seasons. The cycle, which should be thought of in its original form as a continuous frieze, begins with the *Gloomy Day,* corresponding to the old beginning of the year in March. The next picture, lost since the seventeenth century, portrayed spring. It is followed by the *Hay Harvest* (early summer) and

the *Corn Harvest* (late summer), both of which were originally in the Imperial Gallery but are today in the National Gallery in Prague and the Metropolitan Museum of New York respectively. The cycle concludes with the *Return of the Herd* (autumn) and the *Hunters in the Snow* (winter). Each painting is both a self-contained composition and also an integral part of the broader concept of the whole cycle, linked by the sequence of colours beginning with brown/black (*Gloomy Day*), through (probably) blue (Spring), green (*Hay Harvest*), yellow (*Corn Harvest*), ochre (*Return of the Herd*) to white (*Hunters in the Snow*). The transitional nature of the autumn landscape is evoked by the movement of the returning herd from right to left in a diagonal leading to the village and by the division of the picture into two halves: the left-hand side still sunny, and the right-hand half dominated by a gathering storm. The grape harvest depicted in the background is more in the nature of incidental detail, as is the place of execution with wheel and gallows, a ubiquitous feature of those uneasy times.

K. S.

HUNTERS IN THE SNOW
Pieter Bruegel the Elder
(1525/30–1569 Brussels)
1565
Wood; H 117 cm, W 162 cm
Inv. No. 1838

The closing (not opening) painting of Bruegel's series of the seasons is the most well-known and most popular of all the pictures in this cycle, because of its unforgettably inventive form and colouring. The hunters are making their way back to the low-lying village with their meagre bounty, a pack of hounds at their heels; their backs are turned towards us. That, along with the perspective of the row of trees, draws the observer down into the distance, on to the remote, icy mountains on the horizon, and at the same time out of the whole cycle. What was then understood as an illustration of seasonal labour – a pig being singed in front of an inn – comes across only as a secondary scene at the left edge of the painting. The winter idyll is completed by a busy swarm of small figures in the distant plain.　　　K. S.

THE PEASANT AND THE NEST ROBBER
Pieter Bruegel the Elder
(1525/30–1569 Brussels)
1568
Wood; H 59.3 cm, W 68.3 cm
Inv. No. 1020

A beautifully-painted landscape extends into the level distance of the picture; meadowland, fields and a farmhouse with horses in the background, a stream with trees in the foreground. No other painting by Bruegel approaches the depiction of nature in the Dutch landscapes of the seventeenth century as closely as this does. However, this is only the setting for a mysterious scene whose significance is unknown today. All attempts to explain the picture have remained unsatisfactory. A peasant who has walked right up to the edge of the picture looks at the spectator, pointing to a boy who has climbed a tree and is robbing a bird's nest. Is he showing us that the boy, who has just lost his hat, is about to fall? However that may be, he has failed to notice that he himself is about to fall into the stream in front of

him. As so often with Bruegel, the painting probably illustrates a proverb, but as the key is missing, the meaning of the picture remains an enigma.　　　K. S.

PEASANT WEDDING
Pieter Bruegel the Elder
(1525/30–1569 Brussels)
c. 1568/69
Wood; H 114 cm, W 164 cm
Inv. No. 1027

More than any other it is this painting which contributed to Bruegel's fame as a portrayer of Flemish peasant life, earning him the sobriquet of "Peasant Bruegel". The artist here dispenses with the elevated viewpoint affording an overall view and instead leads us straight into the middle of a peasant wedding. The table with the wedding feast leads diagonally through the threshing barn, the largest room in the farmhouse. Piled up high in the background is the harvest, safely gathered in. The bride sits in the middle of the table under a paper crown and near her in a high-backed chair sits the lawyer responsible for drawing up the marriage contract. At the end of the table we see the landowner, dressed in Spanish fashion. The bridegroom is not present; he was not led to the bride until the evening of the wedding day. Two bagpipers, the men carrying the food and the boy pouring the drink lend a true-to-life quality to the scene without descending to the mere comic or caricature.   K. S.

PEASANT DANCE
Pieter Bruegel the Elder
(1525/30–1569 Brussels)
c. 1568/69
Wood; H 114 cm, W 164 cm
Inv. No. 1059

The *Peasant Dance*, the second of Bruegel's large-figured paintings, is not an exact counterpart to the *Peasant Wedding* but is close to it, both stylistically and in its subject. Again we have a scene of rustic celebration, faithfully reflecting sixteenth century Flemish custom. Here we can even see a particular moment in the celebrations: the opening of a Kermesse (village fair) with a traditional dance performed by two couples. Since the spectator is on a level with the figures, the sequence of events is difficult to follow: the large couple in the foreground is hurrying to the dance, with the two couples behind them already dancing; further back a man is pulling his reluctant partner out of a house decorated with a banner in

front of a crowd of onlookers. The scene round the table also needs closer inspection before it becomes clear: a man is stretching out his hand to a beggar on the extreme left, thereby knocking his neighbour, who is either simple-minded or blind, in the face.   K. S.

FIRE
Giuseppe Arcimboldo
(Milan 1527–1593 Milan)
1566
Wood; H 66.5 cm, W 51 cm
Inv. No. 1585

Arcimboldo was court painter to the Emperors Ferdinand I, Maximilian II and Rudolph II from 1562 to 1587. In 1563 and 1566 respectively he executed two cycles of allegorical representations of the seasons and the elements as busts in profile. *Fire* is composed of burning faggots, candles, wicks, fuses, oil lamps, flints, pistols and cannons. Besides the polyvalent interpretation of the concept of fire and the symbolisation of the dependence of human achievement on the forces of Nature, there are also references to the Habsburg dynasty: the Order of the Golden Fleece and the medallion displaying the double eagle, indicating not so much a particular ruler as the omnipotence of the Habsburg dynasty itself.   C. Z.

SPRING LANDSCAPE (MAY) ▽
Lucas van Valckenborch
(Löwen c. 1535–1597 Frankfurt a. M.)
1587
Canvas; H 116 cm, W 198 cm
Inv. No. 1065

In the year 1587, in his capacity as court painter to Archduke Matthias, Valckenborch executed a cycle of twelve paintings, one for each month. Of the seven surviving pictures, five are today in the Kunsthistorische Museum. In *Spring Landscape*

(May), the artist employs the traditional type of a vista landscape with an elevated foreground. The figures are concentrated into the right-hand half of the painting in a wooded landscape where an elegant company has gathered for an alfresco meal. To the left, in the landscape stretching out into the background, one can see the archducal palace in Brussels. While the rest of the landscape bears no similarity to the surroundings of Brussels, the view of the castle is topographically accurate, as can be seen from a contemporary engraving. .   C. Z.

MINERVA VICTORIOUS OVER IGNORANCE
Bartholomäus Spranger
(Antwerp 1546 – 1611 Prague)
c. 1591
Canvas; H 163 cm, W 117 cm
Inv. No. 1133

Bartholomäus Spranger received his artistic training in Antwerp and subsequently spent several years in France, Northern Italy and Rome. Uniquely familiar as he was with all the artistic currents of his time, he seemed predestined to become court painter to Emperor Rudolph II, the outstanding connoisseur of his time, who took a personal interest in the works executed by his court painters, even ordaining their form and complex subject matter. In this picture the victory of wisdom over ignorance is presented in the form of an allegory, the abstract ideas being personified as figures from ancient mythology. Minerva, the warlike protectress of the arts and sciences, places a foot triumphantly on the ass-eared representative of ignorance, who is lying defeated and fettered on the ground. Surrounded by the Muses and personifications of the arts, the goddess exemplifies the power of the Emperor's virtues as a ruler in times of war and peace alike.

K. S.

◁ **VENUS AND ADONIS**
Bartholomäus Spranger
(Antwerp 1546 – 1611 Prague)
c. 1597
Canvas; H 163, W 104.3 cm
Inv. No. 2526

Ovid's *Metamorphoses* recount the ancient myth of the love of the goddess Venus for a mortal, the young shepherd and hunter Adonis. Filled with a dreadful presentiment, Venus tries to keep her beloved from going out to hunt. Yet her warnings are in vain and Adonis is attacked by a wild boar and fatally wounded. Spranger's painting, commissioned by Rudolph II, depicts the hunter bidding Venus farewell. The goddess of love, her left hand resting on her lover's knee, stands at a slight angle to the viewer, bathed in the supernatural light issuing from the depths of the grotto. She displays the naked beauty of her divine form and thus creates a correspondence between the erotic tension of the content and the artistic tension of the formal composition, calculated to please the Emperor's sophisticated tastes.   K. S.

JUDITH DISPLAYING THE HEAD OF HOLOFERNES TO THE PEOPLE ▽
Abraham Bloemaert
(Gorkum 1564 – 1651 Utrecht)
1593
Wood; H 34.5 cm, W 44.5 cm
Inv. No. 6514

EMPEROR RUDOLPH II
Hans von Aachen
(Cologne 1551/52 – 1615 Prague)
c. 1606/08
Canvas; H 60 cm, W 48 cm
Inv. No. 6438

Hans von Aachen was the foremost portraitist among the artists at the court of Emperor Rudolph II (1552–1612). On terms of almost personal friendship with the Emperor, he gained an intimate knowledge of both his outward appearance and his personality. Hence von Aachen was able to avoid any idealisation and his portrait convincingly conveys the complicated character of this highly gifted and cultivated ruler. In the pursuit of his political aims Rudolph vascillated between single-minded determination and lethargy, which led to a feud with his less gifted but ambitious brother Matthias, who virtually deprived him of power in 1608. Nevertheless Rudolphs rôle as promoter of the arts and sciences is indisputable: by offering scholars and artists from all over Europe appointments at his court he made Prague into the cultural centre of Central Europe. His rôle as an art collector is of equal significance; his *Kunstkammer* (Chamber of Art and Marvels), in spite of the great losses sustained in the Thirty Years' War, was one of the most important sources of the Kunsthistorische Museum's collections. K. S.

Abraham Bloemaert is a characteristic representative of late Mannerism in Holland, a style whose aim was to astound the observer by means of elaborate and precisely drawn composition. The painting shows the victorious heroine Judith on her return from the enemy camp, displaying the head of the enemy commander Holofernes to the people of her besieged city Bethulia. Bloemaert turns the scene into a virtuoso showpiece of lighting effects produced by the flickering reflections of the torchlit night. Animated figures, contorted in extreme foreshortening under highlights alternating with deep shadows, imbue the biblical scene with the character of an extraordinary event, its agitation reflected in the gestures of Bethulia's inhabitants. K. S.

◁ THE ADORATION OF THE MAGI
Jan Brueghel the Elder
(Brussels 1568 – 1625 Antwerp)
1598
Copper; H 33 cm, W 48 cm
Inv. No. 617

Jan Brueghel based his many-figured depiction of the *Adoration of the Magi* on compositions of the same theme by his father, Pieter Bruegel the Elder. However, Jan Brueghel's paintings are in no way slavish imitations of his father's ideas. He created his own unmistakeable style, skilfully manipulating the various elements of his models, reducing their dimensions to miniature size, setting off tradition against his own observation of nature. The charm and poetry of his art show him to have broken away from the profound vision of reality that characterizes his work. The minutiousely drawn wealth of delicate little figures, picturesque details and the enamel-like quality of the colours impart to this cabinet piece not only the character of a precious gem but also imbue the Christmas story with an unreal magic, transforming it into a fairy-tale full of grace and romance. G. H.

LANDSCAPE WITH ANIMALS
Roelant Savery
(Courtrai 1576 – 1639 Utrecht)
c. 1618
Wood; H 35 cm, W 49 cm
Inv. No. 1091

Savery's œuvre largely consists of landscapes, animal studies and still-lives. In his predominantly small-scale paintings, possessing the delicacy of miniatures, he combines fantastic elements of landscape and architecture with realistic animal representation, based on exact observation. This was in keeping with the ideas of the Emperors Rudolph II and Matthias, Savery's patrons whose *Kunstkammer* at Prague contained wonders of nature side by side with precious miracles of art. The variety of animals depicted, including numerous exotic species, reflects the results of the voyages of exploration at that time. However,

FLOWERS IN A WOODEN VESSEL
Jan Brueghel the Elder
(Brussels 1568 – 1625 Antwerp)
c. 1606/07
Wood; H 98 cm, W 73 cm
Inv. No. 570

During his lifetime Jan Brueghel had become famous for his brilliantly painted still-lives of flowers, which were prized as collector's pieces all over Europe. Like a microcosm reflecting the splendour and diversity of Creation in the humblest things they brought the beauty of Nature into the secluded world of the *Kunstkammer*. Painted in colours whose luminosity in Brueghel's own words "almost rivals that of Nature", is a bouquet of wild and cultivated, domestic and exotic plants, spring and summer flowers, "so many rare and diverse things that no one has yet painted with such diligence." These he combines into huge, subtly composed arrangements in whose glorious abundance artistic ingenuity and the miracle of nature are felicitously married. G. H.

since mere depiction does not in itself constitute an adequate subject for a painting, Savery gave these pictures superficial content with little scenes in the background: here Orpheus, whose music had charmed the animals, is being torn to pieces by the Thracian maenads.

K. S.

327

VINCENZO II GONZAGA, PRINCE OF MANTUA
Peter Paul Rubens
(Siegen 1577 – 1640 Antwerp)
c. 1604/05
Canvas; H 67 cm, W 51.5 cm
Inv. No. 6084

In 1600, as befitted an ambitious young artist, Rubens left Antwerp for Italy and there entered the service of Duke Vincenzo I Gonzaga of Mantua. This allowed him enough freedom to be able to travel and fulfill commissions from other patrons. From Vincenzo I he received only one large commission: the triptych for the Jesuit Church in Mantua. In the central panel were portrayed the ducal couple, their three sons and two daughters with the Duke's recently deceased parents, all worshipping the Holy Trinity. After Mantua fell to Napoleon the painting was cut up and its remnants dispersed. A fragment with the larger-than-life sized bust of one of the sons, Vincenzo II (1594–1627), was acquired only eighty years ago. Both the broad, pastose application of the paint, calculated to be effective when seen from the back of the church and the colouring, indebted to the Venetian school, point the way to the Baroque pathos of Rubens' later works.   K. S.

THE ANNUNCIATION
Peter Paul Rubens
(Siegen 1577 – 1640 Antwerp)
1609
Canvas; H 224 cm, W 200 cm
Inv. No. 685

Rubens painted this altarpiece for the Jesuit Congregation of Scholars immediately after his return from an eight year sojourn in Italy. The angel Gabriel has burst into the narrow chamber of the Virgin. Mary's incredulous, defensive gesture seems to signify physical fright at the angel's elemental irruption into the earthly sphere, rather than the more traditional modest acceptance. Both react with passionate emotion to the spiritual happening. However, the seductive charm of the angel, with his golden curls and the warm, richly iridescent Venetian colouring of his robes, presents a stark contrast to the severity and reserve of the Madonna in her canonically plain blue and white garments.   W. P.

THE ASSUMPTION OF THE VIRGIN MARY
Peter Paul Rubens
(Siegen 1577 – 1640 Antwerp)
c. 1611/14
Wood; H 458 cm, W 297 cm
Inv. No. 518

This monumental altarpiece is the first of twelve Assumptions that Rubens painted in the course of his career. Originally intended for the high-altar in Antwerp Cathedral, it adorned the Lady Chapel of the Jesuit Church there from 1621 to 1776. Rubens obviously altered the composition during its long genesis. In the oil sketch in Leningrad, a wall composed of disciples, women and cypresses originally closed off the background. In the painting the formal structure of the figural wall was altered: the cypresses were eliminated and the figures were split into two groups. The painting was also cut to form an arch at the top. Stylistic features in the painting also indicate that it was worked on over a long period of time. Aspects of Rubens' early post-Italian style, such as the herculean figures of the Apostles and the iridescent colouring of the women's robes are found alongside traits which indicate his later development. This more classicizing phase of his style is characterized by cool and smooth flesh tones and a more controlled sense of movement. As a whole, this rather early picture is richer in detail and more static than Rubens' later versions, with their flowing diagonal movement and strong sense of drama.   W. P.

THE MIRACLES OF ST. FRANCIS XAVIER
Peter Paul Rubens
(Siegen 1577 – 1640 Antwerp)
c. 1617/19
Canvas; H 535 cm, W 395 cm
Inv. No. 519

Until 1776 this painting was set up alternately with the *Miracles of St. Ignatius Loyola* (also in this Gallery) on the high-altar of the Jesuit church at Antwerp. Francis Xavier is portrayed here as God's missionary to the East Indies protected by the personification of Faith, preaching to the heathens, raising the dead, healing the sick and destroying heathen idols. The whole repertoire of a prospective saint (Francis Xavier was not canonised until 1622), is presented simultaneously. Rubens made careful preparations for the painting, including an oil sketch (also in the Gallery) and drawings; the painting itself was largely executed by his workshop. In the course of the preparatory work, the composition was clarified through the disentanglement of clusters of figures and elimination of unnecessary overlapping, as well as by the greater individualization and heightening of facial expressions. The clarification of the composition also clarified the didactic, propagandistic message of the painting.   W. P.

THE LAMENTATION
Peter Paul Rubens
(Siegen 1577 – 1640 Antwerp)
1614
Wood; H 40.5 cm, W 52.5 cm
Inv. No. 515

The Passion and Redemption of Christ are concentrated and brought together as if under a magnifying glass in the *Lamentation*. Contemplating this painting, which was intended for private devotion, the viewer can make each of the sensuously painted details the starting point for a meditation on the Passion. Noteworthy is the harmony achieved between the intellectual concept of the didactic function of religious painting in the Counter-Reformation and the artistic concept which fuses the ideal and the illusion of a tangible reality. The composition itself provides the ideal of classical form. Rubens' figures, suffused with the warmth of life and in the grip of passion, provide the element of graspable truth.

W. P.

PARK OF A CASTLE
Peter Paul Rubens
(Siegen 1577 – 1640 Antwerp)
Wood; H 52.5 cm, W 97 cm
Inv. No. 696

Although Rubens' main interest lay in large-scale figure compositions, he turned at times to the depiction of landscape and nature. This small picture is one of his late works and depicts a park landscape animated by a gay and lighthearted company of people. Without a trace of pathos Rubens paints the elegant company engaged in amorous play, watched by himself and his wife. The meadow, trees and the fairy-tale castle reflected in the water are rendered with a light, sketchy technique in delicate, translucent pastels. With his evocation of a poetic mood of release Rubens anticipated in his old age the "fêtes galantes", which were to become a favourite theme of Rococo painting a century later.

G. H.

◁ **MEETING BETWEEN KING FERDINAND OF HUNGARY AND THE CARDINAL-INFANTE FERDINAND BEFORE THE BATTLE OF NÖRDLINGEN**
Peter Paul Rubens
(Siegen 1577 – 1640 Antwerp)
c. 1634/35
Canvas; H 328 cm, W 388 cm
Inv. No. 525

To mark the ceremonial entry into Antwerp of the new Governor of the Netherlands, the Cardinal-Infante Ferdinand, brother to Philip IV of Spain, the burghers of the city had the streets decorated with triumphal architecture, as was customary on such occasions. Rubens was appointed artistic director and contributed several paintings himself, one of which was the *Meeting at Nördlingen*. It depicts an event that had occurred immediately prior to the Cardinal-Infante's "entrée joyeuse", namely the unification of his troops in alliance with those of his Habsburg cousin, the future Emperor Ferdinand III. Together they had inflicted a heavy defeat on the Swedes at Nördlingen. The meeting of the two generals is transformed into an event of timeless significance, framed by the allegorical figures of the Danube and Germania with Jupiter's eagles swooping down from the skies. Rubens here glorifies the House of Habsburg, celebrating its dynastic concord in all the magnificence and atmospheric splendour of his mature, painterly style.

G. H.

ILDEFONSO ALTAR
Peter Paul Rubens
(Siegen 1577 – 1640 Antwerp)
c. 1630/32
Wood; centre picture H 352 cm, W 236 cm
each wing H 352 cm, W 109 cm
Inv. No. 678

The *Ildefonso Altar* is the main work of Rubens' late period, when he was finally able to cut the "golden knot of ambition", as he called it, and give up his career as a diplomat and political advisor in order to devote himself exclusively to his art. The altar was commissioned by the Habsburg Regent in the Low Countries, Clara Isabella, in memoriam of her deceased husband, Archduke Albrecht of Austria. Intended for the Ildefonso Brotherhood in Brussels, the altar is in the form of a mediaeval triptych, a form Rubens often used. The altar with its side panels closed shows a pastoral idyll of the *Holy Family beneath an Apple Tree* (also in this Gallery). Opened up, a drama of solemn splendour unfolds in gold-brown and red tones. From the side panels and their show of princely pomp, Rubens moves into the centre of the triptych, a sacred sphere of miracle and vision. Seen kneeling in the wings, the ducal pair, each accompanied by his own patron saint, participate in the heavenly event: in the dusky semi-darkness of a church, the Virgin Mary appears to St. Ildefonso. Surrounded by holy maidens, she presents the pious man with a precious chasuble that he presses to his lips in ardour and humility. Rubens' energetically flowing brushwork is sensual while softening form and transparent while compact. His style attains a hitherto unknown freedom and brilliance through the atmospheric shimmer of the setting and the evocative use of colour to create illusion. Here is the perfect blend of two divergent artistic traditions: the illusionism and colour sense of his beloved Venetians with the enamel-like, near-sighted depiction of body and surface from the Early Netherlandish school, the inheritance of his own Flemish home. One of the greatest masterpieces of all time, the *Ildefonso Altar* embraces the earthly and unearthly, the close and remote. It is a vision of colour and light that combines idealized princely-Catholic patronage with spiritualism and contemplative tranquillity.   G. H.

STORMY LANDSCAPE WITH PHILEMON AND BAUCIS ▽
Peter Paul Rubens
(Siegen 1577 – 1640 Antwerp)
c. 1620/25
Wood; H 146 cm, W 208.5 cm
Inv. No. 690

Behind Rubens' *Stormy Landscape* lie two variations on the theme of natural catastrophe taken from ancient literature. The scene's mythological justification seems to have been added at a later stage: the extra boards carelessly stuck on to all four sides stand witness to an extension of the painting's original concept. Ovid's *Metamorphoses* (VIII, 620 ff.) recount the story of the old couple Philemon and Baucis who alone among the human race give food and shelter to the gods Jupiter and Mercury as they wander on the earth in disguise. The rest of the human race perishes in a flood while Philemon and Baucis are spared and allowed to choose their own death together. They are changed into intertwining trees. Philemon and Baucis' hospitality towards the gods and their subsequent metamorphosis have been the subject of numerous paintings, but only Rubens portrayed the flood and their plea to be spared. The theme of the flood is only mentioned in passing in the story of Philemon and Baucis; it is more than likely that Rubens' conception has its basis in another passage from the *Metamorphoses* (I, 262 ff.), the classic Flood that punished the impious human race, its only survivors being Deucalion and Pyhrra. The real subject of the picture, however, is not the myth but Nature itself in all its elemental violence, "in its most powerful activity, its most strongly human aspect, namely that of destruction" (K. Demus). Only two parts of the landscape remain untouched by the general catastrophe of cloudburst, swollen torrents, flashes of lightning, drowned and drowning figures – the sunny paradisical plain high up on the left in the background, and the wooded spur of rock protected by the gods halfway up on the right. The two sections counterbalance the elemental flood of destruction which plunges diagonally from top right to bottom left. Rubens' *Stormy Landscape* – he painted this subject several times – goes back to a Netherlandish tradition, an early example being Pieter Bruegel's *Gloomy Day* (also in this Gallery) and there are fundamental stylistic influences from the Venetian school, in particular from Titian, Tintoretto and the Bassani, from the German-Roman painter Elsheimer, whom Rubens greatly admired, and from the Carracci. However, Rubens has radically transformed these elements into his own powerfully unique style.

W. P.

THE WORSHIP OF VENUS
Peter Paul Rubens
(Siegen 1577 – 1640 Antwerp)
c. 1636/37
Canvas; H 217 cm, W 350 cm
Inv. No. 684

The Worship of Venus reveals the breadth of Rubens' humanistic learning and his ability to transform completely a diversity of literary and artistic impulses by "free extemporisation" (Jacob Burckhardt) into a vision full of different facets and yet uniquely and inimitably his own. The starting point for this picture was a description of a painting entitled "The Gods of Love" in Philostrates the Younger's *Eikones*. This 3rd century collection of 65 picture descriptions "catalogues" paintings which actually existed in an ancient Neapolitan pinacotheque. There, the picture features an orchard near a grotto from which a stream flows towards some fruit trees. In the orchard stands a cultic statue of Aphrodite, the goddess of love, which the nymphs have decorated. Other features include winged amorinos dancing, picking the apples in the orchard, kissing and romping.

Titian followed the text of the *Eikones* in his *Worship of Venus* (c. 1518/19), which was commissioned by Alfonso I d'Este, Duke of Ferrara, for his *camerino d' alabastro* and is today in the Prado at Madrid. Rubens' extant copy of Titian's painting can be seen in Stockholm.

Rubens reworked the Viennese canvas several times, altering and extending the conception, as can be seen from the additional areas of canvas added on to the top and both sides. Rubens transformed the classical and Renaissance models which celebrate the power of love. He virtually dispenses with Philostrates' rather vague description as a basis and instead presents a modern interpretation of the ancient Roman festival of Venus Verticordia. The festival is described in Ovid's *Fasti* and the 16th century *Immagini de gli Dei* by Vincenzo Cartari. At the beginning of April (the month of Venus), the women of Latium, including prostitutes and brides-to-be, brought flowers and other votive offerings (dolls, mirrors and combs) to Venus who they believed averted immoral desires. They cleaned the statue and performed ritual ablutions – hence the antique architecture and the pool on the left. Rubens' painting is informed by his archaeological and antiquarian interests – as evidenced by the temple and the nymphaeum on the left and the tripod in front of the statue of Venus. Contrasted with this, we find putti, nymphs, satyrs and fauns, half-human, half-mythical beings belonging to Venus' realm, who represent the sphere of unbridled desires where Venus in her aspect as averter of desires has as yet no sway. Above all, Rubens increasingly approaches in his last years the painterly style of Titian's late works, realizing the similarity of their artistic problems. The open brushwork, the richly differentiated effects of colour which unify the atmospheric luminosity of the tones bathed in evening sunlight, and the foreground, teeming with lively figures – all this is an acknowledgement of his indebtedness to Titian's work. Rubens' own achievement on the other hand is the corporeal immediacy, the ecstatic, orgiastic intensity of a vision of antiquity experienced anew in all its actuality.   W. P.

SELF-PORTRAIT
Peter Paul Rubens
(Siegen 1577 – 1640 Antwerp)
c. 1638/40
Canvas; H 109.5 cm, W 85 cm
Inv. No. 527

Posing proudly in elegant dress with gloves, sword and hat, the ageing artist stands before us as a nobleman in this, the last of his rare self-portraits. For many years diplomat and political adviser to the Habsburg governor of the Netherlands and knighted by Charles I of England, Sir Peter Paul fittingly avails himself of courtly forms to present himself to us. However, the disparaging gaze betrays him as the painter himself glancing appraisingly in the mirror while at work, despite the aloof pose and the aristocratic setting.

G. H.

THE FUR
Peter Paul Rubens
(Siegen 1577 – 1640 Antwerp)
c. 1635/40
Wood; H 176 cm, W 83 cm
Inv. No. 688

Rubens himself gave the name *The Little Fur* to this picture of his wife. It is the most intimate portrait of Hélène Fourment whom he married late in life and whose features he often incorporated into his works. Here he achieves a rare and subtle interplay of reality and mythology, the private and the universal. The young woman, in a naturally graceful pose, as if surprised on her way to bathe, at the same time evokes through her pose the classical goddess of love, Venus Pudica. Capturing her in an attitude between posing and withdrawing, revealing and concealing herself, looking out at us and calmly accepting our admiration, Rubens chooses a moment of especial charm, combining sensuous immediacy with the fleetingness of the moment in this homage to his wife's beauty.

G. H.

335

THE FISH MARKET
Frans Snyders
(Antwerp 1579–1657)
c. 1618
Canvas; H 253 cm, W 375 cm
Inv. No. 383

Snyders, a contemporary of Rubens, probably intended his huge and opulent still-lives as decoration pieces for baroque interiors, which were much in demand at that time. He worked in Rubens' studio, specializing in lively, sensuous animal painting. He himself often relied on the assistance of figure painters to complete his numerous market scenes. Here, Snyders painted an extravagant profusion of fish and other sea creatures their shimmering, iridescent forms seeming still to pulsate with life, while Van Dyck added a scene from the New Testament.   G. H.

SAMSON AND DELILAH
Sir Anthony Van Dyck
(Antwerp 1599 – 1641 London)
c. 1628/30
Canvas; H 146 cm, W 254 cm
Inv. No. 512

The story of the Jewish hero Samson is recounted in the Old Testament (Judges, 16:4-21). His lover Delilah had his hair cut off while he slept, thus robbing him of his superhuman strength and leaving him defenceless against the Philistines. Van Dyck follows Rubens' model, but transforms his teacher's composition in his own characteristic way. Instead of portraying Samson's heroic defence, the picture focusses on the moment of discovered betrayal: Samson's wistful leave-taking of the beloved woman who has betrayed him and Delilah's ambivalent affection for the lover whose downfall she has brought about.   W. P.

STUDY OF THE HEAD OF A WOMAN
Sir Anthony Van Dyck
(Antwerp 1599 – 1641 London)
c. 1620
Paper on wood; H 42.9 cm, W 45.9 cm
Inv. No. 514

Compared to his teacher Rubens, Van Dyck painted very few studies of heads. Most were preparatory for multi-figured compositions and fall somewhere between a life-like portrait of a model and its eventual application in a narrative painting. The physiognomy of the actual model, a young woman looking up, is projected onto a more specific iconographic type, eventually becoming that of Mary Magdalen – as suggested by the long hair and the emphatic expression. If the study was to be used in a painting, a further heightening of expression would be achieved by the interposition of other, more powerful models. In the case of this study, Van Dyck used it for the woman swooning in the face of death in the painting *Moses and the Brazen Serpent*, today in the Prado at Madrid. Transferred to the narrative context, madness has replaced measured emphasis. Here, however, the young Van Dyck's confused, "ruffled" brushstrokes of unevenly applied paint are nervous and coarse and seek to achieve a particular effect of expression which will be subsequently heightened even more. The mature Van Dyck was to dispense almost entirely with this type of study. W. P.

PORTRAIT OF A YOUNG GENERAL
Sir Anthony Van Dyck
(Antwerp 1599 – 1641 London)
c. 1624
Canvas; H 115.5 cm, W 104 cm
Inv. No. 490

Following in the footsteps of his teacher, Rubens, Van Dyck spent several years in Italy. The works he produced there, such as the *Portrait of a Young General,* reflect the admiration felt by the young Flemish painter for the Venetian masters. He was fascinated by the nobility of their portrait style, the delicate harmony of their colours, their dynamic brushwork, daring highlights and atmospheric fusing of tones. Van Dyck effectively combines the inspiration he received from the great Venetian painters with his own gift of psychological understanding. With outstanding empathy he reveals the latent unease and hidden conflict of the sitters' character. Here he lays bare the tension between the martial stance and melancholy reserve of the fine-limbed, elegant young nobleman. G. H.

THE VIRGIN MARY WITH CHILD AND SS. ROSALIA, PETER AND PAUL
Sir Anthony Van Dyck
(Antwerp 1599 – 1641 London)
1629
Canvas; H 275 cm, W 210 cm
Inv. No. 482

Van Dyck painted this altarpiece for the Confraternity of Bachelors, a lay brotherhood to which the artist himself belonged. It originally hung in the chapel of the Professed House of the Jesuits in Antwerp. In 1629 the Brotherhood had acquired the relics of St. Rosalia of Palermo, the worship of which the Jesuits had propagated in times of plague. The prominent position in a Jesuit altarpiece of the two "Roman" apostles Peter and Paul reflects the Order's special commitment to the Counter-Reformation: the cult of the Virgin, the worship of the Saints as intercessors, the absolute loyalty to Rome and the Pope. Van Dyck borrows from the Venetians, Titian and Veronese, in the aligning of the compositional elements along the diagonal. However, the ecstatic, fervent tone, the saints' total surrender to their task and the "sentimentalisation", sometimes verging on the hysterical, of the figures' expressions, are features characteristic of Van Dyck.   W. P.

THE VISION OF THE BLESSED HERMANN JOSEPH
Sir Anthony Van Dyck
(Antwerp 1599 – 1641 London)
1630
Canvas; H 160 cm, W 128 cm
Inv. No. 488

The second altarpiece painted by Van Dyck for the Confraternity of Bachelors in Antwerp enables the viewer to participate in a vision, an event whose artistic realisation was ideally suited to the artist's unique gift of rendering extreme psychological states. His art here strikes a note of delicate charm and spiritual release hitherto unknown in paintings inspired by the Counter-Reformation. The composition centres on the touching of hands between the Madonna and the monk. Van Dyck achieves a convincing physical expression of affection and spiritual surrender; the figures strive towards each other, are so closely involved that extrication is unthinkable. Thus, the artistically decisive areas of artistic expression – the hands, eyes, hair and the contours of the draperies – are relegated to the "surface", i. e. the physical periphery.   W. P.

PRINCE RUPERT OF THE PALATINATE
Sir Anthony Van Dyck
(Antwerp 1599 – 1641 London)
1631/32
Canvas; H 175 cm, W 95.5 cm
Inv. No. 484

Rupert (1619–1682) was the son of the Protestant Elector of the Palatinate, later King Frederick V of Bohemia, who emigrated to Holland after the loss of Bohemia and the Palatinate in the Thirty Years War. Van Dyck painted both the sons of the exiled "Winter King". He possessed a keen eye for the distinctive characteristics of youth; although the boy adopts a conventionally adult pose and the requisites of court portraiture are all present, above the wide collar we see a face in which the child-like and the adult are reflected in all their contradictions. The figure itself seems weak and frail, yet is given stability by the traditional architecture in the background. Move-

NICHOLAS LANIER
Sir Anthony Van Dyck
(Antwerp 1599 – 1641 London)
c. 1628/29
Canvas: H 111 cm, W 87.6 cm
Inv. No. 501

Before his appointment to the court of Charles I in London, Van Dyck painted this superb portrait of Nicholas Lanier, who was Master of the King's Musick and adviser on artistic matters to the English monarch. Himself a painter, Lanier is said to have sat for the portrait in Antwerp for seven days. With the inimitable lightness of his virtuoso brushwork, Van Dyck depicts the shimmer of silks and the smoothness of the skin. He portrays the courtier in all his elegance and refinement and also conveys the psychological strain of a man intent on the effect he is creating, revealing both the sitter's ambition and a nervous sense of unease. This and other of Van Dyck's portraits are not only a vivid document of court society under the art-loving Stuart king. They establish the prototype of the aristocratic portrait, and as such decisively influenced the subsequent history of English portraiture.   G. H.

ment and ceremonial repose are here mingled, and evoke the proud and effortless elegance which has remained the epitome of the aristocratic to this day.   W. P.

VENUS AND ADONIS
Abraham Janssens
(Antwerp 1575–1632)
c. 1620
Canvas; H 200 cm, W 240 cm
Inv. No. 728

The Antwerp painter Abraham Janssens was the only Flemish contemporary of Rubens who remained virtually untouched by the great master's exuberant vitality. Janssens continued to follow the idea of severely modelled figures and sharply drawn contours of Caravaggio and the Bolognese school whose art he had admired during his years in Italy. Marble smoothness and statuesque poses impart an almost classical chill to the strictly geometric composition of *Venus and Adonis*. This fascinatingly counterpoints the allusive mood of the lovers' farewell before Adonis leaves for the hunt on which he will meet his death. In keeping with the practice of artistic collaboration, common in the Netherlands at that time, Janssens left the painting of the background to the landscape specialist Jan Wildens, who had also worked for Rubens.

G. H.

THE LAMENTATION OF CHRIST
Gaspar de Crayer
(Antwerp 1584 – 1669 Ghent)
1649/56
Canvas; H 208 cm, W 266 cm
Inv. No. 801

Crayer painted his large figured *pietà* in the spirit of the devout piety of the Counter-Reformation, which aimed at emotional involvement on the part of the believer. His painting is an impressive spectacle, a theatrical display of physical and mental suffering. If Rubens, with whom Crayer occasionally collaborated, had shown the way with his dramatic yet always idealizing art, it was Crayer who introduced populistic elements, with his emphasis on the strikingly graphic depiction of pain, naturalistic rendering of the bloodsmeared body of Christ and episodic, sentimental details. The heightened expressivity of the slight figures and the primarily blue and mauve tones blended with grey indicate that Van Dyck had joined Rubens in representing the two most important artistic sources for contemporary Flemish painting.

G. H.

CHALICE AND HOST ENCIRCLED BY GARLANDS OF FRUIT ▷
Jan Davidsz de Heem
(Utrecht 1606 – 1683/84 Antwerp)
1648
Canvas; H 138 cm, W 125.5 cm
Inv. No. 571

Admiration for the virtuoso technique which could meticulously render the finest details, together with the jesuitical piety of the Counter-Reformation led to the development of the religious still-life, a form of devotional painting characteristic of the Catholic Netherlands. Flowers and fruits in glowing colours, intertwined into garlands and arrangements frame a picture of Christian devotion. Here the sheaves of corn and the bunches of grapes signify the miracle of the Eucharist, the Blood and Body of the Lord in the form of bread and wine. The brilliant composition was intended to guide the eye of the beholder from delight at the abundance and beauty of Nature to contemplation and spiritual understanding. De Heem dedicated the painting with an inscription in Latin to Archduke Leopold Wilhelm, the governor of the Netherlands, whose piety and love of the arts were combined in his especial predilection for the religious still-life.

G. H.

ARCHDUKE LEOPOLD WILHELM IN HIS GALLERY AT BRUSSELS
David Teniers the Younger
(Antwerp 1610 – 1690 Brussels)
c. 1651
Canvas; H 123 cm, W 163 cm
Inv. No. 739

Leopold Wilhelm (1614–1662), the most important collector of paintings among the Habsburgs,
accumulated most of the items in his gallery while
governor of the southern (Spanish) Netherlands
from 1647 to 1656. The times were favourable for
collectors because of the fall of the English
monarchy in 1648. The collections of the English
king and those of numerous British aristocrats
came onto the market in these years. In this
painting, Leopold Wilhelm is portrayed on a visit to
his gallery accompanied by his retinue and
Teniers himself, the director of the gallery and the
archduke's court painter. These "gallery interiors", a traditional genre in the Netherlands,
with their probably fictive portrayals of collections,
were sent as gifts to other princely collectors. This
one was owned by Leopold Wilhelm's brother,
Emperor Ferdinand III in Prague. Almost all of the
fifty-one Italian paintings depicted – their proportions often altered to achieve an impression of
decorative profusion – are today in the Kunsthistorische Museum.   W. P.

THE FEAST OF THE BEAN KING
Jacob Jordaens
(Antwerp 1593–1678)
before 1656
Canvas; H 242 cm, W 300 cm
Inv. No. 786

Jordaens was the only Flemish painter apart from van Dyck who, having assimilated Rubens' overwhelming influence, went on to develop his own unmistakeable style. The exuberant vitality of Jordaens' paintings clearly owes much to Rubens. However, whereas Rubens' sensuously heightened treatment is always idealized in the classical sense, that of Jordaens tends towards a direction only hinted at in Rubens' works, the representation of a robust, often burlesque reality. His art reflects his relish for the vital, rough and ready life of the simple people and epitomizes the typically Flemish enjoyment of sensuous pleasures. In contrast to Rubens, whose direct observation of life is integrated into religious or mythological contexts Jordaens also produced genre paintings. The *Feast of the Bean King* belongs to the tradition, popular in Flanders since Bruegel, of busy scenes of taverns, fairs and overindulgent festivities. This is Jordaens' fourth

and last version of the subject.
While working on the picture Jordaens enlarged the painting, originally conceived as a much smaller work (a practice also employed by Rubens), developing it into a rich, sweeping depiction of a custom associated with Twelfth Night. A cake was served containing a single bean and the guest who found the bean in his slice became the king of the feast. He chose the prettiest woman as his queen and appointed the others present as his courtiers: here small scraps of paper indicate their offices.
Jordaens' treatment of the boisterous celebration overflows with sumptuous luxuriance. Noisy and drunken, old and young, men and women alike are crushed against each other in a wealth of movement that threatens to spill over beyond the frame of the picture. The immoderate and dissolute behaviour and the close, murky atmosphere convey chaos and disorder, yet this is belied by the balanced, almost symmetrical composition. The soft light flooding in through the window not only imbues the scene with a sense of human warmth and intimacy but also disposes the raucous company into groups. Above them hangs a moralizing Latin proverb: "None resembles the fool more than the drunkard." G. H.

ST. JOHN THE BAPTIST PREACHING
Esaias van de Velde
(Amsterdam c. 1591 – 1630 Haag)
c. 1615
Wood; H 69 cm, W 96 cm
Inv. No. 6991

St. John the Baptist Preaching became a favourite subject after the early 16th century in Netherlandish painting encouraged particularly by the Reformation, because of the possibilities it offered for landscape painting. As a pupil of Gillis van Coninxloo, Esaias van de Velde changed the system of sharply differentiated planes characteristic of the Flemish landscape tradition into a more realistic description of landscape using green and strong brown tones. This direct approach to nature is echoed in the figures with their accentuated plasticity and vivid colours, shining brightly in the sunlight and contrasted strongly in the shade.
K. S.

PORTRAIT OF A MAN
Frans Hals
(Antwerp 1581/85 – 1666 Haarlem)
c. 1654/55
Canvas; H 108 cm, W 79.5 cm
Inv. No. 9091

Throughout his long artistic career Frans Hals, the eldest of the great Dutch masters, confined himself almost exclusively to the painting of portraits, which in their faithfulness to reality conveyed a striking and wholly convincing picture of his fellow citizens. The hallmark of his skill as a portraitist is his ability to capture a momentary state. Instrumental to this being his unequalled bold painting technique; he contrasts quickly executed brush strokes, sometimes using a broad, flowing brush, at other times working with short, powerful and seemingly unorganized strokes. All of which are combined to form a complete picture only when viewed at a distance. At the same time his portraits display a sovereign command of colour values, the predominant basis being a deep black and a radiant white; colours which he adapts to achieve a lively surface effect by a virtuoso use of innumerable shades of grey.
K. S.

REMBRANDT'S MOTHER AS THE PROPHETESS HANNAH
Rembrandt Harmensz van Rijn
(Leyden 1606 – 1669 Amsterdam)
1639
Wood; H 79.5 cm, W 61.7 cm
Inv. No. 408

Rembrandt's portraits represent not only the pinnacle of 17th century Dutch art, but the best of European painting as a whole. The portrait of his mother, whom Rembrandt often used as a model, was painted just one year before her death. It shows the slightly bent half-figure of an old woman, enveloped in heavy, precious garments, her hands resting on a walking stick. The Jewish prayer robe identifies her as the prophetess Hannah from the Gospel of St. Luke. This portrait was painted in Rembrandt's middle period, a time of intense artistic growth and rising social prestige. Characteristic of this period are not only his subtle manipulation of colouristic and lighting modulations, but also his use of a wide range of brushstrokes, both exceedingly fine and possessing a strong shape-giving impasto. C. Z.

TITUS VAN RIJN, THE ARTIST'S SON, READING
Rembrandt Harmensz van Rijn
(Leyden 1606 – 1669 Amsterdam)
c. 1656/57
Canvas; H 70.5 cm, W 64 cm
Inv. No. 410

Titus van Rijn, born in 1641, was the fourth child of Rembrandt and his first wife Saskia. As Rembrandt's only child to survive to adulthood, Rembrandt painted him approximately ten times. This portrait was painted at a time when Rembrandt was facing increasing financial difficulties and was living with Titus and Hendrickje Stoffels in the seclusion of their house in Amsterdam. The momentary quality of the depiction is captured in the slightly parted lips of the boy seen in profile, concentrating on the book held in his hands. The broad, generous brushstrokes and the deliberate use of light and dark effects accentuate Titus' forehead, temples, nose and hands bringing them out of the surrounding shadow. Here as always in his works, Rembrandt used the light to heighten the expressiveness of the scene, if only the intimate moment of reading. C. Z.

LARGE SELF-PORTRAIT
Rembrandt Harmensz van Rijn
(Leyden 1606 – 1669 Amsterdam)
1652
Canvas; H 112 cm, W 81.5 cm
Inv. No. 411

Painted in the year his financial troubles began, Rembrandt faces the viewer in the *Large Self-Portrait* in three quarter profile, his hands on his hips, thumbs hooked in his belt. Earlier in his career the artist frequently depicted himself dressed in splendid costumes; in contrast, he here wears a simple artist's smock. The cool grey colouring and fastidious technique of Rembrandt's early works are here replaced by subtly layered, richly modulated scales of brown hues and thickly applied, unifying brushstrokes which hardly differentiate between clothes, hands and background. Only the face is emphasized by the powerful modelling of his brush and the deliberate use of light.   C. Z.

SMALL SELF-PORTRAIT
Rembrandt Harmensz van Rijn
(Leyden 1606 – 1669 Amsterdam)
c. 1657
Wood; H 48.8 cm, W 40.6 cm
Inv. No. 414

During the course of his life, Rembrandt painted more than sixty self-portraits. These paintings have a special significance because they reflect the external circumstances of his life as well as his artistic and personal development. His *Small Self-Portrait* was created in the year of his financial ruin, when the compulsory sale of his property took place. The effect of his close-up seen features is heightened to the utmost by the narrow space within the picture. Rembrandt intensifies the dramatic expressivity of his face by the well aimed use of light which he used almost exclusively in his later work for physiognomical and psychological characterization. The colouring and the brushwork are similar to those of the *Large Self-Portrait,* dating from the same period.
                    C. Z.

LANDSCAPE WITH FENCE
Salomon van Ruysdael
(Naarden 1600/03 – 1670 Haarlem)
1631
Wood; H 37.8 cm, W 54.2 cm
Inv. No. 6972

This view of a roadway among the dunes, flanked by a rough wooden fence and some trees, is typical of the early works of Salomon van Ruysdael. It brings to perfection the characteristics of Dutch landscape painting: the unpretentious, unheroic view into the unembellished and rustic countryside. Ruysdael's palette is limited to earth-coloured tints, ranging from the broken greens of the foliage to the multiple shades of greyish-blue in the vast clouded sky. The distribution of light and shades creates a dramatic effect in itself. The path and peasants remain in the shadow, juxtaposed with the brilliant beam of light which pours through an opening in the fence. The forceful composition of the painting as a whole depends upon the contrast between this illuminated area and the tenderly painted dark path leading out of the picture.

K. S.

STOPPING BY THE INN
Isack van Ostade
(Haarlem 1621 – 1649 Haarlem)
1646
Wood; H 50.5 cm, W 53 cm
Inv. No. 9098

Isack van Ostade was both the younger brother and the student of the prolific genre painter Adriaen van Ostade. He integrated his descriptions of village life with his landscape and genre-painting to create a third, new medium. During his short, ten-year career, Ostade concentrated mainly on pictures of farms or inns with wagons and horses. Here, as in most of his works, the composition followed a diagonal scheme, comprised of the road leading into the painting, the roadside inn and the dark zones in the foreground under the large shade trees. Strong light-dark contrasts and colour accents signify a departure from the monochromatic colouring dominating Dutch landscape painting of the preceding years.

K. S.

RIVER LANDSCAPE WITH CELLAR ENTRANCE ▷
Jakob van Ruisdael
(Haarlem 1628/29 – 1682 Amsterdam)
1649
Wood; H 69.8 cm, W 92 cm
Inv. No. 9807

The many canals and rivers flowing through Holland influenced the character of its countryside to a large degree. It is therefore not surprising that the presentation of canals and water-meadows plays an important part in landscape painting. In this early work by Jakob van Ruisdael all dominant landscape elements are centred on the right side of the picture; in contrast, the left side, giving an open view onto a meandering river is strikingly empty. The strong tonality which characterized Ruisdael's paintings before the middle of the century, has disappeared; the close-up of painted plants includes many shades of green contrasting with the powerful vermilion of the brickwork.

J. R.

"THE GREAT FOREST"
Jakob van Ruisdael
(Haarlem 1628/29 – 1682 Amsterdam)
c. 1655/60
Canvas; H 139 cm, W 180 cm
Inv. No. 426

Netherlandish landscapes of the sixteenth century were not so much literal depictions as rather an accumulative juxtaposition of the various manifestations of Nature. However, around 1600 there

began a new development towards a stricter sense of unity and simplification. The paintings of the Flemish artist Gillis van Coninxloo (1544–1606) already depict lonely stretches of woodland and dispense with the small figures which were conventionally included to give a landscape a human focus. In Coninxloo's paintings, the emphasis lies with the mysterious, almost bizarre thickets; in those of Jakob van Ruisdael half a century later the brushwood is seen from a secure distance. The subject of the painting is the forest itself rather than a mere array of trees. The composition has a simple, lucid structure: in the centre the dense screen of branches thins out towards the background to where the path leads out of the forest into the open. Whereas in Coninxloo's paintings individual leaves were painted in close, almost tapestry-like detail, here the paint is broadly applied over wide areas, the gradations of colour flowing into each other. Man is seemingly insignificant in comparison to the grandeur of Nature: only on closer examination do we notice a traveller resting by the wayside and couple approaching the ford in the centre of the picture. All this contributed to the especial popularity that Ruisdael's paintings enjoyed at the beginning of the Romantic Age in the early nineteenth century.   J. R.

FISHING BY MOONLIGHT
Aert van der Neer
(Amsterdam 1603/04 – 1677 Amsterdam)
c. 1669
Canvas; H 66.5 cm, W 86.5 cm
Inv. No. 6487

The representation of light was a theme which interested many painters in the 17th century. Among these was Aert van der Neer, who was chiefly renowned for his moonlit landscapes. Here

THE PORT OF AMSTERDAM
Ludolf Bakhuizen
(Emden 1631 – 1708 Amsterdam)
1674
Canvas; H 170 cm, W 210 cm
Inv. No. 473

Ludolf Bakhuizen is best known for his numerous depictions of the hustle and activity of ships in the Port of Amsterdam. However, this painting moves beyond a mere depiction of the harbour; it is instead a reportage of a specific event. The ship sailing into the harbour is the "Lejonet", built in the city for King Charles IX of Sweden. The drama of the moment is visually intensified by the Dutch man-of-war on the left firing a salute. The artistic moment is similarly emphasized by the painter in the foreground recording the event. The view of

the variety of detail presented in the picture serves principally to reveal the effects of the light. The brightness, radiating from the disk of the moon, gradually decreases in subtle nuances of colour, varying from yellow ochre to pale violet, towards the edges of the painting, while the banks of the river are largely left in darkness. The accentuated effects of the play of light in the clouds and the reflections in the water help to enliven the picture and endow it with a romantic and poetical quality.　　　　J. R.

the city itself corresponds to the tradition of Dutch paintings of cities.　　　　J. R.

ALLEGORY OF VANITAS
Leonard Bramer
(Delft 1595 – 1674 Delft)
c. 1640/45
Wood; H 80 cm, W 61.3 cm
Inv. No. 413

The ever-present thought of transitoriness in Dutch genre and still-life painting was articulated by Bramer in two companion pieces rich in symbols – an *Allegory of Vanitas* and an *Allegory of Death*. In the first painting a woman is looking in a mirror, while a musician is playing guitar, among carelessly scattered jewels and precious vessels, bits of armour and musical instruments. (In the other a skeleton is gazing at a skull amidst deterioration and decay.) Both paintings are meant to lead man away from pride, the source of all his sins, towards humility, and to divert his heart from love for transient, wordly goods to meditation of eternity and the life hereafter.   K. S.

WOMAN PEELING APPLES
Gerard ter Borch
(Zwolle 1617 – 1681 Deventer)
c. 1661
Canvas on wood; H 36.3 cm, W 30.7 cm
Inv. No. 588

Dutch genre painting, the art of recording scenes of everyday life reached a classical phase in the mid-17th century with the works of ter Borch. The care of children and the responsibility of parents was an often depicted theme in Dutch genre painting. Moralizing symbolic verses and emblems frequently provided the inspiration for such paintings. Ter Borch drew upon his personal experience as well, and used his sister Gesine as a model for his paintings. In *Woman Peeling Apples* Gesine is the mother whom the little girl watches intently. Typical of ter Borch, who often presents the tranquillity of domestic scenes instead of the noisy gaiety of social events, this image is filled with a quiet melancholy.   K. S.

WOMAN AND CHILD WITH SERVING MAID
Pieter de Hooch
(Rotterdam 1629 – 1684 Amsterdam)
c. 1663/65
Canvas; H 64 cm, W 76 cm
Inv. No. 5976

Pieter de Hooch represented urban bourgeois life in Holland in comfortable, orderly houses and sunny backyards. He favoured large rooms with views into the open, heightening their three-dimensional character by surprising light effects. Here, the half-open door at the back gives a view of houses on the opposite side of a canal. The observer is struck by the light which produces a vivid contrast between the illuminated view and the dark shadow of the interior. Images of domestic life were among de Hooch's favourite subjects; the familiar events depicted present a glimpse into the everyday life of Holland's "Golden Age".

K. S.

BEWARE OF LUXURY ("IN WEELDE SIET TOE")
Jan Steen
(Leyden 1625/26 – 1679 Leyden)
1663
Canvas; H 105 cm, W 145 cm
Inv. No. 791

Jan Steen interprets the moralistic truths of Dutch genre painting as a humorist, using images of black comedy, in which realistic action and didactic advice are confused. In his *Beware of Luxury* Steen describes various instances of intemperance in a dissolute household, alluding to common Dutch proverbs and aphorisms. While the housewife has fallen asleep at the table, all around her examples of carelessness and intemperance take place. The key to the meaning is found in the inscription on a slate in the bottom right-hand corner. There is found the first part of a Dutch proverb: *In weelde siet toe*. This means: "At a time of good living, beware", the ending is to be understood as, "and fear the rod". The punishment is also found in the painting in the form of sword and crutches, hanging in a basket from the ceiling. K. S.

THE ARTIST'S STUDIO
Johannes Vermeer "van Delft"
(Delft 1632 – 1675 Delft)
c. 1665/66
Canvas; H 120 cm, W 100 cm
Inv. No. 9128

Vermeer elevated the tradition of Dutch genre to the highest order of artistic achievement by uniting in his paintings pictorial meaning and balanced form. He completely eliminated chance, which had been until then an important characteristic of genre painting. No single element could be altered without destroying the entire concept of the composition irrevocably. The people in his pictures seem to have paused for thought in the middle of their activities, and the wealth of feeling radiating from them creates a thoroughly poetic atmosphere. Vermeer used optical aids, such as a *camera obscura* (an aperture camera) to project the image of the room onto a flat surface – a process which would explain the still-life character of the scene. In *The Artist's Studio* Vermeer went beyond mere genre painting to produce a rich allegory, an allegory of painting in a double sense. For all the numerous allegorical tools of baroque art in it, the painting still might not be convincing were it not a masterpiece of pure painting. Form a darkened room, one looks past a folded back curtain, past the intentionally oversized chair into the luminous studio of the artist. The rich dress of the painter seen from behind is strangely old-fashioned. His model poses with the attributes of Cleo, the Muse of History: the laurel wreath, the trumpet and a book. Equally important to the allegory are the elements of a still-life on the table: treatises on painting, a mask or sculpting study and a sketch book. The map of the seventeen provinces of the Low Countries before their partition in 1581 is also significant. Probably the allegory, in which illusion and reality flow together, is to be understood on many different levels: the Muse of History inspires the painter and proclaims the fame of the region's painting tradition as immortalized in history. From the sale of Vermeer's estate where it was already listed as "The Art of Painting", the picture passed through the collections of Gottfried van Swieten and Count Czernin to find its place in the Picture Gallery of the Kunsthistorische Museum. K. S.

LANDSCAPE IN SUFFOLK
Thomas Gainsborough
(Sudbury 1727 – 1788 London)
c. 1750
Canvas; H 66 cm, W 95 cm
Inv. No. 6271

Those landscapes which the young Gainsborough painted in the middle of the 18th century, mostly in his native Suffolk, reveal the influence of 17th century Dutch landscape painting on his art. This is evidenced in this picture by the winding cart-track meandering into the distance as well as by the towering trees and clouds. However, the firmly built structure of its baroque prototype has given way to a rococo animation and ease. The irregular distribution of patches of light, the graceful figures and the curved outlines of the path, the pool, the tree-trunks and clouds point in this new direction as do the swinging brush-strokes and the gentle honey-coloured hues.

M. H.

THE REVEREND BASIL BURY BERIDGE
Joseph Wright, called Wright of Derby
(Derby 1734 – 1797 Derby)
c. 1780/90
Canvas; H 127 cm, W 101 cm
Inv. No. 6237

The most significant achievements of 18th century English painting are embodied in portraiture. These portraits aptly depict the matter-of-fact qualities of the patrons produced by England's successful and flourishing economy at this time. Joseph Wright, a contemporary of Reynolds and Gainsborough, was not exclusively a portrait painter but was best known for his night scenes with their striking light effects. His success, however, was not immediate. After travelling to Italy, he lived in London for two years, where he met with failure. He returned to Lincolnshire, in 1777, where he specialized in the portraiture of the moguls of Northern England's industrial revolution. The portrait of the *Reverend Basil Bury Beridge,* vicar of Algarkirk in Lincolnshire represents one of the members of this bourgeois society. It is characteristic for its balance between concentration, heightened by a neutral background and dark clothes, and the indolent expression turned towards the observer.

K. S.

THE COIN CABINET

People have long been interested in old coins. Treasure hoards, when they consisted of coins made of precious metal, were always a welcome addition to a sovereign's wealth. Either the coins were melted down and the metal was reused or else they were incorporated into the princely treasure. This was the beginning of many a later art collection. Part of the interest in old coins derived from dynastic and political reasons, since coins give evidence of ancestors and predecessors in office. Thus, coin collections are among the oldest of all museum collections. This is true also of the Vienna Coin Cabinet which has its origins in the Habsburg collection. The Coin Cabinet has been continually expanded and completed and has been extended to include coins of modern times. Over the centuries the collection has increased to approximately 500,000 pieces and has become one of the largest and most important coin cabinets in the world.

The interest of the Habsburg rulers in their own coin portraits and in coins of former days is known to go back at least to Emperor Maximilian I. In 1547, under Ferdinand I, an inventory of the coin collection was drawn up which still exists today. His son, Archduke Ferdinand, who ruled over the Tyrol, was an enthusiastic art collector and also owned a coin collection. His cabinets for storing the coins are still in existence and are today partly at the Vienna Coin Cabinet and partly at Ambras Castle near Innsbruck. During the 18th century the Vienna collection benefited particularly from the numismatic interest of several emperos. Karl VI not only took a great interest in the study of coins but also concerned himself with the coin production of his day, introducing various artistic and technical improvements. He appointed the Swede Carl Gustav Heräus Inspector of Antiquities and entrusted him with the reorganisation of the Cabinet of Coins and Medals. Many new medals commemorating historic or dynastic events were suggested and in some cases even designed by Heräus. His surviving handwritten acquisition journal provides important evidence of the history of the collection of the Vienna Coin Cabinet.

As a collector Karl VI was so interested in coins that he had a book-shaped container (the so-called Numothek) made as a kind of Baroque coin album that enabled him to carry a number of his beloved coins with him when travelling. Karl's son-in-law, Franz I, was an important

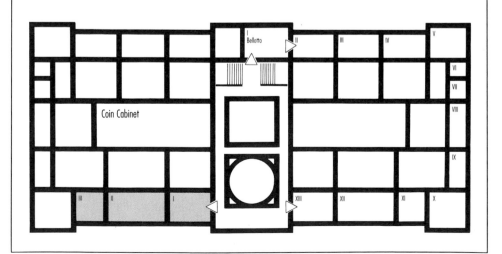

collector of contemporary coins. His position as emperor made it obviously easier for him to acquire rare pieces for his collection from a variety of sources. He found an excellent curator for his collection in Valentin Jamerai Duval, who like Franz himself came from Lorraine. A contemporary inventory of Franz' coin collection has been preserved to this day in two large and beautifully bound volumes. One of the daughters of Maria Theresa and Franz, Maria Anna, was likewise interested in numismatics. She compiled a work on the medals issued in honour of her mother that was published anonymously. After Franz' death Maria Theresa had his collection integrated with the Habsburg collection of coins and medals. Thus, the Imperial Coin Cabinet was established in a form that has essentially remained unchanged ever since. Henceforth it was headed by a succession of learned men with scholarly training. The first of these was Joseph Hilarius Eckhel, who with his work Doctrina numorum veterum established a new scholarly basis for ancient numismatics whose principles are still valid today.

Developments in the historical sciences and the emergence of new points of view during the 19th century have changed numismatics as a field of scholarly research. Monetary history and the function of all means of payment have joined the purely descriptive numismatics of earlier times. This also entailed an expansion of collecting activities: new classes of objects became of interest. Today these include not only coins and medals, but also paper money and securities, primitive money, duty stamps, tokens, seals, coin weights and coin balances, orders and decorations, and historic coin and medal dies.

In addition the Coin Cabinet serves as a repository for all documents relating to money in all its forms and functions which of course includes all the relevant technical and artistic aspects.

The exhibition covers three rooms and comprises approximately 4,500 objects, i. e. about one per cent of the entire collection. It is organized in the following way:

Room I gives an overview of the development of primitive money, coins and paper money from their inception to the present day. The arrangement is by historical periods (Greek, Roman, Byzantine) and by denominations (pfennig, thaler, gold coins, fractions of thalers and smaller denominations). One section of the exhibition documents the circulation of money in Austria from the Celts to this day. Ingot currency, tokens, necessity money and objects relating to the weighing of coins complete this part of the exhibition.

Room II is devoted to medals from their beginnings to the end of the 19th century. They are arranged by stylistic periods, geographic areas and cultural and historical themes.

In Room III 20th century-medals are exhibited. These include orders and decorations of former times as well as those currently awarded by the Republic of Austria. Earlier minting techniques are documented by means of some minting tools and the coins and medals struck with them.   H. J.

STATER
Lydia
7th/6th cent. B. C.
Electrum; WT 4.73 g, Diam. 13 mm
Inv. No. 34 140

Soon after the "invention" of coinage in Asia Minor at the end of the 7th century B. C., the kings of Lydia struck coins in electrum, a naturally occurring alloy of gold and silver. Croesus (561–546), the last of the Lydian kings, was the first to strike coins in pure gold and silver. The obverse of the *stater* depicts the heraldic animal of the Lydian kings, a lion protoma facing left, while the reverse shows two incuse squares, the mark left by the crude punch with which such early coins were struck.   G. D.

TETRADRACHM
Macedonia, Alexander III (the Great)
Silver; WT 16.86 g, Diam. 28 mm
Inv. No. 35 760

The military and political conquests of Alexander the Great (336–323) brought about the first unification of the coinage of the Greek world: its standard denominations were the gold stater and the silver *tetradrachm*. The obverse shows the head of Heracles, the mythical ancestor of the Macedonian kings – in this case clearly bearing Alexander's features – wearing the lion's skin; on the reverse Zeus seated on his throne, with eagle and long sceptre, Alexander's name and various monograms and symbols.   G. D.

DECADRACHM
Sicily, Syracuse
Die-engraver: Euainetos
c. 420 B. C.
Silver; WT 43.11 g, Diam. 36 mm
Inv. No. 6 807

Towards the end of the 5th century B. C. the coinage reached a high point in Syracuse with the two die-engravers Kimon and Euainetos, who created medallions with the monetary value of ten drachms, the *decadrachms*. The obverse of this piece shows the head of the nymph Arethusa crowned with leaves and wearing precious earrings and a necklace, and surrounded by dolphins symbolizing the ocean. The reverse depicts a victorious charioteer in his quadriga being crowned by Victory flying above him; in the exergue the elements of a full suit of armour, the prize for victory in the race.   G. D.

OCTADRACHM
Egypt, Arsinoe II Philadelphos
Gold; WT 27.80 g, Diam. 27 mm
Inv. No. 23 662

Alexander's successors in the various parts of his empire put their own portraits on the coinage. Thus the Ptolemies issued remarkably beautiful coins in gold and silver, e. g. Ptolemy II (285–264) for his wife and sister Arsinoe II. The queen's bust on the obverse of this *octadrachm* is noteworthy not only for its excellent portrait but also for its fine detail and especially its high relief. The reverse depicts double cornucopiae which, made of pure gold, had been dedicated by the queen to a temple. The reverse legend names the queen.   G. D.

TETRADRACHM
Attica, Athens
168/167 B. C.
Silver; WT 16.77 g, Diam. 31 mm
Inv. No. 35 263

From the late 6th century B. C. on, the coinage of Athens showed on the obverse the head of the goddess Athena and on the reverse the owl as her symbol. After a break in the coinage due to the Macedonian supremacy during the 3rd century, Athens started to issue "new style" coins from 196 B. C. on. The obverse of the *tetradrachm* shows the helmeted head of Athena Parthenos right, the reverse the owl standing on an overturned amphora with a club and quiver by its tail, all within an olive-wreath. The legend names not only the city of Athens but also several magistrates. G. D.

AUREUS
Rome, Augustus; mint in Spain
19 B. C.
Gold; WT 7.81 g, Diam. 19 mm
Inv. No. 4 632

The first Roman emperor, Augustus (27 B. C.–14 A. D.), skilfully took the right steps towards installing the monarchy, after Caesar's attempt in this regard had failed. This is also obvious in his coinage, where he mixes the new with the traditional as is demonstrated e. g. by the present piece struck at a mint in Spain. The obverse gives the emperor's titles simply as *CAESAR AVGVSTVS* and shows his slightly idealised portrait; the reverse bears the legend *IOV-TON* (= Iov[i] Ton[anti]) and a hexastyle temple with a cult statue of Jupiter. G. D.

TETRADRACHM
Celts, Noricum, Adnamat
1st cent. B. C.
Silver; WT 9.9 g, Diam. 22 mm
Inv. No. 26 732

The first Celtic coins imitated Greek coins, in particular those of the Macedonian kings, but their style became more and more barbarous. The kingdom of Noricum (situated in what is today Carinthia and Slovenia) issued large and small silver coins, the large ones frequently bearing the names of kings such as *ECCAIO, SUICCA* etc. The obverse shows a male laureate head left, the reverse a horseman with spear galloping right and the name of the king, *ADNAMAT*. G. D.

AUREUS
Rome, Septimius Severus
193 A. D.
Gold; WT 7.05 g, Diam. 21 mm
Inv. No. 14 129

Septimius Severus (193–211) was governor of Upper Pannonia residing at Carnuntum (Lower Austria) at the time of the assassination of the emperor Commodus. Three months later the 14th Legion, which was stationed there, proclaimed him emperor. He was the first of the so-called soldier-emperors. The obverse of this *aureus* shows the laureate head of the emperor surrounded by his titulature; the reverse names the 14th Legion *(LEG XIIII GEM M V* = Legio XIV Gemina Martia Victrix) and shows the legionary eagle between two standards. G. D.

40 NUMMI
Byzantine, Anastasius I; mint of Constantinople
512–517
Copper; Diam. 35 mm
Inv. No. 203 911

4 SILIQUAE
Rome, Constans; mint of Siscia
340–350
Silver; WT 13.22 g, Diam. 38 mm
Inv. No. 32 383

Towards the end of the Roman Empire the coinage becomes slightly monotonous. Silver coins were rarely struck, gold coins are somewhat more common and most of the coinage is in base metal; larger silver denominations which are considered medallions are a rarity. The very low-relief obverse shows Constans (337–350) with pearl diadem and wearing cuirass and paludamentum; on the reverse the emperor is depicted in full figure and in similar attire, holding a sceptre in his left hand and a labarum in his right. The legend *TRIVMPHATOR GENTIVM BARBARVM* expresses a wish rather than a historical fact.   G. D.

Two major reforms of the Byzantine copper coinage occurred during Anastasius' reign (491–518). In 498 large copper multiples of the *nummus* were introduced. In 512 due to a new weight standard for coins, the weights of the copper pieces were doubled. The present coin, although not particularly beautiful, appealed directly to the masses at the time. It was meant for use in daily transactions, and contains all the information necessary for its monetary function: on the obverse the portrait of the emperor, on the reverse the mark of value *M* (= 40 Nummi), the letters *CON* as the mintmark of Constantinople, a △ for the officina (division of the mint) which struck the coin, and stars as an issue mark.   H. J.

DENIER

Frankish Empire, Charlemagne; mint of Mainz?
Silver; WT 1.12 g, Diam. 17 mm
Inv. No. 165 636

King Pepin the Short abolished the bimetallic currency of gold and silver in the Frankish Empire. From 755 on only a silver coin, the denarius or *denier*, was issued. Charlemagne (768–814) gradually increased the weight of the denier until eventually 240 deniers made up one Carolingian pound. All the old coins were withdrawn from circulation. Irrespective of the mint that had issued them the new coins with the king's monogram were to be valid everywhere and to be accepted by everyone. Later the denier came to be known as a pfennig. The present specimen shows the name *CARO/LVS* on the obverse and on the reverse the letters *KD/MAG/C* ∽ indicating the mint. H. J.

PFENNIG

Austria, Leopold VI; mint of Vienna
c. 1210–1230
Silver; WT 0.90 g, Diam. 20 mm
Inv. No. 168 855

The earliest coins of the Babenberg dynasty were struck in 1110/20 at Krems. The extension of their territory to the east, the silver received as ransom for Richard the Lionheart and the fact that Styria came to the Babenbergs in 1192 appear to have led to the establishment of the mint of Vienna in 1193 or 1194. The *pfennige*, most of which do not bear any legend, can only be put into chronological order by analysing coin finds. Almost the entire iconographic repertoire of the Middle Ages can be found on these coins. This specimen shows an eagle and a panther on one side and a lion passant on the other. H. J.

BRACTEATE

Halberstadt, Bishop Ulrich von Reinstein
Silver; WT 0.87 g, Diam. 31 mm
Inv. No. 214 988

Artistically and technically the second half of the 12th century saw the heyday of the *bracteates,* coins whose fabric is so thin that the coin could take only one impression and the design appeared in intaglio on the reverse. Among the many *bracteates* issued there are exquisite examples of Romanesque art, such as this piece struck by the bishopric of Halberstadt in Germany under bishop Ulrich von Reinstein (1149–1160). The currency of Halberstadt, of the abbey of Quedlinburg, the lords of Falkenstein and Arnstein and the counts of Anhalt represented the southern centre of *bracteate* minting, all situated as it was in the Harz mountains rich in silver ore. The specimen illustrated bears the legend *S-S. STEPH – A* Ⴖ *VS – PROTH – OMAR/TIR* and shows the Christian protomartyr St. Stephen half kneeling, half floating up to heaven. H. J.

PRAGER GROSCHEN

Bohemia, Wenceslas II; mint of Kuttenberg
Silver; WT 3.71 g, Diam. 27 mm
Inv. No. 165 004

The decreasing purchasing power of the *pfennig* and the increased need for money due to rising trade led to the issue of *pfennig* multiples, for example the Venetian grosso and the French *gros tournois*. In 1300 during the reign of King Wenceslas II (1278–1305) the *Prager groschen* was issued following the French example. It was struck in great quantities to exploit the rich Bohemian silver mines and circulated widely also in the neighbouring countries. The striking of this denomination was only discontinued under the Habsburg emperor Ferdinand I. The types were influenced by the *gros tournois*. On the obverse is the crown of St. Wenceslas within a double circle of inscription giving the name and titles of the king, on the reverse the legend *GROSSI: PRAGENSES* and the lion rampant of Bohemia.

H. J.

ANGE D'OR

France, Philip VI
1341
Gold; WT 6.32 g, Diam. 32 mm
Inv. No. 21 551 aα

The *ange d'or* was first struck in 1341 under King Philip VI (1328–1350). Its name is derived from the obverse type of St. Michael standing on the dragon. He rests his left hand on a shield with the arms of France. This was the first time that the shield with the fleurs-de-lys was depicted on a French coin. The reverse shows an ornamental design: a floriated cross within a quatrefoil, with four small crowns in the spandrils. The legend *XPC* (Christus) *VINCIT XPC REGNAT XPC IMPERAT* long remained the standard legend on French gold coins. The *ange d'or* represents one of the highest achievements of mediaeval coin art in Europe.

H. J.

FIORINO D'ORO ▷

Italy, Florence
1323
Gold; WT 3.51 g, Diam. 20 mm
Inv. No. 26 782 aα

After the Carolingian currency reform the coinage in large parts of Europe was for some time dominated by the *denier*. The decreasing purchasing power of the denier, an increased need for money, and trade with the east made the city of Florence take up the striking of gold coins in 1252. The coin types were the Florentine lily and St. John the Baptist, the patron saint of Florence. The name of the coin is derived from the emblem of the city depicted on it (fiore = flower). It can be dated by the chalice as the sign of the mintmaster Giano Albizzi, who was responsible for the gold coinage in 1323. The *fiorino d'oro* was much copied and as *florin* it also came to be widespread in Germany.

H. J.

GULDENGROSCHEN
Tyrol, Archduke Sigismund; mint of Hall
Die-engraver: Wenzel Kröndl
1486
Silver; WT 31.94 g, Diam. 42 mm
Inv. No. 164 828

The main commercial currency of this era was the gold *gulden,* and Tyrol, being situated along one of the important North-South trading routes, also issued such gold *guldens* under Archduke Sigismund (1439–1490). However, the striking of gold coins was not profitable, since no gold was mined locally. Archduke Sigismund's financial administrator, Anthoni vom Ross, had eventually the ingenious idea of striking the equivalent of the gold *gulden* in silver, thus using the rich local silver deposits. Artistically the die represents an outstanding achievement of Gothic engraving. Technically, too, it is noteworthy for it involved striking a relatively large and thick piece of metal.

H. J.

TALER
Bohemia, Count Stephán Schlick and his brothers; mint of Joachimsthal
Die-engraver: Melchior Peuerlein ?
c. 1523
Silver, WT 28.97 g, Diam. 41 mm
Inv. No. 5 887 ba

Exercising an disputed coining privilege, the Counts Schlick (Stephán Schlick died in 1526) in Bohemia began to mint coins at Joachimsthal on the Bohemian slope of the Erzgebirge on the model of neighbouring Saxony, where so-called *guldengroschen* had been issued following the example of Hall in Tyrol. Because of their large quantity and the rapid distribution due to the flourishing trade with Saxony these *Joachimstaler* were soon well-known far beyond their place of origin. Shortened to *taler,* the name became a generic term for heavy silver coins in central Europe. The original *talers* show on the obverse St. Joachim, patron saint of the mining town of Joachimsthal, above a coat of arms.

K. Sch.

GULDENGROSCHEN ▷
Austria, Maximilian I, mint of St. Veit
1518
Silver; WT 26.63 g, Diam. 41 mm
Inv. No. 164 261

Emperor Maximilian I (1493–1519) played an important part in the establishment of the new monetary system that had originated in Tyrol. The first coins issued by the mint of St. Veit in Carinthia are dated 1515. The bulk of the coinage was *batzen,* ½ *batzen* and *pfennige.* The *guldengroschen* of St. Veit must be regarded as medallions, since the weights of the individual pieces differ too widely for proper coins. These large Carinthian silver coins are no longer in Gothic style, but show all the characteristics of the Renaissance.

H. J.

TALER
Austria, Leopold I; mint of Vienna
1670
Silver; WT 28.60 g, Diam. 44 mm
Inv. No. 726 bα

Under Leopold I (1657–1705) the issuing of coins was regulated by the so-called *Münzeinrichtungswerk* of 1659, which introduced new denominations that permitted the highest possible profit at the lowest cost for the authority striking the coins. The wars against the Turks led to a financial and monetary crisis, the so-called *kleine Kipperzeit*. This *taler* from the mint of Vienna is an example of a beautiful Baroque coin from the time when each mint was still recognizable by specific artistic and technical characteristics of its coins. Shortly before a new mechanical minting process had been introduced to the mint of Vienna.　　　H. J.

DUCATON
Austria, Maria Theresa; mint of Bruges
(Flanders)
Die-engraver: Jacques Roettiers
1754
Silver; WT 33.12 g, Diam. 41 mm
Inv. No. 170 760

The War of the Spanish Succession ended in 1714 with the Treaty of Rastatt, which gave the Habsburgs possession of the Spanish Netherlands. The *ducaton* had been introduced there in 1618 to be the silver equivalent of the gold ducat. It was one of the finest and heaviest large silver coins of its day until it was discontinued in 1755. On the bust truncation of the graceful portrait of Maria Theresa is the signature of the die-engraver. The reverse shows the crowned arms with laurel branches over two crossed batons, with a small lion underneath as the mintmark of Bruges.
　　　H. J.

DOUBLE VEREINSTALER ▷
Austria, Francis Joseph I; mint of Vienna
Die-engraver: obverse: J. Tautenhayn
reverse: F. Gaul
1866
Silver; WT 36.94 g, Diam. 41 mm
Inv. No. 129 209

The "convention currency" introduced by Maria Theresa in 1753 as a result of a German monetary convention was in use until 1857, when Austria and Liechtenstein concluded a convention with the countries of the German Customs Union, stipulating that the same denominations should be issued in all these countries, viz. gold crown, half gold crown, *double taler* and *taler*. In order to bring the currencies of the 3 large currency areas of the former German Empire into a convenient relationship with each other, Austria slightly lowered its weight standard and called it the Austrian currency standard. The portrait of Emperor Fran-

cis Joseph (1848–1916), which was standardised for all mints, has been worked in low relief but with great precision; the Emperor's motto *(MIT VEREINTEN KRÄFTEN)* is inscribed on the rim.
　　　H. J.

5 DOPPIE
Italy, Genoa
1679
Gold; WT 33.30 g, Diam. 43 mm
Inv. No. 6 463 bα

From 1528 to 1797 the Republic of Genoa was ruled by the Biennial Doges and *Governatori* whose names, however, do not appear on the coins. The coins bear only the mint master's initials, in this case *ILM* (= Ioannes Lucas Maiolus). The *doppia* is the equivalent of the Spanish pistole (double escudo), which played an important role in European trade. The obverse shows the Virgin and Child seated facing in clouds (the Virgin is the patron saint of Genoa), the reverse a floriated cross with quatrefoils at the angles. With the "Casa di San Giorgio" Genoa had one of the first public banks that sometimes even issued silver coins.   H. J.

MEDAL OF ULRICH II MOLITOR
Rafael Ranghieri (medallist)
(Verona ?–after 1595 Prague ?)
1581
Silver cast and partly gilded;
WT 54.21 g, Diam. 53 mm
Inv. No. 12 818 bβ

The artist is presumed to have come to Austria sometime during the 1560s. Together with Antonio Abondio he represents the Italian school of the Austrian medal-making in Vienna and Prague, respectively. Their medals are distinguished by excellent portraiture and detailed chasing. Ulrich Molitor (1526–1585), Abbot of Heiligenkreuz (Lower Austria), is portrayed here at the age of 55. He was born in Überlingen on Lake Constance and after entering the Cistercian abbey of Heiligenkreuz in 1548 was made abbot in 1558. It was under his leadership that the economic decline of the abbey could be halted.   K. Sch.

MEDAL OF ISOTTA DEGLI ATTI ▷
Matteo de' Pasti (medallist)
(Verona c. 1420–c. 1490 Rimini)
1446
Cast bronze; Diam. 85 mm
Inv. No. 435 bβ

Matteo de' Pasti was emulating his fellow-countryman Antonio Pisano (Pisanello), who represents the first high point – with virtually no recent predecessors – of the Renaissance medal in northern Italy. Pasti, who was a sculptor and architect, found a patron in Sigismondo Malatesta, lord of Rimini, whom he portrayed on medals several times. Since her early youth the poetess Isotta degli Atti (1432/33–1474) had been Sigismondo's lover, as is also evidenced by the two matching medals of the couple dating from 1446. If tradition is correct about Isotta's year of birth, she is here portrayed at the age of thirteen. In 1456 she married Sigismondo.

K. Sch.

MEDAL ON THE DANISH NAVAL VICTORY IN THE BAY OF KØGE

Die-engraver: Christoph Schneider
(Germany ?–1701 Denmark)
1677
Gold; WT 1258.8 g, Diam. 128 mm
Inv. No. 249 bβ

This medal represents a considerable technical achievement due to its relief which is unusually high for a struck medal. The medallist Christoph Schneider, who probably originally came from Germany, worked as a die-engraver in Copenhagen. A strong sense of perspective is achieved by the contrast between the high relief of the ships in the foreground and the lower-relief engraving of the background. Moreover there is a wealth of very carefully executed detail. The medal commemorates the three naval victories won by King Christian V of Denmark against the Swedish fleet in 1676 and 1677, in particular the last one in the Bay of Køge on 1 July 1677. The Scandinavian War (1676–79), which had its roots in the enmity between France and Brandenburg, ended in 1679 with the Treaty of Lund.

K. Sch.

MARIA THERESA MEDAL OF HONOUR
Die-engraver: Matthäus Donner
(Essling/Vienna 1704–1756 Vienna)
1743
Silver; WT 87.65 g, oval-shaped 68/60 mm
Inv. No. 1 854 bβ

Such medals of honour were bestowed by sovereigns and princes as honours or to reward particular achievements, similar to orders and decorations today. Whereas in earlier times they had often been cast, in Austria they were struck from the reign of Karl VI onwards. These medals were awarded in precious metal, often gold, on a matching chain or ribbon, and in earlier days they were frequently further embellished by a frame made of precious metal and decorated with precious stones. Different "classes" were indicated by different metals and sizes.

During Maria Theresa's reign there were at first three different sizes of this oval-shaped medal. Before long, however, all newly struck medals were circular. The illustrated medal of honour belongs to the largest size with a weight of 3 ounces (5 Lot). The dies were engraved by Matthäus Donner, a brother of the famous sculptor Raphael Donner, whom he equalled in the excellence of his work. Usually the obverse of the medal of honour shows the portrait of the ruler surrounded by his titulature. In the present case – as the medal was struck before 1745 – Maria Theresa is not yet called Empress, but daughter of Emperor Karl, Queen of Hungary and Bohemia and Archduchess of Austria. The reverse shows Maria Theresa's motto and emblem, which consists of the symbols of the three countries ruled by her: the *Bindenschild* (i. e. the shield representing the Austrian territories), the lion rampant of Bohemia and the patriarchal cross taken from the arms of Hungary. K. Sch.

MEDAL ON THE BAPTISM OF NAPOLEONS'S SON, THE KING OF ROME ▽

Die-engraver: Bertrand Andrieu
(Bordeaux 1761–1822 Paris)
1811
Silver; WT 180.96 g, Diam. 68 mm
Inv. No. 135 168

Napoleon I is holding up his son, who had been given the title King of Rome at birth and who was later to live at the Austrian court as Duke of Reichstadt, over a baptismal font, with a bible leaning against it. The Emperor is standing before a throne whose sides bear Napoleon's emblem. The design of the medal is by the French painter and graphic artist Louis Lafitte, and the die was engraved by Bertrand Andrieu, one of the most prolific die-engravers from the Napoleonic era until the reign of Louis XVIII. Most of the medals that Andrieu engraved were based on his own designs. The reverse bears the names of the 50 cities of the French Empire that had dedicated this medal to their emperor.   K. Sch.

MEDAL OF MARIE VON EBNER-ESCHENBACH

Medallist: Rudolf Marschall
(Vienna 1873–1967 Vienna)
1900
Silber; WT 70.2 g, Diam. 57 mm
Inv. No. 19 953/1914 B

Towards the end of the 19th century a renaissance of the medal began in France which also provided fresh impulses for medals issued in Vienna. The die-engraver Rudolf Marschall, too, had studied in France for a while. In the present example the French influence may be seen in the absence of a rim and the comparatively low relief which almost seems to merge with the background. Despite the realistic treatment of the portrait, faithfulness in every detail is no longer sought after. The en face portrait is unusual for this time. The medal was dedicated to the writer Marie von Ebner-Eschenbach (1830–1916) on the occasion of her 70th birthday.   K. Sch.

MEDAL OF CLEMENS HOLZMEISTER
Medallist: Ferdinand Welz
(Vienna, born 1915)
1961
Cast bronze; Diam. 110 mm
Inv. No. 41 931/1914 B

The contemporary Austrian medal owes decisive impulses to the Viennese artist Ferdinand Welz. For him the cast medal has become an important means of expression after it had long been neglected by medallists in favour of the struck medal. The cast medal offers the artist greater freedom than the more restrictive struck medal. Thus, in his work Welz likes to abandon the precise circular shape and the image itself seems to break through the frame. This way of representation has no doubt been influenced by his training as a sculptor. The present medal shows the world-renowned Austrian architect Clemens Holzmeister (1886–1983) as Rector Magnificus of the Vienna Academy of Fine Arts wearing the appropriate robe and gold chain.   K. Sch.

MEDAL COMMEMORATING THE 20TH ANNIVERSARY OF F.I.D.E.M. ▽
Medallist: André Galtié
(Paris 1908–1983 Issy-les-Moulineaux)
1957
Bronze; Diam. 67 mm
Inv. No. 47 744/1914 B

In 1937 the Fédération Internationale des Éditeurs de Médailles was founded as an association of the issuers of medals. Every few years this association organizes international conferences in conjunction with exhibitions of contemporary medals. The 7th conference of its kind took place in Paris in 1957 on the occasion of the twentieth anniversary of F.I.D.E.M. The official commemorative medal was created by the French medallist Galtié. He loves to give the background an undulating texture rather than leaving it entirely flat, something that modern striking techniques have made possible. This results in a certain similarity of appearance to cast medals.   K. Sch.

COMBINED FORM OF THE GRAND CROSS BREAST STARS OF THE HABSBURG FAMILY ORDERS

c. 1840
Silver, partly gilt and enamelled; H 150 mm,
W 114 mm
Inv. No. 308 E

During the 18th century a transition occurred from the orders of knighthood, such as the Order of the Golden Fleece, to orders of merit, such as the Military Order of Maria Theresa, established by Empress Maria Theresa in 1757. As Queen of Hungary Maria Theresa also founded, in 1764, the Royal Hungarian Order of the Knights of St. Stephen, which again emphasized the aspect of knighthood. Emperor Franz I established in 1808 the Austrian Imperial Order of Leopold and in 1816 the Austrian Imperial Order of the Iron Crown, both of which were intended primarily as orders of merit. The ruling monarch of the Habsburg dynasty was by virtue of his office grand master of all these orders; hence they together with the Order of the Golden Fleece were termed the Habsburg family orders. Since on official occasions the emperor was required to wear the breast stars of all these orders, a special combined form of the four breast stars – of the Order of Maria Theresa, the Order of St. Stephen, the Order of Leopold and the Order of the Iron Cross – with the points of the different stars partly overlapping was created as a less ceremonial version. The arrangement shown here is the one worn by Emperor Ferdinand I (1835–1848).

K. Sch.

THE COLLECTION OF ANCIENT MUSICAL INSTRUMENTS

The Collection of Ancient Musical Instruments at the Kunsthistorische Museum in Vienna differs from other similar collections in that it is housed in ten large rooms of the Neue Burg (the 19th century wing of the Habsburg Winter Palace) – magnificent premises, such as no other collection in the world has. The grand design of the structure with high windows that take in the exterior surroundings makes it possible to better understand the individual items within their overall context. Progressing through these rooms, the observer goes from the visual confrontation with original musical instruments to the various sounds of each instrument and from there to the music of each period; outside, all around him, are the buildings where music history was made: the Vienna State Opera, the Musikverein, the Music Collection of the Austrian National Library and the Imperial Court Chapel, all in the center of town. As far as the individual exhibits are concerned, the special collection of Renaissance instruments is the best in the world. Especially noteworthy is the collection of lutes; they were the most important of all instruments in their time and may be compared in their essential role to that of the piano of the 19th century. The creation of the Viennese ideal of sound was in every way bound to the prolific Viennese piano production, documented here as nowhere else. One special attraction for visitors interested in music are the many instruments that belonged to famous performers and composers.

The history of the collection starts with two significant 16th century inventories, one from Ambras Castle in Innsbruck and the other from Catajo Castle near Padua. The musical instruments in Ambras were mainly show pieces. The Kunst- und Wunderkammer (Chamber of Art and Marvels) of the music-loving Archduke Ferdinand of Tyrol was filled with instruments chosen for their artistic appearance or their rarity. The instruments are not representative of those customarily played in the Renaissance,

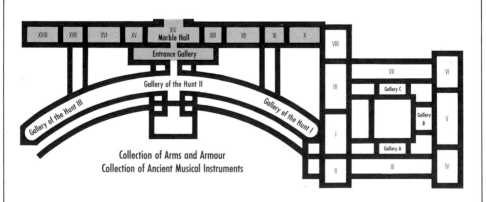

Neue Burg · Heldenplatz

Entrance Gallery: Brass Instruments, Percussion Instruments · Hall X: Wood Wind Instruments, Organs · Hall XI: Clavichords, Virginals, Harpsichords · Hall XII: Plucked Instruments (Lutes, Guitars) · Hall XIII: Bow Instruments · Hall XIV: Pieces of Outstanding Interest, Instruments of Important Musicians · Hall XV: Pianofortes of the 18th century · Hall XVI, XVII: Pianofortes of the 19th century · Hall XVIII: Pianos of the 19th and 20th centuries.

dye eyn ietlicher paur mag kennen ("that every poor farmer may know"). In contrast, the collection of the Este dynasty at Catajo provides an excellent look at those instruments commonly used in the 16th century. Instruments from later periods came into the national collection either from the Emperor's estate or through acquisitions or bequests. Some string instruments in their original state are on loan from the Vienna Hofmusikkapelle (Court Music Chapel). Also among the exhibits the especially splendid workmanship of items from the Rothschild Collection, not to mention other public and private lenders may be seen.

Only in some cases the viewer recognizes that an instrument is also a work of art. More often, the artistry of the maker lies in the aural results, the success of the sound of the instrument as it serves to make music.

The exhibit as a whole is arranged according to the sound production of the various instruments (for example, string instruments, pianos, woodwinds, etc.). This enables the observer to see what various instruments and their sounds have in common with each other. Paintings from the Picture Gallery (and from private lenders) that relate to music document the performance practices of each period. However, the best way to present the sound of the musical instruments is in the concerts sometimes presented in the Marble Hall of the Collection.

G. S.

LARGE BASS VIOL ▽
Ventura Linarol
Padua
1585
BL 100 cm, TL 173 cm
Inv. No. 73

The large bass viol belongs to the family of string instruments with sloping shoulders that is held between the knees. Only by joining many single pieces of wood in a method known as rib construction was it possible to produce an instrument of these proportions. Considering the construction method, this *viola da gamba* is a descendant of the mediaeval fiddle. The sound-holes already resemble the f-holes of the violin which made its triumphal advance from Italy at a later date. This wide-bodied gamba is in excellent condition and all of its parts seem to be original.

G. S.

LIRA DA BRACCIO
Joannes Andrea
Verona
1511
BL 51 cm, TL 80.5 cm
Inv. No. 89

Of the few extant Renaissance liras, a string instrument played while held in the arms, this example from Vienna is the most beautiful. Recently conducted investigations showed conclusively that the table is indeed from the early 16th century. The arching corresponds to the female form – an indication of the relation of love to music. The exquisite sound-holes are not found anywhere else in the world. C-shaped, they are laid out around the bridge, indicating their descent from the round sound-hole as we know it today in the guitar.

G. S.

TORTOISE-SHELL VIOLIN WITH BOW AND SHAPED CASE
Wenzel Kowansky
Vienna
1749
BL 35 cm, TL 57 cm
Inv. No. 638

Maria Theresa bought this violin, made of rare and translucent tortoise-shell, for the Treasury on March 6, 1749. Wenzel Kowansky, known only to have been a case maker, produced this show piece in conjunction with one of the Viennese luthiers. Not of wood, it is unsuitable for playing. It does, however, give a detailed picture of the baroque violin. The purfling is gold. The neck, peg box, fingerboard and tailpiece are of ivory inlaid with gold and tortoise-shell. The bow is of similar construction and along with the violin provides a stunning colour contrast to the red velvet lining of the black leather case.   G. S.

REBEC
Venice
15th century
TL 37 cm
Inv. No. 433

The body was produced from a single piece of wood in a "trough" construction, similar to that of feeding troughs or dugouts. The result is a relatively small but heavy instrument. This kind of small violin was still being played in Austria and Southern Germany in the last century. Its name was *trögl*. The body of this *rebec* is shaped like a Venus figure. Although no longer a complete instrument, it is considered a work of art and is one of the few existing of its kind.   G. S.

VIOLIN
Johann Georg Thir
(Prem 1710 – after 1781 Vienna)
c. 1780
BL 35.4 cm
Inv. No. 580

Johann Georg Thir was considered the best Viennese violinmaker at the end of the 18th century. Like many of his colleagues, he was originally from Füssen in Allgäu (Southern Germany), one of the most important violinmaking centres in the world. The carved lion's head atop the peg box is an ancient Füssen tradition, one that was soon to be replaced in Vienna as well as elsewhere with the scroll, following more and more the Italian influence. The varnish is in mint condition and the fittings are from the 18th century.

G. S.

JOSEPH LANNER'S VIOLIN ▽
Franz Geissenhof
(Füssen 1753–1821 Vienna)
1817
BL 35.6 cm
Inv. No. 713

Franz Geissenhof modelled his violins after those of Stradivarius and is still recognized as the greatest Viennese violin maker of the 19th century. Violins made by Geissenhof were relatively expensive and very popular as early as the beginning of the 19th century. Both Johann Strauss father and son, the main figures in the Viennese dance music tradition, played these violins. The violin of Joseph Lanner, the actual founder of Viennese dance music, is however still in the same state as when he played it and still wins enthusiastic applause from audiences at the museum's matinee concerts. The reaction of the instrument is very sensitive, while the tone itself (according to the Viennese concept of sound) is sweet and delicate.

G. S.

CITTERN FROM ARCHDUKE FERDINAND OF TYROL
Girolamo de Virchi
Brescia
1574
BL 35 cm, TL 73.5 cm
Inv. No. 56

Indisputably the most important instrument in the Viennese Collection, the cittern catches the eye as a prime example of the best in functional construction combined with the finest in artistic execution. The cittern was formerly called "zitter", a name which is noticeably similar to the alpine *zither*. It is played with a plectrum like an mandolin. The use of the most resonant woods has ensured, in this particular case, an exquisitely constructed instrument with a wonderful tone. The splendid, detailed workmanship reflects the wishes of the person who commissioned it. Thus, it became the most exemplary object of Renaissance *Wunderkammern* (Chambers of Marvels). The top is made of very fine-grained spruce with a soundhole shaped like a rosette in ornate openwork. The back has been put together from cuttings of maple and its transparent old Italian varnish is breathtaking. The neck and fingerboard are lavished with different Renaissance elements, like caryatids, putti and acanthus leaves. Most flamboyant, however, are the back and top of the peg box: The customary "nose" at the rear takes on the face of a jester and the naturalistic nude represents Lucretia's death.

G. S.

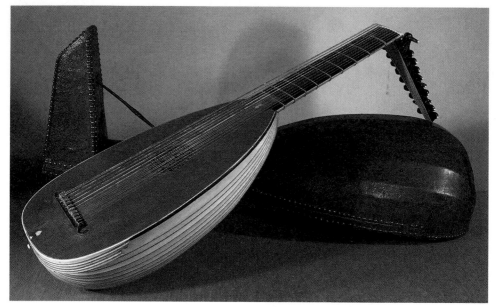

LUTE WITH CASE
Vendelinus Venere
Venice
1626
BL 53 cm, TL 94 cm
Inv. No. 616

According to the latest research, Vendelinus Venere was probably none other than Wendelin
Tieffenbrucker, from Füssen in Allgäu. The ivory
hearts inlaid in the sounding boards are typical for
the Füssen violinmaker's tradition. The body is
made of very thin ivory strips joined together,
responsible for the light carrying power of this
beautifully proportioned lute. The case was custom-made in a similar manner to the lute and
covered in tooled leather. G. S.

LUTE ▽
Blasius Weigert
(d. 1765 Linz)
1740
BL 51.6 cm, TL 88 cm
Inv. No. 719

This recently acquired lute of Linz provenance is
representative of late baroque construction, with a
pear-shaped body. The instrument was originally
many-stringed and was changed by Blasius
Weigert to fit his own performance needs. It was
rebuilt whith six courses of strings, closely resembling the modern guitar with its six single
strings. The rosette is the only ornamental detail
and was formed along mediaeval lines.

G. S.

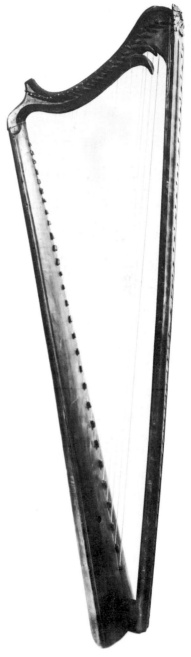

BASS LUTE CITTERN
Germany
c. 1500
TL 175.5 cm
Inv. No. 55

The lute cittern, listed in the Ambras inventory as a "large, rare lute with two necks and three stars" was, even then, considered an oddity. It is still the only one of its kind. Characteristic of the lute is its bent neck and the way of playing it; from the cittern it takes its flat construction. The combination of these two different plucked instruments set in the bass range resulted in an enormous, asymmetrical instrument with a tremendous circumference. The three sound holes are of late gothic tracery.   G. S.

HARP ▷
Italy
16th century
TL 140 cm
Inv. No. 64

The mediaeval harp, known to us from numerous paintings, was still being used in the Renaissance.Only a few examples have survived from the 16th century. The column bears a mascaron and an acanthus ornament. The body consists of two hollowed-out pieces of wood joined together.
                    G. S.

375

DOUBLE GUITAR ▽
Alexandre Voboam
Paris
1690
BL 45 cm and 26 cm, TL 95 cm and 63.5 cm
Inv. No. 53

Playing a guitar in keys that are very different from the key in which the guitar was originally tuned brings increasing intonation difficulties. Alexandre Voboam provided a unique solution to this problem by adding a second guitar tuned a third higher. This cuts down on the time a player would need to constantly be changing instruments. This double guitar concept is unique. Worthy of note is the tailpiece of ivory and ebony as well as the fine workmanship of the two terraced rosettes.

G. S.

GUITAR
Matteo Sellas
Venice
1st half of 17th century
BL 47 cm, TL 98.5 cm
Inv. No. 47

The lute had to be made generally available in a simple version for every musician's pocket, whereas the guitar was for music lovers who could afford to pay more and have a more artistic alternative. This particular instrument is inlaid with ivory in those places on the instrument where it would not affect the resonance. The engraved landscapes on the fingerboard indicate the guitar's Italian provenance. Matteo Sellas, the most famous guitarmaker of the baroque period was originally not from Italy, but, like so many other Italian lutemakers, from Füssen, where he was known as Matthäus Seelos.

G. S.

HARPSICHORD
Joseph Salodiensis
Venice
1559
8', 8', C/E-c^3
TL 184 cm
Inv. No. 630

The painter, Friedrich Amerling, discovered this instrument in 1882 in Venice. It has two stops in the 8-foot register. Like most Italian quilled instruments, it was built, for acoustical reasons, with very thin walls, here of cypress wood. An extra case was necessary to protect it and from that, the painted lid (c. 1580) still exists. 　　　G. S.

HARPSICHORD ▽
Joannes Daniel Dulcken
Antwerp, 1745
8', 8', 4', F$_1$–f^3
L 260 cm
Inv. No. 726

Joannes Daniel Dulcken was, except for the Ruckers family, considered to be the leading exponent of Flemish harpsichord building. In contrast to most Italian instruments, the cabinets of Flemish harpsichords were very stable. The soundboard of this splendid instrument (with two manuals) has floral motive done in gouache, while the cabinet itself is embellished with gold rocaille and flowered garlands painted on a red background. The painting on the lid was probably added later, in Austria, and dates from the second half of the 18th century. 　　　G. S.

CLAVICYTHERIUM FROM THE ESTATE OF EMPEROR LEOPOLD I
Martin Kaiser
Düsseldorf
End of 17th century
8', 8', C_1–c^3
H 282 cm, W 103 cm, D 51.5 cm
Inv. No. 377

In contrast to the harpsichord, whose strings run horizontally, the clavicytherium is strung vertically. The Düsseldorf organ builder, Martin Kaiser, probably of the great luthier family of the same name in Füssen, chose a symmetrical form for this plucked instrument that necessitated a complicated mechanism much like that of an organ. Beautifully embellished and inlaid with ebony, tortoise-shell, mother-of-pearl and ivory, this clavicytherium was used by Emperor Leopold I, a composer of no little merit.   G. S.

ORGAN-PIANO ▷
Franz Xaver Christoph
Vienna
c. 1785
F_1–f^3
H 93 cm, W 163 cm, D 70 cm
Inv. No. 625

After the Florentine Bartolommeo Cristofori built a hammer mechanism into a harpsichord at the beginning of the 18th century, new evolutionary developments followed rapidly from the *clavicembalo* to the *gravicembalo col piano e forte* and eventually to the fortepiano and the modern concert grand piano. Finally the 18th century had a stringed keyboard instrument that equalled the harpsichord in the intensity of its sound and allowed for the dynamic nuances so treasured in the clavichord. The new invention was received with great enthusiasm everywhere – France, England, Germany and Austria – but above all in Vienna. Instruments turned out by the Viennese piano builders of the late 18th and early 19th centuries were preferred by the leading performers of the Viennese Classical period and in turn became world-renowned.

Franz Xaver Christoph was one of the Viennese organ builders who turned to the construction of this popular new keyboard instrument, as is evident in the rare combination of a fortepiano and a positive organ. In concerts with larger audiences, the concert grand form was preferred, whereas for performances at home the square variety was more suitable. The two-part chest-shaped body of this instrument has a mahogany veneer and openwork in gothic motives. Typical for the end of the 18th century is the shape of the keyboard: The lower keys are of ebony and the upper ones of ivory. This results – in contrast to the piano of today – in a relatively dark keyboard and was supposed to emphasize the fair skin of the hands of the ladies playing.

The portrait of Marie Antoinette (Austria, c. 1770, Inv. No. GG 7084) shows her playing a square piano of this sort.   G. S.

BUST OF JOSEPH HAYDN
Franz Thaler
Vienna, c. 1800
TH 30 cm
Inv. No. 350

No portrait of Joseph Haydn could be as life-like as this very plastic sculpture from the hands of Franz Thaler. It was done during Haydn's lifetime, in coloured beeswax with real hair. This priceless memento piece once belonged to Prince Metternich.   G. S.

PEDAL GRAND PIANOFORTE
Josef Brodmann
Vienna, c. 1815
C_1–f^4
H 106 cm, TW 125 cm, TL 240 cm
Inv. No. 646

Pedals were added to the fortepiano, following the idea of a church organ. Only very few such instruments are still in existence. Wolfgang Amadeus Mozart possessed a pedal piano and Robert Schumann composed several works for it. This one from Josef Brodmann, an important name in the Viennese piano making tradition, was decorated in the empire style. The painting above the piano, of Napoleon I (François Gerard, Inv. No. GG 2030), shows very similar furniture pieces.   G. S.

CLAVICHORD ▷
Germany
End of 17ᵗʰ century
C/E–c^3
W 32.5 cm, L 103 cm
Inv. No. 650

It is a trait of the clavichord, that the strings are shortened at certain points while struck. The player was thus able to vary the dynamics with his touch making the clavichord the forerunner of the fortepiano. The so-called fretted instruments of the 17ᵗʰ century are rare. They have few strings and are quite small so that the sound is better than that of the larger models. This clavichord is quite delicate and rests on its own custom-made 18ᵗʰ century stand.

                                              G. S.

GRAND PIANOFORTE
Ludwig Bösendorfer
Vienna, c. 1875
A_2–a^4
H 97 cm, W 147 cm, L 244 cm
Inv. No. 387

Ignaz Bösendorfer was a student of Josef Brodmann and the founder of the Bösendorfer piano factory. His son, Ludwig, built this piano in ebony veneer and richly inlaid with precious woods and metals, on the design of Theophil Hansen, the architect of the Musikverein building. Indeed, many of the details are strikingly similar to the appointments of the large hall of the Musikverein, such as the caryatids on the side of the piano. This splendid instrument was supposedly commissioned by Emperor Francis Joseph I, proof of which may be the double eagle in the crown of the music rack.   G. S.

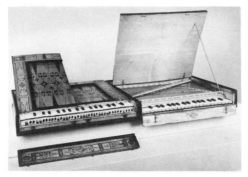

SPINET AND REGAL IN THE FORM OF GAME BOARDS
Anthonius Meidting
Augsburg, 1587
$F–a^2$
H 7.4 cm, L 45.5 cm and 45.5 cm, D 45.1 cm
Inv. No. 119

Emperor Ferdinand I's motto, SIC TRANSIT GLORIA MUNDI, painted on the spinet may refer to the transiency of sounded music. On the other hand, the unusual combination of game board and music instrument shows how important the concept of playing was in the Renaissance. They represent two sides of the same coin: to play a game (checkers, chess and tric-trac) or to play musical instruments, as represented here by a spinet (a small plucked instrument) and a regal (a portable reed organ).   G. S.

CLAVIORGAN
Southern Germany
2ⁿᵈ half of 16ᵗʰ century
$C/E–c^3$
H 25 cm, D 49 cm, L 102 cm
Inv. No. A 132

This claviorgan, already mentioned in the Ambras inventory of 1596, is the oldest still in existence. It is a combination of the positive organ, the regal and the spinet and is a masterful example of

RECORDER
Italy
16ᵗʰ century
TL 45.5 cm
Inv. No. 140

Renaissance recorders are remarkable for their functional but elegant form. Produced on a lathe out of one piece of beechwood, the recorder bears one single linear adornment. The holes are in one row, enabling both playing positions – the modern right-handed position was not the exclusive form then. This is shown by the two holes for the little finger of the lowermost hand: the one that was not needed was closed with wax.   G. S.

southern German organmaking. Through the flue pipes, the reed pipes, and the plucked strings – through these and other possibilities, all the different sounds of the complete instrumental ensemble of the Renaissance could be realized. The built-in „joke stops", like „frog-dance" and „birdsong" provided special effects. The bellows and the cabinet of this instrument are decorated with grotesquery to match the Spanish Hall of Ambras Castle (where it comes from).

                                                        G. S.

SMALL HUNTING HORN
Anton Kerner
Vienna, 1771
Silver, partially goldplated; TL 24 cm
Inv. No. 644

SMALL HUNTING HORN
Michael Leichamschneider
Vienna, 1713
Silver, partially goldplated; TL 19 cm
Inv. No. 598

Small hunting-horns have the advantage of being compact and, in spite of their splendid appearance, reasonably priced. Both of these instruments are from Vienna and are made of solid silver with gold plating. The original mouthpieces have survived in both cases. This type of horn, in a simpler brass version, became known in the 19th century as the post horn.   G. S.

TRUMPET
Anton Schnitzer
Nuremberg, 1581
Brass, silverplated, partially goldplated;
L 70.5 cm, Tube L 206 cm
Inv. No. 248

Nuremberg has been one of the most important centres for instrument-making ever since the Renaissance. One of the most significant instrument-makers there was Anton Schnitzer who is responsible for what must be the most magnificent trumpets in the world. The silverplated tubing of this Schnitzer trumpet from the Ambras collection is embellished and engraved with instrument-laden muses. The ferrules, mouthpiece fitting and the bell are gold-plate. The mouthpiece is unique – its deep cup and the long bell of the instrument give a dark sound.   G. S.

HUNTING HORN ▷
Italy
16th century
Leather with pewter fittings;
TL 25 cm, Tube L 40 cm
Inv. No. 242

Signal instruments were always necessary for the hunt. Originally made of animal horn, they eventually came to be curved, even when – as here –

they were made of two layers of leather with tooled gold decorations. The mouthpiece and the lower end of the bell are pewter. The horn is from Catajo Castle and has a leather strap.
                    G. S.

SIX TRUMPETS
Franz and Michael Leichamschneider
Vienna, 1741 and 1746
Silver, partially goldplated; L 54 cm to 70 cm
Tube L 156 cm to 207 cm
Inv. Nos. 401 to 406

At first exclusively the symbol of the ruler, the trumpet eventually came to be used in court ceremony and military practice, where even today it is responsible for state fanfares. The blaring sound and the precious metals of silver and gold were especially well-suited to represent the splendor of the imperial court. Empress Maria

Theresa purchased these six silver trumpets for the Hofmusikkapelle (Imperial Music Chapel), where they were used up until the end of the 19th century. In the course of their one hundred and fifty years of use, they had to meet many different musical demands. At first the trumpets formed an ensemble of six instruments, tuned in unison. With time, some of them were shortened and outfitted with extra tubing to play in the different keys of the Viennese Classical period. The exquisite gold-plated construction of the twisted, spiral-shaped ferrules, the shaped knobs, and the richly embellished bells have remained unchanged, as well as the original tassled ropes.

PAIR OF KETTLEDRUMS ▽
Vienna
18th century
Copper shells; T 72 and 68 cm
Inv. Nos. 618 and 619

KETTLEDRUMSTICKS
Austria
End of 18th century
Plumwood; L 30.5 cm
Inv. No. 741 a, b

KETTLEDRUM BANNER
Vienna
18th century
Silk brocade; W 112 cm, L 143 cm
Inv. No. 401

The six baroque trumpets of the Viennese Hofmusikkapelle form an ensemble with these two
baroque kettledrums. The flat copper shells were
usually covered by the banner which was fastened along the top edge. The banner bears the
crest of Emperor Franz I Stephan in pure gold silk.
In their own time, the drums were played with
wooden sticks, providing the trumpets with a clear
bass line. The felt heads of drumsticks today
produce a more mellow sound.   G. S.

SERPENT
Italy
16th century
Nut wood, covered with black leather;
H 79 cm, L 180 cm
Inv. No. 237

The body of this instrument is shaped like a
snake. This example is rare in that it includes the
head.
This form permits the player to reach all six holes.
Serpents were important bass instruments in
Austria even up until Joseph Haydn's time and
only with the invention of the valve at the beginning of the 19th century were they replaced by the
lower brass instruments. (The mouthpiece with its
crook is not shown in the above photograph.)
                                            G. S.

SIX TARTOELTEN (DRAGON SHAWMS) WITH CASE

Italy or Southern Germany
16th century
Copper and brass; L 20 cm to 60 cm
Inv. Nos. 208–211

In the Renaissance much value was placed on instruments that imitated the human voice. For this reason, all the different voice ranges were represented in one family of instruments. These dragon shawms form on such family and their construction is totally unique. The double reed mouthpiece is stuck into the end of the tail. The conical metal tubing is wound around like a spiral within the dragon's body thus enabling the short size of the low instrument. It may be supposed that similar instruments were used at the court of Emperor Maximilian I for acoustic and even visual effects in plays of masquerades.
G. S.

TWO RACKETS

Germany
16th century
Ivory; L 12 cm, Tube L 103.5 cm
Inv. Nos. 213 and 214

Technical advances in 16th century woodwind instrument construction made it possible to have different parallel bores in wood or ivory instruments. This meant a more compact size for bass instruments. The double-bored dulcian was the forerunner of today's bassoon. The racket, on the other hand, never advanced beyond the Renaissance and Baroque periods. In this particular case, the nine bores in the ivory cylinder meant that these instruments of twelve centimeters could have an air column nine times that long. The bore diameter is relatively narrow, making the sound very faint, almost as if one were blowing through a comb.
G. S.

THE COLLECTION OF ARMS AND ARMOUR

In the nineteenth century almost all armouries of the Austrian branch of the Habsburgs were united in Vienna establishing the most important collection of its kind in the world. At this time it received the unfortunate designation of Waffensammlung *(Collection of Weapons)*, which even today contributes to some misconceptions; for it is truly a collection of historical military equipment and armaments. The major portion of the exhibited armours and arms served as princely symbols and as examples of courtly sporting equipment. Since the quality and beauty of the weapons illustrated the social rank of their bearers, a princely, especially an imperial armoury, was a collection of the choicest artefacts much like a treasury.

The collection in its present state is a consolidation of three major sources. It has achieved in the richness of its objects the pinnacle of artistic, technical and historical importance and is unique amongst museums of European history. The core of the collection came from the Imperial armoury in Vienna which can be traced back to Frederick III (1425–1493). A large portion comes from the rich armour and arms collection of Maximilian II (1527–1576); it was augmented in the eighteenth century by objects from the armoury in Graz belonging to his brother Karl II of Middle Austria (1549–1590). Although enriched by the ceremonial arms and objects from the Turkish booty of subsequent rulers, the Imperial armoury basically remained unchanged until the mid-eighteenth century. Under Empress Maria Theresa (1717–1780) the entire armoury was moved between 1759 and 1771 to the Imperial arsenal in the Renngasse. Here in museum fashion they were combined with militarily used weapons to form a Baroque Hall of Fame dedicated to the history of the Austrian Habsburgs. After the lootings of 1805 and 1848 the arsenal was demolished and in 1863 the collection was arranged in the new armoury as k. k. Hof-Waffensammlung. It was augmented with ceremonial pieces from the

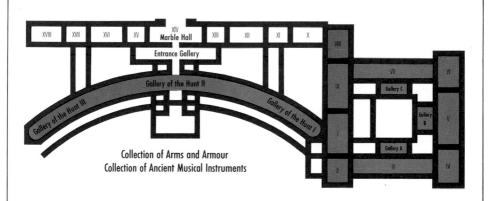

Neue Burg · Heldenplatz

Hall I: Middle Ages 500–1480 · Hall II: Late Gothic 1480–1500 · Hall III: High Renaissance 1500–1530 · Gallery A: Tournament 1480–1530 · Hall IV: Renaissance 1530–1547 · Hall V: Beginnings of Mannerism 1545–1555 · Hall VI: Mannerism and Oriental Art 1550–1566 · Hall VII: Mannerism 1560–1580 · Gallery C: Archduke Ferdinand II 1545–1566 and Sons · Hall VIII: Early Baroque 1620–1630 · Hall IX: Last Flowering of Mannerism 1595–1618 · Gallery of the Hunt I: Early Baroque 1620–1660 · Gallery of the Hunt II: High Baroque 1660–1710 · Gallery of the Hunt III: Late Baroque to Historicism 1710–1914.

Imperial country seat Laxenburg near Vienna. In 1888 during the transfer to the new building of the Kunsthistorische Museum the dynastic armoury and ceremonial arms were for the most part removed. Those pieces remaining in the arsenal were exhibited in 1891 as the k. u. k. Heeresmuseum *(Military Museum)*.

The collection grew enormously through the acquisition of the Armoury from Ambras Castle, the bulk of which went back to Archduke Ferdinand II *(1527–1595)*. Through an inheritance in 1564 he assumed the regency over Tyrol and adjacent lands. After a nineteen years governorship in Bohemia his personal arsenal increased by 347 Zentner *(1 Zentner = 40 kg)* in packed form. It was transferred from Prague to Innsbruck in 1565. After 1580 he placed his valuable collection of personal armour in the Unterschloss at Ambras, in proximity to his famous Kunstkammer *(Chamber of Art and Marvels)*. Almost simultaneously, after 1576, he began according to a uniquely conceived cultural historical concept to build up his Heldenrüstkammer *(Armoury of Heroes)*. With assistance of his secretary, Jakob Schrenk von Notzing, he collected suits of armour and arms of all famous warriors of his time and of previous centuries. Originally the "honourable" (i. e. noble) group encompassed 125 "heroes". In 1601 a printed illustrated catalogue in Latin Armamentarium Heroicum *appeared;* followed in 1603 by a German edition. Ferdinand's successor Karl von Burgau *(1560–1618)*, sold the entire collection of Ambras Castle to Rudolph II *(1552–1612)* in 1606; and hereby it became Imperial property. Rudolf II intended to move it to Prague and combine it with his Kunstkammer. Fortunately, this did not occur, and the collections remained in Tyrol until 1806 when during the Bavarian occupation the collection was moved to Vienna as private and Imperial possessions.

Since 1814 these were exhibited in the Lower Belvedere Palace and were combined in 1888 with the contents of the Kunsthistorische Museum. The final portion was added after the end of the monarchy from numerous objects stored in the Imperial court stables, coming from the former Hof-Jagd-Gewehrkammer *(court hunt and gun chambers)* and from the Hof-Sattelkammer *(court saddlery)*; as well as the numerous pole arms from the depot of the Imperial lifeguard. With these additions the exhibition in the Kunsthistorische Museum no longer satisfied the aesthetic demands of the time; it was transferred in 1934/36 to the expansive galleries of the Neue Burg. Today more objects than ever are displayed in nine halls and six galleries.

C. B.

CRESTED FUNEREAL HELMET ▷
Austria
Mid-14ᵗʰ century
Steel, leather; H 74 cm
Inv. No. B 74

Until 1878 the *Prankher funereal helm* rested over
the grave of the lords of Prankh in the Collegiate
Church of Seckau in Styria. Because of its
noteworthy weight (6.8 kg) this helm was only
used for tournament. This type of closed helmet
was developed in the thirteenth century in order
to afford better protection for the head. Its form
made vision and breathing difficult, and identifying
opponents was only possible from their heraldic
colours and symbols. Of the about fifteen remaining helms only this one and that of the "Black
Prince" (d. 1376) in the Cathedral of Canterbury
have fitting decorations.   J. R.

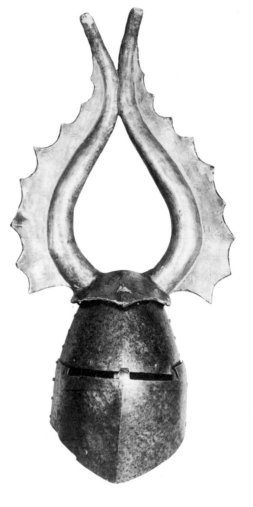

HOUNDSKULL BASNET
Upper Italy
c. 1400
Steel; H 31 cm
Inv. No. A 24

This helmet probably comes from the estate of
Duke Ernst of Austria (1327–1424) father to
Emperor Frederick III. Since knights found that it
was difficult to handle the closed helmet it was
replaced in the fourteenth century by the kettle
hat. The face was protected by a moveable dog
snout shaped visor. The name of the helmet type
is based on its similiarity to the *Gugel,* a pointed
hood of cloth. Although there must originally have
been a large number of houndskull basnets; they
were re-used by infantry soldiers and consequently only fourty have survived.   J. R.

ARMOUR FOR HORSEMAN ▽
Tomaso Missaglia and Workshop
(Milan ment. 1430–1452)
c. 1450
Steel; H 189 cm
Inv. No. A 2

In 1451 to wear at his inauguration, the Elector Frederick of the Palatinate (1425–1476) ordered a suit of armour from the then leading workshop of the Missaglia family in Milan. Even before 1300 Milanese armourers had started to protect the body with steel plates, and by 1400 the development to plate armour was complete. The *Frederick cuirass* as a typical quattrocentro armour conveys a feeling of power and massiveness. However, in keeping with the French taste the Elector was also fitted with sabotons, a large helmet with rounded visor (grand bacinet), symmetrical shoulders and discs to protect them. J. R.

CEREMONIAL SADDLE
Southeastern German
1438–1439
Wood, ivory; H 40 cm
Inv. No. A 73

This saddle was made for the Holy Roman King Albrecht II (1397–1439), the first Habsburg who ruled not only over the Empire but also over Bohemia and Hungary. The crests of these countries are also used in the decoration of the saddle. Pictured on both sides of the bowed horn is a dragon, the symbol of the Order of the Dragon founded in 1408 to defend Christianity. The style of the decoration with many small figures framed by thistle leaves is reminiscent of south German textile work of the time, c. 1430. The two slits on the seat are for the attachments of the stirrups, girth and seat cushion.   J. R.

CEREMONIAL MACE
German
c. 1474
Brass; L 65 cm
Inv. Nos. A 153 and A 162

In 1474 Duke Charles the Bold of Burgundy besieged the fortification of Neuss. A relief force of the Holy Roman Empire led by Emperor Frederick III (1415–1493) and his sixteen year old son, Maximilian, later emperor, moved against the duke. These two similiar maces were probably made in commemoration of the event. The mace was already used as a sign of rank in ancient Egypt; and from it evolved the scepter and the marshall's baton. The gracefully bizarre form of these two maces clearly indicates that they were not intended to be used as weapons. A gameboard with pieces was stored in each of the hollowed shafts.   J. R.

CUIRASSIER ARMOUR
Lorenz Helmschmied
(Augsburg, ment. 1467–1516)
c. 1485
Steel, brass; H 172 cm
Inv. No. A 62

In 1484 Duke Siegmund of Tyrol (1427–1496) married Katherina of Saxony. The bridegroom received this cuirass made by Lorenz Helmschmied as an Imperial gift for the occasion. Augsburg had become a center for the manufacture of ceremonial armour, and Helmschmied was the preferred armourer of the Emperors Frederick III and Maximilian I. This German armour clearly differs from the Missaglia armour. Following Burgundian fashion the proportions are slender with an extenuated narrow waist. The sallet, a form of helmet, protects the head. The continuity of construction is interrupted by numerous bands with cruciferous flowers; rippling and fluting underline the angular and unusual impression of the piece.   J. R.

CUIRASSIER ARMOUR ▽
Master I P
Italian
1490/1500
Steel; H 167 cm
Inv. No. A 5

This armour belonged to King Ferdinand of Aragon (1452–1516), grandfather of Charles the Bold, who laid the foundations for the world wide Spanish empire. The armour is in the style of the Italian quattrocento; it contrasts with the armour of Frederick of the Palatinate which was fashioned in the French mode. The head of the king was protected by an armet, a pivoted visor helmet. In keeping with stylistic developments Ferdinand's armour is devoid of the accentuated heaviness of the older armour. The Spanish taste of the patron can be seen above all in the shift of the breastplate and the Arabic influenced decorative studs on the edges.   J. R.

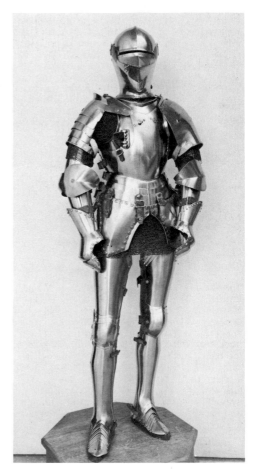

CUIRASSIER ARMOUR
Lorenz Helmschmied
(Augsburg, ment. 1467–1516)
c. 1494–1500
Steel; H 109 cm
Inv. No. A 7

This cuirass of Lorenz Helmschmied does not appear in the sketch book of the master under the armours made for Emperor Maximilian, and it is assumed to have belonged to King Philip (1478–1506). Upon the death of his mother, Maria of Burgundy, this son of the "Last Knight" inherited the lands of his grandfather, Charles the Bold. With the marriage to Juana, daughter of King Ferdinand of Aragon, Philip became the founder of the Spanish branch of the Habsburgs. The decoration of the armour relates to Burgundy and the Order of the Golden Fleece. The cross of St. Andrew is etched on the breast and back plates; on the upper ridge are gold appliqued insignia of the Order, flint and steel as well as flames, and again the cross of St. Andrew.   J. R.

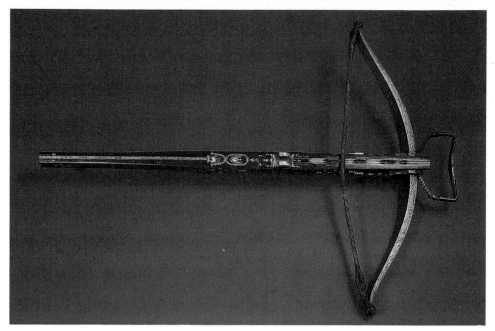

CROSSBOW FOR THE HUNT
Spanish
1499–1514
Steel, wood, ivory; L 104 cm
Inv. No. D 1

The decoration of the shaft with porcupines, the insignia of the Order of King Louis XII (1462–1515) indicates that this weapon was meant for the French king. The gift could not be sent because of political tensions and came to the Habsburg armoury from King Philipp. Since the fourth century A. D. the crossbow had been widely used as an effective distance weapon in the field and on the hunt; its penetration power was a factor in the development of plate armour. Initially the bow was drawn by a claw and belt, then with emergence of the steel bow other devices were used, in the west above all the cranequin.

J. R.

FALCONHOOD AND FEATHER LURE
Milan
1494–1508
Leather; H 6 cm (Hood), 13 cm (Lure)
Inv. Nos. D 6, D 44, D 46

The falconry equipment was made in Milan for Emperor Maximilian and his second wife, Bianca Maria. Falconry was considered the most distinguished of all forms of hunting, because in it the animal had to bow to the wIll of man. The falcon's hood served to rob him of the gift of sight so that the bird would sit quietly on the falconer's hand. After flight the falcon was lured back by swinging a padded feather weight. The embroidery on this lure reminds one that the falcon was a constant symbol in courtly love poetry. A falconer's garniture included a hunting bag with whose contents the bird of prey was fed after a successful hunt.

J. R.

393

ADARGA ▽
Spanish/Moorish
Before 1492
Leather; H 92 cm
Inv. No. C 195

In 1492 Granada, the last Moorish stronghold in Spain, fell and the "reconquista" had reached its climax. This *Adarga,* a leather shield, was amongst the booty which fell into the hands of King Ferdinand. It probably belonged to Boabdil IV, the last king of Granada. Through Ferdinand's son-in-law, King Philipp, son of Emperor Maximilian I, the piece found its way into the imperial armoury. Although the *Adarga* originally belonged to the light cavalry, this royal ceremonial piece is generously embroidered on the back side with silk and quill work. This kind of ornamental art strongly influenced Renaissance workmanship.

J. R.

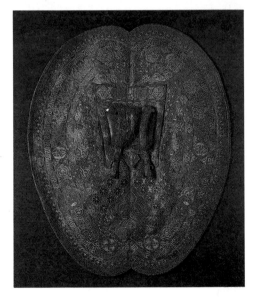

CEREMONIAL SWORD
Milan
1494
Steel; L 108 cm
Inv. No. A 170

In 1494 Emperor Maximilian I (1459–1519) married for the second time, Bianca Maria, daughter of the Duke Galeazzo Maria Sforza of Milan. He most likely received this valuable Milan sword on that occasion. This ceremonial sword was exclusively a symbol of knighthood. The gilded etching clearly alludes to love and marriage. The broad blade with a strong central ridge is characteristic of Italian swords, while the grip with an oval pommel and mother of pearl inlay is reminiscent of German workmanship. This reflects the geographic position of Milan, situated in Italy but belonging to the Holy Roman Empire.

J. R.

BOY'S DRESS ARMOUR
Konrad Seusenhofer
(Innsbruck, ment. 1500–1517)
1512/14
Steel; H 142 cm
Inv. No. A 109

In 1512 Emperor Maximilian I ordered for his nephew, later Emperor Charles V (1500–1558), a pleated skirt armour from his Innsbruck armourer, Konrad Seusenhofer. It was delivered in 1514. Seusenhofer is presumably the originator of this type of armour which imitated contemporary fashion in steel. Initially a mask visor probably not suiting the infante's taste must have belonged to the helmet, because in 1514 a simple visor was added to the armour, which is still in the collection. The decoration of the bands inlaid with gilded silver in clever imitation of cloth trim and the etching were done in Augsburg.   J. R.

JOUSTING ARMOUR (STECHZEUG)
Kaspar Rieder
(Innsbruck, ment. 1455–1499)
1483/84
Steel; H 103 cm
Inv. No. S VIII

For the occasion of his second wedding in 1484 Archduke Siegmund of Tyrol ordered a large number of jousting armours from the Innsbruck armourer Kaspar Rieder. Towards the end of the fifteenth century specialized armours were developed for the various forms of knightly tournament. The aim of the joust *(Stechen)* was to lift the opponent out of the saddle with the strenght of the tilt. Neck, chin, breast, left shoulder and both hands were particularly endangered. The helmet permanently attached to the armour, is strongly reminiscent of the fourteenth century close-helmet. The heavy lance with its characteristic three pronged point, the coronel, lay on the lance rest. A queue on the backplate gave added resistance. The vamplate protected the right hand of the rider. The shield, the targe, was tied unto the breast-plate. It was particularly difficult to find suitable horses, even though the chanfrons had no eyelets to prevent the horses shying. Some tournaments had to be cancelled because of reluctant horses.   J. R.

JOUSTING ARMOUR (RENNZEUG)
Matthes Deutsch
(Landshut, ment. 1485–1495)
1498
Steel; H 114 cm
Inv. No. R IV

In 1498 Emperor Maximilian staged a joust in honour of Duke John of Saxony. In honour of the occasion this jousting armour may have been made for the Saxon sovereign by the Landshut armourer Matthes Deutsch. *Rennen* was next to *"Stechen"* the second most desirable form of the knightly tournament on horse. Its aim was not so much to knock the opponent out of his saddle, but rather to prove the accuracy of the lance. The armour bears a strong resemblance to field armour; the large shield and the semi-circular vamplate made arm protection unnecessary. The thighs were protected by two large plates, the tilting sockets; a leg garniture was generally not worn. Emperor Maximilian invented numerous variations for this type of tournament. The various garnitures for these are accurately depicted in a series of woodcuts of the Emperor's "Triumph" printed in 1512. One example, *Geschiftscheibenrennen,* a successful tilt resulted in the release of wedges attached to the breastplate by a pressurized spring. Such a mechanism is preserved in the Vienna collection.   J. R.

397

COSTUME ARMOUR ▽
Brunswick
c. 1526
Steel; H 188 cm
Inv. No. A 78

In 1526 Albrecht of Brandenburg, Grand Master of the Teutonic Knights (1490–1568), married Dorothea of Denmark; and the land grant in Prussia was secularized. For this occasion the pleated skirt armour in the Innsbruck style was made in Brunswick. The etched design of a bride and groom on the backplate bears witness to the occasion. The armourer's work is by far not as subtle and expansive as in the work of Seusenhofer. Bizarre and fantastic forms clearly dominate from the too broad sabotons to the helmet which is fitted with a grotesque mask visor and wings.   J. R.

FLUTED ARMOUR
Lorenz Helmschmied
(Augsburg, ment. 1467–1516)
1516
Steel; H 169 cm
Inv. No. A 239

The Augsburg armourer Lorenz Helmschmied fashioned this armour in the last year of his life for the later Elector Otto Henry of the Palatinate (1512–1559). An armour made thirty years previously for Archduke Siegmund is still in the late Gothic style, while this piece of the master resembles in every detail a classical suit of armour, much like the one his son Colman had made before 1511 for Andreas von Sonnenburg. Rounded forms dominate and the proportions are those of the human body. Some time after 1510 the surface was decorated en suite with fine ridges. With this fluting homage was paid to fashion, since it never appears again after 1530.
                                                J. R.

COSTUME ARMOUR
Colman Helmschmied
(Augsburg 1471–1532)
c. 1525
Steel; H 134 cm
Inv. No. A 374

During his tenure in Spain (1522–1529) Wilhelm von Roggendorf (1481–1541) received this armour as a symbol of recognition from Emperor Charles V. During several sieges against the Moors Roggendorf had become a general and captain of the Emperor's lifeguard. The armour was part of a garniture which on stylistic grounds could have been made by Colman Helmschmied of Augsburg. In a clever manner the armourer imitated in steel the costume of the *Landsknechte* with its characteristic puffy sleeves. In those places where according to the model coloured fabric shows through slits, the shiny steel is darkened by etched indentations.

J. R.

ARMOUR "ALLA ROMANA" ▽
Filippo Negroli
(Milan, active 1532–1545)
1532
Steel, leather; H 90 cm
Inv. No. A 498

The half armour made for Duke of Urbino, Francesco Maria della Rovere-Montefeltre (1490–1538) is the earliest dated work of the famous Milanese embosser Filippo Negroli. Its form corresponded to the self-image of the Italian Renaissance princes, who saw themselves as the legitimate successors of the classical heroes. Negroli modelled it on Roman and oriental Mameluke examples; the open morion was shaped to resemble a curly Moor's head with naturalistic ears. He signed and dated this piece in the neck area. The body armour is of lamellae, the lames are interlaced with mail. C. B.

FIELD ARMOUR
Wolfgang Grosschedel
(Landshut, ment. 1517–1562)
c. 1535–1540
Steel, leather; H 128 cm
Inv. No. A 376

This armour was made by the Landshut armourer Wolfgang Grossschedel for Konrad von Bemelberg und Boyneburg (1494–1567), one of the important *Landsknecht* leaders of Charles V. The open morion and cuisses reaching to the knees is typical for *Landsknecht* armour. The high quality etching is signed by Ambrosius Gemlich (ment. 1527–1542) of Munich and Landshut. He used a mixture of Christian and classical themes in the style of the German Renaissance. On the breastplate is found a kneeling *Landsknecht* praying to the crucified Christ; this scene is encircled by medallions with portraits of classical heroes, mythological characters and grotesqueries. C. B.

MEDUSA SHIELD AND MORION
Filippo Negroli
(Milan, active 1532–1545)
1541
Blued iron; H 35 cm, Diam. 80 cm
Inv. No. A 693

According to the inscription on the rondache this magnificent ensemble was given to Charles V (1500–1558) by his brother Ferdinand I (1503–1564) in remembrance of the 1541 campaign he led to Algiers. It was from here that the notorious Khayr al-Din Barbarossa (d. 1547), as a vassal of the "Sublime Porte" and in conjunction with France, effectively interrupted Christian sea traffic on the Mediterranean. Both ceremonial pieces are the work of the Milanese embossers Negroli, who by using richly gilded figurative decoration alluded at all times to the owner. The helmet's visor was shaped like the Nemean lion, and hence the owner became the new Hercules. Fighting, riding or music making Tritons and Nereids are to be found on the helmet and on the shield. On the outer frieze of the shield these figures are sectioned off by four medallions picturing the Roman heroes of African campaigns, Scipio, Caesar, Augustus and Claudius. As their successor Charles V in a Perseus-like fashion was to turn his enemies to stone with the central Medusa medallion.   C. B.

"EAGLE GARNITURE"
Jörg Seusenhofer
(Innsbruck, ment. 1528–1580)
1547
Steel; H 180 cm
Inv. No. A 638

In 1546 the later Emperor Ferdinand I (1503–1564) ordered this garniture from the Innsbruck armourer Jörg Seusenhofer for his son Archduke Ferdinand of Tyrol (1525–1595). The garniture named after its decoration cost the enormous sum of 1258 *Gulden,* twelve times the annual salary of a court official. About 463 *Gulden* alone were spent for the gilding. Hans Perckhammer (ment. 1527–1557) completed the etching in

unique perfection. In the first half of the sixteenth century using as many of the original parts as possible it was attempted through exchange pieces to keep step with the development of various specialized garnitures. Retained were the original parts of the armours which needed a queue for resting the lance, the field armour, and the armor for heavy infantry. For all tournaments on horse (armour for free tilt and free tournament) the left side inclined to the opponent had to be strenghtened. Combat armour with its characteristic tonlet was the armour used for foot tournaments and no queue was needed. The remaining queue-less armour types (light cavalry, foot soldier, boy armour) could be made by combining various pieces. J. R.

CUIRASS FOR HORSEMAN ▽
Desiderius Helmschmid
(Augsburg 1513–1579)
1544
Steel, Leather; H 141 cm
Inv. No. A 574

Charles V ordered this cuirass as part of a splendid large garniture for his son Philipp II of Spain (1527–1589) from his court armourer De-

siderius Helmschmid. In 1527 the cuirass was given by Madrid to the *Heldenrüstkammer* in Ambras Castle, during this process the original helmet was mistakenly exchanged for another, and like the main part of the garniture is still in Spain today. The Augsburg etcher Ulrich Holtzmann (ment. 1539–1568) decorated the armour very delicately with broad vertical blackened bands etched with a plait design, intertwined tendrils and leaf work finished off by narrow gold etched edging stripes.   C. B.

CHANFRON AND CRINET
In the style of Desiderius Helmschmid
Augsburg
c. 1555
Steel; H 70 cm
Inv. No. A 639

The anonymous armourer working in the style of Desiderius Helmschmid, (1513–1579) and the etcher Jörg T. Sorg, both resident in Augsburg, gave free rein to their mannerist imaginations while collaborating on this piece. Chased leafwork and etched tendrils surround a centrally placed sculptured and chased dolphin's head. The nose guard is chased with a crawling dragon. The entire surface is decorated with expansive foliage and etched tendrils. Hinged extension pieces shaped like scales are attached from the top of the forehead and are etched like the neck lame with an alternating design.   C. B.

403

HALF ARMOUR
Kunz Lochner
(Nuremberg c. 1510–1567)
c. 1555
Steel, leather; H 103 cm
Inv. No. A 1412

In 1555 the famous armourer Kunz Lochner crafted for the Grand Chancellor and Marshall of Lithuania, Nicholas IV Radziwill (1515–1565) a magnificent garniture for field and tournament. Only half of the double armour is preserved, which through the assemblage of various exchange pieces was used either as a field, tourna-

COMBAT ARMOUR ▽
Matthäus Frauenpreiss the Elder
(Augsburg, c. 1505–1549)
1549
Steel, leather; H 178 cm
Inv. No. B 73

It was evident at the Augsburg Imperial Diet in 1548 that Maximilian II (1557–1576) would be elected King of Bohemia in the following year. For this occasion a combat armour for foot tournament was ordered from the armourer Matthäus Frauenpreiss the Elder. It is a masterpiece with its curved tonlet and puffed out leg garniture. Not less noteworthy is the extremely fine gold etching found in the broad bands filled with grotesqueries, fabled creatures, trophies and tendrils. The etcher Jörg T. Sorg (1522–1603) completed this work in 1550.   C. B.

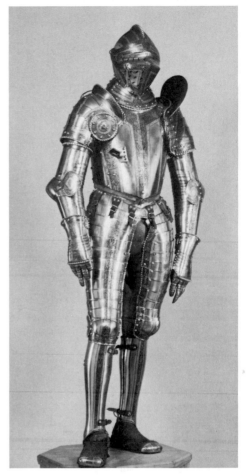

FIELD ARMOUR FOR HORSEMAN
Matthäus Frauenpreiss the Younger
(Augsburg, ment. 1555–1573)
1551
Steel, leather; H 177 cm
Inv. No. A 500

ment of jousting armour. The highly colourful, tapestry-like decoration was achieved through etching and enamel work according to eastern taste. Presumably the Polish King Sigismund II (1520–1572) ordered his identically decorated garniture for the same occasion (now in the *Livrustkammaren* in Stockholm).   C. B.

There was until 1945 in the Thun-Hohenstein Estate Library a manuscript on armour, which as a type of pattern book had been passed around amongst various Augsburg armourers since the mid-sixteenth century. This magnificent armour made in 1551 was pictured under the works of M. Frauenpreiss the Younger. It had been made for the "Printzen de Asz Gully" (= Ascoli). Presumably we are dealing with Luis de Leiva, the oldest son of the Duke of Ascoli, Antonio de Leiva. Unfortunately the etcher who decorated this piece with a magnificent band design, in which grotesqueries are mingled with figures, animals and trophies, is not known.   C. B.

"BLUE ARMOUR" ▷
Upper Italy (Mantua)
c. 1550/55
Iron, leather, clothe; H 250 cm
Inv. No. A 1398

The *Blue Armour* is one of five differently coloured embroidered parade armours for man and
horse used by Ferdinand II (1529–1595) as
Viceroy of Bohemia. The rich embroidery work of
the coats and the horse blankets, the caparisons,
are unequalled in their splendour, and perhaps
even intended to surpass the painstakingly executed embossed work. Ferdinand had this garniture made in four other colours – ashgray, red,
black and white. Even the helmet is covered with
velvet and was carried on festive occasions by
pages on horseback, clad in the same colour as
their master, although the embroidery was simpler. Embossing was limited to the chanfron and
saddle mounts, which consisted of partly silvered
or gilded tendrils of hops and half-figures on
blued ground. The design is repeated in cut iron
over the appropriate ground on the bridle, stirrups, spurs and sword. The embosser is presumed to be a follower of the school of the
Mantuan master Caremolo Modrone
(1498–1543); the embroidery was done by the
Mantuan silk embroiderer Giovanni Battista Ligo-
za who came to the court of Ferdinand II in 1565.
Even if only partially preserved, this series of
parade armours gives the best impression of the
splendour of the Renaissance princes.   C. B.

FIELD ARMOUR FOR HORSEMAN
North German (Brunswick)
1559
Steel, leather; H 135 cm
Inv. No. A 400

Neither the armourer nor the etcher of this superb
field armour are known. It is certain, however that
it was worn by Heinrich von Rantzau (1526–1598)
on the Dietmar Campaign of 1559. Particularly
attractive is the gilt etching on a blued ground.
Mythological creatures, animals, and roundels
with gilded monograms of the owner *HR* surrounded by foliage are found in the bands. Etched
in gold on the breast and back plates respectively
are the Virgin and St. John standing on an arch
flanking the crucified Christ, and Adam and Eve
flanking the tree of knowledge from which the
serpent wife gives Adam the apple.   C. B.

◁ **MILANESE ARMOUR ("MAILÄNDER
RÜSTUNG")**
Giovanni B. Serabaglio
(Milan, ment. 1560–1592)
1559
Steel, leather; H 250 cm
Inv. No. A 785

Seldom has a piece of art been better
documented than the famous *Milanese Armour* of
Ferdinand II (1529–1595). Thanks to the bill we
know the embosser, the damascener, the price,
the year of manufacture and the patron of this best
preserved and most complete Italian ceremonial
armour for man and horse. Giovanni B. Serabaglio
was the embosser, whom Marc Antonio Fava had
summoned for the execution of the expansive
gold damascening. It cost the enormous sum of
"2,400 Welsch Kronen", an amount for which 120
oxen could be purchased in Vienna in 1560.
Through his glamourous court Ferdinand, Viceroy
of Bohemia, resident in Prague since 1547, won
the sympathy of the Bohemians. The quality and
beauty of certain weapons can only be understood as indications of rank. Ferdinand had this
parade armour sent to Prague from Milan. All parts
are blued, embossed, gold and silver damascened. Although the details are nearly unrecog-
nizable, there is an unusually rich but confused
program of scenes, persons, allegorial or
mythological characters, creatures from Greco-
Roman mythology to the Old Testament. Typo-
logically the armour is completely fitted for a
mounted infantry officer – with its round shield,
the boar spear as the sign of command, the mace,
sword and saddle, to which was mounted a
dagger, and the luxuriously fitted horse armour.
C. B.

WHEEL-LOCK PISTOL
Brunswick
1555
Steel, wood; L 64.5 cm
Inv. No. A 525

The pistol with its silver monkey puffer was made
in Brunswick and came from the armoury of
Archduke Ferdinand of Tyrol. This type of wheel-
lock was an Italian invention of the first half of the
sixteenth century and was still rather rare in 1555.
When ready for firing the wheel was wound, the
lid of the flash pan pushed off, and upon pulling
the trigger the piece of sulphur quartz struck the
rotating wheel producing the igniting spark. Although a pictorial program is not identifyable in
the silver inlay work certain religious as well
mythological figures are recognizable. The classical hero Mucius Scaevola symbolizes fire; the
hunt scenes on the shaft are reminders that
pistols were originally weapons of the hunt.   J. R.

WHEEL-LOCK CARBINE
Brunswick
1549–1556
Iron, ivory; L 99 cm
Inv. No. D 71

This carbine is easily dated by its heraldic marks.
In 1549 Emperor Maximilian was crowned King of
Bohemia; in 1556 he became a member of the
Order of the Golden Fleece, whose chain does
not appear in the crest. Hence this weapon must
have been manufactured in Brunswick between
these two dates. The ivory relief on the firing side
shows the story of Perseus and Andromeda, a
myth which had already been illustrated on the
Medusa shield of his uncle Emperor Charles V.

Here it symbolizes the fight of the oppressed
Christians. The style is reminiscent of late classical ivory work and is intended to underline the
imperial claims of the owner.   J. R.

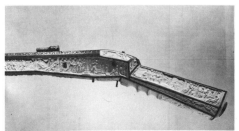

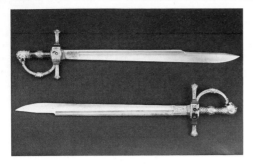

TWO COLTELAGGI PISTOLS
French
1555/60
Steel; L 83 cm
Inv. No. A 2248

The large number of hybrid forms attests to the fascination exerted by the wheel-lock in the sixteenth century. Although intended to be functional in their original form and as firearms, the *Coltelaggi* were probably non-functional either as knives or as pistols. *Coltelaggi* is a large knife which was incorrectly presumed to be a Roman weapon and hence its classical attributes. The wheel-lock is encased in a little box on the cutting point by the hilt and quillon. The barrel is on the back edge of the blade. The decoration indicates that it was made for the Parisian court.   J. R.

CEREMONIAL RAPIER ▷
Spain (Barcelona?)
c. 1550
Gilded cast iron, enamel, steel; L 120 cm
Inv. No. A 588

Without a doubt the *Gold Rapier* of Maximilian II (1527–1576) belongs to the most beautiful ceremonial weapons in the world. It was fashioned by a Spanish goldsmith and fitted with a Milanese blade. The hilt is of the highest quality gilded cast iron; finely worked leaves, clouds and angels' heads covered with a shiny coloured enamel enhance the sculptured gold decoration. To protect such richly worked parts, the weapon could be dismantled by unscrewing the pine nut on the pommel and by opening several nuts in the shape of rosettes. A storage case for the parts came with the weapon. A first quality blade has the maker's mark on the ricasso and his signature that of Antonio Piccinino (Milan 1509–1589) on the hollow grind. According to his wardrobe inventory Maximilian II as King of Bohemia received this sword together with a now lost dagger in 1552 from his Bohemian Chamberlain Wratislaw von Pernstein (1530–1582). This wealthy Bohemian nobleman had, like his king, married a Spaniard and may have brought the *Gold Rapier* back from his travels in Spain, where such gilded cast iron rapier mounts were frequently made.   C. B.

CEREMONIAL RAPIER
Damiano da Nervi
(Liguria)
Italian–French
c. 1555
Steel; L 114 cm
Inv. No. A 586

This *rapier* is decorated with the finest gold and silver damascening. The entire surface of the hilt is covered with undulating tendrils, cityscapes, hunt or war scenes, as well as the capture of Cerberos by Hercules and the heroic deeds of Mucius Scaevola. On the blunt edge of the blade the artist engraved *DAMIANVS DE . NERVE . ME . FECIT,* indicating that this was the work of Damiano da Nervi, a master who is otherwise unknown, apart from a similarly decorated ceremonial dagger also in the Viennese collection.
                    C. B.

CARTOUCHE SHIELD ▽
Eliseus Libaerts
(Antwerp, ment. 1557–1569)
1555/60
Steel; H 69 cm
Inv. No. A 562

The goldsmith Eliseus Libaerts used the designs of the French court artist Etienne Delaune (1518/19–1582) in decorating this ceremonial shield, a pure *Kunstkammer* object. A studded frame edges the cartouche-shaped shield whose corners are ending in faun and satyr heads. Five inlaid medallions are symmetrically placed and show in highest perfection embossed scenes of war and victory. These are surrounded by shackled prisoners and trophies. An exact duplicate of this shield can be found in Skokloster Palace in Sweden.　　　　　　　　　　　　C. B.

HELMET AND ROUNDSHIELD
Milan
c. 1560
Steel, velvet; H 31 cm, Diam. 64 cm
Inv. No. A 936

Karl of Styria (1540–1590), youngest of Ferdinand's I three sons, favoured this parade ensemble. The unknown embosser of exceptional talent worked in the style of Giovanni Battista Serabaglio (ment. 1560–1592). Helmet and shield are decorated with heroes from antiquity, like Marcus Curtius and Horatius Cocles, as well as with countless medallions of emperors and trophies.　　　　　　　　　　　　C. B.

▽ ARMOUR FROM THE "BLUE-GOLD GARNITURE"
Augsburg
1557
Steel, brass; H 172 cm
Inv. No. A 578

Neither the armourer nor the goldsmith of this beautiful *Blue-Gold Garniture* made for Maximilian II (1527–1576) are known. In imitation of Spanish court dress appliqued vertical gold bands are set on deeply blued ground and edging stripes of gold. Mythological figures, fabled creatures, masks and fruit fill the bands. Around the neck opening of the breast plate lies the chain of the Order of the Golden Fleece. At one time an armour with helmet and round shield belonged to this very elegant ensemble which with exchange pieces could also be used for foot tournament.

C. B.

"HERCULES ARMOUR"
Eliseus Libaerts
(Antwerp, ment. 1557–1569)
c. 1555
Steel, leather; H 168 cm
Inv. No. A 1400

The goldsmith Eliseus Libaerts decorated this armour according to sketches by the French court artist Etienne Delaune (1518/19–1582) for Maximilian II. As an expensive *Kunstkammer* object it was most likely never worn. On grayed ground are finely chaste tendrils which end in animal heads, masks and half figures; interspersed are fabled creatures, snakes, satyrs, or hanging fruit. Admidst this there are figurative scenes showing some of the Herculean Labours. On the lower part of the breastplate two double tailed Bohemian lions hold a coat of arms as proof of Maximilian's kingship, which he had since 1549.

C. B.

ARROW AND QUIVER CASE
Turkish
c. 1550
Leather, linen; L 38 cm
Inv. Nos. C 5, C 5a

During the reign of Sultan Suleyman the Magnificent the Ottoman Empire was not only at its largest but also culturally at its zenith. The extremely unusual craftsmanship of the period is recognizable in the consumate ornamentation technique of this quiver case. The unknown master embroidered a closely worked arabesque of fine spiral tendrils on a light background with many coloured silk threads. The edging band and the center medallion are on a red background. The fine tendrils end in blue leaves or golden blossoms.   C. B.

HALF ARMOUR
Central Europe (Prague?)
c. 1560
Steel, leather; H 98 cm
Inv. No. A 609

As Grandduke of Transsylvania and King of Poland since 1575, Stephan Bathory (1522–1586) became the owner of this Turkish conical helmet richly decorated with gold damascened arabesques, leaves and buds of unusual quality. The dark blued half armour seems to have been ordered by Bathory in Prague (?), where an unknown master used gold damascening in broad bands to complement the helmet. On the central band a Crucifixion was damascened in front of a city panorama with numerous church spires as one finds in Prague or Cracow.   C. B.

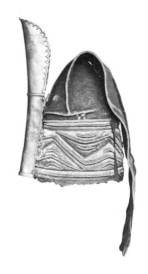

PAPAL CEREMONIAL SWORD, HAT AND BELT
Rome
1581
Steel, velvet; L 182 cm, H 35 cm
Inv. No. 989

In 1556 Archduke Ferdinand of Tyrol led a campaign against the Turks in an attempt to raise the siege of the fortress of Sziget in Hungary. Although the campaign was uneventful, the Archduke was hailed as a hero in the fight against the Turks. Pope Pius V sent him this sword and hat. Since the middle of the fourteenth century such garnitures were consecrated every Christmas and used to honour a defender of Christendom. For example, in 1511 the society sworn to defend the Pope received such accolades for a battle against Bologna. Even though swords from this period exist, contemporary hats are very rare. In 1582 Archduke Ferdinand received another belt and sword from Pope Gregory XIII.   J. R.

◁ KETSCHE
Turkish
c. 1550
Felt; H 36 cm
Inv. No. C 135f

In 1566 Sultan Suleyman the Magnificent (1494–1566) undertook his last campaign in Hungary. At this time the Imperial Field Marshall Lazarus Schwendi and his troops secured northern Hungary from Turkish incursions. Schwendi sent some of his booty to Archduke Ferdinand of Tyrol for his collection in Ambras. The *Ketsche* was the headdress of higher Turkish military official. Its form is similar to the headdress worn by the Janissaries, the elite infantry of the Ottomans; it is a late development of the pointed cap of the oriental horsemen. The broad gold border with its zig zag pattern aims to copy the winding design of the turban cloth; the high gilded silver tube served as a plume holder.   J. R.

ARMOUR GARNITURE
Jakob Topf
(Innsbruck, ment. 1573–1597)
1582/83
Steel; H 181 cm
Inv. Nos. A 1277, A 1205, A 1170

In 1582 for his second marriage Archduke Ferdinand of Tyrol ordered from the Innsbruck armourer Jakob Topf a garniture of two suits of armour for his son Karl (1560–1618). Several fatal accidents like that involving the French king Henry II (1559) had led to a simplification of the multifaceted nature of the tournament, and the sporting duel became eventually a colourful show. Following contemporary fashion armour in the middle of the century was crafted with a lowered pointed beltline, the peascod. The luxurious decoration of the court goldsmith Elias Stark is in the Italian style with a series of bands with delicate tendrils and roundels with figures.   J. R.

"ROSEPEDAL GARNITURE" ▽
Franz Grosschedel
(Landshut, ment. 1556–1581)
1571
Steel; H 176 cm
Inv. No. A 474

In 1571 Archduke Karl of Middle Austria married Maria, daughter of Duke Albrecht V of Bavaria. A tournament was staged in August in Vienna; and for the occasion the brother of the groom, Emperor Maximilian II, ordered this garniture which was named after its etched pattern. In contrast to the *eagle garniture* a complete suit of armour exists for each of the five tournament types, making exchange pieces virtually unnecessary. From 1550 onwards the Landshut armourers Wolf and Franz Grosschedel provided strong competition for the Augsburg masters. Especially noteworthy is the sparse use of etching to underline the sculpted form thereby giving an imperial glow to the garniture.   J. R.

"FLECHTBAND GARNITURE"
Augsburg
1571
Steel; H 153 cm
Inv. No. A 886

For the on the left page mentioned wedding of 1571 uniting the Catholic powers of Bavaria and Austria, the sons of the Emperor, Rudolph (1552–1612) and Ernst (1553–1595), were outfitted with specially designed armours. The Archdukes received similarly etched Augsburg armour garnitures for jousting, foot and free tournament, making the brothers indistinguishable in combat. The etched design with its interwoven bands *(Flechtband)* and hop leaves covers the entire surface of the armour like a textile pattern. The mannerist taste shows itself not only in the lavish ornamentation but also in the dropped narrow waist and in the large gauntlets.   J. R.

MATCH-LOCK MUSKET ▽
Hans Paumgartner
(Graz, ment. 1563–1590)
1570
Steel, wood, ivory; L 122.5 cm
Inv. No. 2305

In 1570 the Graz gunsmith Hans Paumgartner made this weapon for Archduke Karl (1540–1590). The match-lock ignites when a cock with flint held in its jaws strikes a vertically hinged plate over the pan. Weapons with such simple locks were used by the infantry and were seldom ceremonial weapons. Match-lock guns were unsatisfactory as hunting weapons, since game could smell the slow-match. These guns were often used as target rifles, hence the ornamentation is of feasts and merriment and not of the hunt or of war. The verse and representation of Orpheus on the firing side proclaims the healing effects of music. The classical hero Marcus Curtius symbolizes fire.   J. R.

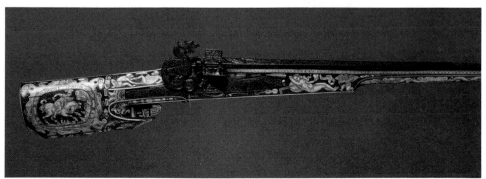

PARADE ARMOUR
Lucio Piccinino
(Milan, ment. 1570–1595)
c. 1578
Steel; H 250 cm
Inv. No. A 1132

Duke Alessandro Farnese (1545–1592), Field-marshall of the Spanish in the war against the Netherlands, wrote to Archduke Ferdinand of Tyrol of a beautiful armour in Namur which he wanted to send him to Ambras. Farnese probably meant the ceremonial armour made by the Milanese master Lucio Piccinino; sketches of which have survived. The sculpted forms are pronounced and plump but clearly formed so as to offer ample space for the rich and full decoration. The embossing corresponds to the use of decorative bands in the costumes of the time. Only close scrutiny reveals the almost confusing richness of the allegorical figures.   J. R.

ARMOUR FOR FOOT TOURNAMENT
Master I O
Milan
c. 1600
Steel; H 95 cm
Inv. No. A 1712 and A 1529

The two similar foot tournament armours were probably made for the wedding of the later Emperor Ferdinand II (1578–1637) to the Duchess Maria Anna of Bavaria in 1600. Of all tournament types the foot tournament corresponded most closely to actual combat. Divided by a barrier the two opponents fought with a lance and sword, in contrast to older foot combat rules, hitting below the belt was not allowed. The mark of Castello Sforzesco shows that the amour was made in Milan. In according with French taste the decoration was in the form of small rhomboids covering the whole armour.   J. R.

**HALF PARADE ARMOUR
WITH ROUND SHIELD** ▽
Upper Italy
c. 1570
Steel
Inv. No. A 1408

The parade armour comes from the Imperial arsenal, but its original owner has long since been forgotten. Undoubtedly, it must have been a person of high rank, because the entire surface is subtly damascened with gold and silver. This eastern technique was widespread in Europe during the sixteenth century. The metal ground was roughened in a criss-cross fashion with well placed gashes; then wires, leaves of gold and silver were layed on in a design and hammered in. After grinding and polishing this particularly fine armour was enriched with engraving.   J. R.

RAPIER WITH MOORS' HEADS
Upper Italy
1600/10
Steel; H 118 cm
Inv. No. A 1029

As the sword became an object of fashion in the sixteenth century, so increased the quality of workmanship of luxurious sword mounts. A large number of patterns were used for this. Towards the 1600's this white arm was made in Northern Italy; its hilt is decorated with Moors' heads. Surely imagination grounded in magic played a role in this. As the decapitated Medusa protects the hero Perseus from his enemies, so the bearer of this weapon is protected from bad luck by the Moors' heads. The Age of Discovery brought knowledge of foreign people and habits and awakened an interest in the exotic. Such painstakingly executed rapiers were not intended for fencing but became part of the *Kunstkammer*.
                                          J. R.

WHEEL-LOCK RIFLE
Daniel Sadeler and Hieronymus Borstorffer
c. 1600
Wood, ivory; L 121 cm
Inv. No. D 92

Prague and Munich were the centers of crafts-manship in the 1600's. The "iron worker" Daniel Sadeler was active at the court of Rudolph II until 1610 when he moved to the Bavarian capital. The barrel of the rifle was made by Hieronymus Borstorffer who became a master craftsman in Munich after 1598. Pictures and scenes from Ovid's *Metamorphoses* cover the entire weapon. Depicting lovers in the age of alchemy was thought not only to have erotic significance but also symbolized the unity of opposites. On a central spot on the firing side is found the abduction of Europe, who was led across the sea to Crete by Zeus disguised as a tame bull.   J. R.

WHEEL-LOCK RIFLE ▽
Adam Vischer
(Munich, ment. 1599–1617)
c. 1610
Steel, wood; L 111.5 cm
Inv. No. D 105

Adam Vischer became a master gunsmith in Munich in 1599. The impressively engraved de-coration of the inlaid ivory comes from the en-graver Johannes Sadeler. Surprisingly these are not mythological representations, but rather scenes from the Old Testament. On the butt is the flight of Lot from Sodom; the verse speaks of fire which was to be the fate of Lot's wife. Especially noteworthy is the representation preceding it. Perhaps the fatricide of Cain is a reflexion of the Habsburg fraternal strife between Rudolph II and his brother Matthias, under way since 1580.
J. R.

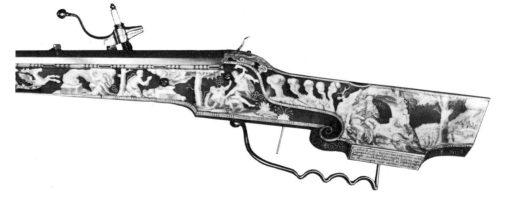

SILVER RIFLE
Daniel Sadeler and David Altenstetter
Prague, 1607
Iron, silver; L 114.8 cm
Inv. No. D 209

SILVER RIFLE WITH FLASK
Hans Schmidt
(Ferlach, ment. 1624–1669)
1628
Iron, wood, silver; L 109.5 cm
Inv. Nos. D 93 and D 93a

It is not surprising that weapons became art objects at the end of the sixteenth century, the age of the *Kunst- und Wunderkammern* (Chambers of Art and Marvels). The Augsburg goldsmith Daniel Sadeler used the same decoration on a clock (preserved in the Collection of Sculpture and Decorative Arts) as on this silver rifle. The silver plates are decorated with coloured enamels based on patterns by Etienne Delaune. The decorative element is prominent, especially accentuated by the unusual shape of the powder flask. The firing side is enhanced by a medallion showing the peace of Szitva Torok, November 1606, ending the Turkish Wars. It is executed in the style of Turkish war scenes by Hans of Aachen. J. R.

In 1628 Hans Schmidt finished a "target tube", i.e. a target rifle, for Archduke Leopold V (1586–1632). Schmidt came from Riedlingen near Ulm and moved in 1624 to Ferlach in Carinthia, which had since the middle of the sixteenth century been a centre for gunsmithing. The barrel and lock, as swell as the powder flask, are heavily decorated; and it is said that the master let it be known that he would never expend such effort again. The cock has the shape of an eagle's head, and a small lion's head attempts to hinder with his teeth the movement of the wheel. Leaves, tendrils and all forms of the hunt are inlaid in silver on the shaft, the underside of the barrel is even decorated with elephants. J. R.

BOY'S ARMOUR ▽
Christoph Krämer
(Innsbruck, ment. 1639–1662)
1641
Steel
Inv. No. A 1356

The last Innsbruck court armourer, Christoph Krämer, made this boy's armour for Archduke Ferdinand Karl. He modelled it on the blued armour, which his father-in-law, Hans Jacob Topf, had made for Archduke Leopold V. In comparison to the stark armour, this one is richly decorated. The breast plate carries the inscription *LEGES URBANITATIS*, laws of courtly behaviour. The knight's way of life, of which the young bearer was to be constantly reminded, no longer required armour, and towards the end of 1650 the traditional armour craft ended in Europe.   J. R.

ARMOUR FOR HEAVY CAVALRY
Hans Jakob Topf
(Innsbruck, ment. 1605–1628)
c. 1625
Steel; H 137 cm
Inv. No. A 1528

This armour belonged to Jacob Hannibal von Hohenems (1595–1645), nephew of the Archbishop of Salzburg, Markus Sittikus. The armour was made by the court armourer of Archduke Leopold V, Hans Jacob Topf, for the occasion of Leoplod's wedding in 1626. The so-called lock free armour belonged to equipment for heavy cavalry during the Thirty Year's War, in which Hohenems fought with his own regiment. Even though parts of the body were protected against pistol shots, the weight of over forty kg soon led to the abandonment of such armour.   J. R.

TELESCOPE AND COMMANDER'S BATON
German
1648
Ivory, silver, enamel; L 74 cm, Diam. 2.9 cm
Inv. No. A 1166

Emperor Ferdinand III (1637–1657) was presented with this curious commander's baton at the Westphalian Peace Treaty in 1648. On either end there is a removable silver gilt and partly enamelled cap. The upper cap in the shape of a helmet with moveable visor is thickly set with rubies. When the visor is opened the ivory head shows the visage of its imperial owner. The base of the lower cap has the encised monogram *F3ML* which points to specific date. Ferdinand III and his second wife, Maria Leopoldine, were married in 1648, but she died already in 1649. When both covers are removed the spiral shaped hollowed ivory stave provided with sets of lenses is useable as a telescope.   C. B.

WHEEL-LOCK GUN ▽
Johann Conrad Tornier
(Massevaux, ment. 1630–1646)
1646
Iron, wood; L 148.8 cm
Inv. No. D 144

While the metal parts of the firearm were made by gunsmiths, the luxuriously decorated woodwork came from a gun joiner. One of these was Johann Conrad Tornier, who was active in Massevaux in Alsace Lorraine, the French German border area; this geographical position can be recognized in this gun. The lock is in the French style, the mainspring is placed into a recess of the stock, giving the weapon a slender and elegant shape. The decoration with its scattered animal and flower motifs is in the German taste. Like most joiners Tornier also made other decorative pieces like gameboards, strong boxes and small cabinets.

                                        J. R.

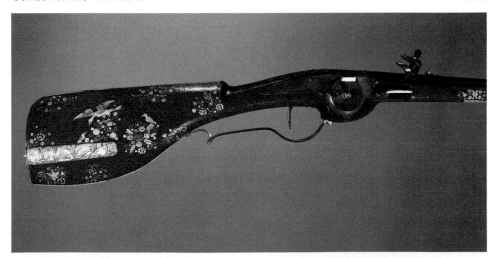

SNAP-MATCHLOCK GUN
Lazarino Cominazzo
(Brescia 1600– after 1661)
1660
Steel, wood; L 112.5 cm
Inv. No. A 1453

Brescia in Lombardy was one of the centres of firearm manufacture. The family Cominazzo was active as gunsmiths for almost four hundred years in this city. The extremely slender stock made of burled nutwood is the identifying characteristic of weapons made there. The pointed decoration with cut iron strenghtened the delicate impression. In the snap-matchlock the igniting spark results when the trigger is released and a flint strikes the steel plate hinged over the flash pan. These metal parts are primarily decorated with small sculpted dragons, even the trigger is in the shape of an animal.   J. R.

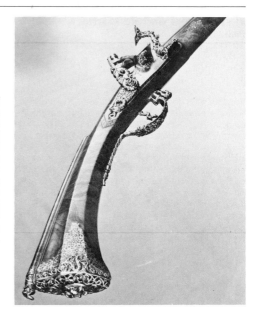

PAIR OF FLINTLOCK PISTOLS ▽
Christoph Treffler
Augsburg
c. 1660
Brass, ivory; L 54.5 cm
Inv. Nos. A 1472 and A 1473

Christoph Treffler of Augsburg probably came from a Dresden family of gunsmiths. In the beginning of the seventeenth century the flintlock was developed from the snap-matchlock. With the flintlock ignition results from the activated flint striking a steel plate, here however the steel and pan cover are one element. Since the mid-seventeenth century and for 150 years this simplified lock was the favoured ignition mechanism for the hunt and military weapons. For the most part Treffler in shaping the stock abstained from decoration, so that the patterning of the ivory is prominent. The barrel and lock are also sparingly engraved.

J. R.

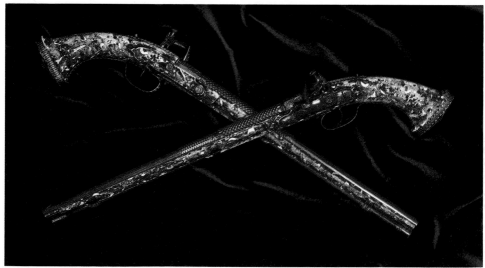

WHEEL-LOCK GUN AND FLASK
Michael Gull
(Vienna 1619–1679 Vienna)
c. 1665
Steel, ivory; L 105.5 cm
Inv. Nos. D 239, D 146

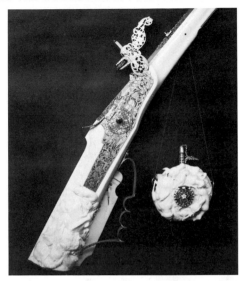

Along with Dresden, Munich and Nuremberg, Vienna became a centre for ivory work. An unknown artist crafted the stock and the powder flask of this weapon for Emperor Leopold I (1640–1705). The entire surface is covered with fighting and biting animals in relief. The mark of the Viennese gunsmith, Michael Gull, is found on the barrel. The trigger in the style of the iron cutter from Eger clearly alludes to a political situation. The dolphin, a symbol of the French enemy, is in combat with the Habsburg lion. The clock mounted in the powder flask underlines the *Kunstkammer* characteristics of this weapon. J. R.

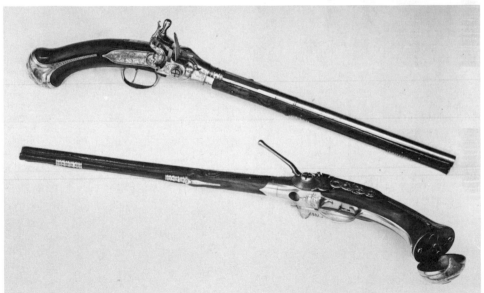

SET OF TWO FLINTLOCK REPEATER PISTOLS AND GUN
Michele Lorenzoni
(Florence, ment. 1683–1733)
1695
Steel, wood; L 54 cm
Inv. Nos. A 1446, A 1447 and D 374

The wish for a quicker firing rate led to various modifications and inventions in the course of the century. The Florentine gunsmith Michele Loren- zoni invented in the mid-seventeenth century a system, named after him. Two magazines, one for the powder and one for the balls, were in the butt of the gun; and a priming magazine was attached to the lock. Two apertures in the breech were aligned with the two magazines in the butt allow- ing ball and powder to fall into the chamber. This very simple system had the disadvantage that the barrier between the two sections was insufficient to prevent an explosion if a remnant spark was present during reloading. J. R.

SADDLE AND RIDING GEAR
Turkish
c. 1680
Leather; H 85 cm
Inv. No. C 153

In 1683 the Turks for the second time besieged Vienna. On September 12th of that year they were beaten at the gates by Imperial forces strengthened by Polish troops. The luxurious camp of the Ottomans fell into the hands of the victors. The major part of the Turkish booty is kept today in the *Heeresgeschichtliche Museum*. However, a few special mementos are in the Collection of Arms and Armour, among them the saddle and riding gear of the high commander, the Grand Vizier Kara Mustafa. The precious pieces of armament were made in the court workshop in Constantinople. The leather is covered with brocade, and turquoises are set in silver gilt inlay.   J. R.

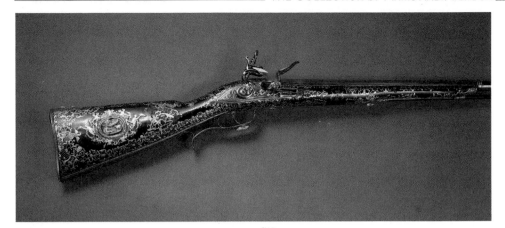

FLINTLOCK GUN
Diego Ventura
(Madrid, ment. 1720–1762)
1722
Steel, tortoise shell, wood; L 144.5 cm
Inv. No. A 1758

With the end of the Spanish Succession War the areas adjoining Italy and Belgium became part of the Austrian hereditary lands. Although the desire to make Emperor Karl VI (1685–1740) King of Spain was unrealized, Spanish influence was felt throughout the Habsburg Empire. In 1721 the Emperor recognized in the Peace Treaty of the Hague the Bourbon Philipp V as King of Spain. This weapon was made in 1722 by Diego Ventura in Madrid. Durability was the distinguishing characteristic of Spanish stocks and locks; the tortoise covered butt came from Imperial Naples.

J. R.

BREECHLOADING RIFLE
Joseph Werndl
(Steyr 1831–1889)
1870
Steel, nutwood; L 116 cm
Inv. No. G 722

In 1871 the gunsmith Joseph Werndl presented this ceremonial rearloader to Emperor Francis Joseph I. Werndl came from a long line of gunsmiths, and studied the newest mechanisms and mass production from Colt and Remington in the United States. After his return to Steyr (Upper Austria) he purchased several grinderies and founderies and established in 1853 the still existing munitions factory. It developed into one of the most important weapons' factories in Europe and remained such until the end of the monarchy. A weapon similar to this target rifle was exhibited by Werndl at the 1889 Paris World Fair.

J. R.

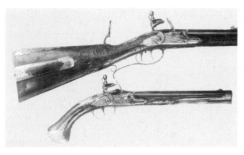

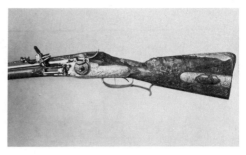

**FLINTLOCKGUN AND A PAIR OF
FLINTLOCKPISTOLS**
Georg Keiser
(Eger 1647–1740 Vienna)
1731
Steel, wood; L 112 cm
Inv. Nos. A 1760–1763

Like his father Leopold Emperor Karl VI was also
an avid hunter, even though he was short sighted.
After a hunting accident, a monocle was affixed on
the top of the butt of the imperial weapons.
Towards the end of the seventeenth century a
great surge in Viennese gunsmithing was seen.
The strict regulations of the guild were partially
responsible for this; it demanded that a gunsmith
make all the iron parts of a gun. Johann Georg
Keiser from Eger played a leading role in this
guild. With pride he marked his unusually advanced age on the weapon: *ALT 84 JAHR.*
J. R.

WHEEL-LOCK GUN
J. S. Hauschka
(Schmalkalden 1695–1775 Wolfenbüttel)
1733
Steel, nutwood; L 111 cm
Inv. No. D 171

In 1708 the later Emperor Karl VI married Christine of Brunswick-Wolfenbüttel, mother of the
Empress Maria Theresa. The court gunsmith of
the duke of Wolfenbüttel, J. Sebastian Hauschka,
made this gun for the Emperor in 1733. Like most
of the weapons the duke had commissioned for
foreign monarchs, portrait medallions also per-
sonalized the stock of this gun. The shaft of this
gun is decorated with such medallions. The oval
pastel miniature on the neck of the butt shows the
wife of the Emperor, Elisabeth Christine. While
flint-lock guns were made almost exclusively in
the rest of Europe, the wheel-lock was still
favoured for its precision in Germany.
J. R.

AIRGUN
Bartolomeo Girandoni
(Cortina 1744–1799 Vienna)
1778
Iron, nutwood; L 96 cm
Inv. No. G 327

Bartolomeo Girandoni invented a magazine airgun in 1778, with which part of the Imperial army

was equipped. At the end of the sixteenth century
a gun using compressed air as a means of
propulsion had already been constructed. This
weapon had the distinct advantage on the hunt
because it had a quieter discharge and left no tell
tale smoke. Because of the constantly changing
air pressure in the bottle these air guns were not
always reliable, and consequently the production
of this first repeating military weapon was halted.
J. R.

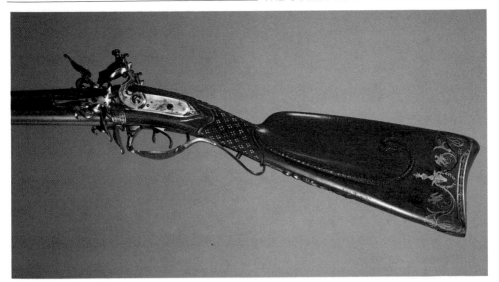

FLINTLOCK WENDER RIFLE
Joseph Devillers
(Luttich, ment. 1799–1819)
1808
Steel, wood; L 120.7 cm
Inv. No. G 501

The French occupied the Netherlands in 1797 in the course of the revolutionary wars. An unknown inhabitant of todays Belgium commissioned this

weapon from Joseph Devillers, and presented it to his former head of state, Emperor Franz II (I) (1768–1835). Latin quotations underscore his imperial loyalties, and along with the decoration shows the classical taste of the Empire Period. The *Wender* was a further attempt to design a multi-firing weapon. After firing the two adjacent barrels by means of a double lock the barrels could be turned and fired twice again.

J. R.

BOXED SET OF PERCUSSION PISTOLS
Karl Pirko
(Vienna, ment. 1831–1867)
c. 1830
Steel, wood; L 41 cm
Inv. No. G 602

The boxed set of percussion pistols comes from the estate of Duke of Reichstadt (1811–1832). He was the son of Napoleon Bonaparte and the Archduchess Maria Louise and went to live with his grandfather Emperor Franz I after the fall of the French emperor. Lung problems resulted in an early death at Schönbrunn Palace. During the nineteenth century the sword was no longer part

of daily dress and duels were fought with pistols; not surprisingly the property of a fashionable gentleman necessarily included a set of duelling and target pistols with their accoutrements.   J. R.

LEFAUCHEUX DOUBLEBARREL RIFLE
Heinrich Dasch
(Graz, ment. 1826–1853)
c. 1840
Steel, wood; L 113 cm
Inv. No. G 561

Emperor Ferdinand I (1793–1875) purchased this rifle at the 1841 Regional Trades Fair in Graz. For centuries the loading of firearms was a compli-cated procedure. With multiple motions, powder, ball and ram rod had to be placed in the barrel. This procedure was simplified after the invention of the percussion lock which replaced flint and steel as a quicker and more efficient ignition system. Here only the barrel needed to be tilted for loading. The Paris gunsmith Lefaucheaux used paper patches to contain the fulminate. This system was widely used for hunting weapons.

J. R.

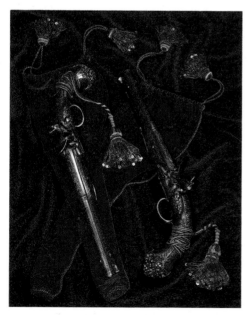

FLINTLOCK PISTOLS
Claude Bizouard
(Marseille, ment. 1840–1866)
1857
Steel, nutwood; L 40.7 cm
Inv. Nos. A 1679, A 1680

In 1857 the Bey of Tunis presented this weapon to Emperor Francis Joseph I (1830–1916). While Oriental swords were world reknowned, their firearms never attained this quality. For this reason the Turks and Arabs often used guns fashioned in southern Europe. The Bey ordred this presentation gun from a smith in Marseille, Claude Bizouard, a sign of the French influence in Tunisia after the French conquest of Algeria in 1830. The Europeans favoured richly dam-ascened barrels, and captured Turkish weapons were often refitted with a new stock and lock. J. R.

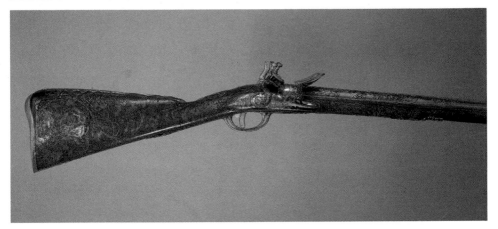

FLINTLOCK GUN
C. Chasteau
(Paris, ment. 1675–1727)
Beginning of 18th century
Steel, wood; L 157.2 cm
Inv. No. A 1759

Under the reign of Louis XIV (1638–1715) Parisian gunsmiths were leading in the manufacture of ceremonial weapons. It is surprising however that these weapons found their way to the Imperial armoury in Vienna, since the Habsburg empire constantly had to resist the aggressions of the Sun King. The decoration of the gun is geared more towards war than the hunt. On the richly decorated stock above the chamber the antique hero Hercules is pictured, and a scribe is writing down on the back of time the emperor's honourable feats of war. Characteristic for Parisian work are the inlaid silver delicate tendrils covering the butt.   J. R.

CENTRAL-FIRING REVOLVER/GUN
Johann Gasser
(Vienna 1847–1896 Vienna)
c. 1890
Steel, nutwood; L 97 cm
Inv. No. G 14

The loading chambers of a revolver are attached on an axis so as to permit rotation and multiple firing with just one barrel and ignition mechanism. Examples from as early as the 1600 are known, but the weapon did not prevail because of technical problems, especially insulating the loading chamber. It was not until percussion and firecaps that this invention was truly useable. Leopold Gasser comes from an old family of Carinthian gunsmiths and in 1869 he developed in Vienna a revolver which was introduced into the Austro-Hungarian army. After his death his brother Johann took over his factory-sized workshop in Vienna.

                                                      J. R.